T0414211

Italian Communication on the Revolt in the Low Countries (1566–1648)

Library of the Written Word

VOLUME 109

The Handpress World

Editor-in-Chief

Andrew Pettegree (*University of St. Andrews*)

Editorial Board

VOLUME 88

The titles published in this series are listed at *brill.com/lww*

Italian Communication on the Revolt in the Low Countries (1566–1648)

by

Nina Lamal

BRILL

LEIDEN | BOSTON

Cover illustration: 'L'assedio della città di Herlem in Hollanda', a news print published by Antoine Lafréry in Rome in 1573. Courtesy Rijksmuseum Amsterdam, RP-P-OB-79.236

The Library of Congress Cataloging-in-Publication Data is available online at https://catalog.loc.gov
LC record available at https://lccn.loc.gov/2022060694

Typeface for the Latin, Greek, and Cyrillic scripts: "Brill". See and download: brill.com/brill-typeface.

ISSN 1874-4834
ISBN 978-90-04-53806-1 (hardback)
ISBN 978-90-04-53807-8 (e-book)

This book is printed on acid-free paper and produced in a sustainable manner.

MIX
Paper from
responsible sources
FSC
www.fsc.org FSC® C004472

PRINTED BY DRUKKERIJ WILCO B.V. - AMERSFOORT, THE NETHERLANDS

Contents

Acknowledgments

This book has been long in the making and I am pleased I can finally thank many people for their support along the way. My supervisor Hans Cools was instrumental for my own fascination with (early modern) Italy. Discovering Rome as a third years bachelor's student, following the itineraries of early modern travel guides, was in many ways an eye-opener. I am grateful to Hans for his trust and his guidance. In St Andrews, I was fortunate to be welcomed by Andrew Pettegree from the very start, and it has been a real privilege to work with him. His generous advice has been invaluable for my understanding of the early modern book world and my development as a historian. Helmer Helmers has commented on different drafts of the book and I want to thank him especially for his encouragements and unfailing optimism.

Throughout the years, I have been fortunate to have many supportive colleagues and friends in several insitutions. I am grateful to all my collegeaus on the fifth floor of Erasmus House in Leuven. I have fond memories of the numerous coffee breaks, birthday celebrations, and lunches. In St Andrews, I enjoyed the many conversations with John Condren, Jessica Dalton, Marc Jaffré, Nikolas Funke, Graeme Kemp, Jan Hillgärtner, Drew Thomas, and Arthur der Weduwen. Thanks also goes to all the other members of USTC and Reformation Institute for making it such a stimulating place to work. A special thanks to Shanti Graheli and Róisín Watson for their unwavering friendship since we first met in St Andrews.

I am grateful to the members of my committee Joad Raymond, Bart van den Bossche, Guy Rowlands, and Violet Soen for their thoughtful questions and suggestions. Along the way, I have benefitted from conversations with other scholars and would like to thank them for their help and inspiration: Paul Arblaster, Maurizio Arfaioli, Sara Barker, Sebastiaan Derks, Pierre Delsaerdt, Gert Gielis, Emma Grootveld, Geert Janssen, Guido Marnef, Jan Machielsen, Emily Michelson, Judith Pollmann, Christophe Schellekens, Lieke van Deinsen, Maartje van Gelder, Klaas van Gelder, Henk van Nierop, Djoeke van Netten, Heleen Wyffels.

My doctoral research, from which this book evolved, was made possible by the funding of Flemisch Research Council. My thanks to the Dutch Art Historical Institute in Florence and the Academia Belgica in Rome for accommodating me at several points during my many research trips. Thanks to all the dedicated staff of all the different institutions who have helped me navigate their precious collections.

A huge thank you to Arnout, Ilse, Fauke, Dien, Karel, Achilles and Juno for welcoming me into the family and for always making me feel at home. I am greatly indebted to my parents who have encouraged me to pursue my love for history, for their lasting support, and enthusiasm. Lastly, I would like to thank Klaas for his trust, his patience, and for continuing to be my *rots in de branding* (tower of strength). I dedicate this book to him.

Illustrations

Abbreviations

AAV	Archivio Apostolico Vaticano	
	NI	Nuntiature d'Inghilterra
	NF	Nuntiature di Fiandra
	SdS	Segreteria di Stato
ASCR	Archivio Storico Capitolina, Rome	
ASF	Archivio di Stato di Firenze	
	CS	Carte Strozziane
	MdP	Mediceo del Principato
	MM	Miscellanea medicea
AGS	Archivio General de Simancas	
ASMo	Archivio di Stato di Modena	
	CD	Cancelleria Ducale
ASMn	Archivio di Stato di Mantova	
	AG	Archivio Gonzaga
ASTo	Archivio di Stato di Torino	
ASVe	Archivio di Stato di Venezia	
BA	Biblioteca Ambrosiana di Milano	
BAV	Biblioteca Apostolica Vaticana	
BCB	Biblioteca Civica Berio, Genoa	
BL	The British Library, London	
BNM	Biblioteca Nazionale Marciana, Venice	
BMKF	Bibliothek Museum für Kommunikation, Frankfurt	
BNB	Biblioteca Nazionale Braidense, Milan	
BNCF	Biblioteca Nazionale Centrale di Firenze	
BNCR	Biblioteca Nazionale Centrale di Roma	
BNUT	Biblioteca Nazionale Universitaria di Torino	
BUA	Biblioteca Universitaria Alessandrina, Rome	
BRT	Biblioteca Reale di Torino	
BV	Biblioteca Vallicelliana, Rome	
DBI	*Dizionario Biografico degli Italiani* (100 vols., Rome: Istituto della Enciclopedia italiana, 1960–2020), online <https://www.treccani.it/biografie>	
EDIT16	*Censimento Nazionale delle Edizioni Italiane del XVI secolo*, online <https://edit16.iccu.sbn.it/>	
KBR	Koninklijke Bibliotheek van België, Brussels	

RCT   Royal Collection Trust, London

STCV   *Short Title Catalogue Vlaanderen*, online <https://www.stcv.be/>

VD17   *Das Verzeichnis der im deutschen Sprachraum erschienenen Drucke des 17.*
         Jahrhunderts, online <https://www.vd17.de>

USTC   Universal Short Title Catalogue, online <https://www.ustc.ac.uk/>

Notes on Conventions

The conflict in the Low Countries, which started around 1566 and lasted until 1648, is known in the English language and among international scholars as the Dutch Revolt. While it certainly has the advantage of brevity, I have chosen to use the more encompassing 'Revolt in the Low Countries'. The term reflects more accurately the current state of research which interprets the conflict as a chaotic religious and civil war in the Low Countries, which eventually (and not intentionally) united seven provinces in the northern part. To reflect the multinational nature of the forces fighting in the Low Countries, I will mostly use terms such as the Spanish-Habsburg, Habsburg or royal army, instead of the Spanish army. I will refer to Philip II and his successors as the king of Spain as both in the Low Countries and on the Italian peninsula it was widely used by contemporaries.

In early modern Italian sources, the Low Countries are most often referred to as *Fiandra* and sometimes as *Germania Inferiore*. *Fiandra* is used as a *pars pro toto* for the whole of the Netherlands, and not only to refer to the county of Flanders. I will mostly use the terms 'the Netherlands' or 'the Low Countries' when they used *Fiandra*. From the 1590s onwards, the term *Olanda* appeared more frequently in Italian sources to refer to the Seven United Provinces and not specifically to the province of Holland. I will use the Dutch Republic or United Provinces as a translation for *Olanda*. Similar problems arise when using Italy, as in the early modern period, it was not a political entity but consisted of many different states. When I use the term Italy, I do so to refer to the Italian peninsula and when I speak of Italian rulers, this is also meant as an encompassing term, referring to all its different territorial states and its dynastic houses.

In referring to the proper names of members of the ruling houses in Italy and the Low Countries, the English form of their names is used. Therefore it is Alexander Farnese, and not Alessandro Farnese. Italian sources will be cited in translation; original quotes are in the footnotes. All translations are my own unless otherwise indicated. In the translation of idioms, I have chosen to use a translation which suits best the meaning of that idiom. I would like to thank Dr. Shanti Graheli for helping me to translate Italian into English, and all remaining mistakes are my own. Quotes from primary sources are given in the original and often varying spelling. I have only standardized i/j and u/v to modern usage for archival sources. For the news publications and books I have tried to keep the original spelling of the book to facilitate finding them in catalogues.

Introduction

The young papal nuncio Guido Bentivoglio arrived in Brussels in August 1607 at a crucial moment. For more than forty years revolt had raged in the Low Countries, and now the Habsburg Netherlands and the Seven United Provinces were trying to negotiate a peace treaty that would bring an end to the conflict once and for all. In a letter to Rome, the twenty-seven-year-old admitted that he needed time to become a skilled diplomat, 'although I came here my ears so full of the Low Countries, it almost seemed as if, even before my arrival, I had also seen it with my own eyes'.[1] Guido did not exaggerate. Like so many young Italian aristocrats, several generations of his Bolognese patrician family had joined the Spanish-Habsburg army in their quest for military glory and personal advancement. When Guido was only five years old, his half-brother Ippolito was besieging the crucially important city of Antwerp under the command of Alexander Farnese; the first of several of Guido's brothers and nephews to fight in the Low Countries.[2] Stories about the Revolt in the Low Countries, then, must indeed have accompanied Guido Bentivoglio through-out his youth, so much so that he concluded that 'its concerns grew so familiar to me, that nothing now remained but to come here and to become entirely Netherlandish myself'.[3] During his time as foreign envoy at the archducal court in Brussels, Bentivoglio wrote several political reports on the war of the Low Countries for the papal curia, and after his tenure, he published a three-part history of the conflict, the closing chapter on a life-long fascination.[4]

---

1   Guido Bentivoglio, *Raccolta di lettere scritte dal Cardinale Bentivoglio in tempo delle sue nun-tiature di Fiandra e di Francia* (Cologne: s.n., 1631), USTC 2522134, pp. 8–9: 'Ma io son nuovo, e bisogno inanzi ch'io parli, ch'ascolti ben prima. Se bene ho portate quà le orecchie si piene di Fiandra, che prima di giungervi, mi par quasi d'haverla anche habitata con gli occhi'. For Bentivoglio's career as papal envoy: Raffaelo Belvederi, *Guido Bentivoglio e la politica euro-pea del suo tempo (1607–1621)* (Padua: Liviana editrice, 1962), and bio see A. Merola in *DBI*, 8 (1966).

2   In ASMo, CD, 44: letters by Ippolito Bentivoglio sent from the battlefield to the Alfonso II d'Este between 1584–1588; BAV, Barb Lat 5776, contains several letters written by Guido Bentivoglio in 1639 recommending his nephews, Hermes and Francesco, see for instance from Rome on 15 January 1639 to Marchese d'Este in Brussels, fol 48: 'ad immitatione d'altri della nostra casa in cotesta esercito a Sua Maestà, et alla Real Corona di Spagna'.

3   Bentivoglio, *Raccolta*, p. 9: 'Onde quasi nascendo hò udito parlar di Fiandra, e nel crescer de gli anni mi si son fatte in modo familiari le cose di qua ch'appunto non restava altro, che il venir qua io medesimo per diventar Fiammingo del tutto'.

4   Guido Bentivoglio, *Relationi fatte dall'ill.mo, e reu.mo sig.or cardinal Bentiuoglio in tempo delle sue nuntiature di Fiandra, e di Francia. Date in luce da Erycio Puteano* (Antwerp: Meerbeeck,

© KONINKLIJKE BRILL NV, LEIDEN, 2023 | DOI:10.1163/9789004538078_002

Bentivoglio's history was only one of the most famous of a wide variety of contemporary histories of the Revolt in the Low Countries by Italian authors, which has led scholars such as Alberto Clerici to remark that 'Italians were, together with the Dutch, amongst the keenest narrators and interpreters' of these wars.[5] As Bentivoglio's case suggests, these historical narratives were the result of a deep Italian engagement with the Revolt, for Bentivoglio's familiarity and fascination with the conflict were shared by many Italians. Throughout the long, eighty years war, Italians engaged with it in a variety of ways and discussed it incessantly.[6] This book studies the deep and protracted Italian engagement with the Revolt in the Netherlands.

The presence of several generations of Italian soldiers in the Low Countries led to a growing awareness of these ongoing events across Italian states and society. It was not just patrician families like the Bentivoglios who were eagerly awaiting the latest news from the military front, but families of all stations. Fighting alongside Ippolito Bentivoglio in the siege of Antwerp was a certain Giovanni Pietro Becharia from Spanish-held Milan, whose brother Sebastiano was deeply worried by the reports of the most recent attacks with a large fire ship and the lack of news from his brother.[7] News of military actions often created uncertainty in Italian cities, and thanks to local chroniclers we know that

---

1629), USTC 1001516; and *Della guerra di Fiandra* (Cologne: s.n., 1632–1639), for USTC numbers, consult bibliography.

5   Alberto Clerici, 'Ragion di Stato e politica internazionale. Guido Bentivoglio e altri interpreti italiani della Tregua dei Dodici Anni (1609)', *Dimensione e problemi della ricerca storica*, 2 (2009), p. 190: 'È noto che gli italiani furono, assieme agli olandesi, tra i primi e più acuti narratori ed interpreti'.

6   Silvia Moretti, 'La trattatistica italiana e la guerra: il conflitto tra la Spagna e le Fiandre', *Annali dell'Istituto storico italo-germanico in Trento/Jahrbuch des italienisch-deutschen historischen Instituts in Trient*, 20 (1994), pp. 129–164; Cees Reijner, *Italiaanse geschiedschrijvers over de Nederlandse Opstand, 1585–1650. Een transnationale geschiedenis* (Unpublished PhD, University Leiden, 2020). See special issue B. Boute, H. Cools, M.A. Visceglia (eds.), 'Fiandre e Italia tra monarchia universale e stati territoriali: cultura politica e dinamiche sociali', *Dimensioni e problemi della ricerca storica*, 2 (2009) and H. Cools, 'Some Italian voices on Dutch liberties', in P. Brood, R. Kubben (eds.), *The Act of Abjuration. Inspired and Inspirational* (Nijmegen: Wolf Legal publishers, 2011), pp. 1–13.

7   On 6 June 1585 in Milan, Sebastiano Becharia wrote a letter to Ambrosio Landriano requesting news about his brother (he lacked news since 24 March) and a letter to his brother expressing his distress about hearing about the attempt to destroy Farnese's bridge across the river Scheldt. These two letters are kept in BMKF, D10, 2 and have only survived because they are part of one or more posts intercepted en route from Milan to the Low Countries in the late 1580s. On this remarkable and unique collection consult Karl Sautter, 'Auffindung einer grossen Anzahl verschlossener Briefe aus dem Jahre 1585', *Archiv für Post und Telegraphie*, 4 (1909) pp. 97–115 and Andrew Pettegree, *The Invention of News. How the World Came to Know About Itself* (New Haven/London: Yale University Press, 2014), pp. 174–177. I would like to

rumours circulated for days in the streets of Modena about the death of numerous Italian soldiers at the battle of Nieuwpoort in 1600, including Cornelio and
Alessandro Bentivoglio.[8] Passages in the rare surviving letters between siblings
and friends as well as chronicles demonstrate that many Italian contemporaries experienced the Revolt in the Netherlands indirectly and followed its
course very closely.[9] Rumours and snippets of news of battles and epic long
sieges, unexpected skirmishes, violent sacks, murder and mutinies, as well
as failed peace initiatives reached the ears and eyes of many and were hotly
debated at Italy's courts and on Italian squares. The stream of letters and news
reports also produced a wider culture of reflection in Italian court circles where
those with experience of the events and their wider political context weighed
the impact of these distant convulsions on Habsburg policies and the fate of
the Italian states. They inevitably also came to the attention of Italian history
writers, who produced several monumental histories of *Guerre di Fiandra*.

This book provides the first comprehensive study of Italian information and
communication on the Revolt in the Low Countries, casting an entirely new
light on the keen Italian interest in this protracted conflict. It traces both how
news was disseminated, and by whom, in order to analyse how the flow of
information shaped political debates and historical discourses of the Revolt on
the Italian peninsula. Drawing upon a range of different sources in both manuscript and print, including newsletters, printed pamphlets, political treatises
and historical narratives, it studies Italian views of, and debates on, the conflict
in a varied media landscape. In doing so, this study firmly demonstrates that
the complex political constellation of the Italian peninsula, and the influence
of the Habsburg monarchy, shaped the Italian news, debates and interpretations of the Revolt in the Low Countries. Examining all of these textual sources
together also shows to what extent authors exploited the news coming from the
Netherlands for their own purposes. Charting the influence of news reporting
on contemporary political writing and historical discourse helps us to understand how the history of news was connected to the wider political culture in

---

thank the Director Jürgen Küster and Bärbel Menke for their warm welcome and kind assistance in the library.

8   Giovan Battista Spaccini's fascinating chronicle has been published: A. Bioni, R. Bussi,
    C. Giovannini (eds.), *Cronaca di Modena, anni 1588–1602* (Modena: Franco Cosimo Panini,
    1993), pp. 380–381, 389–390, 394–396.

9   A seventeenth-century chronicler of Asolo, a city in the hinterland of Venice, recorded that
    a certain doctor Bevilacqua, one of his fellow citizens, would start 'discussing the war in
    the Low Countries and other things from news reports', quoted by Mario Infelise, *Prima dei
    giornali: alle origini della pubblica informazione, secoli XVI e XVII* (Rome/Bari: Laterza, 2002),
    p. 146.

the Italian states. By reconstructing how news from the Low Countries reached the Italian states, as well as their reception and (re-)use, I argue that to many Italians, the Revolt against Spain was a political matter of the first order, and crucial in building the theoretical framework of contemporary political and historical thought in a fragmented Italy.

1   Entangled Histories

Since the late Middle Ages, Italian cities and the Low Countries were bound by strong commercial and cultural ties.[10] Following the Peace of Cambrai in 1529, which consolidated Habsburg power in Milan and Southern Italy, commercial relations between the Low Countries and Italy recovered and intensified. Antwerp as the commercial hub hosted a sizeable community of 250 merchants and bankers from the Italian peninsula mainly exporting English cloth and importing silk.[11] These connections became tighter when the two distant regions were integrated into the Spanish-Habsburg composite monarchy with the peace treaty of Cateau-Cambrésis in 1559.[12] Ending the wars between the Habsburgs and the Valois over the control of the Italian peninsula, the treaty left Philip II in control of Milan, Naples and Sicily as well as his Burgundian inheritance in the Low Countries.

Even before this formal integration, the gradual expansion of the Habsburg empire under Charles V had created an urgent need to organise communication efficiently between the different regions and viceroyalties. A crucial development was the establishment of regular public postal services by the Tassis family.[13] The Tassis postal route was the backbone of communication in Europe, connecting Habsburg possessions in the Low Countries with the

---

10   Literature on the topic is vast, for an overview see Emma Grootveld and Nina Lamal, 'Cultural translation and glocal dynamics between Italy and the Low Countries during the sixteenth and seventeenth century', *Incontri. Rivista europea di studi italiani*, 30 (2015), pp. 6–8.

11   P. Stabel, 'Italian Merchants and the Fairs in the Low Countries (12th–16th centuries)', in P. Lanario (ed.), *La pratica dello scambio. Sisteme di fiere, mercanti e città in Europa (1400–1700)* (Venice: Marsilio, 2003), pp. 131–160 and P. Subacchi, 'Italians in Antwerp in the second half of the sixteenth century', in H. Soly, A.K.L. Thijs (eds.), *Minderheden in Westeuropese steden (16de-20ste eeuw). Minorities in Western European Cities (sixteenth-twentieth century)* (Rome: Belgisch Historisch Instituut Rome, 1995), pp. 73–90.

12   John Elliott, 'A Europe of Composite Monarchies', *Past & Present*, 137 (1992), pp. 48–71.

13   The most important contribution to date on the Tassis postal services is Wolfgang Behringer, *Im Zeichen des Merkur: Reichspost und Kommunikationsrevolution in der Frühen Neuzeit* (Göttingen: Vandenhoeck & Ruprecht, 2003).

Italian peninsula via the Holy Roman Empire. From Antwerp and Brussels, via Augsburg and Trent, the routes continued to Milan, Venice and Rome. This postal infrastructure shaped the flow of information between the two regions. Crucially it made Italy into a conduit between the Low Countries and Spain. News of the Revolt often made it to these Italian cities first, before reaching the Spanish court in Madrid.[14]

These routes were also vital for the passage of troops and other military supplies to the Low Countries.[15] Once the Revolt erupted in 1566, as Geoffrey Parker has demonstrated in his ground-breaking study on the Army of Flanders, Italy became of crucial importance for the Habsburg strategy in the Low Countries. Genoa, Lombardy and Piedmont were of strategic importance for the 'Spanish road'. Genoese merchants played a key role in sustaining the Habsburg war effort in the Netherlands by lending enormous sums of money to the Spanish crown to finance the war effort.[16] Italy's primary engagement with this war, however, was through its soldiers. Two of the more successful and famous Habsburg army generals, Alexander Farnese and Ambrogio Spinola, hailed from the Italian peninsula. Since the peace of Cateau-Cambrésis had ended the Italian wars only shortly before the conflict erupted in the Low Countries, Italy had troops to spare; many feudal families had specialised in the military profession and were now eager to join the Spanish-Habsburg cause.[17]

Throughout the entire conflict, between ten to twenty percent of the army consisted of Italians.[18] Both Farnese's and Spinola's time as military commanders saw significant increases in the number of Italian troops. In 1581, Farnese ended Spanish dominance in the high command of the army by introducing some significant changes to its internal structure: he allowed the Italian infantry to be organised in their own *tercios*.[19] These Italian *terzi* were primarily recruited from territories within the direct control of the Spanish-Habsburg

---

14   N. Schobesberger, P. Arblaster, M. Infelise, A. Belo, N. Moxham, C. Espejo and J. Raymond (hereafter Schobesberger etc.), 'European Postal Networks', in J. Raymond, N. Moxham (eds.), *News Networks in Early Modern Europe* (Leiden: Brill, 2016), p. 41.

15   Geoffrey Parker, *The Army of Flanders and the Spanish Road 1567–1659* (Cambridge: Cambridge University Press, 1972), pp. 70–90.

16   See articles in R. Belvederi (ed.), *Rapporti Genova-Mediterraneo-Atlantico nell'età moderna* (Genoa: University of Genoa, 1985) and Thomas Allison Kirk, *Genoa and the Sea: Power and Policy in an Early Modern Maritime Republic* (Baltimore: John Hopkins University Press, 2005).

17   For a brief overview of Italian condottiere: David Parrott, *The Business of War: Military Enterprise and Military Revolution in Early Modern Europe* (Cambridge: Cambridge University Press, 2012), pp. 40–46.

18   Parker, *The Army of Flanders*, pp. 237–239.

19   Mario Arfaioli, 'Bastion of Empire: The Italian *terzo vecchio* of the Army of Flanders (1597–1682)', *Journal of Military History*, 85 (2021), pp. 27–50.

monarchy, mainly from Milan and Naples. Soldiers were levied across the
Italian peninsula, including Tuscany, Urbino, Modena, or the Papal States.[20]
As men of all social classes joined the large, multinational Habsburg army, the
Netherlands increasingly became a training ground, a 'school' for those who
wished to enter the business of war. It was also a place where the old tensions
and the competition amongst members of powerful Italian families reap-
peared. Going to the Netherlands became an essential part of the curriculum
of Italian aristocrats, enabling them to gain favours from the king or receive a
prestigious position in the administration of Habsburg Italy.[21]

While they did not share a single border with the Low Countries, Italian
states became important players in the Revolt in the Low Countries. Given
these ties and connections, it is rather strange that Italian perceptions of the
wars have hitherto been largely ignored. National or nationalist frameworks
and perspectives in both Dutch and Italian historiography have prevented such
an approach so far. Like many historical events, the Revolt in the Netherlands
has largely been studied from the perspective of the victors. Historical attention has accordingly focused on the Dutch rebels and their success in establishing a new state. Geoffrey Parker brought the perspective of the Habsburg
monarchy back into the picture by arguing that the course of the conflict
had been significantly influenced by Philip II's involvement in the wars in
the Mediterranean and France.[22] Following Parker's observations, in the last
two decades, the historiography of the Dutch Revolt has turned its attention
more to the international dimensions of the conflict.[23] Even so, recent celebra-

---

20   See the different contributions in G. Bertini (ed.), *Militari Italiani dell'esercito di Alessandro
      Farnese* (Guastalla: Mattioli, 2013); Giuseppe Bertini, 'La nazione italiana nell'esercito di
      Alessandro Farnese nei Paesi Bassi: Nuove prostettive', *Philostrato*, 1 (2018), pp. 258–295.
      Research for Spinola's tenure is more scant: D. Maffi, 'Cacciatori di gloria: La presenza
      degli italiani nell'esercito di Fiandra (1621–1700)', in P. Bianchi, D. Maffi, E. Stumpo (eds.),
      Italiani al servizio straniero in età moderna (Milan: Angeli, 2008), pp. 73–103.
21   This is one of the reasons why the number of Italians in the French army during this
      time declined, D. Parrott, 'Italian soldiers in French service 1500–1700. The Collapse of a
      Military tradition', in P. Bianchi, D. Maffi, E. Stumpo (eds.), *Italiani al servizio straniero in
      età moderna* (Milan: Angeli, 2008), pp. 15–39.
22   Geoffrey Parker, 'Spain, her Enemies and the Revolt of the Netherlands', *Past & Present*,
      99 (1970), pp. 72–95, republished in *Spain and the Netherlands 1559–1659. Ten studies*
      (London: Collins, 1979), pp. 17–43.
23   For an overview of historiographical trends: Judith Pollmann, 'Internationalisering en
      de Nederlandse Opstand', *Bijdragen en Mededelingen betreffende de Geschiedenis der
      Nederlanden*, 124 (2009), pp. 515–535; Judith Pollmann, 'Hogenberg's Ghost: New books on
      the Eighty Years' War', *Early Modern Low Countries*, 4 (2020), pp. 124–138 and Anne-Laure
      van Bruaene, '50 jaar Tachtig Jaar Oorlog in de BMGN', *Bijdragen en Mededelingen betref-
      ferende de Geschiedenis der Nederlanden*, 136 (2021), pp. 124–134.

tions marking the 450th anniversary of the 'birth of the Netherlands' show the durability of the old nationalist paradigm.[24] The historiography also remains largely influenced by the rebels' perspective: Calvinist communities, networks, propaganda, and the inspiring model of the Dutch Republic have received by far the most attention. Hugh Dunthorne's study on the relationship between Britain and the Low Countries exemplifies these trends.[25] Dunthorne studied the publication of the rebels' pamphlets, traced contemporary opinions on the conflict, and showed that this made the revolt a source of inspiration both during the British Civil Wars and during the Glorious Revolution.

It is only fairly recently that scholars such as Violet Soen, Monica Stensland, Yolanda Rodríguez-Pérez have turned their attention to the perspective of the Habsburg monarchy.[26] More recently still, Raymond Fagel has turned his attention to the view from the Spanish trenches, studying the Spanish army commanders' perceptions of the war during the first decade. His work serves as important reminder that there was not a single unified Spanish narrative of the conflict.[27] All these contributions represent a serious attempt to move away from more traditional Dutch historiography which has been shaped by rebel propaganda in the sixteenth century and memory campaigns in the seventeenth century and beyond.[28]

Studying Italian perspectives and experiences of the conflict not only adds another layer to the story but also provides further encouragement for changing that story altogether. As such, it answers Judith Pollmann's recent call to

---

24   https://geboortevannederland.nl/ and more specifically the overview of events in 1572 which does not mention the sack of Mechelen, the first city to be punished by the Duke of Alba in this year: https://geboortevannederland.nl/gebeurtenissen-1572/.

25   Hugh Dunthorne, *Britain and the Dutch Revolt 1560–1700* (Cambridge: Cambridge University Press, 2013). See also H. Dunthorne, 'Resisting Monarchy: The Netherlands as Britain's School of Revolution in the Late Sixteenth and Seventeenth Centuries', in R. Oresko, G.C. Gibbs, H.M. Scott (eds.), *Royal and Republican Sovereignity in Early Modern Europe: Essays in Memory of Ragnhild Hatton* (Cambridge: Cambridge University Press, 1997), pp. 125–148.

26   Violet Soen, *Vredehandel: Adellijke en Habsburgse verzoeningspogingen tijdens de Nederlandse Opstand* (Amsterdam: Amsterdam University Press, 2013); Yolanda Rodríguez Pérez, *The Dutch Revolt Through Spanish Eyes: Self and Other in Historical and Literary Texts of Golden Age Spain (c.1548–1673)* (Bern: Peter Lang, 2008); Monica Stensland, *Habsburg Communication in the Dutch Revolt* (Amsterdam: Amsterdam University Press, 2012).

27   Raymond Fagel, *Protagonists of War. Spanish Army Commanders and the Revolt in the Low Countries* (Leuven: Leuven University Press, 2021), and R. Fagel, L. Francés Álvarez, B. Santiago Belmonte (eds.), *Early modern war narratives and the Revolt in the Low Countries* (Manchester: Manchester University Press, 2020).

28   Jasper van der Steen, *Memory Wars in the Low Countries, 1566–1700* (Leiden: Brill, 2015).

move away from the canonised moments of the Revolt, which have remained more or less static ever since Frans Hogenberg published his influential illustrations of what he considered to be key scenes in the late sixteenth century.[29] 'There are still worlds to be discovered', Pollmann argued, 'for those who are prepared to look beyond the scenes that Hogenberg selected'.[30] Italy provides one of those worlds that challenges Hogenberg's canon. Cross-examining different archives allows us to retrace the sixteenth-century contemporary stories and reflections on the repercussions of events. For instance, where the standard historiography considers the declaration of independence by the States General, the Act of Abjuration (1581), as a seminal moment, the event barely registered at all with Italian political commentators. Chapter Two demonstrates that political observers and thinkers on the Italian peninsula instead highlighted that the damage had already been done in 1577 when the States had invited other foreign rulers to intervene. The events of 1577 have fallen pretty much into oblivion, but for Italian contemporaries, they were key to understanding the Revolt.

If Dutch historians have traditionally ignored the extensive Italian engagement with the Revolt, the same is true for Italian historians. The peace treaty of Cateau-Cambrésis in 1559 is generally seen as the beginning of a *Pax Hispanica*, a sixty-year-long period of peace in Habsburg-controlled Italy.[31] The Duchy of Milan and the Kingdoms of Naples and Sicily were all under direct Spanish-Habsburg rule.[32] Except for the Republic of Venice, the other states, such as the Republic of Genoa, the Grand Duchy of Tuscany, the Duchy of Parma-Piacenza, the Duchy of Urbino, the Duchy of Mantua-Monferrato, the Duchy of Ferrara (Modena), the Duchy of Savoy, and even the papacy fell to varying degrees under the Spanish-Habsburg sphere of influence.[33] Italian

---

29   Hogenberg's prints were already used to illustrate Emanuel van Meteren's history of the Revolt in 1599, and continue to be used to this day. Ramon Voges has argued against uncritical use of these prints in *Das Auge der Geschichte: Der Aufstand der Niederlande und die Französischen Religionskriege im Spiegel der Bildberichte Franz Hogenbergs (ca. 1560–1610)* (Leiden: Brill, 2019).

30   Pollmann, 'Hogenberg's Ghost', p. 138.

31   T. Dandelet, J. Marino (eds.), *Spain in Italy: Politics, Society, and Religion 1500–1700* (Leiden: Brill, 2007).

32   On the imperial system consult: Aurelio Musi, *L'impero dei viceré* (Bologna: Il Mulino, 2013).

33   Venice is invariably presented as the exception, it was the only state to maintain a certain level of independence. See J.J. Martin, 'The Venetian territorial State: Constructing Boundaries in the Shadow of Spain', in T. Dandelet, J. Marino (eds.), *Spain in Italy: Politics, Society, and Religion 1500–1700* (Leiden: Brill, 2007), pp. 226–248. For opposing views about the influence of Spain on the papacy: Thomas Dandelet, *Spanish Rome 1500–1700* (New Haven/London: Yale University Press, 2001) and M. Pattenden, 'Rome as a 'Spanish Avignon'? The Spanish Faction and the Monarchy of Philip II', in P. Baker-Bates,

historians have long neglected this period which was seen as a period of political, economic and cultural decadence and decay.[34]

Since the 1980s, this negative view has gradually been reassessed, but the extent of the Spanish-Habsburg political and military dominance is still debated by historians: were the various Italian rulers mere vassals or rather independent actors from Spanish-Habsburg rule?[35] Michael Levin has gone so far as to question the existence of Habsburg hegemony during the reigns of Charles V and Philip II. He argued that there were several instances where Italian princes, and especially the Grand Duke of Tuscany, showed they had political ambitions of their own.[36] Yet historians have increasingly argued that Habsburg hegemony brought opportunities, identifying the advantages for the Italian mercantile and political elites of being incorporated or affiliated with the Habsburg empire.[37] Rather than Italian subservience to Habsburg intentions, Italian states (to varying degrees) and Madrid were mutually dependent on one another. Many individuals and entire social groups on the Italian peninsula benefitted from the relationship with Europe's most powerful monarchy.[38] The participation of Italian soldiers and officers in the wars in the Low Countries is now understood in this light.[39] By granting Italian noblemen titles, land or pensions, or by brokering favourable marriage alliances,

---

M. Pattenden (eds.), *Spanish Presence in Sixteenth-Century Italy: Images of Iberia* (Farnham: Ashgate, 2015), pp. 65–78.

34 For a discussion on anti-Spanishness as part of Italian identity, see essays in A. Musi (ed.), *Alle origini di una nazione. Antispagnolismo e identità italiana* (Milan: Guerini, 2003).

35 E. Fasano Guarini, 'Italia non spagnola e Spagna nel tempo di Filippo II', in L. Lotti, R. Villari (eds.), *Filippo II e il Mediterraneo* (Rome: Laterza, 2003), pp. 5–23. For an overview of recent literature consult M. Levin, 'Italy and the Limits of the Spanish Empire', in W. Reger, T. Andrade (eds.), *The Limits of Empire: European Imperial Formations in Early Modern World History. Essays in Honor of Geoffrey Parker* (Farnham: Ashgate, 2012), pp. 121–136.

36 Michael Levin, *Agents of Empire. Spanish Ambassadors in Sixteenth Century Italy* (Ithaca/London: Cornell University Press, 2005). Francesco Angiolini, 'L'Italia nell'età di Filippo II. Osservazioni preliminari', *Rivista Storica Italiana*, 92 (1980), pp. 432–469 already highlighted how Spain feared that political changes might affect its dominant position.

37 Angelantonio Spagnoletti, *Le dinastie italiane nella prima età moderna* (Bologna: il Mulino, 2003).

38 Manuel Herrero Sánchez, 'The Business Relations, Identities and Political Resources of Italia Merchants in the early-modern Spanish monarchy: some introductory remarks', *European Review of History*, 23 (2016), pp. 1–12. In her study of the Genoese presence in Southern Italy, Céline Dauverd has called it 'symbiotic imperialism' in *Imperial ambition in the Early Modern Mediterranean: Genoese merchants and the Spanish Crown* (Cambridge: Cambridge University Press, 2015).

39 Gregory Hanlon, *The Twilight of a Military Tradition: Italian Aristocrats and European Conflicts, 1560–1800* (London: UCL press, 1998); Giampiero Brunelli, *Soldati del papa. Politica militare e nobiltà nello Stato della Chiesa (1560–1644)* (Rome: Carocci, 2003); Angelantonio

Philip II and his successors hoped to keep his allies close, to be guaranteed their continuing support and to ensure that Italian rulers were reluctant to break definitely with the Habsburg state.[40] The old rivalry with France over the domination of the Italian peninsula did not resurface until the early seventeenth century. Louis XIII and Richelieu embarked on an active policy of establishing alliances with Italian states, but only with limited success and sometimes disastrous consequences for the Italian dukes who had aligned themselves with France.[41]

In pondering the relationship between their own states and Habsburg power, members of the Italian elites recognized both danger and opportunity.[42] The leading members of Italian society were by and large well-disposed towards Spanish-Habsburg power but also recognized the challenge of manoeuvring within the complex Habsburg system and tried to mark their positions vis à vis the king and his administration.[43] Italian observers of the Revolt in the Netherlands saw that conflict through the lens of their own experience of Habsburg influence, while Spanish officials in Italy worried that it might seep into the peninsula. Crucial to Levin's argument above is that Spanish ambassadors stationed in Italy were constantly worried about the intentions of Italian princes.[44] The evolution of the Revolt in the Netherlands played a crucial role in their worries as the Spanish-Habsburg diplomats and secretaries feared that the war could potentially threaten Habsburg dominance and peace on the Italian peninsula.

This book will not reconstruct the involvement of each of the different Italian territories in the war in the Low Countries and their respective (changing) relationships with Madrid, but look at it from a very specific angle. One of its main arguments, following Levin, is that Habsburg rulers and agents did

---

Spagnoletti, 'Le dinastie italiane e la guerra delle Fiandre', *Storia e società*, 125 (2009), pp. 423–443.

40   For relations under Philip III consult J. Martinez Millán, M.A. Visceglia (eds.), *La monarquía de Felipe III: los reinos* (Madrid: Fundación Mapfre, 2008).

41   Sven Externbrink, *Le Coeur du monde. Frankreich und die norditalienischen Staaten (Mantua, Parma, Savoyen) im Zeitalter Richelieus 1624–1635* (Munster: Lit Verlag, 1997) and Anna Blum, *La Diplomatie de la France en Italie du nord au temps de Richelieu et de Mazarin* (Paris: Garnier, 2014).

42   A. Spagnoletti, 'Paz y quietud in Italia negli anni di Filippo II', in G. di Stefano, E. Fasano Guarini, A. Martinengo (eds.), *Italia non spagnola e monarchia spagnola tra '500 e '600. Politica, cultura e letterature* (Florence: Olschki, 2009), pp. 29–41.

43   P.P. Merlin, 'Spagna e Savoia nella politica italiana ed europea da Cateau-Cambresis a Vervins (1559–1598)', in J. Martinez Millán (ed.), *Felipe II (1527–1598): Europa y la Monarquía Católica* (Madrid: Parteluz, 1998), pp. 513–530.

44   Levin, *Agents of Empire*, pp. 1–13.

not take the allegiances of the Italian princes for granted, and that Habsburg policy in the Low Countries subsequently had to be explained and defended on the Italian peninsula. The focus, therefore, lies on the circulation of information about the Revolt in the Low Countries to, from, and within the different Italian states. This approach is not entirely new; the importance of rapid and reliable information gathering for the survival of Italian dynastic states has been hinted at by Daniela Frigo and Alessandra Contini.[45] Driven by political and military preoccupations, as well as pursuing dynastic prestige, the rulers of smaller states such as the duchies of Urbino, Modena and Mantua, as well as the Grand Duchy of Tuscany, wanted to be constantly updated with the latest information. Comments in secretarial guides illustrate why it was important to collect all the available news, as Panfilo Persico advised in his work *Del Segretario* (1620):

> The interests of princes are connected, and often depend on minor events which become great successes, so nothing can be neglected, but every movement, every novelty needs to be reported, so that often through close comparison with *avvisi* from other parts, the light shines on secret matters.[46]

The surviving impressive collections of handwritten newsletters (*avvisi*) illustrate the access of these princes to a wealth of news and political information.[47] The bulk of my material comes from the archives of Italy's ruling dynasties: Della Rovere, Medici, d'Este, Gonzaga, and to a lesser extent Farnese and Savoy. This is partly due to the survival and nature of their archives. In the case of

---

45   See the contributions in D. Frigo (ed.), *Politics and Diplomacy in Early Modern Italy. The Structure of Diplomatic Practice, 1450–1800* (Cambridge: Cambridge University Press, 2000).

46   Panfilo Persico, *Del Segretario del sig. Panfilo Persico libri quattro, ne'quali si tratta dell'arte, e facolta del segreatrio, della istituione, e vita di lui nelle republiche e nelle corti* (Venice: Zenaro, 1643), USTC 4017857, p. 196: 'Ond'essendo gl'interessi dè prinicpe tanto l'un coll'altro congiunti, e pendendo spesso da lievi momenti successi di grandissima importanza, niuna cosa par, che si deva trascurare, ma ogni moto, ogni novità, avisar si poiche spesso confrontandosi con gli avisi d'altri parti aprono lume a maneggi non penetrati'.

47   When I started research on these collections in 2011, very few had been studied, with the exception of Cornel Zwierlein, who studied the collections in Mantua, Modena and the Vatican library. See his *Discorso und Lex Dei. Die Entstehung neuer Denkrahmen im 16. Jahrhundert un die Wahrnehmung der französischen Religionskriege in Italien und Deutschland* (Göttingen: Vandenhoeck & Ruprecht, 2006), pp. 214–240. More recently Paola Molino, 'Connected News. German Zeitungen and Italian avvisi in the Fugger collection (1568–1604)', *Media History*, 22 (2016), pp. 267–295 and the EURONEWS project, dedicated to researching *avvisi* in the Medici archives: https://www.euronewsproject.org.

the dukes of Savoy, archivists in the eighteenth century have separated newsletters from diplomatic correspondence and these have since disappeared.[48]
Individual members of the Farnese family played a key role during the Revolt
in the Netherlands, but sadly large parts of their rich archive were destroyed
during the bombardments of Naples in 1943. The detailed archival guide compiled by the Belgian historians Alfred Cauchie and Léon van der Essen in 1911
provided some guidance to the original contents.[49] By establishing the importance of access to information on the Low Countries for these different Italian
princely rulers, this study firmly demonstrates that the complex political constellation of the Italian peninsula, and the influence of the Habsburg monarchy and its agents, shaped the Italian news, debates and interpretations of the
Revolt in the Low Countries.

2   Early Modern Communication

While this book contributes to the history of the Revolt in the Low Countries
and Habsburg-Italian relations, is also a study of political communication and
information in the early modern period. Throughout the sixteenth century, the
existing media landscape began to change. Regular postal services allowed for
a steady flow of information at a time when the demand for news was growing due to the ongoing confrontations with the Ottomans and the devastating
religious and civil wars in both France and the Low Countries. Political information became regularly and readily available in a variety of different genres,
such as handwritten newsletters, printed news pamphlets, prints and contemporary histories.

Scholarship on this key period in the history of news has in recent years
been both extensive and transformative; documenting the rapid development
of international news networks and markets in the sixteenth and seventeenth
centuries.[50] Importantly, recent research has increasingly examined the oral

---

48   Zwierlein, *Discorso und Lex Dei*, p. 249.
49   Alfred Cauchie and Léon Van der Essen, *Inventaire des archives Farnésiennes de Naples*
       (Brussels: Libraries Kiessling et Company, 1911); Michel Dierickx, 'Les "Carte Farnesiane"
       de Naples per rapport à l'histoire des anciens Pays-Bas, après l'incendie du 30 septembre
       1943', *Bulletin de la Commission Royal d'Histoire/ Handelingen van de Koninklijke Commissie
       voor Geschiedenis*, 112 (1947), pp. 111–126.
50   B. Dooley, S.A. Baron (eds.), *The Politics of Information in Early Modern Europe* (London/
       New York: Routledge, 2001); J. Koopmans (ed.), *News and Politics in Early Modern Europe
       (1600–1800)* (Leuven: Peeters, 2005); J. Raymond (ed.), *News Networks in Seventeenth
       Century Britain and Europe* (London: Routledge, 2006); B. Dooley (ed.), *The Dissemination
       of News and the Emergence of Contemporaneity in Early Modern Europe* (Burlington:

transmission of news, the circulation of news in manuscript newsletters and the interactions between different media.[51] From these studies, a new picture emerges: information constantly moved between different places and media regardless of political, linguistic or religious boundaries.[52]

The present study contributes to a growing body of work on the circulation of political information in early modern Europe that moves beyond state actors and takes a more expansive approach to the making of news including the development of public political and historical discourse. It questions the recent emphasis on a lack of borders in the flow of information and takes inspiration from Filippo de Vivo's important more micro-historical work on information in Venice in studying how political and confessional allegiances of individual actors and institutions shaped both the media and the message.[53] It particularly draws attention to one crucial yet missing piece in the news puzzle: the role played by letters. Although scholars recognize that correspondence was essential for the transmission of news, letters have been studied separately from other news media.[54] The use of diplomatic correspondence

---

Ashgate, 2010); Johann Petitjean, *L'intelligence des choses. Une histoire de l'information entre Italie et Mediterranee (XVIe–XVIIe Siècle)* (Rome: Ecole Française de Rome, 2013); Pettegree, *The Invention of News*; S. Davies, P. Fletcher (eds.), *News in Early Modern Europe: Currents and Connections* (Leiden: Brill, 2014); J. Raymond, N. Moxham (eds.), *News Networks in Early Modern Europe* (Leiden: Brill, 2016); Paul M. Dover, *The Information Revolution in Early Modern Europe* (Cambridge: Cambridge University Press, 2021).

51   On the interactions between different media see Robert Darnton, 'An Early Information Society: News and Media in Eighteenth-Century Paris', *American Historical Review*, 105 (2000), pp. 1–35; Joad Raymond, 'Newspapers: a National or an International Phenomenon', *Media History*, 11 (2012), pp. 1–9; Rosa Salzberg and Massimo Rospocher, 'Street Singers in Italian Renaissance Urban Culture and Communication', *Cultural and Social History*, 9 (2012), pp. 9–26; Daniel Bellingradt and Massimo Rospocher, 'A History of Early Modern Communication', *Annali dell'Istituto storico italo-germanico in Trento/Jahrbuch des ialienisch-deutschen historischen Instituts in Trient*, 35 (2019), pp. 7–22.

52   Most notably J. Raymond and N. Moxham, 'News Networks in Early Modern Europe', in J. Raymond, N. Moxham (eds.), *News Networks in Early Modern Europe* (Leiden: Brill, 2016), pp. 1–16; J. Raymond, 'News Networks: Putting the 'News' and 'Networks' Back in', *News Networks*, pp. 102–129; D. Bellingradt, 'The Dynamic of Communication and Media Recycling in Early Modern Europe: Popular Prints as Echoes and Feedback Loops', in M. Rospocher, J. Salman, H. Salmi (eds.), *Crossing Borders, Crossing Cultures. Popular Print in Europe (1450–1900)* (Oldenbourg: De Gruyter, 2019), pp. 9–32.

53   Filippo De Vivo, *Information & Communication in Venice. Rethinking Early Modern Politics* (Oxford: Oxford University Press, 2007) and more recently his article: 'Microhistories of Long-Distance information: Space, Movement and Agency in the Early Modern News', *Past & Present*, 242 Supplement 14 (2019), pp. 179–214.

54   J. Boutier, S. Landi, O. Rouchon (eds.), *La politique par correspondance. Les usages politiques de la lettre en Italie (XIVe–XVIIIe siècle)* (Rennes: Rennes Presses Universitaires, 2011); James Daybell, *The Material Letter: Manuscript Letters and the Culture and Practices*

illustrates this trend. Contemporaries described diplomats as the 'eyes and the ears of their prince' as they had to provide their ruler and his allies with recent and reliable news.[55] Yet their letters have been primarily and selectively analyzed to reconstruct the conduct of foreign policy instead of studying the role diplomats and their secretaries played in disseminating, manipulating and controlling news.[56]

In the case of news coming from the Low Countries, Italian rulers faced a serious disadvantage as they did not have any official representatives in the Low Countries. I argue that Italian military commanders acted as alternative 'eyes and ears' for a variety of Italian princely rulers filling the gap left by the absence of regular diplomatic correspondence.[57] Their letters provided a reliable source of information and were particularly important to shaping the first narratives of battles and sieges. Their letters were often excerpted, copied and repurposed in handwritten news reports and other (printed) media. By incorporating these more confidential letters, a variety of agents involved in the transmission of news, as well as the patronage relationships governing the epistolary exchanges become much clearer and the impact of political and confessional differences will come into focus for the first time.[58]

Building on the recent scholarship, this book advances an integrated approach to the history of news or a more 'entangled history of media'.[59] Its main presupposition is that to understand the Italian media coverage of the Revolt, it is essential to study how news is both being reused as well as

---

of Letter-Writing in Early Modern England, 1580–1635 (Basingstoke: Palgrave, 2012); Gary Schneider, The Culture of Epistolarity: Vernacular Letters and Letter Writing in Early Modern England, 1500–1700 (Newark: University of Delaware Press, 2005); P. Findlen, S. Sutherland (eds.), The Renaissance of Letters. Knowlegde and Community in Italy, 1300–1650 (London: Routledge, 2020).

55 Persico, Del Segretario, p. 196: 'Perciò si chiamano gli ambasciatori occhi, & orecchi dè Principi'.

56 For exceptions and growing recognition of their importance see: T. Sowerby, 'Elizabethan Diplomatic Networks and the Spread of News', in J. Raymond, N. Moxham (eds.), News Networks in Early Modern Europe (Leiden: Brill, 2016), pp. 305–327; J. Peacey, '"My Friend the Gazetier": Diplomacy and News in Seventeenth-Century Europe', in News Networks, pp. 420–442 and Helmer J. Helmers, 'Public Diplomacy in Early Modern Europe: Towards a New History of News', Media History, 22 (2016), pp. 401–420.

57 Nina Lamal, 'Communicating conflict: early modern soldiers as information-gatherers', Journal of Medieval and Early Modern Studies, 50 (2020), pp. 13–31.

58 For a recent case study of how religious differences influenced the flow of information between England and Rome, see Charles R. Keenan, 'English News in Papal Rome: Cross-Confessional Information Exchange in Reformation Europe', Journal of Early Modern History, 23 (2019), pp. 350–366.

59 This term has been proposed by Bellingradt, 'The Dynamic of Communication', p. 31.

repurposed in different written news media. Epistolary news, handwritten mis-cellaneous summaries of news, and single event news reports, both in manu-script and print, were part of the same media system. These forms of news, however, had different functions within the media landscape and were subject to different social relationships and production mechanisms. Paying attention to these different communicative functions and contexts allows uncovering how a variety of actors contributed to constructing and promoting a specific narrative of an event.

Close examination of correspondence, handwritten newsletters, political treatises and printed output is also essential to trace the influence of news on wider political discourse on the conflict. The arrival of fresh news fueled Italian political debate on how to solve the ongoing war. Most of the authors of the manuscript treatises on the conflict in the Low Countries were mostly not well-known political thinkers, and have so far escaped the attention of intel-lectual historians who have preferred to study more canonical texts. In these scribal publications, political intelligencers applied reason of state thinking and discourse to contemporary events to analyse potential outcomes.[60] This specific framework, the *discorso* method, shaped how Italian perceived and interpreted information about the conflict and their discussion of how to pre-serve the Spanish reputation and monarchy.[61]

Finally, letters and news reports were also a form of contemporary history writing. These texts offer us the first accounts of political and military events in the Low Countries. Contemporary history writers, who were often themselves active as intelligencers, gave these first drafts of history an afterlife in their own historical accounts.[62] This study traces how news in all its different forms was reused and repurposed in histories in ways that left a lasting influence on its content. It examines the different ways in which Italians described events they had either heard or read about, witnessed or participated in – and how they remembered them afterwards.

To show the variety and depth of Italian engagement with the Revolt in the Low Countries from 1566 to 1648, each chapter pays attention to a specific genre of

---

60   For reason of state see Maurizio Viroli, *From Politics to Reason of state: The Acquisition and Transformation of the Language of Politics, 1250–1600* (Cambridge: Cambridge University Press, 1992).

61   For this method: Zwierlein, *Discorso und Lex Dei*.

62   See Brendan Dooley, *The Social History of Skepticism. Experience and Doubt in Early Modern Culture* (Baltimore: John Hopkins University Press, 1999) and Joad Raymond, *The Invention of the Newspaper: English Newsbook 1641–1649* (Oxford: Clarendon Press, 2005), pp. 270–313.

information organised chronologically. Throughout the chapters, I trace how different events were explained and interpreted in Italy and how this shaped the Italian perception of the conflict as a whole. The first chapter explores the dissemination of information about the conflict, both in handwritten newsletters as in more confidential letters. The next chapter offers a first case study of how the Revolt in the Netherlands filtered into Italian political discourse. It analyses how the eruption of unrest in 1577 in the Low Countries dominated Italian news reports and shaped Italian political discussions. The third chapter examines occasional printed news reports from the start of the revolt in 1566 until the death of Alexander Farnese in 1592. Examining which events were printed in which Italian cities, I argue, tells us a great deal about Habsburg communication on the peninsula. The fourth chapter explores the 'afterlives' of letters and how news reports were used in the first Italian historical narratives of the Revolt. Chapter Five turns to the Italian debates on how to pacify the conflict in the Low Countries between 1598 and 1610. While in 1577 Habsburg authority and reputation were not questioned, some thirty years later during the peace negotiations leading to the Twelve Years' Truce in 1609, it was. Chapter six investigates the changes in the genre of occasionally printed news accounts in the early seventeenth century. These printed news reports presented more coherent narratives and increasingly became polemical instruments. The final chapter argues that the past reports and debates influenced the development of a moderate Catholic narrative of the Revolt in the Low Countries in the various Italian histories printed in the first half of the seventeenth century. The historical accounts were the end products of Italian communication on the Revolt in the Low Countries.

Italian News Networks

In the 1570s, the Florentine tailor Bastiano Arditi regularly visited the *Mercato Nuovo* to hear the latest news.[1] This international economic centre at the heart of the city was an ideal place to stay up to date: merchants exchanged the most recent information and couriers arrived here with letters from all over Europe.[2] On 18 December 1576, Arditi noted in his diary that letters from Lucca had arrived in Florence with news of events in Antwerp.[3] He did not record the exact content of these letters, but it was probably related to the previous month's sack of Antwerp by the Spanish troops. Arditi, however, did remark that he did not believe the reports. Indeed, at this stage, it was unclear what exactly had happened, as some accounts circulating in Italian cities reported that the army of the States General had attacked Antwerp.[4]

The outbreak of plague in Northern Italy had delayed the arrival of postal couriers, which created more uncertainty and speculation about what had happened in Antwerp. Arditi thus decided to wait for further confirmation. A few days later, several news reports coming from a number of places arrived in Florence offering a very different version of the events. It turned out that it was not the army of the States General that had attacked Antwerp, but mutinous Spanish-Habsburg soldiers: they had sacked the city, setting parts alight, killing numerous inhabitants and plundering the houses. For the merchants at the *Mercato Nuovo*, this was particularly bad news since these mutinous soldiers had not spared the Florentine and other foreign merchants residing in Antwerp.

This news was exceptionally dramatic, but what Arditi described in his diary is otherwise a typical example of how news arrived in Florence: hear-say,

---

1 Roberto Cantagalli (ed.), *Diario di Firenze e di altre parte della cristinità (1574–1579)* (Florence: Istituto nazionale di studi sul Rinascimento, 1970). For more on Arditi consult D. Rosenthal, 'The Tailor's Song: Notes from the Savonarolan Underground in Grand-Ducal Florence', in P.F. Howard, C. Hewlett (eds.), *Studies on Florence and the Italian Renaissance in Honour of F.W. Kent* (Turnhout: Brepols, 2016), pp. 359–372.

2 Also see Petitjean, *L'information des choses*, pp. 70–75.

3 *Diario di Firenze*, pp. 134–135.

4 BA, D188 INF, fol 183: *Di Venetia il primo decembre 76*, fol 184: 'Lettere d'anversa ne per via d'Augusta ne per altra si sono ricevute due settimane passate, onde si dubita o che la citta sia assediata dall'essercito de stati, o che il pressidio de Thedeschi accordatisi con spagnuoli non habbiano fatto qualche gran novità dentro della città ne dalla corte cesarea habbiamo lettere questa settimana'.

© KONINKLIJKE BRILL NV, LEIDEN, 2023 | DOI:10.1163/9789004538078_003

combined with mercantile and diplomatic letters as well as *avvisi* from various European cities. This chapter traces how news of the Revolt in the Low Countries reached Italian courts, cities, and squares. With the development of handwritten newsletters, known in Italian as *avvisi*, Italian rulers, merchants, and citizens received regular weekly updates on events occurring in the rest of Europe.[5] These handwritten newsletters started to play a crucial role in the intelligence gathering of Italian ducal families, their ambassadors and administrations.[6] Reports from Antwerp became a regular feature in these *avvisi*, as the Revolt in the Netherlands unfolded and the Italian demand for news on the political and military conflict grew incessantly. These *avvisi* offered the first factual, albeit often fragmentary, narratives of the Revolt in the Low Countries shaping the initial perceptions in Italian states.

As the news of the sack of Antwerp arriving in Florence in 1576 indicates, rumours and divergent accounts circulated very frequently. The reliability of news reports was one of the major problems for news consumers in this period.[7] Alongside the new periodic medium of handwritten newsletters, Italian rulers relied on their diplomats stationed at foreign courts to obtain regular, trustworthy, and current information. They faced a significant problem in gathering accurate news from the Low Countries: they lacked their own diplomatic representatives in Brussels or elsewhere in the region. This chapter investigates how the Medici, rulers of Florence, dealt with this challenge and obtained confidential news from the Low Countries during the opening decade of the conflict (1566–1576).

In a seminal article, Alessandra Contini has already shown that Cosimo I de' Medici understood the power of information.[8] To legitimise his state and his power, he relied on diplomats 'to gather the information he needed to police his internal and external enemies', as well as established complex and flexible networks which were largely based on informal patron-client relationships.[9] While Contini has focused almost exclusively on the careers of ambassadors

---

5   Infelise, *Prima dei giornali*, pp. 3–20.

6   S. Barker, '"Secret and Uncertain": A History of *Avvisi* at the Court of the Medici Grand Dukes', in J. Raymond, N. Moxham (eds.), *News Networks in Early Modern Europe* (Leiden: Brill, 2016), pp. 716–738.

7   Pettegree, *Invention of News*, p. 13.

8   A. Contini, 'Dinastia, patriziato e politica estera: ambasciatore e segretari medicei nel cinquecento', in D. Frigo (ed.), *Ambasciatori e nunzi: figure della diplomazia in età moderna* (Rome: Bulzoni, 1999), pp. 57–131. For a recent overview of Cosimo de' Medici consult A. Assonitis, H. Th. Van Veen (eds.), *A Companion to Cosimo I de' Medici* (Leiden: Brill, 2021).

9   A. Contini, 'Aspects of Medicean Diplomacy in the Sixteenth Century', in D. Frigo (ed.), *Politics and Diplomacy in Early Modern Italy. The Structure of Diplomatic Practice, 1450–1800* (Cambridge: Cambridge University Press, 2000), p. 59.

and secretaries of state, this chapter outlines the careers of two Medici correspondents in the Low Countries and their reasons for sending letters with news to Florence. These trusted informants provided the Medici with valuable and credible reports to ascertain with some sense of certainty how the conflict was evolving. I argue that, compared to other ruling Italian houses, the Medici were particularly well-informed on the first phase of the revolt and that their access to different sources of news provided this ruling house with a political advantage over other dynastic rulers on the Italian peninsula.

1   A New Medium

One of the Italian terms for news in the sixteenth century was *avviso*. This term has various and interrelated meanings: an *avviso* can either be a notice, an announcement, information or a news sheet.[10] This last meaning of a news sheet containing information about a contemporary event was new in the sixteenth century, as it started to emerge as a news medium in Italian cities to meet the growing demand for information.[11] It is a handwritten bulletin of the latest news, organized under headlines and divided into paragraphs, ranging from two to eight pages.[12] The heading is one of the defining formal features which consisted of a place and a date: for instance, 'from Antwerp 13 July 1566'. The location mentioned is not necessarily the city where the events occurred, but the place where the news was first received or gathered. The information was divided into short paragraphs, each paragraph dedicated to a different bit of news, and often characterised by a dry factual style without any further comment or analysis. These handwritten newsletters lacked standard epistolary greetings and the writer of the news report did not sign off with their name. During the sixteenth century, this standard *avviso* emerged in Venice and Rome, where the first commercial news agencies were established offering customers a regular subscription service.

---

10   On the terminology see J. Hayez, 'Avviso, informazione, novella, nuova: la notion de l'information dans les correspondances marchandes Toscanes vers 1400', in C. Boudreau, K. Fianu, C. Gauvard (eds.), *Information et société en occident à la fin du Moyen Age* (Paris: Publication de la Sorbonne, 2004), pp. 113–133; Johann Petitjean, 'Mots et pratiques de l'information. ce que aviser veut dire (XVI–XVIIᵉ Siècles)', *Mélanges de l'école française de Rome, Italie- Méditerranée*, 122 (2010), pp. 107–121.

11   Avvisi were 'discovered' in the first half of the twentieth century: Salvatore Bongi, 'Le prime gazette in Italia', *Nuova Antologia*, 11 (1896), pp. 31–46 and René Ancel, 'Étude critique sur quelques recueils d'avvisi', *Mélanges d'archéologie et d'histoire*, 28 (1908), pp. 115–139.

12   Infelise, *Prima dei giornali*, pp. 3–20; Dooley, *Social History of Skepticism*, pp. 9–23.

It is important, however, to remember that standardization was a gradual process. A significant number of newsletters from the second half of the sixteenth century still diverged from this standard *avviso*-form. We find several examples still being signed by their compilers. The Venetian news writer, Hieronimo Acconzaioco, signed his newsletters to the Fuggers between 1575–1576.[13] Even more common are anonymised copies of more personal letters with a typical heading. Letters from the battlefield by soldiers regularly formed the basis of anonymised newsletters: in 1576 an *avviso* had the headline 'from Antwerp with letters from a soldier'.[14] A practice which offers some glimpses into the close ties between more personal letters and this new medium.

The origins of this new information service have been the subject of some debate. Some scholars have pointed to the mutual exchange of news by merchants as political and military events could disrupt international trade.[15] Others have questioned whether merchant correspondence provides a sufficient explanation for the emergence of handwritten newsletters.[16] The development of diplomacy in Italian city-states and the practice to send the latest news regularly by diplomats to their governments are particularly relevant for the commodification of news.[17] As is the development of regular postal services, between different Italian cities and by the Tassis family which 'formed the spine of news communication, shaping all printed and manuscript forms that follow, including periodicity'.[18] The postal infrastructure facilitated the

---

13   See Oswald Bauer, *Zeitungen vor der Zeitung. Die Fuggerzeitungen (1568–1605) und das Frühmoderne Nachrichtensystem* (Berlin: Akademie Verlag, 2011), p. 118.

14   For other anonymised personal letters with an *avviso*-style headline: ASF, MdP 4254, fol 206r–v; 246r–247r.

15   See Georg Christ, 'A Newsletter in 1419? Antonio Morosini's Chronicle in the Light of Commercial Correspondence between Venice and Alexandria', *Mediterranean Historical Review*, 20 (2005), pp. 35–66; Juraj Kittler, 'Caught between business, war and politics: late medieval roots of the early modern European news networks', *Mediterranean Historical Review*, 33 (2018), pp. 199–222.

16   M. Infelise, 'From Merchants' Letters to Handwritten Political Avvisi: Notes on the Origins of Public Information', in F. Bethencourt, F. Egmond (eds.), *Cultural Exchange in Early Modern Europe: Correspondence and Cultural Exchange in Europe, 1400–1700, Volume 3* (Cambridge: Cambridge University Press, 2007), pp. 33–52; Z. Barbarics-Hermanik, 'The Coexistence of Manuscript and Print: Handwritten Newsletters in the Second Century of Print, 1540–1640', in G. Kemp, M. Walsby (eds.), *The Book Triumphant. Print in Transition in the Sixteenth and Seventeenth Centuries* (Leiden: Brill, 2011), p. 359, points to the relevance of developing humanist epistolary practices.

17   For the development of diplomacy, consult Isabella Lazzarini, *Communication & Conflict. Italian Diplomacy in the Early Renaissance, 1350–1520* (Oxford: Oxford University Press, 2015), related to letter writing specifically see pp. 202–212 and in relation to *avvisi*: Zwierlein, *Discorso und Lex Dei*.

18   Schobesberger etc., 'European Postal Networks', pp. 59–60.

transmission of information between Europe's main commercial and political centres and the arrival of the postal courier on set days influenced the regular appearance of handwritten newsletters in a given city.

Italian rulers received newsletters from a very diverse range of agents and places. Most of the ruling Italian dynasties received newsletters from their ambassadors across Europe. Cosimo Bartoli, the Florentine ambassador in Venice between 1562 and 1572, for instance, personally compiled a standard type of *avviso* every week, which he signed before sending them to Florence.[19] Most ambassadors would dispatch anonymised *avvisi* alongside their dispatches. They were encouraged and expected to relay the information available to them, as it might just prove to be the missing bit of information required to distinguish fact from fiction. To ascertain their veracity, it was a common practice to compare reports from different places. It explains why Bernardo Canigiani, Medici ambassador in Ferrara between 1564–1577, forwarded Roman newsletters to Secretary of State, Bartolomeo Concino, while at the same time newsletters were sent from Rome by Cardinal Ferdinand de' Medici.[20] For the same reason, most Italian dukes further employed specific agents in Rome and Venice, who would send them *avvisi* regularly. Between 1572 and 1593, for example, the Farneses received newsletters from Carlo Stuerdo and Benedetto Gallo, their agents in Rome.[21] In addition to the newsletters these rulers received from their own agents and ambassadors, they also had subscriptions to more commercial newsletters which were compiled by professional scribes in Venice, Rome, and later also in Genoa.[22] Italian dukes, cardinals and noblemen regularly received and read the same or very similar news reports, potentially originating from the same scribal offices.[23]

---

19   ASF, MdP 3079–3081; Judith Bryce, *Cosimo Bartoli (1503–1572): The Career of a Florentine Polymath* (Geneva: Droz, 1983), pp. 113–129; R. Cantagalli and N. de Blasi, 'Cosimo Bartoli', in *DBI*, 6 (1964). Bartoli's son, Curzio, would continue this service: ASF, MdP 3082.

20   ASF, MdP 4026, fol 155v: 'All Ill. mio Signore en Pron. Col. Il Sig. Bernardo Canigiani Ambasciatore dell Alt. Di Toscana Ferrara' was further addressed to Concino. Also see: E. Fasano Guarini, '"Rome, workshop of all the practices of the world": from the letters of Cardinal Ferdinando de' Medici to Cosimo I and Francesco I', in G. Signorotto, M.A. Visceglia (eds.), *Court and Politics in Papal Rome, 1492–1700* (Cambridge: Cambridge University Press, 2002), pp. 53–77.

21   Cauchie and Van der Essen, *Inventaire des archives Farnéssiennes*, pp. lix–lx, 37–38, 41, 49, 50–51, 82–83.

22   Genoa has not yet received any attention as a centre for writing of *avvisi*, the Gonzaga family received a lot of handwritten newsletters from Genoa, see for instance ASMn, AG, 1982; 1983.

23   For a comparison see the *avviso* from Antwerp 2 November 1566: ASF, MdP 4254, fol 210r; BAV, Urb Lat 1040, fol 299v and ASMo, CD, Avvsi 6, fol 475. In ASMo, CD, Avvisi 12–13, the

The majority of these professional news writers, called *reportista* in Venice or *menante* in Rome, remained anonymous. That such anonymity was taken for granted is shown by a comment, on the verso of an *avviso* from 1585 sent to the Duke of Urbino, one finds the comment: 'newsletter from the new news writer'.[24] These news writers had good reasons to hide their involvement. Between 1567 and 1572, the authorities of Venice and Rome took different legal punitive measures against this new professional group. In both cities, bans were renewed, but ultimately the authorities were unsuccessful in controlling their circulation. Being a news writer certainly became a risky occupation with many requesting help or protection from their powerful clients when new measures were being promulgated.[25] Occasionally news writers were arrested and severely punished, but only in very exceptional cases were news writers sentenced to death.[26] The known cases are of rather high-profile news writers suspected of informing foreign protestant rulers in the years between 1586 and 1589.[27] Annibale Cappello, for instance, who had begun his career as a secretary to Cardinal Cesare d'Este, and supplied both d'Este's and Gonzaga's with handwritten newsletters from Rome, was sentenced to death in 1587 for his contacts with Elizabeth I and Elector of Saxony.[28]

Hiring the services of a *menante* was a costly enterprise. According to Mario Infelise prices were kept relatively high to restrict the access to news to an elite audience.[29] The surviving collections of *avvisi* in archives confirm that the recipients all belonged to the ruling elite in Italy: the various ruling

---

same *avvisi* in two different hands are quite frequent from 1582 to 1585: one was addressed to Alfonso II d'Este, Duke of Ferrara, and the other to Cardinal Luigi d'Este.

24 BAV, Urb Lat 1053, fol 286v: 'avvisi del nuovo menanti'.

25 See ASF, MM, 29, fol 20 in 1572 from Venice and a request for protection by a news writer from Rome in BAV, Urb Lat, *Di Roma li xv di febraro 1576*, fol 50r: 'è in grandissima colera contra questi Menanti contra platici li quali mettano mano ad ogni cosa che le venga nella mente imaginata, ond' se bene questa non è mia professione, et scrivo senza entrar' in sagrestia, nondimeno supplico V.E. Ill. à tener la mia protettione bisognando poiché non ho altro refugio che l' ombra dall' arbori colae die quelle saporitissime ghiande dell' età dell'oro, perche non si niega à nessuno di scrivere à Principe, tenga Agentes, at negotiorum gestores'.

26 Infelise, *Prima dei giornali*, pp. 154–158.

27 Simone Testa, 'Death of a political informer. Camillo Volta, Roman agent of Louis de Gonzague Duc de Nevers', *Lives and Letters*, 2 (2010), pp. 1–8.

28 In ASMo, CD, Avvisi, 128 and ASMn, AG, 1988. For more on Cappello, see entry by M. Giansante in *DBI*, 18 (1975).

29 M. Infelise, 'News Networks between Italy and Europe', in B. Dooley (ed.), *The Dissemination of News and the Emergence of Contemporaneity in Early Modern Europe* (Farnham: Ashgate, 2010), pp. 57–58.

dynasties, powerful noble families and cardinals.[30] The collection of Gian Vincenzo Pinelli, now in the *Biblioteca Ambrosiana* in Milan, is an exception.[31] Pinelli was a learned nobleman and avid bibliophile living in Padua. He received newsletters from Venice and collected them in an organised way at least from 1566 onwards. While Pinelli did not have a political or ecclesiastical career, he was still a member of the higher echelons of Italian societies. A rare example of the wider circulation are two handwritten newsletters from 1566 and 1567 sent from Venice to Giovanni Rossi, a printer active in Bologna.[32] Rossi may have received those from a friend in Venice, where he had been operating as a printer a few years earlier before moving to Bologna. He was active in exchanging newsletters, Rossi sent some to the humanist and Medici court historian Lodovico Domenichi, which are still kept in the Medici archive.[33] These surviving exemplars point to a wider exchange of the latest news between friends, business relations, and other acquaintances, which has left very few traces otherwise. Rossi may also have had a far more professional interest in receiving *avvisi* from Venice when he moved to Bologna, as during these years, quite a few of those manuscript versions were reprinted.[34] These copies of *avvisi* were mostly printed anonymously, and the practice seems to have disappeared almost entirely around 1570–1571, directly following the promulgation of more strict censorship laws in both Rome and Venice.[35]

---

30   Cardinal Morone collected Roman newsletters, see BAV, Cod. Vaticano, 6436; The Orsini-Bracciano collected *avvisi*: ASCR, Archivio Orsini, I, 398–399. See G. Brunelli, 'Canali di informazione politica degli Orsini di Bracciano fra cinque e seicento', in E. Fasano Guarini (ed.), *L'informazione politica in Italia (secoli XVI–XVIII): Atti del seminario organizzato presso la scuola normale superiore Pisa, 23 e 24 Giugno 1997 (Pisa: Scuola Normale Superiore, 2001)*, pp. 281–301.

31   Angela Nuovo, 'Manuscript Writings on Politics and Current Affairs in the Collection of Gian Vincenzo Pinelli (1535–1601)', *Italian Studies*, 66 (2011), pp. 198–200.

32   My thanks to Rebecca Carnevali, to whom I owe this precious reference. The newsletters are kept in Archivio di Stato di Bologna, Fondo Alidosi, vol 50–51. On Rossi consult the entry by R. Spina in *DBI*, 88 (2017).

33   Between 1555 and 1556 Rossi sent Domenichi newsletters from Venice, see ASF, MdP 3079. For more on Domenichi consult A. Piscini's entry in *DBI*, 40 (1991).

34   For example: *Copia d'alcuni avisi venuti novamente di Francia, di Oriliens d'inghilterra, & d'Alemagna, d'Amosin, Lione, &Viena* (Bologna: Benacci, 1569), USTC 804647; *Copia de diuersi auisi de Roma, Napoli, e Mesina, Spira, Anuersa, & Cipro* (Venice: s.n., 1570), USTC 762012; *Copie di avvisi venuti di Anversa, di Spira, di Roma, di Venezia, di Spagna, di Francia, & di Costantinopoli* (Florence: s.n., 1570), USTC 804715.

35   The latest example I have found is from 1575: *Tutti gli avisi novi di tutte le parti di Europa, et massime di Roma, di Fiandra, et di Francia. Ne quali s'intende i preparamenti di guerra & ciò che si crede dell'armata turchesca* (Brescia: s.n., 1575), USTC 805264.

It was mainly through oral circulation that manuscript news sheets reached a broader audience.[36] An edict published in Rome in 1590 prohibiting priests from talking about the news in their sermons indicates that the clergy played a role in the dissemination of news to a wider public from the pulpit.[37] The diary of the Florentine tailor Arditi, discussed above, illustrates how foreign news reached different social groups. Places such as the *Mercato Nuovo* in Florence, the *Rialto* and *San Marco* in Venice, and the statue of *Pasquino* in Rome, to mention just a few examples, were ideal spots in the urban fabric to hear the latest news. In various Italian cities, barbershops and pharmacies were often frequented by people from different social backgrounds to exchange and to read the news together.[38] In the early seventeenth century, the famous Venetian friar Paolo Sarpi regularly met with German, Netherlandish and other foreign merchants in the shop *Nave d'Oro* to discuss the latest news.[39] Just a few years earlier, in 1596 Pietro Vecchi, a Bolognese citizen had requested the Senate to supply a specific venue where 'avvisi from all parts of the world' would be read out loud.[40] In his petition, Vecchi claimed that his service would be aimed at a wide public consisting of 'virtuous people, gentlemen, citizens and other people, who would like to know and hear daily what happens in the different parts of the world'.[41] Unfortunately, we do not know whether the Senate in Bologna approved his request. Nevertheless, Vecchi's suggestion does point to a growing desire for news and the continuing importance of oral communication.

---

36   On importance of orality see for instance the articles in the special issue 'Oral Culture in Early Modern Italy: Performance, Language, Religion' in *The Italianist*, 34 (2014).

37   *Editto che predicatori non trattino nelle loro prediche, de reporti, & avvisi* was published as a broadsheet and as a pamphlet: (Rome: Blado, 1590), USTC 821034 and (Rome: Blado, 1590), USTC 870002.

38   Filippo de Vivo, 'Pharmacies as Centres of Communication in Early Modern Venice', *Renaissance Studies*, 24 (2007), pp. 505–521 and Fabrizio Nevola, *Street Life in Renaissance Italy* (New Haven/London: Yale University Press, 2020), pp. 187–226.

39   Filippo de Vivo, 'Paolo Sarpi and the Uses of Information in Seventeenth-Century Venice', *Media History*, 11 (2005), p. 41.

40   P. Bellettini, 'Pietro Vecchi e il suo progetto di lettura pubblica, con ascolto a pagamento, delle notizie periodiche di attualità (Bologna 1596)', in P. Bellettini (ed.), *Una città in piazza: comunicazione e vita quotidiana a Bologna tra cinque e seicento* (Bologna: Compositori, 2000), pp. 68–76.

41   Bellettini, 'Pietro Vecchi e il suo progetto di lettura pubblica', p. 71: 'de virtuosi, gentil'homini, cittadini, et. altre persone, che desiderino di sapere, et intendere quello, che alla giornata occorra in diverse parti del mondo'.

2   Antwerp in the Headlines

Handwritten newsletters, containing news from a variety of European cities, were primarily copied and compiled in Rome and Venice. Recent research suggests that during the second half of the sixteenth century the *avvisi* network and practice expanded outside Italian cities.[42] By counting the number of headlines in the famous *Fuggerzeitungen* (1568–1605), the most well-studied collection of handwritten newsletters collected by Octavian Secundus and Philipp Eduard Fugger, historians have shown that in 1572 Antwerp became the third main information hub after Rome and Venice.[43] These scholars have all linked Antwerp's appearance in these newsletters to the city's rise as an economic and commercial centre in 1572.[44] By this time, however, the city had been an economic hub for almost half a century, and its economy was in decline because of the revolt in the Netherlands. The appearance of Antwerp in *avviso*-headlines, instead, was a direct result of the escalating situation in the Low Countries rather than the city's economic rise. In 1572, numerous cities in the provinces of Zeeland and Holland declared for William of Orange, who was preparing a new invasion on two fronts, with the potential support of the French king.[45]

Antwerp's rise to prominence in Italian manuscript newsletters had already started a few years earlier: around 1566 and coincided exactly with the outbreak of the revolt. The number of newsletters in the Vatican Library for the year 1566, collected by German merchant Ulrich Fugger, provide one demonstration of this phenomenon: newsletters from Antwerp and Brussels only appeared after April 1566, as a direct result of the noble petition to Margaret of

---

42   Cornel Zwierlein, 'Fuggerzeitungen als Ergebnis von italienisch-deutschem Kulturtransfer 1552–1570', *Quellen und Forschungen aus italienischen Archiven und Bibliotheken*, 90 (2010), pp. 1–56.

43   Z. Barbarics-Hermanik and R. Pieper, 'Handwritten newsletters as means of communication in early modern Europe', in F. Bethencourt, F. Egmond (eds.), *Cultural Exchange in Early Modern Europe: Correspondence and Cultural Exchange in Europe, 1400–1700, Volume 3* (Cambridge: Cambridge University Press, 2007), pp. 74–75; Bauer, *Zeitungen vor der Zeitung*; Katrin Keller and Paola Molino, *Die Fuggerzeitungen im Kontext. Zeitungssammlungen im Alten Reich und in Italien* (Vienna: Böhlau, 2015).

44   The presence of merchants and the availability of information have often been associated with one another: John J. McCusker and Cora Gravesteijn, *The Beginnings of Commercial and Financial Journalism* (Amsterdam: Centraal Boekhuis, 1991), p. 85.

45   For an overview of the conflict see Geoffrey Parker, *The Dutch Revolt* (Hamondsworth: Penguin, 1979). For an overview of the events in the year 1572, see Judith Pollmann and Raymond Fagel, *1572. Burgeroorlog in de Nederlanden* (Amsterdam: Promotheus, 2022).

Parma, the first critical public event of this tumultuous year in which a wave of iconoclasm would sweep through these territories.[46] In total, 12 *avvisi* have a headline 'from Antwerp', whereas 46 *avvisi* have the headline 'from Rome'. The following year, in this collection, the numbers datelined Antwerp started to rival those of Rome: 38 from Antwerp and 42 from Rome. This trend is confirmed in the year 1568, when the counts of Egmont and Horne were publicly executed by the Duke of Alba, and William of Orange formally entered into a rebellion against Philip II. In this year, 44 newsletters came from Antwerp (with a total of 53 from the Netherlands) whereas 50 came from Rome. These figures indicate the same periodicity: on average, once a week, news came from Rome and Antwerp. Antwerp's appearance in the newsletters thus cannot be explained exclusively by its economic and commercial importance, but should properly be linked to the outbreak of the revolt.

A large proportion of news in the Italian collections came from Antwerp, but it was not necessarily compiled in Antwerp. There is no evidence of the existence of professional news agencies in Antwerp based on the Italian model. As late as 1626, the famous Baroque painter and diplomat Pieter Paul Rubens wrote to Pierre Dupuy in Paris: 'here [in Antwerp] it is not a practice to amploy news writers (novellanti), but everyone informs himself as best as he can'.[47] The majority of newsletters in Italian collections were composed in the same scribal hand, and contained news from a range of other places, in the following (varying) sequences: Antwerp, Augsburg or Vienna or Prague and Venice/Rome.[48] Throughout the years, there is noticeable consolidation of news centres in handwritten newsletters, and the most common series in Italian archives contained news with heading from Antwerp, Cologne and Venice.[49] These sequences closely resembled the cities the postal couriers passed through on their way from the Low Countries to Italy and suggest that

---

46   BAV, Urb Lat 1040, similar numbers can be obtained by a comparison to the collection of Pinelli for 1566, BA, G276 inf and the *avvisi* sent by Bartoli from Venice in ASF, MdP 3080.

47   M. Rooses, C. Ruelens (eds.), *Correspondance de Rubens et documents épistolaires concernant sa vie et ses œuvres, publiés, traduits, annotés. Tome troisième du 27 juillet au 22 octobre 1626* (Antwerp: Maes, 1900), p. 469: 'quì ove non s'usa d'impiegar novellanti ma ciascuno s'informa al meglio che pò'.

48   ASF, MdP 4254. See also Petitjean, *L'information des choses*, pp. 102–103.

49   During the siege of Antwerp (1584–1585), Cologne became a crucial node for the transmission of news to and from the Italian peninsula, as sending and receiving correspondence in Antwerp was monitored closely and made nearly impossible. The appearance of Cologne as a place of correspondence in the *avvisi*-headlines was due to the war in the Low Countries and the Cologne war (1583–1589): see O. Bauer, 'Reichspolitik in den Fuggerzeitungen (1568–1605) – Der Kölner Krieg (1583–1589) als Medienereignis mit Reichspolitischer Relevanz', in J. Burkhardt (ed.), *Die Fugger und das Reich – Ein neue*

news coming from these various places was collected, copied or compiled by a single professional news writer in a single city, most likely Venice or Rome. Some *avvisi* offer additional crucial clues, on the verso, it was often noted that the reports came from Venice, and in rare cases with the name of the *novellante*.[50]

The process of how news reports from Antwerp or the Netherlands made their way into the hands of news agents and were compiled into *avvisi* is rather difficult to trace as many pieces of the puzzle seem to be missing, yet occasionally some of the surviving newsletters provide a glimpse of the different actors involved in this process. The newsletters of the year 1572 in the archive of the Dukes of Mantua and Monferrato, for example, specify the sources of news items: 'from Brussels 23 June 1572 from Branc and Mariano', 'from Antwerp 5 July 1572 from Tassis', and 'from Brussels 20 July 1572 from the Catholic Ambassador'.[51] The Gonzaga secretary in Venice received and collated specific information from other news writers (Brancane and Mariano), the postal courier Ruggiero Tassis, and Diego Guzmán de Silva, the Spanish ambassador in Venice. We can safely presume that these are typical examples of how reports were disseminated. It reveals a complex information landscape in which the news agents shared information, but would increasingly disguise the original source of information to their readers.

Looking at the sources of newsletters of 1572, postal services and embassies, in particular, emerge as important spaces for the flow of political information. Postal couriers frequently provided news from the Low Countries to professional compilers in Italian cities. As the headline of an *avviso* from 1578 indicates 'news given orally by a courier coming from the Low Countries'.[52] The postmaster, as the first point of contact in cities for sending and receiving letters, had privileged early access to the news.[53] It explains why people were advised to befriend the postmaster and why those working in post offices were

---

     Forschungsperspektive zum 500jährigen Jubiläum (Augsburg: Wissner-Verlag, 2008), pp. 269–288.

50   See particularly the avvisi from 1583 written by 'Ariosto' from Venice in ASMo, CD, Avvisi, 12.

51   ASMn, AG, 1981, fol 427: *Da Brusselles li 23 Jugno 1572 havuti dal Branc et dal Mariano*; fol 436: *D'Anversa li v luglio 1572 havuti dal Tassis*; fol 465: *Di Bruselles alli 20 di luglio 72 havuti dal S. Ambasciatore Cattolico*.

52   ASF, MdP 4254, fol 605–606r: *Advisi dati in voce da un corriero venuto di fiandra questo di viiij di settembre 1578*.

53   For a more comprehensive picture of a postmaster's involvement in the news market during seventeenth century see Heiko Droste, *The Business of News* (Leiden: Brill, 2021), pp. 231–271.

recruited as informers.[54] Postal officials often ran more personalised information services as well. Ambrogio Vignati, the postmaster in Bologna, regularly supplied copies of news sheets to both Francesco de' Medici and Francesco Maria II della Rovere.[55]

Foreign embassies were hubs of information as ambassadors and their secretaries received and wrote multiple letters. Incoming letters with valuable information were often copied and summarised. Such summaries were forwarded to other agents, allied governments and other interested parties. In Venice, the secretaries of Spanish ambassador Guzmán de Silva in 1572 and 1573, were particularly active in copying and, crucially, anonymising news coming from the Low Countries. As Rodríguez-Salgado has argued Guzmán de Silva circulated information critical of Duke of Alba's policy of repression in anonymised *avvisi*.[56] The Duke of Urbino received such anonymised Spanish reports which are kept in his collection of *avvisi* together with copies of Alba's letters.[57] The Spanish embassy in Venice continued to play a crucial role in producing and distributing newsletters about the Low Countries to various Italian rulers. In 1584 and 1585 the Duke of Urbino regularly received sheets labelled as 'successi di Fiandra' from a certain Salazar in Venice.[58] Presumably, the author is Cristóbal de Salazar, who had been secretary to Guzmán de Silva's various embassies, including Venice, and from 1580 was the acting secretary in Venice in the absence of an ambassador.[59] This example serves as an important reminder of the early involvement of diplomats, and their secretaries, in circulating and manipulating news and concealing their involvement quite successfully.

---

54   In 1607, the Mantuan soldier Sebastiano del Pio recruited Henrico Glauwe (Glaussee), who worked in post office in Brussels, as a news writer for Vincenzo I Gonzaga, see ASMn, AG, 575, fol 802, with his newsletters, fol 810–836.

55   Barker, 'A history of *Avvisi*', p. 721, 724, 726; BAV, Urb Lat 1069, fol 662r, same anonymised copy on fol 682r; Urb Lat 1070, fol 256; Urb Lat 1071, part 1, fol 166.

56   See M.J. Rodríguez-Salgado, '"Do not reveal that I wrote this": Diplomatic correspondence, news and narratives in the early years of the civil war in the Low Countries', in Fagel (eds.), *Early Modern War Narratives*, pp. 18–35.

57   For example in BAV, Urb Lat 1043, fol 61–62: *Relación delo sucedido enla entrada del socorso del ducque de Alva ala isola d'Walcheren*, fol 88: *Copia de un capitano dela carta de S. duque Alva de Brusselas 30 de Junio 1572*, fol 102: *Copia dela carta del duque de Alva de los 14. De julio 1572*; fol 103–104: *Relacion de lo sucedido en la batalla que se gano Jueves 17 de Julio 1572*.

58   See BAV, Urb Lat 1052, fol 297, 348r, 417v, 432v, 514v: 'Quello che importa di successi di Fiandra sara qui allegato nel foglio del S. Salazar'; Urb Lat 1053, fol 6v, 29v, 42v.

59   Information based on overview of archival material in the archive of Simancas, see: Ricardo Magdaleno, *Papeles de Estado de Venecia* (Valladolid: Martin, 1976) and Jean-Michel Laspéras, 'La biblioteca de Cristóbal de Salazar, humanista y bibliófilo ejemplar', *Criticón*, 22 (1983), pp. 5–132.

The practice of anonymising a range of letters written by different individuals influenced the tone and content of *avvisi*. These news sheets were filled with impersonal statements and passive statements such as 'it was heard', 'it is said'. Historians have therefore described the style of *avvisi* as factual and plain without any personal opinions or added commentaries.[60] Italian newsletters employed fairly neutral terms, without overtly negative connotations to describe the rebels in the Low Countries, such as Calvinists, Huguenots, Beggars.[61] This does not, however, render the news reports impartial, as they are also often labelled as 'our enemies' and the Spanish-Habsburg army as 'our side'. Delving deeper into the content of some newsletters, there are clear traces of comments offering interpretations of events. One telling early example is a newsletter from Brussels dated 28 August 1567, describing the arrival of Duke of Alba and his Spanish troop in the city, which included the following comment: 'And as we will see, the administration of these countries will be taken away little by little and given to the Spaniards, as is done in Milan, Sicily and Naples, and it is very bad for the Prince who is not respected by his subjects.'[62] It predicts that the Low Countries will share the same fate as Habsburg-controlled Italy and ends with a political truism which suggests that the overall sentiment is hostile towards the Spanish. It is just one example of many newsletters which offered some guidance to its readers and thus shaped Italian perceptions of these events.

A newsletter from Antwerp dated 30 May 1572, for instance, sent to both Della Rovere and d'Este, explained the renewal of civil disobedience and unrest, by referring to the enormous anger of the population about the introduction of the tenth penning by the Duke of Alba. Significantly, it included the comment that the Duke had now definitely lost the love of the people.[63] This *avviso* may well have been one coming from Guzmán de Silva's Venetian embassy, which was trying to advocate a different solution to deal with the unrest in the Low Countries. Depending on the perspective and agenda of the now anonymous letter writers and their compilers, readers of *avvisi* got different impressions of the situation on the ground. A news report from Antwerp

---

60   Bauer, *Zeitung vor der Zeitungen*, p. 153.

61   The word Geuzen in Dutch, Gueux in French translated into Italian as 'Goi' and 'Gheusi', the Sea Beggars as 'vatergus' and 'guattergus' (watergeus) or 'pirati ugonotti' and more conventionally 'corsari'.

62   ASMo, CD, Avvisi 6, fol 578: 'Et à quel che si vede sarà levato à poco à poco à tutti le aministrationi di questi paesi, et data alli spagnoli, come si fa a Milano, Sicilia et Napoli, et è malissima cosa al Principe che non viene stimato da suoi sudditi.'

63   ASMo, CD, Avvisi 7, fol 876–879: *D'Anversa l'ultimo di maggio 1572;* BAV, Urb Lat 1043, fol 69–70: *D'Anversa l'ultimo de Maggio 1572*, 69v: 'perso l'amor de i popoli'.

dated 28 August 1572 offers an indication of this phenomenon, as it was written
from a Catholic perspective.

> The evil that our enemies are doing in Holland is incredible. They are
> ruining and sacking the churches and treating the unfortunate religious
> people so cruelly that it is enough to say that the Turks would not do what
> they are doing.[64]

In July, when the soldiers of William of Orange ransacked Roermond several
Carthusians had been murdered, and nineteen friars were hanged and dis-
membered at Den Briel. These facts are not recounted in this newsletter, but
by highlighting that even the Ottomans would not commit such cruelties,
the anonymous author makes it sufficiently clear to any (Italian) Catholic
reader how barbaric the protestant rebel forces were. This comparison to the
Ottomans, as we will see in the next chapters, will be exploited further in news
pamphlets and contemporary histories.

Avvisi did, at times, use specific and powerful imagery to convey their message and were far from factual accounts. In order to give sense to contemporary events, without extensive details, references to the past were common.
A similar use of analogy occurs in some of the newsletters reporting on the
sack of Antwerp in 1576. Instead of chronicling at length what had happened
in the city, a Roman *avviso* dated 19 December 1576 stated that letters from
Antwerp had arrived for Cardinal Granvelle containing news that: 'the sack
lasted for four days in a row with greater damage than the Germans and soldiers of Bourbon had caused in Rome'.[65] Similarly, an *avviso* from Genoa stated
that 'this sack is of great importance, and the sack of Rome was little, or nothing compared to this one'.[66] By comparing the sack of Antwerp to the sack of
Rome by Charles v's troops in 1527 *avvisi* appealed to living memory on the
Italian peninsula.[67] The comparison between both events was based on clear

---

64   ASMn, AG, 1981, fol 514: 'Il male che fanno gli nostri nemici nella Olanda è incredibile.
      Ruinando et sacheggiando le chiese trattando gli poveri religiosi tanto vituperosamente
      che non si basta a dir piu basta che gli turchi non farebbono quello che loro fanno.'
65   BAV, Urb Lat 1045, fol 203r: 'Il Card. Granvela ha ricevuti lettere d'Anversa delli 10 del pas-
      sato con avviso che il sacco era durato in quella città 4 giorni continui con maggior danno
      che non fecero li Thedeschi et Borboni à Roma'. Unfortunately Morillon's surviving let-
      ter to Cardinal Granvelle describing the sack of Antwerp is incomplete: see C. Piot (ed.),
      Correspondance du cardinal de Granvelle, 6: 1576–1577 (Brussels: Hayez, 1887), p. 166.
66   ASMn, AG, Avvisi 1988: 'questo sacco, e di grandissima importanza, et quello di Roma fu
      poco, o, nulla rispetto a questo'.
67   For an overview of the events in Rome in 1527: Judith Hook, *The Sack of Rome* (London:
      Palgrave, 1972), pp. 156–180; for the humanist interpretations of the sack of Rome:

similarities: like Rome, Antwerp was plundered for days by unpaid soldiers, who set the city alight, raped and murdered. Yet by identifying Antwerp with Rome, the analogy was far from innocent: in the fifty years separating both events, the plundering of Rome had become synonymous with Spanish arrogance and cruelty.[68] A single reference was enough to tell the ruling elite and citizens of Italy exactly what had taken place in Antwerp, and how to interpret it. Looking closer at the content of newsletters, it becomes clear that comparisons were employed as a tool of analysis. *Avvisi* were not dispassionate factual accounts, by using comparison as a tool of analysis, these reports shaped to a considerable degree how the unfolding events were understood.

3   Florentine Correspondents

Receiving letters and *avvisi* from their various diplomatic agents stationed across Europe, the Medici also obtained more in-depth information from a few trusted correspondents in the Low Countries. The former Florentine merchant Giovanni Battista Guicciardini and the military commander Gian Luigi di Niccolò Vitelli, better known as Chiappino (The Bear), stand out for their systematic letter-writing activities. In the early stages of the Revolt in the Low Countries, (bi-)weekly Guicciardini and Vitelli provided the Medici with privileged information gathered in Brussels and near or on the battlefield. Their letters, like all epistolary exchanges in this period, were strongly influenced by client-patron relations in early modern Italian society. While they each had a very different social relationship with the Medici rulers, their letters abounded in expressions of fidelity, obligation, obedience and duty. For instance, in December 1567, Vitelli wrote that 'he would not miss an opportunity to fulfil his duty to write every week what he had heard'.[69] The exchange of news in letters served to establish and maintain the personal ties or patronage relationship with the Medici rulers.[70] Here, their letters are studied primarily as carriers of

---

Kenneth Gouwens, *Remembering the Renaissance: Humanist Narratives of the Sack of Rome* (Leiden/Boston: Brill, 1998). On the importance of wars and sacks in collective memory: J. Pollmann and E. Kuijpers, 'Why remember terror?' Memories of violence in the Dutch Revolt', in J. Ohlmeyer, M. Ó Siochrú (eds.), *Ireland 1641: Contexts and Reactions* (Manchester: Manchester University Press, 2013), pp. 176–196.

68   Massimo Firpo, *Il sacco di Roma del 1527 tra profezia, propaganda politica e riforma religiosa* (Cagliari: Ceuc editrice, 1990), pp. 37–41.

69   Vitelli to Francesco de' Medici, Antwerp 14 December 1567, ASF, MdP 649, fol 111r: 'non manchar dal mio debito ogni settimana scrivarò tutto quello ch'io intendaro'.

70   On news as a social resource: Droste, *The Business of News*.

information to inform the Medici. It seeks to establish how the information was evaluated and used by the Medici. In contrast to the *avvisi* circulating at various courts, Guicciardini's and Vitelli's letters were meant to be confidential with some directly addressed to the (Grand) Duke and others to the various secretaries of state. It is important to stress that while treated as a separate form of news exchange, as these letters were not meant to be disseminated publicly, such letters did form an integral part of the early modern world of information, as these letters were continuously excerpted, anonymised, summarised and copied by various political actors and information professionals.

3.1   *A Former Merchant*

Thanks to the numerous Florentine merchants active in Antwerp, the Medici were in a privileged position compared to other Italian territorial rulers to be kept abreast of the developments.[71] Several of these merchants maintained contact with their hometown and its ruler: Giovanni Battista Guicciardini, brother of Lodovico, the far more well-known author of the *Descrittione dei Paesi Bassi* (Descriptions of the Low Countries), was one of them.[72] Already in 1559, Giovanni Battista had started writing letters regularly to Cosimo I containing the latest news from Brussels, and with the outbreak of the revolt in 1566, he quickly became the Medici's trusted news agent or 'information broker'.[73]

---

71   On this diaspora see Richard A. Goldthwaite, *The Economy of Renaissance Florence* (Baltimore: John Hopkins University Press, 2009), pp. 36–230; for their ties with Florence: Christophe Schellekens, *Merchants and their hometown: Florentines in Antwerp and the Duchy of Florence* (ca 1500–1585), (Unpublished PhD thesis, European University Institute, 2018).

72   Lodovico Guicciardini, *Descrittione di tutti i Paesi Bassi altrimenti detti Germania Inferiore. Con piu carte di geographia del paese, & col ritratto naturale di piu terre principale* (Antwerp: Silvius, 1567), USTC 405351. For most recent biography consult D. Aristodemo (ed.), *Descrittione di tutti i paesi Bassi* (2 vols., Rome: Edizioni di Storia e letteratura, 2020), I, pp. 3–40.

73   Most of the letters have been edited by Mario Battistini (ed.), *Lettere di Giovan Battista Guicciardini a Cosimo e Francesco de Medici scritte dal Belgio dal 1559 al 1577* (Brussels/Rome: Academia Belgica, 1949). I have come across additional letters by Guicciardini in ASF, MdP 650, fol 1, 146, 147, 179r–v, 180r–v, 185, 200, 201, 212r–v, 225, 239, 246–247, 254r–v, 264, 267, 272, 286r–v, 290r–v. For biographical information consult: D. Aristodemo, 'Giovan Battista Guicciardini', *DBI*, 61 (2004); Monique Jacqmain, 'Een minder bekende "vlaamse" G.: G.B., de korrespondent van de Medici's', *Ons erfdeel*, 18 (1975), pp. 321–396 and Nina Lamal, 'Nieuws en informatienetwerken: De Medici en de eerste jaren van de Nederlandse Opstand (1566–1568)', *Handelingen – Koninklijke Zuid-Nederlandse Maatschappij voor taal- en letterkunde en geschiedenis*, 66 (2012), pp. 63–77. For the concept of brokers: M. Keblusek, 'Double Agents in Early Modern Europe', in M. Keblusek and B. Noldus (eds.), *Double Agents: Cultural and Political Brokerage in Early Modern Europe* (Leiden: Brill, 2011), pp. 1–9.

For some, yet unknown reason, he stopped writing letters in 1571, only to resume in 1576 for another year.[74]

Before Giovanni Battista started his letter-writing activities in 1559, he ran the family company in Antwerp, importing wine from France and exporting grain to Italy.[75] He had arrived in Antwerp in 1527, when the city was becoming a thriving commercial and cosmopolitan city, attracting merchants from all over Europe.[76] The Guicciardini firm was, however, never very successful and had gone into liquidation in 1543, after their ships had been taken by pirates. At the request of the most powerful Italian merchant and banker in the Low Countries, Gaspare Ducci from Pistoia, the money and the goods of the company were seized. Only fifteen years after the bankruptcy, in 1559, Giovanni Battista started corresponding with Cosimo I, and by now he had moved from Antwerp to Brussels, the main hub for political information as all governmental bodies and the governor-general were located in the city. Brussels was situated at the crossroads of different commercial and postal routes and so it was no coincidence that the family Tassis established its postal headquarters in the city.[77]

The pending court case with Ducci might have been one of the reasons to explain why Giovanni Battista started his role as an intelligencer, as he might have hoped to gain their support in his ongoing litigation. So far, there is no evidence of any financial compensation given to Giovanni Battista in return for his services. This lack of evidence, however, does not mean that he was not hoping to get a pension or other types of rewards for his services. Crucially, the members of Guicciardini family had, unlike other Florentine patrician families, not actively opposed Medici rule in the previous decades.[78] In two letters written at end of February 1568, Giovanni Battista reminded both Francesco and Cosimo I de' Medici that his family were old and trustworthy servants of

---

74   It remains unclear what happened between 1570 and 1576: did he stop writing letters or has this correspondence simply been lost? Substantial parts of the minutes of the replies to his letters are kept in ASF, MdP 51, 261, 262.

75   For a more detailed account of the mercantile company see Richard Goldthwaite, *Private Wealth in Renaissance Florence, A Study of Four Families* (Princeton: Princeton University Press, 1968), pp. 145–155.

76   On Italian merchant colonies in Antwerp: Jan-Albert Goris, *Etude sur les colonies marchandes méridionales à Anvers de 1488 à 1567* (Leuven: Librairie Universitaire, 1925), pp. 70–95 and Subacchi, 'Italians in Antwerp', pp. 74–84.

77   P. Arblaster, 'Antwerp and Brussels and Inter-European Spaces in News Exchange', in B. Dooley (ed.), *The Dissemination of News and the Emergence of Contemporaneity in Early Modern Europe* (Burlington: Ashgate, 2010), pp. 195–198.

78   Goldthwaite, *Private Wealth*, pp. 151–152.

the Medici.[79] They were rewarded for their loyalty, in 1570, his brother Lorenzo was nominated as a senator.[80]

In 1564, Cosimo instructed Guicciardini to write directly to his son Francesco, who had taken over most of the day-to-day affairs and would become Grand Duke in 1574.[81] Guicciardini performed his duty to keep Francesco informed of the ongoing events by writing letters regularly: at least twice a month, mostly on a Sunday or a Monday, just in time to hand them over to the Tassis courier leaving for Italy.[82] His letters were entirely dedicated to the recent news from the Netherlands and he rarely touched upon personal matters. The one major exception to this rule was when his brother Lodovico was imprisoned by the Duke of Alba in 1569. More than two months after Lodovico's incarceration, he started to include pleas for help.[83]

Giovanni Battista's letters shed some light on how he gathered news and how his letters arrived at the Florentine court. He relied mainly on his closest family members to obtain information and to pass on his own letters. He received news from Antwerp from his brother Lodovico, who acted as a consul of the Florentine trading nation throughout this period, and news about England from his brother Vincenzo, who resided in London until 1567. The access to

---

79   One letter to Francesco and a different one to Cosimo de' Medici from Brussels on 22 February 1568, in *Lettere di Giovan Battista*, p. 306–308. He described his family as 'antichi et fedeli servitori'. In 1568, he still had many debts from the bankruptcy and the trial: Goldthwaite, *Private Wealth*, pp. 149–150.

80   ASF, MdP 4253, fol 21r.

81   Letter to Francesco from Brussels 8 September 1564 is extensive expressing 'il desiderio grande che ho di farle servitio', see *Lettere di Giovan Battista*, pp. 233–238.

82   Brussels 11 September 1566: 'io mando le lettere per via di Trento e per mani di G. Batista Bordogna de Tassis, maestro de poste, et così feci sempre da molti anni', in *Lettere di Giovan Battista*, p. 275.

83   According to Giovanni Battista, Lodovico had consulted citizens and merchants in Antwerp on the introduction of the tenth penning and had written down some of the grievances against this new tax to present to the secretary of the Duke of Alba. Before he went to Brussels, he had shown it to some magistrates in Antwerp and one of them had taken a copy, which arrived in Brussels before Lodovico had the chance to present his piece of writing. On top of this unfortunate pre-circulation of his petition, the Antwerp Magistrate refused to comply with Alba's demands using the arguments from the petition. Alba immediately arrested Lodovico and imprisoned him in the castle of Vilvoorde. Both Cosimo and Vitelli intervened on Lodovico's behalf, but to no avail. He was only freed from prison in September 1570, probably through the mediation of Anne of Austria, who was on her way to Spain to marry Philip II. See his letters to Francesco, Brussels 12 June, 25 July, 9 September, 10 October 1569 in *Lettere di Giovan Battista*, pp. 339–343. A similar version of the events in the history written by the Genoese merchant Gerolamo Conestaggio printed in 1614 who accused Jeronimo Curiel, a Spanish merchant and intelligencer for Philip II, of copying the text and showing it to the Duke of Alba.

news about English matters was an important asset to the Medici, because just like in the Low Countries, they did not have a permanent diplomatic representative at the English court until the beginning of the seventeenth century.[84] His brothers were not only involved in supplying him with information, but also in the delivery of his letters to Florence. Until 1570 he sent copies of his letters to Ferrara, addressed to his brother Lorenzo.[85] Upon his return to Florence, Lorenzo remained a crucial intermediary in passing information coming from London and the Low Countries to the grand ducal administration.[86]

In addition to these strategically placed family members, Giovanni Battista also maintained contacts with the well-informed Bolognese architect Francesco de Marchi, a confidant of Margaret of Parma, governor-general in the Netherlands.[87] De Marchi frequently wrote letters to Giovanni Battista Pico, the secretary of the Duke of Parma, and Cardinal Alexander Farnese, relating the ongoing political affairs.[88] He probably did so on the express demand of Margaret, who also wished to keep her family members informed.[89] Before the arrival of the Duke of Alba in the Low Countries in 1567, the Farnese family was very well-positioned and received information regularly. Margaret's return to the Italian peninsula and the arrival of the Duke of Alba created an information disadvantage for the powerful Farnese dynasty. For in-depth knowledge of the situation in the Low Countries, Cardinal Farnese had to rely upon the letters of one of his agents in Paris, Guido Lolgi.[90] Margaret received regular updates from Cardinal Granvelle and the Spanish ambassadors in Venice, but it seems that the Farnese family did not have any personal correspondents in

84   Contini, 'Aspects of Medicean diplomacy', pp. 89–93; Anna Crinò, 'Avvisi di Londra di Petruccio Ubaldini, Fiorentino, relativi agli anni 1579–1594, con notizie sulla guerra di Fiandra', *Archivio Storico Italiano*, 127 (1969), pp. 461–581. See also: Keenan, 'English News in Papal Rome', pp. 350–366.

85   Due to the possibility of problems occurring along the postal routes, this was a common practice, ASF, MdP 650, fol 179r–v, 180r–v, 212r–v, 254r–v, 272, 286r–v.

86   Crinò, 'Avvisi di Londra di Petruccio Ubaldini', pp. 461–581.

87   Alfred Cauchie, 'Episodes de l'histoire de la ville d'Anvers durant le second semestre de l'année 1566. Correspondance de Daniel di Bomalès avec François di Marchi', *Analectes pour servir à l'histoire ecclésiastique de la Belgique*, 7 (1892), pp. 20–60.

88   For a biography see D. Lamberini, 'Francesco de Marchi', in *DBI*, 38 (1990); for his letters Amadio Ronchini (ed.), *Cento lettere del capitano F. Marchi Bolognese* (Parma: F. Carmignani, 1864).

89   Louis Prosper Gachard, 'Les archives Farnéssienes, à Naples', *Compte Rendu des séances de la commission royale d'histoire*, 11 (1870), pp. 301–311. For a biography of Margaret see George Henri Dumont, *Marguerite de Parme bâtarde de Charles Quint (1522–1586). Biographie* (Brussels: Le Cri, 1999).

90   Logli wrote to Cardinal Farnese from 1562 until 1588 detailed letters on the events in the Low Countries: Cauchie and Van der Essen, *Inventaire*, pp. 19–22.

the Netherlands until the arrival of Alexander Farnese in 1578. The Medici, on the other hand, alongside Guicciardini, now had another valuable source of information with the arrival of Gian Luigi di Niccolò Vitelli, one of Cosimo's closest confidants, in the Duke of Alba's army in 1567. Between 1567 and 1571, the Medici thus had one correspondent on or near the battlefield and one on the ground in Brussels offering them weekly updates.

3.2 Medici Confidant and Military Commander

In 1567 the majority of soldiers in Alba's army heading for the Netherlands were Spanish. Cosimo sent Vitelli, along with a contingent of Tuscan soldiers, to Genoa to join the royal army. Originally from a family of well-known *condottieri* from Città di Castello in Umbria, Vitelli had played a key role in the establishment of the Duchy of Florence as a territorial state. He had joined Cosimo's entourage at court when the latter came to power in Florence in 1536 and became one of Cosimo's most trusted military advisors.[91] In 1555 Vitelli had played an important role in the conquest of Siena and was rewarded for his services with the marquisate of Cetona in 1558 and he was made a member of the new chivalric order the Knights of Saint Stephen in 1562.

In sending his confidant, Cosimo demonstrated his support for Alba's punitive expedition. The ties between the Medici family and the Toledo's were very close, as in 1539, Cosimo had married Eleonora de Toledo, daughter of the then viceroy of Naples, Pedro Alvarez de Toledo.[92] This marriage was advantageous for both Charles V and Cosimo I because on the one hand, Charles hoped to ensure Cosimo's support for the Habsburg monarchy, and on the other, the Medici were now very close to one of the most powerful Spanish noble families and factions at the court. In supporting Philip's attempt to crush the rebellion, Cosimo showed himself as a devout Catholic ruler and a loyal trustworthy ally of the Spanish-Habsburg crown.

Vitelli served as the *maestro de campo general* of the infantry from 1567 until he died in 1575, and during this time he wrote letters to Florence regularly.[93]

---

91   More recently Francesca Mavilla has studied the patronage of Vitelli: 'Committenti e collezionisti tra l'Italia e le Fiandre, il ruolo di Paolo e Chiappino Vitelli nel contesto artistico e culturale del Cinquecento' (unpublished doctoral dissertation, Università degli Studi di Perugia, 2016).

92   C.J. Hernando Sanchez, 'Naples and Florence in Charles V's Italy: Family, Court and Government in the Toledo-Medici Alliance', in T. Dandelet, J. Marino (eds.), *Spain in Italy: Politics, Society, and Religion 1500–1700* (Leiden: Brill, 2007), pp. 135–180.

93   His letters are kept in ASF, MdP 649–651; Maurizio Arfaioli, 'Alla destra del Duca: la Figura di Chiappino Vitelli nel contesto degli affreschi Vasariani del Salone dei Cinquecento', *Mitteilungen des Kunsthistorischen Institutes in Florenz*, 51 (2007), pp. 271–278. I would like to thank Maurizio Arfaioli for generously sharing his knowledge of Vitelli with me.

His letters are kept in the Florentine State Archives in three separate volumes, each some 300 folios thick. The careful contemporary archiving of Vitelli's letters bound in separate volumes reveals the importance given to his letters by the Medici because normally correspondence was either archived among secretarial papers or in the duke's correspondence, but not separately. Vitelli's letters form a unique collection, they offer a window into Vitelli's reporting and understanding of the conflict for almost an entire decade. He witnessed some of the most crucial episodes in the early revolt, such as the imprisonment and execution of Egmont and Horne, and he fought during various battles such as Jemmingen (1568) and the siege of Mons (1572), where he got wounded.[94]

Upon his arrival in the Low Countries, Vitelli immediately became integrated into the existing Florentine circles. Giovanni Battista Guicciardini was instructed to present himself to Vitelli and to forward his letters.[95] He often enclosed Vitelli's letters with his own and received letters on his behalf.[96] Vitelli also had regular contact with his brother Lodovico, initially related to matters of the Florentine trading nation in Antwerp.[97] Lodovico must have gained his trust and developed a closer relationship throughout these years, as in 1575, Vitelli informed Francesco I that Lodovico had the right to open his letters and to execute what the grand duke asked when he was away on the battlefield.[98] Vitelli's use of personal messengers to Florence reveals his reliance on a tight-knit Florentine network. The letter bearers were almost always Florentines (or Tuscans), either merchants or soldiers.[99] Raffaelo Barberini was one such messenger, who had come to Antwerp for business

---

94   Vitelli to Francesco, Brussels 17 September 1567, ASF, MdP 649, fol 70r–72v; Brussels 6 June 1568, fol 200: 'per il conto che gle ne do per l'incluso foglio', the same letter in ASF, MdP 4254, fol 317; and from Jemmingen 22 July 1568, fol 212–215.

95   Guicciardini to Francesco, 10 and 24 August 1567, see *Lettere di Giovan Battista*, pp. 299–300.

96   Guicciardini to Francesco, 7 September 1567 and 25 January 1568: *Lettere di Giovan Battista*, p. 300, 305–306. This practice explains why some of Guicciardini's letters are still bound together with those of Vitelli in Florentine state archive see footnote 73, and based on the arguments and material in my PhD thesis: Francesca Mavilla, '"Sua signoria è qua in molta buona riputatione con ciascuno": Chiappino Vitelli e i fratelli Guicciardini', *Horti Hesperidum*, 8 (2018), pp. 321–348.

97   Vitelli was often involved in solving the problems of the Florentine mercantile nation in Antwerp: Brussels 10 January 1569 in ASF, MdP 649, fol 273r–v; Brussels 13 February 1569, MdP 650, fol 14–15.

98   Antwerp 8 May 1575, ASF, MdP 651, fol 310r.

99   Brussels 17 October 1567 by Roberto Ridolfi, ASF, MdP 649, fol 80–82; Brussels 24 February 1568 by Giovanni Battista Fortini, fol 149; 's Hertogenbosch 17 June 1574 by Cosimo Strozzi, MdP 651, fol 276.

reasons just like the Guicciardini brothers.[100] He mostly traded with Russia
and is now known for the reports of his voyages to Russia.[101] With the arrival
of the Spanish-Habsburg army in 1567, Barberini joined the forces, and quickly
became part of Vitelli's entourage, as two years later, he had accompanied
Vitelli on a diplomatic mission to the English court.[102] After Vitelli's death, he
also started to write letters to Florence between 1576 and 1577, addressed to the
Tuscan secretary of state, Antonio Serguidi.[103] It shows that Florentine citizens
understood the need for information of the Medici, and used letters as a tool
to convey information and retain patronage relationships with the rulers of
their hometown.

Vitelli repeatedly stressed that he saw it as his duty to keep his prince continuously informed.[104] He reassured that his own writings were 'not without
truth'.[105] Such assertions were common in correspondence: the most important criterion for news reporting was that it had to be trustworthy. He regularly admitted he found it difficult to distinguish fact from fiction, especially
when he was away from the Duke of Alba.[106] During his time in Antwerp, for
instance, he complained 'the merchants talked as much as it pleased them,
especially in Antwerp, where there are merchants from all different sects'.[107]
His comment about gossiping protestant merchants reveals a preoccupation
with the credibility of news and that he found his task burdensome.

100   ASF, MdP 651, fol 328.
101   His *Relazione di Moscovia* appeared in a modern edition in 1996 by M.G. Barberini and
      I. Fei. Some of his letters sent from Antwerp between 1564 and 1565 describing his jour-
      neys in BAV, Barb Lat 5369, fol 1–4.
102   Letters from Barberini from Brussels 10 and 11 December 1569 in ASF, MdP 650, fol 149,
      fol 156–157.
103   ASF, MdP 1179 and 1180.
104   Brussels 7 September 1567, in ASF, MdP 649, fol 68r–v: 'no lassaro giornalmente tenire
      avisato V.E.'; Brussels 10 May 1568, fol 184: 'Io non lasciaro scrivere continuamente a Vostra
      Ecc. Ill. quanto occorrà alla giornata'.
105   Brussels 30 August 1567, in ASF, MdP 649, fol 47: 'quello che io scrivo a V.E. no e senza
      fondamento'; Brussels 6 February 1569, MdP 650, fol 19: 'Le avvisi che corrano delle cose di
      qua sono si varij, che mi mettano in confusione, ne si puo fare d'essi giuditio alcuno'.
106   Antwerp 9 January 1568, ASF, MdP 649, fol 114v: 'Questo è, per hora s'intende et per voce
      universale, et per lettere di Mercanti, n'io posso darle altra certezza, per ritrovarmi lon-
      tano dall' Ecc. del S. Duca d'Alva'; Antwerp 24 January 1568, fol 125v: 'Questi sono nuove de
      mercanti et come altre volte ho fatto intendere all Ecc. Vostra Ill. ritrovandomi qui non le
      posso servere il certo come farei s'io fusse in Brusselles'.
107   Antwerp 7 December 1567, in ASF, MdP 649, fol 109r: 'Poiche io mi trovo assente dal s.
      Duca d'Alva, havaro pocho che scriverli di nuovo con fundamento perche tra li mercanti
      si parla à volunta, e in Anversa particolarmente, che vi sono di tutte le sette'.

His letters were very often divided into different paragraphs with news items coming from different parts of the Low Countries, England, France and the Holy Roman Empire. The use of such paragraphs closely resembles the style of *avvisi*. Vitelli regularly enclosed separate anonymised news sheets.[108] He also acted as an intermediary for news obtained elsewhere, for instance, he received letters from his nephew Giovanni Battista del Monte, who was fighting in France in 1567, and passed them onto Florence.[109] Apart from sending news, Vitelli also sent other types of information. Together with the military engineers Gabrio Serbelloni and Francesco Paccioto, he was responsible for the erection of the citadel in Antwerp.[110] Very shortly after he arrived in the Netherlands, he went to Antwerp to inspect the possible sites for a five-bastioned star-shaped pentagonal citadel.[111] In October 1567, Francesco wrote to Vitelli that he really would like to see the design of this citadel, upon which Vitelli enclosed the various plans of the citadel in the next postal packets.[112] Vitelli did the same for the other citadels whose construction fell under his responsibility such as those in Valenciennes, Cambrai, and Maastricht.[113]

The Medici had developed a great interest in fortifications. The Italian historian Giorgio Spini describes the military architecture as a characteristic product of Medici rule.[114] One of the earliest examples of an urban fortress, *Fortezza da Basso* was built in Florence between 1534 and 1537 to solidify Medici rule. Cosimo was also the first to erect a whole belt of fortifications using the *trace italienne* design at the borders of his state. The drawings, maps and proposals

---

108 ASF, MdP 4254, fol 319–321; Antwerp 14 December 1567, ASF, MdP 649, fol 111v: 'Mando à V.E. Ill. la copia delli avvisi del Alemagnia', Brussels 27 February 1568, fol 146: 'Se non qualche intenderà dal Concino al quele per fastidir meno l'Ecc vostra Ill. scrivo quelle nuove che si sono intesse doppo l'altre mie', to Concino, Brussels 22 February 1568, fol 148: 'Vederà V.S. per l'incluso foglio le nuove che io ho di qua di Franca, pregola strettamente à farne parte all'Ecc'. On 21 July 1570, he promised to send a printed copy of Alba's general pardon to Florence from Antwerp: ASF, MdP 650, fol 240v.

109 ASF, MdP 4254, fol 217–219v: Giovanni Battista del Monte from Sogny to Chiappino Vitelli in 1567. For references to the inclusion of letters and news from France: ASF, MdP 649, fol 124r–v, 156–161v, 173, 174.

110 Charles van den Heuvel, *'Papiere bolwercken'. De introductie van de Italiaanse stede- en vestingbouw in de Nederlanden (1540–1609) en het gebruik van tekeningen* (Alphen aan de Rijn: Canaletto, 1991), pp. 30–51.

111 The idea of a citadel in Antwerp itself was highly contested in the Low Countries, but in the rest of Europe it would become one of the most studied and admired pentagonal citadels: Martha Pollak, *Cities at War in Early Modern Europe* (Cambridge: Cambridge University Press, 2010).

112 ASF, MdP 229, fol 27; MdP 649, fol 76, 94.

113 ASF, MdP 649, fol 273.

114 Giorgio Spini, *Architettura e politica da Cosimo I a Ferdinando I* (Florence: Olschki, 1976).

sent by Vitelli were of enormous value for the spread of knowledge on fortifications using the new *trace italienne* design, and it was in the interest of the Medici and the development of their grand ducal state to have access to such information. This was especially valuable since the designs of citadels and bastions were relatively confidential operations in early modern Europe.[115] Thanks to Vitelli, they were able to follow closely the new technological developments and innovations.

During this period, other Italian territorial rulers received letters far more sporadically from Italian military engineers or soldiers.[116] Concurrently with Vitelli, Ottavio Gonzaga-Guastalla was in the Low Countries from 1567 to 1570 and wrote to the Duke of Mantua and the Duke of Urbino. Ottavio's relationship was very different from the privileged relationship between Vitelli and the Medici. He was a member of the cadet branches of the Gonzaga family who were on good terms with the Spanish-Habsburg monarchy, he served in various military campaigns including the Mediterranean and the Low Countries.[117] He wrote letters to these two different rulers, primarily to obtain favours and to present himself as a faithful and loyal servant. Interestingly, he did not write the same letters to these two dukes, suggesting different ties led to a selection in coverage. His dispatch to Guidobaldo II della Rovere, Duke of Urbino about the imprisonment of Egmont and Horne in 1567, was a long one compared to the one sent to Mantua. In his letter, he explained that he wrote at great length because he wanted to make sure that the duke knew everything in detail, even reconstructing the dialogues between Egmont, Horne and their respective captors.[118] Some of his letters sent to Urbino imply a more regular exchange of information, as can be seen in one of his letters to Guidobaldo II: 'that I will not miss any opportunity to inform your Illustrious Excellency of the events happening here and that in future I will continue to do so as you have commanded me in your letter of 3 May'.[119] Yet, it is unclear whether he kept both rulers abreast of the developments regularly or whether he only wrote about momentous events such as the imprisonment of Egmont and Horne.

---

115   On the confidentiality: Pollak, *Cities at War*, pp. 3–4, 11–28.

116   Two letters written by Bartolemeo Picco to Mantua in 1567 and 1569: ASMn, AG, 573, fol 1–2.

117   Giuseppe Bertini, *Ottavio Gonzaga di Guastalla. La carriera di un cadetto al servizio della monarchia spagnola (1543–1583)* (Guastalla: Biblioteca Maldotti, 2007).

118   Brussels 13 September 1569, ASF, DU, I, 198, fol 67–68v, published in Bertini, *Ottavio Gonzaga*, pp. 86–87.

119   Brussels 20 June 1569, ASF, DU, I, 198, fol 72r: 'Io non lasio occasione nisuna ch'io non dia conto a V. Ecc. Ill. delle cose che qui pasano et il medesimo faro per l'avenire poi che lei nella sua di 3 di maggio me lo comanda'.

Keeping one's patron informed was one of the many tasks of a military commander, especially from high-ranking status. Just like ambassadors whose task consisted in writing regular newsletters to their respective governments, military commanders were expected or instructed to write to their peers and their (potential) patrons. These military men and their letters were of crucial importance in the provision of news about political and military events. The letters of the prominent Milanese military engineer Gabrio Serbelloni from the Low Countries, between 1567 and 1569, serve as a case in point. They were frequently summarised and copied into separate newsletters.[120] It is yet unclear who was responsible for this process, but it may have been a chancellery or embassy, as both d'Este and Medici regularly received these specific summaries with headlines such as 'notices from Antwerp on 30 May 1568 from Gabrio Serbellone'. In Serbelloni's case, his authorship was not omitted, perhaps to lend greater credibility to these specific digests, as he was well-known and well-connected, having served both the Medici and papacy before entering the service of Philip II. When Serbelloni returned to the Low Countries in 1578, this practice resumed with anonymised copies of his letters, but also letters addressed to him are kept in the newsletter collection of d'Este's and Gonzaga's.[121]

Under the governorship of Alexander Farnese, more military engineers and soldiers from the Italian states joined the Spanish-Habsburg army.[122] Their presence offered the opportunity to other Italian rulers to receive information from people on the battlefield more regularly.[123] Yet in the early phase of the revolt, the Medici were ahead of the game with their network of Florentine correspondents in the Low Countries. These correspondents were in contact with each other and were part of the Florentine community. None of the other Italian rulers had access to a comparable diverse range of correspondents in the Netherlands.

4   The Uses of Information in Medici Florence

How exactly did the Medici process and use the information coming their way through *avvisi* and letters? By this point, so much information was arriving in Florence that it would have required a considerable time to read and digest it

---

120   See ASMo, CD, Avvisi, 7, fol 5–6. For a biography see F. Biferali in *DBI*, 92 (2018) and on his activities in the Low Countries: Van den Heuvel, '*Papiere bolwercken*', pp. 157–158.

121   ASMo, CD, Avvisi, 9 and ASMn, AG 1983. Numerous references to Serbelloni writing to Cardinal San Giorgio, his brother in Rome in 1579: BAV, Urb Lat 1047, fol 255v; 258v; 280r.

122   Bertini, 'La nazione italiana nell'esercito di Alessandro Farnese', pp. 258–295.

123   Lamal, 'Communicating Conflict', pp. 13–31.

all. Scholars considering the information network developed by Philip II have spoken of information overload.[124] Contemporaries regarded Philip's style of governing, the sedentary ruler surrounded by a mass of paper, as most unusual. But this image of a spider king or paper king has also been applied to Cosimo I, who like Philip II, wanted to have control over the stream of information and government decisions.[125] Incoming information from Low Countries was processed at the Medici court by Bartolomeo Concino, one of Cosimo's most trusted advisors and secretary of state. Concino made summaries of the news he had received (and read).[126] In the margins of these surviving secretarial summaries, Cosimo sometimes scribbled a few words or short sentences, which sometimes reveal glimpses of his geopolitical views. In 1568, reading reports of William of Orange's attempts to court the German princes, Cosimo noted in the margins 'Noi siamo Spagnioliaimo', suggesting that Florence was supportive of the Spanish side.[127]

From the surviving summaries, it is clear that Concino made a selection from the incoming correspondence and *avvisi* he received and highlighted the importance of some of the events described. For instance, in November 1566, he included the news of a second wave of iconoclasm in 's Hertogenbosch and the subsequent power grab by the reformed in the city a month earlier. These events had been the subject of various letters written by Guicciardini who had emphasised these were worrying developments due to the important location of the city, a point which Concino reiterated in his summary.[128] Concino frequently summarized the content of Vitelli's letters, but sometimes also attached them to his summaries for Cosimo to read in their entirety.[129]

---

124 C. Borreguero Beltrán, 'Philip Of Spain: The Spider's Web of News and Information', in B. Dooley (ed.), *The Dissemination of News and the Emergence of Contemporaneity in Early Modern Europe* (Burlington: Ashgate, 2010), pp. 23–50; P.M. Dover, 'Philip II, Information Overload, and the Early Modern Moment', in W. Reger, T. Andrade (eds.), *The Limits of Empire: European Imperial Formations in Early Modern World History. Essays in Honor of Geoffrey Parker* (Farnham: Ashgate, 2012), pp. 99–120.

125 Contini, 'Dinastia, Patriziato e politica estera', p. 77.

126 ASF, MdP 610; 612.

127 ASF, MdP 612, fol 360.

128 ASF, MdP 612, fol 286: 'In Bolduch in Fiandra non solo hanno deturpase le chiese et buttatsi a terra le figuere, & il santo sacramenti ma scacciati li ansiani, & battuti li governatori, cosa che per l'importanza del luogo è tenuto malissima perche è passo del frontiera di Cleves, di Gheldria, d'Hollanda, & di Brabante', compare to 'per esser la villa di Bolduche una delle 4 ville capitali di Brabante, et frontiera, si può dire a Ghelderi, et a Holanda, et tanto vicina al ducato di Cleve et altri potentati, è cosa di grandissima importanza' see Guicciardini's letters from 20 October 1566, *Lettere di Giovan Battista*, pp. 276–277. See other letters from 3 and 17 November 1566 on pp. 277–279.

129 ASF, MdP 610, fol 16, 25, 65, 189, 215, 277, 295, 329, 339.

This practice indicates that Vitelli's letters were considered to be important sources of information.

Where different letters and news reports contradicted one another in a significant way, Concino often noticed this fact. In 1570, for instance, he wrote that he had received news from Milan that Gabrio Serbelloni had reported that large numbers of inhabitants were fleeing from the Low Countries and that the Duke of Alba was devolving responsibilities to his son Fadrique.[130] He remarked that this report was contradicted by Vitelli, who had given a far more positive state of affairs. In this instance, by comparing Concino perceived a clear difference between Serbelloni and Vitelli's accounts. His observations highlight the necessity for early modern rulers and their administration of having access to different sources of news to have a more accurate sense of the unfolding events.

Italian rulers, including the Medici, often received a variety of information of the conflict. In these early stages of the revolt, Orange's apology for his resistance against Alba in 1568 circulated in Italian translations and was copied into handwritten newsletters.[131] While the Italian dukes were tied more closely to Spanish-Habsburg power than a number of the German princes, it thus remained paramount to convince them of the necessity of his actions and policies. The Duke of Alba was acutely aware of the importance of correspondence in shaping his persona and maintaining support for his decisions.[132] Vitelli's letters and views were shaped by his proximity to the Duke of Alba and often presented an official, as well as a more positive assessment of the political and military situation. He claimed, just like Alba, that the war would be over soon.[133]

The close ties of Medici with Alba influenced the tone of the reports they received, certainly compared to those received by other Italian rulers. The postscript to an anonymous letter from Brussels in 1572 to Alfonso II d'Este stated that if the Spanish publish something to their advantage, it was best to believe

---

130   ASF, MdP 610, fol 25.

131   ASF, MdP 3081, fol 293: *Dichiarazione et prostestazione del Principe di Oranges et d'altri principe et signori: sopra quelli che hanno prese le armi per opporsi alla Tirannide et oppossione del Duca d'alva et de spagnoli nelli paesi bassi*. Also in MdP 4026, fol 57–58r; BAV, Urb Lat 874, fol 258-v; ASMo, CD, Documenti di stati e città, estero, 164.

132   Monique Weis, *Les Pays-Bas Espagnols et les états du Saint-Empire (1559–1579): priorités et enjeux de la diplomatie en temps de troubles* (Brussels: Université de Bruxelles, 2003), pp. 253–363.

133   For Alba's view see R. Fagel, 'The Duke of Alba and the Low Countries 1520–1573', in M. Ebben, M. Lacy-Bruijn, R. van Hövell (eds.), *Alba: General and Servant to the Crown* (Maastricht: Karwansaray, 2013), pp. 279–282.

the opposite.[134] In the same letter, the unknown author employed an intriguing image of the inhabitants of the Low Countries, when writing that it was a generally held opinion in Brussels and also his own that: 'they are no longer the daft tools of the past years, they have been purged from the beer they have been drinking and now they show their teeth to the duke'.[135] Ever since Tacitus, it was a well-established trope that the inhabitants of the Low Countries consumed a lot of beer and a result were terrible fighters.[136] Yet according to this anonymous letter writer, this weakness had been conquered and they were now ready to take up arms and fight. During the conflict, this image of warriors would gain even more resonance and come to play an important role in political discourse. In this instance, it offered the first indication that this war would not be as easily won as the Duke of Alba and Vitelli had claimed.

Around the same time, Vitelli's optimistic tone also changed. He wrote that money was urgently needed to pay the troops and to launch a new war offensive against the rebels. He reported that they had lost control over a large part of Zeeland, but also the cities Mons and Valenciennes located at the border with France.[137] In his letter to Concino dated 27 May 1572, Vitelli confided that the situation was far worse than he would be able to say and that the secretary could imagine. He even described the danger that Philip II might lose all his states.[138] Vitelli's letters offered crucial information to the Medici about how worrying the situation actually was, at a crucial moment in their relationship with Spain. Philip II was worried about their potential support to the French crown, and Cosimo's recent elevation as Grand Duke by Pope Pius V had caused even further distrust.[139] Offering the Duke of Alba an enor-

---

134   ASMo, CD, Avvisi 7, fol 873: 'Signore, egli è una regula generale. Che quando i spagnuoli pubblicano qualche cosa al loro vantaggio bisogna credere tutto l'opposito'.

135   ASMo, CD, Avvisi 7, fol 872v: 'Ma la commune opinione, et la mia particolarmente e che costoro non siano de i sciocchi instromenti de gli anni passati, et che se siano bene purgati della biera che haverano bevuta di sorte che li mosteraranno i denti al detto duca'.

136   Some Italian authors, such as the fourteenth century Florentine chronicler Villani, had related an overconsumption of alcohol to the lack of any military fighting skills, see Joey De Keyser, *Vreemde Ogen. Een kijk op de Zuidelijke Nederlanden (1400–1600)* (Antwerp: Meulenhof/Manteua, 2010).

137   Vitelli to Concino, Brussels 14 April 1572 and 3 June 1572, in ASF, MdP 651, fol 51–52v; 55r.

138   ASF, MdP 651, f36: 'Io so ben' qualche dico, che mi trovo in fatto, et son ser di Alt, come v.s. alla quale dico liberamente che la necessità e grandemente, et il stato in che ci trovamo-molto peggiore di qualche io saprei dire, et lei imaginarsi. Crucially, Vitelli did not include both these comments in the letter he wrote to Francesco on that very same day, see fol 33.

139   Angiolini, 'L'Italia nell'età di Filippo II', pp. 462–463 and G. Galasso, 'L'Italia una e diversa nel sistema degli Stati Europei (1450–1750)', in G. Galasso (ed.), *Storia d'Italia vol XIX: L'Italia moderna e l'unità nazionale* (Turin: Einaudi, 1998), p. 116.

mous loan of 200,000 *scudi* was an ideal to present themselves as loyal and trustworthy allies of Philip II.[140] It also offered the possibility to bargain and obtain recognition of their Grand ducal status. With this prestigious title, the Medici became the most important family on the Italian peninsula, outranking the much older dynastic families of Este, Gonzaga and Savoy.[141] This rapid rise to prominence of a former banking family caused diplomatic difficulties between the Italian ruling houses across European courts. Both Philip II and Maximilian II were reluctant to recognize this new title and especially the Emperor disputed the Pope's authority in granting such titles.[142] However, after the Medici's huge loan of 1572, Philip II abandoned his protest and formally recognized the Medici as grand dukes of Tuscany. In this way, the combination of having access to multiple sources of information, and their financial capacity greatly helped the Medici rulers to outmanoeuvre their peers politically on the Italian peninsula.

The Medici received first-hand information from their different trusted correspondents, who had either a mercantile or a military background, but all belonged to the same Florentine network. Their allegiance to their home town, Florence, and its rulers was a crucial feature of this network. In writing letters, they regularly performed their loyalty and allegiance to the ruling house. Thanks to these correspondents, the Medici were amongst the first to know exactly what was happening both on the battlefield and in Brussels. Having access to reliable people on the ground and their observations gave the Medici concrete political advantages over their Italian peers. Due to their access to different news reports and letters, the Medici secretary of state was able to weigh the incoming information and assess what was going on and how the situation would evolve.

---

140   A. Contini, P. Volpini (eds.), *Istruzioni agli Ambasciatori e inviati Medicei in Spagna e nell'*
      "Italia Spagnola" (1536–1648) Tomo I: 1536–1586 (Rome: Beni Culturali, 2007), pp. 344–346.
      Letters from Brussels written by Macinghi in ASF, MdP 575, fol 256; MdP 576, fol 302;
      MdP 577, fol 256, 261, 282.

141   Toby Osborne, 'The Surrogate War between the Savoys and the Medici: Sovereignty and
      Precedence in Early Modern Italy', *The International History Review*, 29 (2007), pp. 1–21.

142   G. Spini, 'Il Principato e il sistema degli stati europei', in G.C. Garfagnini (ed.), *Firenze e la*
      Toscana dei Medici nell' Europa del' 500, Strumenti e veicoli della cultura relazioni politiche
      ed economiche (Florence: Olschki, 1983), III, p. 191, 198; D. Marrara, 'I rapporti giuridici fra
      la Toscana e l'impero (1530–1576)', in *Firenze e la Toscana dei Medici*, I, pp. 217–222, and
      N. Scott Baker, 'The Emperor and the Duke: Cosimo I, Charles V; and the Negotiation of
      Sovereignty', in A. Assonitis, H. Th. Van Veen (eds.), *A Companion to Cosimo I de' Medici*
      (Leiden: Brill, 2021), pp. 115–159.

For the dissemination of news from the Low Countries to Italian cities, *avvisi* were of crucial importance. As soon as the conflict erupted in 1566, news from Antwerp became a standard headline offering readers a digest of the latest occurrences. In describing the political and military situation in the Low Countries, specific images and references to the past were made, both in *avvisi* and in correspondence, which appealed to the Italian political imagination and historical memory. The evolution in the use of long-established stereotypes, as we will see in the next chapters, would exert considerable influence over the subsequent Italian debates concerning the state of the Low Countries and their impact on Habsburg power in Italy.

'Much to the Dislike of Italy': The First Political Debates (1577–1578)

In his popular history *Cronologia del mondo* (chronology of the world) printed in 1580 in Venice, Francesco Sansovino attempted to list all the important events in history.[1] For the year 1577, he summarized the situation in the Low Countries as follows:

> [The Low Countries] having attained liberty, first asked King Matthias and the Prince of Orange for help, and later the Duke of Alençon brother to the King of France. They defend themselves, weapons in hand against their lord Philip King of Spain, much to the dislike of Italy, possibly fearful that this fire might penetrate these lands and disturb our long-lasting peace.[2]

The year 1577 had an almost unusually peaceful start for Philip II and the Spanish-Habsburg monarchy in general: in February Philip's half-brother, Don John, had concluded a peace deal in the Low Countries and secret peace talks with the Ottomans were underway. In the summer, however, the situation in the Netherlands escalated rapidly and dramatically. Fearing an attack upon his life, Don John marched with his remaining men into the citadel of Namur. The States General accused Don John of violating the peace agreement and Catholic nobles had approached Matthias of Austria, the younger brother of Emperor Rudolf II, to become the new governor-general. Meanwhile, negotiations were ongoing with Francis of Valois, Duke of Anjou and Alençon, brother of the French king Henry III for support.

Apart from describing Matthias of Austria and the Duke of Anjou's ill-fated ventures in the Low Countries as failures, this volatile period has received little

---

1 Paul Grendler, 'Francesco Sansovino and Italian Popular History 1560–1600', *Studies in the Renaissance*, 16 (1969), pp. 139–180.

2 Francesco Sansovino, *Cronologia del mondo* (Venice: Sansovino, 1580), USTC 854821, p. 87: 'La quale postasi in libertà, chiamato in suo aiuto prima il Re Matthias, il Principe d'Orange, & poi il Duca di Lanson fratello del Re di Francia si difende con l'armi in mano contra Filippo Re di Spagna suo signore: con dispiacer dell' Italia, dubbiosa forse che quell' incendio non penetri in queste parti, & disturbi la nostra lunga pace'.

attention from historians working on the Revolt in the Low Countries.[3] Both Violet Soen and Arthur Weststeijn have focussed on the conciliatory efforts of some members of the Netherlandish nobility and Spanish councillors during this period. At this time, they argue, the beleaguered Spanish authorities were more open to peace initiatives than has previously been acknowledged, and these initiatives themselves merit more scholarly attention.[4] By looking at the Italian perspective it becomes clear that the revolt was now being perceived as a war with major international repercussions.

While the events in 1577, in the end, did not seriously alter the course of the war itself, this chapter argues that they nevertheless had a profound and lasting impact on the Italian perceptions of the conflict. In this year, news from the Low Countries came to dominate the Italian headlines and chronicles show that observers across diverse social groups became particularly alert to the unfolding events.[5] The question of how to solve the conflict became a hot topic in political debates. Most historians identify the famous Act of Abjuration in 1581, when the States General officially declared their independence from Philip II, as a watershed moment. Yet because the Italian perspective has been rather neglected, so far they have missed out on just how shaken the international public was by these earlier events. William of Orange's famous *Apology* and the subsequent legal abjuration of Philip II did not generate any contemporary counterattacks in Italian states as they had done in Spain, where Pedro Cornejo wrote a vicious pamphlet against William of Orange's text. Instead, it was in 1577 that the conflict and its potential dangerous repercussions dominated the news cycle and political debates in different Italian states and cities.[6] For most Italian political thinkers and other observers, radical steps were already taken in 1577 by openly inviting foreign princes to rule without Philip II's consent.

---

3 Howard Louthan, *The Quest for Compromise. Peacemakers in Counter-Reformation Vienna* (Cambridge: Cambridge University Press, 1997); Mack Holt, *The Duke of Anjou and the Politique Struggle during the Wars of Religion* (Cambridge: Cambridge University Press, 1986); Frédéric Duquenne, *L'entreprise du duc d'Anjou aux Pays-Bas de 1580 à 1584. Les responsabilités d'un échec à partager* (Villeneuve d'Ascq: Septentrion, 1998).

4 Soen, *Vredehandel*, pp. 117–130; Arthur Weststeijn, 'Antonio Pérez y la formación de la política española respecto a la rebelión de los Países Bajos, 1576–1578', *Historia y Política*, 19 (2008), pp. 231–254.

5 The Florentine tailor Arditi, who had been chronicling events in Florence since 1574, started to pay particular attention to the news arriving from the Netherlands: *Diario di Firenze*, pp. 161–170, 174, 183.

6 See Anton Van der Lem and Bahar Turkoglu, 'L'anti-apologie de 1581 de Pedro Cornjeo', *LIAS*, 31 (2004), pp. 185–237 and Yolanda Rodríguez-Pérez, 'The Pelican and its ungrateful Children: The Construction and Evolution of Dutch rebelliousness in Golden Age Spain', *Journal of Early Modern History*, 11 (2007), pp. 286–302.

Italian observers recognised that these political initiatives could have repercussions for the Italian peninsula and even the potential to alter the balance
of power in Europe. Given the potentially far-reaching consequences of the
events of 1577, political thinkers and agents on the Italian peninsula started to
debate the situation in earnest. Various Italian political observers, some with
close ties to the papacy, wrote *discorsi* on how to resolve the escalating situation in the Low Countries. These political tracts were used as crucial tools
to interpret incoming news reports and to grasp the present state of affairs.[7]
Combining information from newsletters with historical examples and political axioms, these analyses tried to predict potential outcomes and influence
decision-making. Steeped in reason of state thinking, they show a significant
shift from the overall positive image of the Low Countries and its inhabitants.
Though these texts were primarily addressed to a restricted audience of poli-
cymakers and were not meant to circulate in wide circles, many nevertheless
did and became part of *Thesoro politico*, a hugely popular collection of different political writings first printed in 1589.[8] These treatises are a crucial part
of the story and give insight into how Italian contemporaries perceived and
interpreted the Revolt in the Low Countries.

1   From Pacification to Rupture

In Papal Rome, the discussions at the Spanish court on how to resolve the problems in the Netherlands were followed closely. The papacy feared that the Low
Countries might become entirely dominated by Calvinists and had its own
agenda as Pope Gregory XIII wanted to play a more pro-actively role in international politics.[9] Many at the papal curia were convinced that the solution for

---

7   Zwierlein, *Discorso und Lex Dei*, pp. 538–540.
8   The *Relatione degli Stati di Fiandra* was included in the first edition: *Thesoro politico cioè*
    relationi instruttioni trattati, discorsi varii d'amb.ri pertinenti alla cognitione, et intelligenza
    delli stati, interessi, et dipendenze de più gran Principi del Mondo (Cologne [Paris]: Alberto
    Coloresco, 1589), USTC 806507. On this collection see Jean Balsamo, 'Les Origines Parisiennes
    du *Tesoro politico* (1589)', *Bibliothèque d'Humanisme et Renaissance*, 57 (1995), pp. 7–21;
    Simone Testa, 'Per una interpretazione del Thesoro Politico (1589)', *Nuova Rivista Storica*, 85
    (2001), pp. 347–362; Simone Testa, 'Did Giovanni Maria Manelli publish the Thesoro Politico
    (1589)?', *Renaissance Studies*, 19 (2005), pp. 380–393. Numerous editions appeared with each
    containing a different selection of texts, for an overview consult Simone Testa, 'From the
    "Bibliographical Nightmare" to a Critical Bibliography: Tesori politici in the British library',
    The Electronic British Library Journal, 1 (2008), pp. 1–33.
9   M.A. Visceglia, 'The International Policy of the Papacy: Critical Approaches to the Concepts
    of Universalism and *Italianità*, Peace and War', in M.A. Visceglia (ed.), *Papato e politica inter-*
    nazionale nella prima età moderna (Rome: Viella, 2013), pp. 17–62.

the revolt in the Low Countries was intimately connected to England arguing it could only be resolved by neutralizing the rebels' principal ally, Elizabeth I.[10] An enterprise to remove the English Queen had been firmly on the mind of the previous pope, Pius V, and had now captured the interest of Gregory XIII. When Don John of Austria was appointed as the new governor-general in 1576, hopes were high in Rome that the hero of Lepanto would be able to appease the situation in the Low Countries and prepare for a war with England.[11]

Upon his arrival in the Low Countries in November 1576, Don John was immediately confronted with an extremely difficult set of circumstances.[12] Mutinous unpaid Habsburg troops had just sacked the city of Antwerp, and all the provinces had agreed to the Pacification of Ghent. This important treaty temporarily suspended religious persecution and called for the removal of Spanish troops from the Low Countries.[13] Despite the deep mistrust between Don John and the States, they negotiated a peace settlement largely based on the Pacification in February 1577.[14] In the Perpetual Edict, Don John ratified most of the terms of the Pacification of Ghent. He agreed that the Spanish and Italian troops would soon leave the Netherlands, but insisted on the recognition of Catholicism as the only official religion.

When the news of the Perpetual Edict reached Rome, Gregory XIII appointed Filippo Sega, Bishop of Ripatransone, as extraordinary nuncio to the Netherlands.[15] Sega was assigned a double mission. Officially, he declared

---

10   AAV, SS, NI, vol 1, fol 3–14; 16o: 'Stando tuttavia S.S.tà nel suo antico proposito, che il muo-
      vere le armi contro Inghilterra fosse per essere rimedio di molta salute alla intiera quiete
      delli paesi di Fiandra'; AAV, Fondo Borghese III, vol 129d: *Relatione del negotiato di Mons
      Sega, nuntio in Fiandra, havuta dallo stesso, fatto cardinale alli 7 di Novembre 1595.*

11   See Bernard De Meester, *Le Saint-Siege et les troubles des Pays-Bas 1566–1579* (Leuven:
      Bibliothèque de Louvain, 1934), p. 107 and Violet Soen, 'Philip II's Quest. The Appointment
      of Governors-General during the Dutch Revolt (1559–1598)', *Bijdragen en Mededelingen
      betrefferende de Geschiedenis der Nederlanden*, 126 (2011), pp. 3–29.

12   For a biography see Bartolomé Bennassar, *Don Juan de Austria. Un héroe para un imperio*
      (Madrid: Temas de Hoy, 2004) and with particular focus on his time in the Netherlands,
      see Fréderic Wauters, *L'audience de Don Juan d'Autriche: essai sur le séjour dans les Flandres
      (1576–1578)* (Brussels: Le Cri éditions, 2000).

13   See M. Baelde and P. Van Peteghem, 'De Pacificatie van Gent (1576)' in *Opstand en
      Pacificatie in de Lage Landen. Bijdrage tot de studie van de Pacificatie van Gent* (Gent:
      Snoeck, 1976), pp. 1–62.

14   Gustaaf Janssens, *Brabant in het verweer. Loyale oppositie tegen Spanje's bewind in de
      Nederlanden van Alva tot Farnese, 1567–1578* (Kortrijk: Heule, 1989). Manuscript copies in
      BAV, Urb Lat 1045, fol 264r–v: *Copia delli Articoli della pace fatta in Fiandra col Signore Don
      Giovanni d'Austria, in nome del Re Catholico, l'una, et con tutti li stati di fiandra, l'altra parte,
      la qual fù publicata alli 17 di febraro 1577 à Bruselles* and fol 265–266r: *Capitolatione tra il
      S. Don Gio d'Austria et li Diputati delli stati di Fiandra.*

15   BAV, Urb Lat 1045, fol 262r–263v: *Di Roma li xvi di febraro 1577.*

to the States General that he came to support Don John's pacification strategy.[16] However, Sega had to prepare and finance an expedition against Elizabeth I.[17] Don John's personal mission was to establish Mary of Scotland as Queen of England and to marry her.[18] However, very soon, these ambitious plans were brought to an abrupt end by the deteriorating situation in the Low Countries.[19]

The papal curia was kept abreast of the developments thanks to the excellent information network of Cardinal Granvelle, who resided in Rome, and their extraordinary nuncio.[20] In his letters to the papal Secretary of State, Tolomeo Gallio, Sega described the confusing and tense situation. He mainly blamed William of Orange for this state of affairs because the prince refused to recognize the Perpetual Edict.[21] Sega further reported that due to the absence of persecution more and more *tristi* were flocking to Antwerp and Ghent. The word *tristo* can best be translated as wicked or as the treacherous nature of humans and is often used by Italian writers to refer to the Calvinists.[22] Sega was convinced Don John had to undertake swift action because this situation would otherwise create 'an open door to exterminate the Catholic faith in these lands'.[23]

---

16 N. Japikse (ed.), *Resolutiën der Staten Generaal. Eerste deel 1576–1577* (Den Haag: Nijhoff, 1915), p. 324.

17 Angel Fernandez Collado, *Gregorio XIII y Felipe II en la nunciatura de Felipe Sega (1577–1581). Aspectos político, jurisdiccional y de reforma* (Toledo: Estudios teologicas de San Idlefonse, 1990), pp. 138–140.

18 Per Olof de Törne, *Don Juan d'Autriche et les projets de conquête de l'Angleterre: Étude historique sur dix années du seizième siècle (1568–1578)* (Helsinki: Acta Academia Aboentis, 1915–1928).

19 Some would continue to argue that it was necessary to move the war to England to solve the conflict in the Low Countries, see for instance the Spanish treatise written by Francesco de Vera on 29 September 1577 in a collection of manuscripts of Minucci (vol 22, fol 229–241v), see A. Kohler, P.P. Piergentili, G. Venditti (eds.), *I codici Minucciani dell'Istituto Storico Germanico. Inventario* (Rome: Online Publication of the German Historical Institute, 2009), p. 156.

20 Sega's letters were also a key source of information for Cardinal Granvelle who summarised their content in his letters to Margaret of Parma: *Correspondance du cardinal de Granvelle 6*, pp. 222–223, 241–243. See also G. Janssens 'Cardinal Granvelle and the Revolt in the Netherlands. The evolution of this thought on a desirable political approach to the problem 1567–1578', in K. De Jonge, G. Janssens (eds.), *Les Granvelle et les anciens Pays-Bas* (Leuven: Universitaire Pers, 2000), pp. 135–156.

21 Sega's letters from 23 March and 23 July 1577: AAV, SdS, NI 1, fol 338–372.

22 Macchiavelli used the term 'tristi' in this way: Q. Skinner, R. Price (eds.), *The Prince* (Cambridge: Cambridge University Press, 1988), pp. 59–62. For other examples related to context in the Low Countries: ASF, MdP 4254, fol 206v, 228; BAV, Urb Lat 1047, fol 83.

23 Sega to Gallio, Mechelen 4 July 1577, AAV, SdS, NI, vol 1, fol 348v: 'Et io destramente tengo persuaso, che non si faccia, poiché questa è la porta aperta al' esterminio de la religione Cattolica in questi paesi'.

Sega went further than simply reporting about the ongoing developments: he regularly sent intercepted letters and other texts (*scritture*). Attached to his letter of 1 June 1577 was a treatise outlining the various reasons for the outbreak of the revolt under Margaret of Parma's governorship in 1566.[24] According to Sega, in this account, one could clearly see how the Protestants had returned to good behaviour out of 'their fear of punishment'.[25] Without making the comparison explicitly, he suggested that to end these new troublesome and confusing times a new rigour needed to be applied. It was clear to Sega that no good was to come or could be expected from the present liberties. The two other intercepted writings, Sega had included in this letter put forward the arguments of the States General and the bishops in defence of the Pacification of Ghent. Sega warned Gallio that the members of the States General did not know he had intercepted these texts; he counselled that it was best not to circulate them.[26]

Such warnings were needed as these dispatches were not restricted to the pope and his secretary of state, but were sometimes read in the consistory. The arrival of Sega's letters in Rome was newsworthy in itself and recorded by several news writers.[27] One claimed that the news that Sega wrote to the pope had been published or made public.[28] The practice of sharing and copying information from official correspondence certainly blurred the lines between more confidential and public information. Due to Sega's activities in the Low Countries, the political arguments put forward by the States General in defence

---

24 Sega to Gallio, Brussels 1 June 1577, AAV, SdS, NI, vol 1, fol 344–345v. Unfortunately, these documents are no longer kept together with Sega's letters in the Vatican Archives, which makes it difficult to know exactly which texts he sent to Rome. The *Principio et causa della guerra di Fiandra* (BAV, Urb Lat 1206, fol 126–138) is a strong contender based on Sega's short summary. In his letter, Sega remarked that the reform of the bishoprics was not mentioned at all in this treatise, while others consider it as one of the main reasons for the outbreak of the revolt.

25 Sega to Gallio, Brussels 1 June 1577, AAV, SdS, NI, vol 1, fol 344v: 'che li tristi havranno più presto in questo intermedio cessato da questa maledittione "formidine penae" che che siano cessati e ritornati al bene "virtutis amore"'.

26 Sega to Gallio, Brussels 1 June 1577 in AAV, SdS, NI, vol 1, fol 344v: 'Queste scritture non si sa da huomo delli Stati che siano capitate alle mie mani, e perciò non è bene ce si publichino'. The term *pubblicare* (to publish) was mostly used in the sixteenth century in relation to the publication of a printed book, but was sometimes also used for the dissemination of manuscript copies. Richardson, *Manuscript culture*, p. 31.

27 BAV, Urb lat 1045, fol 432–433r: *Di Roma li 14 d'Agosto 1577*.

28 BAV, Urb lat 1045, fol 438–439r: *Di Roma li xvij d'Agosto 1577*: 'si è publicato l'avviso scritto del Nuntio Sega a S. Sta'. On the circulation of news in Rome consult John M. Hunt, 'The Conclave from the "Outside In": Rumor, Speculation, and Disorder in Rome During Early Modern Papal Elections', *Journal of Early Modern History*, 16 (2012), pp. 355–382.

of their decisions were circulating in handwritten newsletters and other political tracts on the Italian peninsula. As we will see, several political thinkers used
these texts to counsel on which policy should be pursued in the Netherlands.

The political and military situation changed quickly and halted Sega's prepa-
rations for an English enterprise. On 24 July 1577, fearing an attack upon his life,
Don John marched his remaining men into the citadel of Namur. To make matters even worse, he recalled the troops from Lombardy on his own initiative.
The States General accused Don John of violating the Perpetual Edict. These
sudden military actions caused consternation in the Low Countries and the
rest of Europe. Anonymous manuscript news reports with specific titles such
as 'particular account of the new uproars in the Low Countries' began to circulate to explain this uncomfortable turn of events.[29] Ottavio Gonzaga-Guastalla,
an important military officer and close advisor to Don John, penned various
letters to the Duke of Urbino and the Duke of Mantua and Monferrato, and
important noblemen in Rome, such as the Roman Capilupi family, to explain
and above all to justify Don John's actions.[30] His letter of 26 July to Guglielmo
of Gonzaga, Duke of Mantua and Monferrato, is highly revealing of how he
used historical examples to explain the dangerous situation without going into
much detail. According to Ottavio, Don John had received intelligence 'that
they wanted to start a Sicilian vesper', referring to the bloody events that took
place on Easter Monday in Palermo in 1282.[31] In that year, thousands of French
men and women had been killed by the Sicilians in a collective uprising against
French rule on the island. In drawing this comparison, Ottavio made it clear to
Guglielmo that the general attitudes toward Don John and his entourage were
very hostile and that they were fearing for their lives. He concluded his letter by stating that they were 'in a land which knew neither God nor King'.[32]
Incoming *avvisi* confirmed this hostile atmosphere and reported about a total
collapse of Spanish authority.

These news reports heightened the fears that events in the Netherlands
would have serious repercussions for the *Pax Hispanica* on the Italian peninsula. These fears were not unfounded: its fragility had been demonstrated only

---

29   BAV, Urb Lat 1045, fol 388–389r: *Particolare Relatione de nuovi tumulti suscitati in Fiandra*.
      For Arditi: *Diario di Firenze*, pp. 166–167: 'e la Fiandra tutta liberata dalle man di Spagnoli,
      che avevono dominato undici anni detta Fiandra'.
30   Bertini, *Ottavio Gonzaga*, pp. 133–155. For an example of a copy of a letter by Ottavio
      Gonzaga sent to Capilupi from Namur on 19 September 1577: BAV, Urb Lat 1045, fol 470–471v.
31   Copies of Gonzaga's letters to the Duke of Mantua were sent to the Duke of Urbino: BAV,
      Urb Lat 1045, fol 405r: 'che volevano fare un vespro siciliana'.
32   BAV, Urb Lat 1045, fol 407r: 'in paese che non conosce ne Dio ne il Re'.

two years earlier by an uprising in the Genoese Republic.[33] According to some newsletters Philip II, seeing how matters in the Netherlands were going from bad to worse, was secretly trying to keep many Genoese nobles in the city on friendly terms.[34] Genoese financial support was crucial for Philip II to mobilize and pay troops to keep a firm hold over all his possessions.[35] Contemporary observers worried that the unrest might spread from the Netherlands to their Italian possessions, especially to Milan, the gateway to Italy, a crucial city for Habsburg dominance on the Italian peninsula.[36] If Milan was threatened, Philip II would ultimately be unable to retain dominance over Naples and Sicily, which would, in turn, be more vulnerable to attacks from the Ottomans. These growing political fears on the Italian peninsula for war explain why contemporary observers started writing about potential solutions to the conflict.

2   Di Castro and Reason of State

In the autumn of 1577, the worrying developments in the Low Countries and their international repercussions dominated the political agenda in Rome. Whilst various cardinals were already gathered at the house of Cardinal Morone, a senior member of papal curia responsible for German affairs, to discuss the escalation in the Netherlands, some unexpected and more unwelcome news from Vienna arrived in the city on 25 October.[37] Archduke Matthias of Austria, brother of Emperor Rudolf II, had secretly left Vienna for Brussels where he was to become the new governor general as the States General had renounced Don John's governorship.[38] This move sent shockwaves through

---

33   On this episode: Claudio Costantini, *La Repubblica di Genova* (Turin: UTET, 1986), pp. 101–122.

34   The discontent in the city over the plots to hand the republic over to the Spanish was still simmering in 1577: BAV, Urb lat 1045, fol 421r.

35   Parker, *The Army of Flanders*, pp. 127–128.

36   C. Capra, D. Sella (eds.), *Il Ducato di Milano dal 1535 al 1796* (Turin: UTET, 1984), pp. 4–5 and see also Stefano d'Amico, *Spanish Milan. A City within the Empire 1535–1706* (New York: Palgrave, 2012).

37   ASMn, AG, Avvisi 1982, fol 450–451: *Di Roma li xxv di ottobre 1577*. For more on Morone, see Adam Patrick Robinson, *The Career of Cardinal Morone* (Burlington: Ashgate, 2002), pp. 206–213 and on the Congregatio Germanica: Guido Braun, *Imagines Imperii: Die Wahrnehmung des Reiches und der Deutschen durch die römische Kurie im Reformationjahrhundert (1523–1585)* (Münster: Aschendorf Verlag, 2014), pp. 312–326. Nuncio Delfino wrote letters from Vienna, see: A. Koller (ed.), *Nuntiaturen des Giovanni Delfino und des Bartolomeo Portia (1577–1578)* (Tübingen: De Gruyter, 2003), pp. 264–267, 283.

38   The Duke of Aerschot had lobbied for the help of Archduke Matthias, to counter William of Orange's growing influence in the States General: Soen, *Vredehandel*, pp. 97–116.

the various European courts. As a member of the Habsburg dynasty, Matthias acted without the approval and support of Philip II, who was not intent on replacing Don John. Keen to avoid a direct confrontation with his cousin Philip II, who was angered by this move, Rudolf II made it known that he had not consented to his brother's departure.[39]

Treatises reflecting on this new state of affairs were written with a sense of urgency. Less than ten days after the news of Matthias' escape had reached Rome, Scipio di Castro, a political advisor to Giacomo Boncompagni, the illegitimate son of Pope Gregory XIII, had already composed his political discourse on the matter.[40] Several other political advisors and thinkers affiliated with Giacomo Boncompagni wrote treatises discussing the current state of affairs and predicting the course of the conflict.[41] Boncompagni had good reasons to worry about this worsening situation, as he was a commander of the Spanish-Habsburg army in the Duchy of Milan, where a large proportion of Habsburg troops from the Low Countries were stationed.[42]

Scipio di Castro is an intriguing character: he was a former spy, a suspected heretic and one of the most important political intelligencers active in Rome.[43] He had studied in the Eremite convent in Naples. From 1550 to 1555, he was active as an informant and a spy for Ferrante Gonzaga in Milan, after which he spent a short time in Switzerland. Later, he became a political adviser to several Sicilian viceroys, including Medinacelli and Garcìa de Toledo. In 1576, he

---

39   Louthan, *Quest for Compromise*, pp. 143–154.

40   The autograph is in BAV, Boncompagni-Ludovisi, D10, fol 323–327. The document is dated 3 November 1577. This authorship is disputed by Minucci, who wrote on his copy of the treatise in 1586 that it was actually written by the French ambassador in Venice: 'Seguitano alcune consideration fatte sopra l'andata dell'arciduca Matthia in Fiandra, delle quali pare che s'honerasse don Scipio de Castro, ma però ne fu autore monsignor di Messen, ambasciatore del re di Francia in Vinetia già neli anni ove stava anco quest'anno '86', quoted *I codici Minucciani*, p. 154.

41   U. Coldagelli, 'Giacomo Boncompagni', in *DBI*, 11 (1969); Boncompagni was well known for his interest in political tracts: G. Brunelli, 'L'eco di un paradigma: *Gli avvertimenti politici di Vincenzo Vitelli a Giacomo Boncompagni*', in C. Ossola, M. Verga, M.A. Visceglia (eds.), *Religione cultura e politica nell' Europa dell' età moderna, studi offerti a Mario Rosa dagli amici* (Florence: Olschki, 2003), pp. 251–261; and for a broader context of political discussions in Rome: M. Rosa, 'The World's Theatre: The Court of Rome and Politics in the first half of the seventeenth century', in M.A. Visceglia, G. Signorotto (eds.), *Court and Politics in Papal Rome, 1492–1700* (Cambridge: Cambridge University Press, 2002), pp. 78–98.

42   On the situation see M. Rizzo, 'Milano e le forze del principe. Agenti, relazioni e risorse per la difesa dell'impero di Filippo II', in J. Martinez Millán (ed.), *Felipe II (1527–1598). Europa y la Monarquía Católica* (Madrid: Parteluz, 1998), pp. 743–759.

43   Biographical details are based on Roberto Zapperi, *Don Scipio di Castro. Storia di un impostore* (Rome: Carucci Beniamino, 1977) and his entry 'Scipio di Castro', in *DBI*, 22 (1979).

was arrested and sentenced by the Roman Inquisition on suspicion of heresy, a sentence which he was allowed to serve in the Roman monastery of Santa Maria del Popolo. During his confinement, he became a political advisor to Giacomo Boncompagni and wrote this treatise on Matthias of Austria. His various writings were addressed to Giacomo, but in most cases, Gregory XIII was the final recipient. Di Castro probably aspired to be an advisor to Philip II.

Di Castro's political thinking and writing were shaped by the language of reason of state. Although the term *ragion di stato* (reason of state) was established and popularised by the former Jesuit and political thinker Giovanni Botero in his work *La Ragion di Stato* published in 1589, this strand of political thinking was flourishing on the Italian peninsula decades earlier.[44] In this period, reason of state was developing to formulate an alternative more in line with the Catholic Church's moral thinking and increasingly directed against the ideas of Niccolò Machiavelli on statecraft.[45] Yet, di Castro's treatise on the rule of a state entitled *Delli fondamenti dello stato et delle parti essentiali che formano il principe* (On the fundamentals of the state and on the essential parts that form a ruler) it is clear that he was strongly influenced by Machiavelli's realistic view on politics.[46]

His treatise discussing the situation now that Matthias was on his way to the Low Countries, was based upon maxims of reason of state, rather than on accurate and in-depth knowledge of the problems in the Low Countries.[47] Di Castro suggested that Matthias did not pose a threat to the leadership of Philip II and Don John.[48] Matthias, he argued, lacked the essential qualities required of a prince, namely prudence, force and reputation. According to di Castro, Matthias was, too young to have any knowledge of how to govern a state. His young age and inexperience would prevent him from navigating

---

44   For Botero's political thinking, see amongst others: E. Baldini (ed.), *Botero e la "Ragion Di Stato": atti del convegno in memoria di Luigi Firpo (Torino 8–10 Marzo 1990)* (Florence: Olschki, 1992) and Romain Descendere, *L'état du monde. Giovanni Botero entre raison d'état et géopolitique* (Geneva: Droz, 2006).

45   Robert Bireley, *The Counter-Reformation Prince: Anti-Machiavellianism or Catholic Statecraft in Early Modern Europe* (Chapel Hill/London: University of North Carolina Press, 1990).

46   For this analysis, see also Simone Testa, *Scipione di Castro e il suo trattato politico. Testo critico e traduzione inglese inedita del seicento* (Rome: Vecchiarelli, 2012), pp. 31–73. The word 'principe' can be best translated as a ruler, although I have sometimes translated it as 'the prince'.

47   Zapperi, *Don Scipio di Castro*, pp. 101–102.

48   For a more in-depth analysis: Testa, *Scipione di Castro e il suo trattato*, pp. 43–51.

the private interests of his counsellors.[49] A ruler had to rely on his own judgments and not those of his ministers, and this was simply not possible for the young Matthias.

In addition to a lack of prudence and experience, di Castro predicted that Matthias' power in the Low Countries would be restricted by agreements with the States. The limitations of this power would also have an impact on his financial and military capacities. In a country devastated by war, the States General would be unable to provide him with enough money and troops. Di Castro compared Matthias' position to that of Peter of Aragon. In an attempt to free themselves from French rule after the Sicilian Vespers in 1282, the Sicilians had called upon Peter of Aragon.[50] If Peter had relied only on the resources of the Sicilians, his chance of winning Sicily would have been slim. In addition, Matthias would be unable to solicit any foreign support. According to di Castro, neighbouring states such as France and England would prefer a weak leader in the Low Countries and the German princes would be reluctant to back one of the Austrian Habsburgs to rule the Netherlands.[51] Matthias' restricted power and authority in strained economic circumstances meant that he would not pose a threat to Philip II.

In his treatise, di Castro also offered advice to Philip II on how to win this conflict. He claimed Philip II should use 'severe cruelty with those who resist and exemplary humanity with those who surrender'.[52] The king had to move all his troops to the Low Countries, which was possible because all the other parts of his empire were currently at peace. Di Castro considered Don John a capable general: his *felicità* (felicity or good fortune) to conduct this war successfully was based upon the valour of its army and the righteousness of the cause.

Di Castro's manuscript treatise was addressed to Boncompagni, but its readership was by no means confined to this addressee or even to the circles around Boncompagni in Rome. This text was immediately copied and sent to

---

49   'Discorso del Signor D. Scipione di Castro sopra l'andata dell'Arciduca Matthia d'Austria in Fiandra', appeared in 1605 in another anonymous edition of the famous 'Tesoro Politico': *La terza parte del tesoro politico. Nella quale si contengono Relationi, Instruttioni, Trattati, et Discorsi non meno dotti et curiosi, che utili per conseguire la perfetta cognitione della Ragione di Stato. Non prima dati in luce* (s.l.: Turnoni, 1605), USTC 6801413, pp. 129–130. I will reference the relevant pages of this printed edition.

50   'Discorso sopra l'andata', p. 131.

51   'Discorso sopra l'andata', p. 133.

52   'Discorso sopra l'andata', p. 134: 'crudele severità con chi resiste, & esemplare humanità con chi si rende'.

other recipients.[53] Scribal copies of his political treatises circulated quickly on a wide scale, and almost instantly provoked debates on the nature of the inhabitants as well as on the right course of action to solve the conflict in the Low Countries.

3   Understanding the Low Countries

Immediately anonymous authors rebutted the arguments set forward by di Castro arguing that Philip II should opt for a peaceful solution rather than consider another devastating war.[54] It was necessary to draw lessons from the experience of ten years of warfare and the king needed to consider the enormous loss of lives and the high cost of warfare. According to one anonymous author, the expenses 'were worth more than the state itself'.[55] Several Italian political commentators considered the nature of the Netherlandish people to be a key factor that had to be taken into account.

Understanding the climate of the land and its inhabitants was a crucial aspect of political theory in this period.[56] For any ruler to preserve his territories successfully, it was paramount to understand the passions of the different people they were ruling. Between 1577 and 1579, a flurry of different treatises providing general overviews of the Low Countries were written on the Italian

---

53   Other copies can be found in the following collections: BNCF, Capponi N 109, cart 181; AAV, Pio 199, fol 229–232; AAV, Borghese I 429–448, fol 327–404v; BAV, Vat Lat 7021, fol 204–208. See: Harold Love, *Scribal publication in seventeenth-century England* (Oxford: Clarendon Press, 1993).

54   Copies in ASF, MdP 4254, fol 565–568; KBR, Manuscript II 5193; AAV, Pio 77, fol 9–16.

55   KBR, Manuscript II 5193, fol 62v–63: 'Fresche le piaghe de la guerra che già tanti anni hà havuto con quella natione, che ogni volta che se ridure à memoria la difficulta passate, le spese notabili, che si può dire, piu di quanto vale quello stato, la perdita di tanta gente et la necessità in che finalmente s' è trovato di fare una pace tanto vantagiosa al nimico, non si vede come possa facilmente resolvessi al nuovo sbarraglio'. Upon his return from Madrid in 1576 the Venetian ambassador Lorenzo Priuli had told the Venetian senate that: 'Nè si vede modo per il quale S.M. per via della forza possa ricuperar quegli stati [...] A questi mali e pericoli adunque non potendo rimediare il re con la guerra, come per esperienza di tanti anni si è veduto, ed essendo già fatto il male molto vecchio e quasi incurabile, sarà necessitata S.M. mettervi fine con quelle condizioni di pace che potrà aver migliori' in E. Albèri (ed.), *Relazioni degli ambasciatori veneti al senato. Relazioni degli stati Europei, tranne l'Italia, Serie I Tome III* (Florence: Grazzini, 1860), p. 234.

56   F. Lestringant, 'Europe et théorie des climats dans la seconde moitié du XVIe siècle', in F. Lestringant (ed.), *Écrire le monde à la Renaissance. Quinze études sur Rabelais, Postel, Bodin et la littérature géographique* (Caen: Paradigme, 1993), pp. 255–275.

peninsula.[57] Their appearance and wide circulation at this particular juncture point to the urgent need to understand the unfolding events.[58] In compiling their treatises Italian commentators relied heavily on Lodovico Guicciardini's *Descrittione* (1567). In less than ten years, Guicciardini's work had become the standard work of reference for knowledge about the Netherlands.[59] He had dedicated a section to the characteristics of the inhabitants and had sketched a very positive picture of the Low Countries as a peaceful and devout place. He considered them to be learned and very diligent people.[60] Combining climate theory with the precepts of Galenic medicine, he had noted these people were cold-natured. Following this line of thinking, he mentioned in passing that they were easy to trick, distrustful and sometimes even a bit obstinate.[61] These elements of his discourse became more prominent in contemporary analyses to explain the situation. It is at this very moment in time that a clear shift in Italian perception emerges. The idea that the Low Countries were a pleasant and even idyllic place had to be reinterpreted. An anonymous tract serves as an example: although there had been a time when the inhabitants of

---

57   An earlier example is BAV, Vat. Lat. 7080, fol 230–262: *Discorso sopra la Fiandra, delli costumi, richezze, forze, qualità, sito et modo di governo delli Paesi Bassi.*

58   They circulated widely on the peninsula and had varying titles but were based on two main versions: *Relatione de gli stati et governi di Fiandra* (Report of the states and the government of the Low Countries), probably written by Scipio di Castro for the Sicilian nobleman, Charles of Aragon, the Duke of Terranova, who was the main Habsburg negotiator at the peace talks in Cologne in 1579. It also has been ascribed to the Venetian ambassador Michele Suriano see BAV, Boncompagni D10, fol 433r–442v. For other copies see MA, cod CLXXXVI CIVI; AAV, Borghese I 618, fol 136–158v and BAV, Barb Lat 5235, fol 257–276. Other titles for the same treatises include *Relatione delli stati e governi di fiandra in tempo di Filippo II, anno 1578* and *Compedio delli stati et governo'. Relazione in forma di discorso de costumi, de richezze, forze, qualità, sito e modo di governo delli paesi bassi* (Report in the style of a discourse on the costumes, the richness, the forces, the quality, the cities and the way of government of the Low Countries); the identity of the author of this work is unknown. ASF, CS I, fol 198–215; BAV, Vat. Lat. 7080, fol 231–261v.

59   For instance, Sansovino advised his readers of *Cronologia* to consult Guicciardini's *Descrittione* if they wanted to know more about the Netherlands, p. 165: 'particolarmente con molta diligentia da Lodovico Guicciardini, nipote per fratello dello Historico, al quale rimettiamo il lettore'. The *Descrittione* was first published in Italian in Antwerp in 1567 (two new revised editions in 1581 and 1588). Although it was never reprinted in its entirety on the Italian peninsula, it reached the Italian market via the Frankfurt book fair, see Ian Maclean, 'Ciotti and Plantin: Italy, Antwerp and the Frankfurt Book Fair', *La Bibliofilía*, 115 (2013), pp. 135–146. Only Guicciardini's extensive description of Antwerp was printed together with two other discourses: *Tre discorsi appartenenti alla grandezza delle città. L'uno di m. Lodovico Guicciardini. L'altro di m. Claudio Tolomei. Il terzo di m. Giovanni Botero* (Rome: Martinelli, 1588), USTC 835453.

60   Guicciardini, *Descrittione*, p. 27.

61   Guicciardini, *Descrittione*, p. 30.

the Low Countries were used to pleasure and comfort, in the recent wars they had shown a willingness to pick up arms to fight the Spanish.[62] For these ideas on the people of the Low Countries, this anonymous author might have been inspired by a recent news report from Antwerp of 29 October 1577 which stated something similar.

> If ever these lands have craved for war, now they crave for it more than ever, [...] these people nurtured and raised in *otium*, now have become more than ever experts in warfare, as they are determined to fight until death, so that the Spanish can never again set foot in these regions as dominators.[63]

The recent wars had had a clear impact on the reputation of the Low Countries and its inhabitants. Most authors arguing against another war effort used Julius Caesar's description of this nation as the most bellicose of Gaul. These ideas would also gain more traction in political discourse and wider reception of the conflict as the war dragged on.

In another treatise entitled *Discorso sopra l'andata dell' arciduca Mathia in Fiandra* (Discourse on the journey of Archduke Matthias to the Netherlands), an unknown author also elaborated upon the nature of people in the Low Countries to argue against di Castro's advice.[64] One also needed to consider that Matthias had been invited by the people of the Low Countries 'who had obstinately and fiercely resisted, for many years, the scourge of the death, fires and extortions of the Spanish, to maintain their liberty'.[65] The author insisted that these inhabitants were united by their passions in their struggle against the Spanish. One of these shared passions was their natural hatred of the Spanish and another was their ancient struggle to uphold their privileges and liberties.

---

62   KBR, Manuscript II, 5193, fol 65v: 'Nella diversita de costumi che vanno introdotto le commodita et le delitie de tante e cosi belle citta che da quello tempo in qua hanno dato nuova forma a quel paese ha pero estinta in tutta la loro natura fierezza per che ogni volta l' occasione li hà chiamati all' armi si sono mostrati molto pronti à pigliarle, et la guerra passata con la lunga continuatione, [...] oltre che col dare à questa lor rivolta titolo di libertà, si può credere et combatterebbono tanto piu ostinatamente, giuntovi l'odio naturale che portano alla Natione spagnola, et il tenersi da quella in piu modi offesi'.

63   ASMn, AG, Avvisi 1982, fol 458: 'Se mai questi paesi bramorno la guerra, hora la bramano piu che mai [...]: questi popolu che nutriti et allevati nell'otio, hora son piu esperti che mai nel guereggiare sendo resoluti di volere combatere fin che haranno vita, accio mai piu gli spagnoli mettino passo in queste bande come dominatori'.

64   AAV, SdS, NF, vol 7, fol 25–28.

65   AAV, SdS, NF, vol 7, fol 26v: 'tanto arditi et tanto ostinati con le prova di tanti anni continui alla sferza delle morti, delli incendij, et delle rapine delli spagnuoli, a mantenere la libertà loro'.

In his work on political thought during the Dutch Revolt, Martin Van Gelderen has shown how the rebels represented their struggle mainly as a defence of traditional liberties rather than a religious conflict.[66] The 'constitutional trinity of liberty, privileges and the States General' present in rebel pamphleteering found resonance in Italian political discourses.[67] This particular author was one of several who echoed arguments presented by the States General now circulating on the Italian peninsula partly due to the activities of papal nuncio Sega's in 1577. Some Italian authors also rehearsed part of rebel discourses by referring to the brutal Spanish mutinies in the Low Countries. The unknown author concluded that present and past examples had shown the extent to which these people would stand up and fight for their privileges and rights. He was firmly convinced that the people of the Low Countries were very capable of waging war against Philip II on their own.

Whereas some political commentators considered the Netherlandish combative spirit a virtue, others turned it into a vice and mainly saw obstinacy. The anonymous writer of a *Relazione in forma di discorso* offers a beautiful illustration of this phenomenon:

> but their virtues are stained, corrupted and tainted by one vice, which springs from their natural kindness: that they lend faith to anyone in whatever case, so they can easily be tricked, as they have been recently by the Prince of Orange and other rebels to their own detriment. Furthermore, they are suspicious, and very obstinate in their opinions and judgements.[68]

He argued that the inhabitants were gullible and that William of Orange was clearly exploiting this characteristic to his own advantage. This would become one of the most dominant vices ascribed to the inhabitants in Italian (and also Spanish) discourse on the revolt.[69] Depending on the author's position in the debate pro or against a new war, Guicciardini's account offered them material

---

66   Martin van Gelderen, *The Political Thought of the Dutch Revolt 1555–1590* (Cambridge: Cambridge University Press, 2002), pp. 133–146.

67   Van Gelderen, *Political Thought*, p. 138. On liberties and privileges in Guicciardini, see Aristodemo (ed.), *Descrittione*, pp. 57–65.

68   BV, N22, fol 2v: '[...] ma queste loro virtù sono macchiate corotti, et guaste da un' vitio, che nasce da natural bontà, usè, che prestano fede di qualunque cosa ad ogn'uno, onde con poca fatica possono esser gabbati, come sono stati ultimamente dal Principe d'Orange, et altri ribelli con tanto suo danno: sono di più sospettosi, et nelle sue opinioni, et impressioni molto ostinati'.

69   In Pedro Cornejo's history, who also relied heavily on Guicciardini, the same vices became important in Spanish discourse: Yolanda Rodríguez Pérez, *De Tachtigjarige Oorlog in Spaanse ogen* (Nijmegen: Vantilt, 2003), pp. 56–59, 62–64.

to pick and choose from to highlight particular characteristics of the inhabitants to explain the ongoing situation and determine the right course of action.

4   Debating Practical Obstacles

Some treatises reacted to di Castro's analysis by considering the practical obstacles Philip II had faced in this war so far. The anonymous author of *Risposta al manifesto, che fa facilissima l'impresa di Fiandra* (Answer to the manifesto that the enterprise in the Low Countries is easy) offered a thoughtful treatment of the problems of ruling an empire and specifically the repercussions of Habsburg policy for the Italian peninsula.[70] First of all, he maintained that the geographic position of the Low Countries made it much easier for the rebels to be supplied than for the Habsburg troops. Philip II did not have enough food supplies as the land was 'burnt, ruined, trampled by foreign armed troops'.[71] Nor could he rely on neighbouring territories to help him with provisions given their animosity against Philip II. By referring to recent historical examples, such as Charles V's German and Italian campaigns, this commentator made his case that it was impossible to win a war without having adequate provisions.

In discussing the attitudes of the neighbouring countries, the author recognized the naval superiority of the rebel forces: he went as far as to state that the Prince of Orange and Elizabeth I could bring together a more powerful military fleet than Philip II, as the Spanish king would have to fight with his fleet on two fronts. Here the author is thinking about the potential repercussions for the 'Italian liberties' if Philip II would withdraw his ships from the Mediterranean. It was a dangerous scenario, as Philip II he had to fight or at least prevent the Ottomans from attacking the Italian coasts once again.

Another major problem was the king's financial situation, since the lack of funds to pay the soldiers had already caused 'difficulties', a euphemism for the numerous mutinies by unpaid soldiers.[72] In addition, due to the cold weather in winter, the campaigning season was relatively short, while the king still had to pay his soldiers in garrisons without making any significant progress. The offensive war Philip II now had to pursue would again cost him a great deal of money and his income, albeit vast, would not suffice to finance siege warfare.

---

70   'Risposta al manifesto, che fa facilissima l'impresa di Fiandra' in BAV, Urb Lat 836 Pars I, fol 177–184v, is published in G. Brom (ed.), *Archivalia in Italië belangrijk voor de geschiedenis van Nederland* (3 vols., The Hague: Stockum, 1908–1914), II, pp. 216–220.
71   *Archivalia in Italië*, II, p. 217: 'Fiandra arsa, rovinata, calpestrata da genti straniere armate'.
72   *Archivalia in Italië*, II, p. 218: 'sicome è chiaro a qualunque sa le difficoltà occorse in Fiandra per non esservi stato da pagare i soldati'.

All in all, this anonymous author presented a dire but realistic assessment of Philip II's position, directly contradicting di Castro's arguments.[73]

This author acknowledged that Philip II was superior to his adversaries in one respect: his cause was righteous. The king, as their natural lord, was after all defending his claims on the Low Countries and he was also protecting the Catholic religion. These people, however, had rebelled because of the many errors committed, not least by the Duke of Alba, who had had some difficulty in maintaining the 'strada di mezo' (middle way).[74] By this stage, critique of Alba's rule amongst those advocating pacification became rather common. Cardinal Granvelle, for instance, was convinced that the inhabitants had become obstinate due to the bad treatment and constant plundering.[75] Such views on Alba's rule were not only present amongst political advisors and thinkers but also across different social groups in Italian society.[76] In Florence, the anti-Medicean tailor Arditi noted that the revolt had started with the 'cruel injustices' committed by the Duke of Alba.[77] Alba's reputation of being merciless and cruel from his military campaigns on the Italian peninsula, before his punitive expedition in the Low Countries, certainly contributed to such views.[78]

The anonymous author of the *Risposta* pledged to find a peaceful solution for the conflict, 'better with the arms of prudence than with those of iron' and was in favour of peace talks under the auspices of the Holy Roman Emperor.[79] The treatises advocating peace talks prompted another set of discourses written by members of the circles surrounding Giacomo Boncompagni. All the treatises emerging from the Boncompagni circle encouraged Philip II to undertake an

---

73   Cardinal Granvelle equally raised these considerations in letters to Philip II (31 October and 18 November 1577), see *Correspondance du cardinal de Granvelle 6*, pp. 280–285, 289–303.

74   *Archivalia in Italië*, II, p. 220.

75   In various letters, Granvelle had been very critical of the rule of Duke of Alba see Janssens, 'Cardinal Granvelle and the Revolt in the Netherlands', pp. 143–146.

76   In another discourse *Summario d'un discorso sopra le cose di Fiandra* a similar observation was made: 'per la rigidità d'alcuni ministri regii in quel paese e per la poca intelligenza di quelli humori', quote taken from *Archivalia in Italië*, III, p. 270.

77   *Diario di Firenze*, p. 202.

78   Henry Kamen, *The Duke of Alba* (New Haven, London: Yale University Press, 2004), p. 67 and M.J. Rodríguez-Salgado, 'Capo dei Capi: the Duke of Alba in Italy', in M. Ebben, M. Lacy-Bruijn, R. van Hövell (eds.), *Alba: General and Servant to the Crown* (Maastricht: Karwansaray, 2013), pp. 227–255. In their contribution to this same volume Judith Pollmann and Monica Stensland show that in Dutch rebel discourse, Alba was in a more forceful way blamed for igniting the rebellion see 'Alba's reputation in the early modern Low Countries', pp. 308–325.

79   *Archivalia in Italië*, II, p. 220: 'meglio sarebbe con l'arme di prudenza che con il ferro'.

offensive war rather than opt for a peace treaty. It seems that these authors were trying to shift the tide at the papal court, where Gregory XIII was leaning more towards the necessity of peace talks with the support of Emperor Rudolph II.[80]

One of the authors advocating a more aggressive stance was the Florentine poet Lionardo Salviati. Salviati had recently joined Boncompagni's household on the initiative of Francesco I de' Medici, Grand Duke of Tuscany, and operated as an intelligencer in Rome for his old patron in Florence between 1578 and 1582.[81] He wrote *Discorso intorno alla ribellione di Fiandra* (Discourse on the rebellion in the Netherlands) at the end of 1577 as a direct refutation of the anonymous *Risposta*. In the first part of his treatise, Salviati discussed the various reasons given by those who tried to dissuade the king from starting a new war. One of these arguments was the danger of a French attack on Milan, a persistent fear in Italy in the sixteenth century that frequently surfaced in manuscript newsletters. According to an *avviso* of May 1576, the whole of Milan seemed to have been in a state of panic when rumours spread that an army of French Huguenots was marching towards the city.[82] The argument that France might profit from the war in the Netherlands connected it to the *Pax Hispanica* on the Italian peninsula. Boncompagni might have feared that the war would have a destabilizing effect on Milan itself. Salviati tried to allay these fears, arguing in the second part of his discourse that the French king would not have the forces to attack Milan.

Salviati further claimed the inhabitants of the Low Countries would become tired of waging war in defence of their own liberties. He dismissed the argument that the inhabitants were united and would continue to be united in their striving for liberty. Another treatise advocating for war entitled *Summario d'un discorso sopra le cose di Fiandra* (Summary of a discourse on the matters in

---

80   In June 1578, the pope had dispatched Ludovico Madruzzo as papal nuncio to Rudolph II to convince the emperor to recall Matthias as it had been 'too great an affront to such a great king' in order to restore the relationship between the two Habsburg nephews. See the instruction by Como to Madruzzo in June 1578, translation of 'essendo di troppo gran affronto a si gran re'.

81   BAV, Vat lat 6160 f192–212v; Barb lat. 5242 fol 35–50v for copies of *Discorso del cavallier Salviati all' Eccellentissimo S. Giacomo Buoncompagni, suo signore*. It has been published by L. Manzoni (ed.), *Prose inedite del Cav. Salviati* (Bologna: Romagnoli, 1987), pp. 59–77 on the basis of another version kept in the University Library of Bologna. For more information on Salviati: Peter M. Brown, *Leonardo Salviati: A Critical Biography* (Oxford: Oxford University Press, 1974).

82   BA, D188 INF, fol 98: *Di Milano 27 maggio 1576* and accounts such as *Discorso a la Maestà del re Christianissimo esortandolo a far guerra contra il re Cattolico* (Discours to the Christian King urging him to start a war against the Catholic King) circulated in manuscript in Italy.

the Low Countries) further elaborated on this point.[83] The opposition between William of Orange's private interests and those of the general public would ultimately break their unity and confidence.

Salviati concluded it would be 'neither useful nor honourable' for the king to pursue a peaceful solution.[84] The king should send all his troops to the Low Countries in order to be able to win the war. Salviati ended by advising the king to go there in person to reconcile the discord amongst the inhabitants.[85] In his treatise, Salviati revived the old solution of a royal visit, which had been advocated by various royal counsellors and the papacy since the start of the revolt in 1566. In trying to prove that the inhabitants of the Low Countries faced more difficulties than Philip II, Salviati and other authors proposing military action demonstrate a lack of realistic political insight into the complicated situation on the ground. The author of *Summario*, for instance, reasoned that the rebels would not be able to find a new ruler who would openly favour and support them. Even if there had been some justification for a revolt to restore ancient privileges, according to this author, this cause had now become 'detestable because of their manifest rebellion in front of the whole world, thus setting a very bad example'.[86] This remark indicates how the appointment of Matthias of Austria as governor-general was considered a turning point in the conflict: it was only now that these provinces were perceived to have openly rebelled against the authority of their king.

Other political writers advocating an offensive war show a far more realistic understanding of the complex situation. One anonymous writer, possibly Scipio di Castro himself, congratulated the king for undertaking a just war against 'the rebels to God'.[87] At the same time, he warned Philip II that it would have been wiser if Don John had not taken it upon himself to speak about religious matters since 'until now in all their published writings to justify their deeds, the inhabitants of the Low Countries have tried to present themselves as Catholics'.[88] This piece of advice illustrates that Italian commentators and observers were well aware of the arguments put forward by the States General

---

83   BAV, Boncompagni D5 and it has been published in *Archivalia in Italië*, III, pp. 268–270.

84   *Prose inedite del Cav. Salviati*, p. 77: 'nè utile, nè onorevole il consenso dell' accordo'.

85   Violet Soen, '"C'estoit comme songe et mocquerie de parler de pardon". Obstructie bij een Pacificatie-maatregel (1566–1567)', *Bijdragen en Mededelingen betreffende de Geschiedenis der Nederlanden*, 119 (2004), pp. 309–328.

86   *Archivalia in Italië*, III, pp. 269–270.

87   BAV, Boncompagni D10, fol 343: 'che si e dato alla giusta guerra, che v.M. e sforzata di far in fiandra contra li ribelli di Dio'.

88   BAV, Boncompagni D10, fol 343: 'Ma sarebbe forse stato meglio passare con silentio il particolare della religione, si perché in tutte le scritture publicate fin qui da' Fiaminghi per loro giustificatione hanno sempre voluto mostrarsi catholici'.

defending their actions in inviting Matthias of Austria. For a number of reasons, it was better not to wage this war on religious grounds according to this author. Firstly, it might entice Protestant leaders to come to the rebels' aid and secondly, it might alienate a number of the German and Swiss mercenaries serving in the Spanish-Habsburg army. The king needed to maintain good relationships with the Swiss to have access to the Alpine passes, without which it would be impossible to conduct this war. In these observations we see a real sense of the wider geopolitical ramifications. Many Italian observers understood the international importance of the ongoing conflict well and related it to their own position within the larger Habsburg empire.

5   Fear of French Involvement

The invitation of Matthias of Austria had caused a stir in 1577, with worries of a potential rupture in the House of Habsburg, a few months later, the potential involvement of Francis of Valois, Duke of Anjou led to frantic speculation, news reports, and diplomatic initiatives.[89] The intertwining of the religious wars in France with conflict in the Low Countries had already been a cause for concern in 1572 when William of Orange's brother was negotiating with the French king.[90] Alongside fears over the expansion of Calvinism, the revival of the old antagonism between Valois France and Habsburg Spain had to be avoided at all cost. Anjou's involvement could even cause an enormous shift in the European balance of power. The French king Henry III still had no heir, therefore his brother the Duke of Anjou was the next in line to the French throne. In addition to this, there were rumours about a potential marriage negotiations with Elizabeth I.[91] Anjou's involvement could unite France, England and the Netherlands, a prospect which was very worrying. When Anjou announced in April 1578 he wanted to become the protector of the Netherlands, the newsletters aptly captured the general mood in Italian cities with comments as 'this

---

89   Rosanne Baars describes it as a 'major news event', see *Rumours of Revolt: Civil War and the Emergence of a Transnational News Culture in France and the Netherlands, 1561–1598* (Leiden: Brill, 2021), pp. 138–143, 153–157. Rumours of the negotiations with Anjou had been circulating as early as November 1576 and in July 1577, the nuncio Sega in Brussels had intercepted correspondence between the Duke of Anjou and the States and especially with the city of Brussels: Holt, *Duke of Anjou*, pp. 73–74, 350.

90   On these negotiations see René van Stipriaan, *De Zwijger. Het leven van Willem van Oranje* (Amsterdam/Antwerpen: Querido, 2021), pp. 358–359, 378–381, 391–394.

91   Natalie Mears, 'Love-making and Diplomacy: Elizabeth I and the Anjou Marriage Negotiations, c. 1578 1582', *History*, 86 (2001), pp. 442–466.

war could harm the whole of Christianity'.[92] A month later, rumours were spreading in Milan and Genoa that the French king had broken the Peace of Cateau-Cambrésis (1559) and was preparing a 'great war' against Philip II.[93] Other reports denied this rumour and claimed that Henry III had shown himself to be a good and loyal friend of Philip II. In his diary, Arditi noted that the continuing rumours and reports about Anjou raised the question to what extent the French king supported his brother's intervention.[94]

This was one of the main questions Scipio di Castro discussed in his treatise on the Duke of Anjou's engagements in the Low Countries.[95] He addressed three questions: whether the duke was acting with the consent of the French king; secondly, whether Anjou had been asked by several states to come to their help or one state in particular; and thirdly whether this would ultimately result in further trouble. Di Castro argued that it was unimaginable that Henry III would support such an enterprise as it was too dangerous for his own position. The rebels in the Netherlands had close contacts with the French Huguenots, who also posed a threat to the stability of the French kingdom. Di Castro said he did not have any reason to believe Anjou had been asked by all the provinces. For the future he predicted, as he had done in his discourse on Matthias of Austria, that Philip II could easily win this war. According to di Castro, the most important thing was not the conquest of the territories, but their reconciliation with the king.

Not everyone shared this rather positive assessment of the situation, reports of the arrival of more troops under guidance of another foreign prince, the staunch Calvinist John Casimir of Palatinate, reached the Italian peninsula.[96] A total escalation of the situation seemed almost unavoidable. Gregory XIII saw it as his mission to guarantee peace between Christian princes and therefore decided to send Fabio Mirto Frangipani as extraordinary envoy to Paris to dissuade Anjou from joining the rebel forces.[97] The Venetian Republic and the

---

92   ASMn, AG 1983, fol 116: *Di Roma xi aprile 1578*: 'di questo guerra, dipende il danno di tutta la christianità'. A similar comment by Pope Gregory XIII, quoted by Granvelle in his letter to Margareta of Parma, from Rome 3 June 1578, in C. Piot (ed.), *Correspondance du cardinal de Granvelle, 7: 1578–1579* (Brussels: Hayez, 1889), p. 100: 'allumera ung feu en la chrestienté'.

93   ASMn, AG, 1983, fol 172.

94   *Diario di Firenze,* p. 183.

95   For copies see BAV, Urb Lat 854 Pars II, fol 413–418; BAV, Barb Lat 5215, fol 62–67; AAV, Pio 77, fol 1–7v; AAV, Borghese I 429–448, fol 339–345v.

96   Morillon to Granvelle, Cambrai, 2 June 1578 in *Correspondance du Cardinal de Granvelle 7*, pp. 97–98: 'les champ sont couverts de gens de guerre'.

97   De Meester, *Le Saint-Siege et les troubles des Pays-Bas*, p. 132. For biography and his time as nuncio in Paris see: A. Martin Lynn, 'Fabio Mirto Frangipani and Papal Policy in France.

Duke of Savoy followed the papacy's lead: the Venetian Senate chose Giovanni Michiel and the Duke of Savoy dispatched Louis Oddinet, count of Montreal.[98] The importance these Italian and Catholic powers attached to this mission is clear from the profile of their special envoys as they sent some of their more experienced diplomats: Michiel was now undertaking his third extraordinary mission to France and Frangipani had already been a nuncio in France between 1566 and 1572.[99]

In July 1578, however, Anjou had left France and travelled to Mons in haste to avoid meeting the papal delegate. Numerous special envoys chased him to Mons in a last attempt to dissuade him from undertaking any further action. Their exhortations and appeals were unsuccessful. A month after his arrival, the States appointed Anjou 'as defender of the liberty of the Netherlands against the tyranny of the Spanish and their allies'.[100] His first intervention failed as his troops became affected by disease, and he was forced to return to France at the end of 1578, but the disaster was not yet adverted.

For the seasoned Venetian ambassador Michiel the widespread foreign support for the rebels was an important factor to take into account in assessing the situation in the Low Countries.[101] The events in 1577 and 1578 illustrated a ruler could lose the love (and obedience) of his people by being too harsh. and Michiel presented that political lesson as a warning to other rulers. In his final report to the Venetian Senate on 15 November 1578, he summarised this point eloquently:

> To their aid, without any respect for the king, came England, France and Germany. I do not know whether this has happened before, or whether other subjects have had so much support and favour in their struggle

The case of an independent minded nuncio', *Archivum Historiae Pontificae*, XVII (1979), pp. 197–240.

98   The Senate of Venice instructed Giovanni Michiel on 29 June 1578: 'for the sake of the common welfare, all Christian Princes ought to do their utmost to dissuade him: we, therefore, according to our ancient custom, being most desirous for the preservation of peace amongst the Princes of Christendom, have followed the pious and wise counsels of the Supreme Pontiff'. Quote taken from R. Brown, G. Cavendish Bentinck (eds.), *Calendar of State Papers Relating to English Affairs in the Archives of Venice, Vol 7, 1558–1580* (London: Her Majesty's Stationery Office, 1890), pp. 575–579; available via *British History Online*.

99   Ivan Cloulas, 'La diplomatie pontificale médiatrice entre la France et l'Espagne: La mission de l'archevêque de Nazareth auprès de François d'Anjou (1578)', *Mélanges de la Casa de Velázquez*, 5 (1969), pp. 451–459.

100 Holt, *Duke of Anjou*, p. 104.

101 His final report is edited by Albèri in *Relazioni degli ambasciatori veneti al senato, serie I volume IV*, pp. 377–404.

against their natural lord, as they have had, thus becoming not equal in strength but even superior to the king. This could serve as an example to all other rulers to respect their subjects and not to treat them with so much harshness.[102]

Italian observers, such as Michiel, were also astounded about the foreign involvement in internal matters. The supposed absence of any historical examples to draw upon reinforces how unusual it seemed to these contemporaries that several different countries were offering assistance to the States General against Philip II, who was still the sovereign ruler of the Netherlands.

Looking back in 1581, the papal nuncio Filippo Sega observed in the instruction to his successor at the court of Madrid that the interventions of Matthias of Austria and Francis of Valois had been 'a flash in the pan'.[103] His assessment aligns with how later historians have generally treated this particular episode, but whichever position Italian observers in 1577–78 took in the burgeoning debate, they shared one conviction: the Low Countries had renounced their allegiance towards the king. The discourses and the replies these events generated indicate that Habsburg policy in the Low Countries was energetically debated on the Italian peninsula and that the Revolt was of crucial importance to the Italian States.

In these debates, the analysis of the nature of the Netherlandish people became an important point of discussion. The Netherlanders had become ferocious enemies who were willing to die for their liberties. Some used this image to advocate a more peaceful strategy. While in Sega's letters from 1577, heresy was seen as the main cause of the problems, the analysis of all these political writers put a clear emphasis on political issues, rather than on religious ones. The various texts containing the arguments of the States General, some sent secretly by Sega, were crucial bits of information for political commentators who started to write treatises on the best policy for the Low Countries. The States' emphasis on the maintenance of privileges, love of liberty and hate for the Spanish surfaced in Italian political discourse. These authors recognised it as an important catalyst for their continued and dogged resistance against the Spanish-Habsburg empire. To several of these Italian political observers, the

---

102 *Relazioni degli ambasciatori veneti al senato, serie I volume IV*, p. 399: 'Ma a favor loro, senza alcun rispetto verso il Re, si è mossa l'Inghilterra, la Francia, e la Germania, che non so se sia occorso, o si sia mai più veduti in altri sudditi di aver tanto seguito e favor contra il loro principe naturale quanto hanno questi fatti non pur eguali ma superiori alle forze del re. Il che potrà servire per esempio a tutti gli altri principe di riconoscer i sudditi, e di non trattarli con tanta asperità'.

103 *Archivalia in Italië*, II, p. 385: 'fuoco di paglia'.

past wars had clearly shown that it was not as easy to defeat the rebels authors such as di Castro and Salviati continued to predict. By pointing to the practical obstacles, always with an eye towards the repercussions of a long conflict for the Italian peninsula. While none of the authors questioned Philip II's authority and power, they put forward varying opinions on how to win the war. All observers recognised that it would be difficult for the king to regain his lands now that he had lost their love and obedience.

Promoting Spanish-Habsburg Power through Print

Having traced the circulation of information in confidential letters, hand-written newsletters, and *discorsi*, this chapter focuses on the first occasional news reports as well as illustrated prints on the conflict produced in different Italian towns and how these shaped contemporaries' perceptions. Italian cities were among the first places outside of the Low Countries where accounts of Spanish-Habsburg military victories as well as edicts and peace treatises appeared in print.[1] While manuscript *avvisi* had a certain regularity, mostly weekly or bi-weekly, printed news appeared only occasionally. From the continuous stream of information, certain events such as festivities, processions, miracles, natural disasters, battles and sieges were singled out to be printed.[2] In the second half of the sixteenth century, the market for brief prose accounts was flourishing on the peninsula and was in output even comparable in size to France and the Low Countries.[3] Due to the predominant focus on manuscript newsletters in Italian historiography, scholars have largely ignored both

---

1   The first printed publication on the Revolt in Low Countries was not a conventional news pamphlet recounting a battle, but an Italian translation of *Ordonnance et edict provisional sur la pacification des troubles de la ville d'Anvers* (Antwerpen: Silvius, 1567), USTC 13178, promulgated on 28 May 1567 in Antwerp by Margaret of Parma, governor-general of the Low Countries: *Ordinatione et editto provisionale, fatto per sua maesta catolica sopra la pacificatione delli tumulti della citta d'Anuersa, circa il fatto della religione, e quello che ne dipende* (Rome: Accolti, 1567), USTC 809780; *Ordinatione del catolico re Filippo per la pacificatione della villa d'Anversa, sopra il fatto della religione* (Bologna: Benacci, 1567), USTC 809779. For more information on this specific edict consult Gustaaf Janssens, 'De ordonnantie betreffende de pacificatie van de beroerten te Antwerpen (24 mei 1567): breekpunt voor de politiek van Filips II ten overstaan van de Nederlanden', *Handelingen van de Koninklijke Commissie voor de Uitgave der Oude Wetten en Verordeningen*, 50 (2009), pp. 105–132.

2   For Italian cities, there is no general bibliographic overview of this specific genre. Only the news pamphlets preserved in a few Roman libraries have been catalogued by Tullio and Sandro Bulgarelli: Tullio Bulgarelli, *Gli avvisi a stampa in Roma nel Cinquecento* (Rome: Istituto Nazionale di Studi Romani, 1967); Sandro Bulgarelli and Tullio Bulgarelli, *Il giornalismo a Roma nel Seicento* (Rome: Bulzoni, 1988). See also the three volumes of Ugo Belocchi, *Storia del giornalismo italiano* (Bologna: Edison, 1974–1984). Belocchi's work is not a systematic survey of the available material in Italian libraries and archives, but it contains some facsimile of news pamphlets. For a brief overview of other studies in European countries, Henry Ettinghausen, *How the Press Began. The Pre-Periodical Printed News in Early Modern Europe* (Coruña: Janus, 2015), pp. 26–29.

3   Based on the USTC which offers the possibility to search for 'news books', a feature which is not available in EDIT16, the survey of Italian publications in the sixteenth century. Data for

the production and the function of these occasional news pamphlets and news prints.[4]

Hitherto the production in Rome and Venice, the two major centres of news writing and printing on the peninsula, has attracted the most attention. Rome was shaped and formed by its position as the centre of the Catholic world, whereas Venice played an important role in the provision of news on the Ottomans.[5] In this chapter, I demonstrate that Milan, one of the Spanish-Habsburg strongholds on the Italian peninsula, played a crucial role in the dissemination of printed news on the Revolt in the Netherlands. Here, government edicts, peace treatises as well as occasional news pamphlets were printed to promote Spanish-Habsburg power by officially appointed printers.

Cataloguers and historians have frequently compartmentalised these different types or genres of news. Government publications, for instance, have for a long time been dismissed as ineffective means of communication and excluded from studies on early modern media and politics.[6] To explain why such official texts were often translated into other vernaculars, scholars of early modern news have suggested recently that they had a news function, offering

---

news books from 1500 to 1600 in USTC: 1238 printed items for the Italian States, 1300 items for France and 1345 items for the Netherlands (last accessed 6 January 2021).

4   For this point see H. Ettinghausen, 'Los avvisi a stampa: las relaciones de sucesos italianas, en relación con las españolas', in G. Andres (ed.), *Proto-giornalismo e letterature: avvisi a stampa, relaciones de sucesos* (Rome: Francoangeli, 2013), pp. 14–15. For the fifteenth century: Margaret Meserve, 'News from Negroponte: Politics, Popular Opinion, and Information Exchange in the First Decade of the Italian Press', *Renaissance Quarterly*, 59 (2006) pp. 440–480 and Kate Lowe, 'Africa in the News in Renaissance Italy: News Extracts from Portugal about Western Africa Circulating in Northern and Central Italy in the 1480s and 1490s', *Italian Studies*, 65 (2010), pp. 310–328. For later periods: A. Buono and M. Petta, 'Il racconto della battaglia. La Guerra e le notizie a stampa nella Milano degli Austrias (secoli XVI–XVII)', in A. Buono, G. Civale (eds.), *Battaglie. L'evento, l'individuo, la memoria* (Palermo: Associazione Mediterranea, 2014), pp. 187–248; N. Lamal, 'Promoting the Catholic cause on the Italian Peninsula: Printed Avvisi on the Dutch Revolt and the French Wars of Religion, 1562–1600', in J. Raymond, N. Moxham (eds.), *News Networks in Early Modern Europe* (Leiden: Brill, 2016), pp. 675–694.

5   P. Burke, 'Rome as Center of Information and Communication for the Catholic World, 1550–1650', in P.M. Jones, T. Worcester (eds.), *From Rome to Eternity: Catholicism and the Arts in Italy, ca. 1550–1650* (Leiden: Brill, 2002), pp. 253–269; P. Burke, 'Early Modern Venice as a Center of Information and Communication', in J. Martin (ed.), *Venice Reconsidered: The History and Civilization of an Italian City-State, 1297–1797* (Baltimore: Johns Hopkins University Press, 2000), pp. 389–419. For Italian book market in general, consult Angela Nuovo, *The Book Trade in the Italian Renaissance* (Leiden: Brill, 2013).

6   See contributions in A. Pettegree (ed.), *Broadsheets: Single-sheet Publishing in the First Age of Print* (Leiden: Brill, 2017); N. Lamal, J. Cumby, H.J. Helmers (eds.), *Print and Power in Early Modern Europe* (Leiden: Brill, 2021).

information on a foreign conflict to audiences across Europe.[7] The separation between illustrated and non-illustrated printed material is even more profound. Illustrated news prints were not as common on the Italian peninsula compared to the Netherlands and the German lands, but engravings and etchings of foreign wars were not entirely absent.[8] Most engravings on current events, often accompanied by verbal accounts, were published in Rome, where that technique was flourishing thanks to the likes of Antoine Lafréry.[9]

The different genres need to be considered as part of the same commercial market for news on the Italian peninsula.[10] These texts and images informed a broad public on foreign events, and each individual publication offers insight into what both the religious and political authorities as well as printers thought was an event worth to be publicised. Following the specialisation of individual centres and printing houses, this chapter traces how the marketplace of print was deployed by political forces to disseminate information and shape the perceptions of the conflict.

1   A Developing Market for News

In Italian scholarship, printed prose accounts are known as *avvisi a stampa*. The term underlines the close relationship between the manuscript newsletters and printed brochures of news.[11] Terms such as *relatione* (report),

---

7   S.K. Barker, '"Newes Lately Come": European News Book in English Translation', in S. Barker, B.M. Hosington (eds.), *Renaissance Cultural Crossroads: Translation, Print and Culture in Britain, 1473–1640* (Leiden: Brill, 2013), pp. 227–244.

8   See for instance Christi M. Klinkert, *Nassau in het nieuws: nieuwsprenten van Maurits van Nassaus militaire ondernamingen uit periode 1590–1600* (Zupthen: Walburg, 2005) and Voges, *Das Auge der Geschichte*.

9   Christopher L.C.E. Witcombe, *Copyright in the Renaissance: Prints and the Privilegio in Sixteenth-Century Venice and Rome* (Leiden: Brill, 2004).

10   Print publishing in Rome and Venice has received considerable attention from art historians, see for instance Christopher L.C.E. Witcombe, *Print Publishing in Sixteenth-Century Rome. Growth and Expansion, Rivalry and Murder* (Turnhout: Brepols, 2009). So far many of these prints have been ignored by scholars working on Italian news. This can partly be explained because many of the surviving news prints are found in map collections. One of the largest and also unique collections containing a lot of Italian news prints was assembled by brothers Cassiano and Carlo Antonio dal Pozzo in seventeenth-century Italy, now in RCT: Mark McDonald, *The Print Collection of Cassiano dal Pozzo. 2: Architecture, Topography and Military Maps* (London: Royal Collection Trust, 2019).

11   For terminology: Petitjean, 'Mots et pratiques de l'information', pp. 107–121; Arblaster et al., 'The Lexicons of early modern News', in J. Raymond, N. Moxham (eds.), *News Networks in Early Modern Europe* (Leiden: Brill, 2016), pp. 64–69.

raguaglio (report, information) and *discorso* (discourse) appear more frequently on title pages than the word *avvisi* (notices). It was mainly through the development of standardized layout during the second half of the sixteenth century, that these printed news pamphlets became a distinct and recognizable product on the Italian news market.[12] Like the German *Neue Zeitungen* or Spanish *Relaciones de sucesos*, the majority of these printed news accounts described a single event in continuous prose.[13] They were four to eight pages long and were printed in a small format (mostly in quarto), which emphasized the novelty as well as reliability of the report by including words such as 'latest' and 'true' in the title. This air of reliability was strengthened by other elements on the title page: they frequently contained a woodcut illustration of a coat of arms, mostly the coat of arms of the Habsburg family or the imperial eagle of the Holy Roman Emperor, and frequently contained statements that they were published with the consent of the authorities.

The fact that these accounts were printed does not necessarily guarantee a huge readership. Especially for ephemeral publications such as news reports, it is notoriously difficult to assess in which numbers they were printed and how widely they were disseminated since many printed news pamphlets have been lost and the majority of the surviving copies are known to be unique copies.[14] It is impossible to give exact numbers of print runs for sixteenth or seventeenth century Italy, but Sandro Bulgarelli estimated that pamphlets of this sort must have been printed in several hundred copies.[15] It furthermore appears that these news accounts were frequently reprinted in different Italian cities since pamphlets often mentioned the earlier places where the text had been published. This practice allows scholars to document the dissemination of these news accounts on the Italian peninsula even when no or few copies survive.

---

12   M. Petta, 'Wars News in Early Modern Milan: the birth and shaping of printed news pamphlets', in J. Raymond, N. Moxham (eds.), *News Networks in Early Modern Europe* (Leiden: Brill, 2016), pp. 287–290.

13   See the various conference volumes of SIERS (Sociedad Internacional para el Estudio de las Relaciones de Sucesos) and more in particular V. García de la Fuente, 'Relaciones de Sucesos en forma de carta: estructura, temática y lenguaje', in H. Ettinghausen (ed.), *Las Relaciones de sucesos en España (1500–1750)* (Alcalá de Henares: Universidad de Alcalá, 1996), pp. 175–184.

14   Alexander S. Wilkinson estimates that as many as 64% of Spanish news pamphlets survive in a unique copy, 'Bum Fodder & Kindling: Cheap Print in Renaissance Spain', *Bulletin of Spanish Studies*, 90 (2013), pp. 871–893. For an idea of lost news reports also see Alexandra Hill, *Lost Books and Printing in London 1557–1640: An Analysis of the Stationer's Company* (Leiden: Brill, 2018), pp. 65–101.

15   Bulgarelli, *Il giornalismo a Roma nel Seicento*, p. XIII.

FIGURE 3.1 *Ordinatione del Catolico Re Filippo per la Pacificatione della villa d'Anversa sopra il fatto della Religione* (Bologna: Benacci, [1567]), USTC 809779. Universiteit Gent, Acc. Meul 1567 (4)

A good illustration is a news pamphlet on the siege of Ostend printed in Siena in 1604.[16] According to the title page, this news report had been printed earlier in Rome, Bologna, and Florence. While there are no known surviving copies of the Bolognese and Florentine editions, the Roman edition, like the one in Siena, survives in one single copy.[17] We may therefore safely assume that this particular pamphlet, which is by no means exceptional, was indeed printed in at least four cities.

The surviving copies in libraries and archives, then, suggest that publishers in towns across the peninsula seized upon the growing appetite for information. In some cases, two different reports on the same event were printed in the same city by two different publishers. In Bologna, for instance, two different news pamphlets on the conquest of Maastricht by Farnese in 1579 were printed.[18] The almost simultaneous appearance of these two accounts in Bologna, which was a vibrant urban centre with a renowned university at the crossroads of various postal roads, points to the existence of a public interested in current affairs.[19]

The publication of news pamphlets was a profitable business that mostly required a small investment both in terms of materials (these were short, even crammed texts, often printed on cheap paper) and in terms of other resources, as printers frequently produced letters and other news accounts which were already circulating. The two different accounts on Maastricht printed in Bologna serve as a case in point. Whereas one printer, Bonardi, reprinted an anonymous letter describing the final attack and subsequent surrender of the city based on information coming from Cologne, the other one, Benacci, seems

---

16   *Relatione dell'assedio della fortezza d'Ostenden posta nella Fiandra. Assediata del sereniss. arciduca Alberto d'Austria alli cinque di luglio 1601. Et resa all' illustrissimo. & Eccellentis-simo Sig. Marchese Francesco Spinola genovese alli 21. Di settembre 1604* (Siena: s.n., 1604), in BUA.

17   *Relatione dell'assedio della fortezza d'Ostenden posto nella Fiandra; assediata del sereni-simo arciduca Alberto d'Austria, alli 5. di luglio 1601. Et resosi all'illustriss. & eccellentiss. sig. marchese Spinola genouese, alli 22. di Settembre 1604* (Rome: Facciotti, 1604), in Biblioteca Angelica in Rome.

18   *Copia de gli ultimi avisi venuti di Fiandra all'Illustrissimo & Eccentissimo Signore Duca di Parma & Piasenza &c. dove s'intende minutamente tutti gli assalti, sacaramucie, che sono occorse, sotto la fortezza di Mastrich. Con la presa, & il vero disegno della fortezza* (Bologna, Benacci, 1579), USTC 805472; *Raguaglio della citta di Mastrich assediata, & presa, per il Principe di Parma. Generale dell'Essercito del Rè Philippo Catholico nella Fiandra* (Bologna: Bonardo, 1579), USTC 805508.

19   C.H. Caracciolo, 'L'informazione a Bologna tra cinque e seicento: il caso degli avvisi a stampa', in P. Belletini (ed.), *Una Città in piazza: comunicazione e vita quotidiana a Bologna tra Cinque e Seicento* (Bologna: Compositori, 2000), pp. 77–88.

to have had access to a more privileged source of information.[20] His news pamphlet was a compilation of some letters by the captain Hercole Magno sent to Alexander Farnese's father Ottavio Farnese, Duke of Parma and Piacenza.[21] Magno's letters circulated in different manuscript copies and Benacci might just have obtained such a copy to print.[22] Subsequently, other printers would and could easily (re-)produce accounts relatively quickly and cheaply.[23]

The growing demand for news on the Revolt in the Low Countries was not only apparent in the competition between printers, but it also appears in dedications. Giorgio Marescotti, a French-born printer active in Florence, claimed to have translated and printed the conditions of surrender of Antwerp in 1585 'as so many gentlemen and friends wanted to have a copy'.[24] While some of these statements might exaggerate the demand for such publications, in this specific case, another less elaborate version of the text had already appeared in print in Florence by the ambulant and blind publisher Francesco Dini.[25] Marescotti's dedication to Leonardo Santacroce highlights the importance of authenticity as a potential selling point, as he thanked Santacroce for giving him access to the French text printed by Plantin in Antwerp.[26] Readers of Marescotti's translation were reassured there was a very close relationship to the source text.

Dedications and other paratextual evidence illustrate that timing could be a crucial element. It was important for printers to be the first to publish

---

20 *Ragguaglio*, USTC 805508, A1: 'Et per quanto si è inteso per lettere di Colonnia, delli 4 di Luglio'.

21 This pamphlet was reprinted in Padua: *Copia de gli vltimi auisi venuti di Fiandra all'illustrissimo, & eccellentissimo sig. duca di Parma, Piasenza, &c. doue s'intende minutamente tutti gli assalti, scaramucie, che sono occorse, sotto la fortezza di Mastrich. Et con la presa di detta città* (Padua: Pasquato, 1579), copy in Biblioteca Palatina in Parma.

22 Letter by Hercole Magno, Maastricht 10 June 1579, in ASF, MdP 4254, fol 661r–v.

23 P. Stallybrass, 'Little jobs: broadsides and the printing revolution', in S. Alcorn Baron, E.N. Lindquist, E.F. Shevlin (eds.), *Agent of Change: Print Culture Studies after Elizabeth L. Eisenstein* (Amherst: MA, 2007), pp. 315–341. See also Kevin M. Stevens, Paul F. Gehl, 'Cheap print: A look inside the Lucini/sirtori stationery shop at Milan (1597–1613)', *La Bibliofilía*, 112 (2010), pp. 281–327. I would like to thank Professor Kevin M. Stevens for sending me an offprint of this article.

24 *Articoli et condizioni del trattato fatto, & concluso infra l'altezza del Principe di Parma & Piacenza* (Florence: Marescotti, 1585), USTC 763655.

25 *Ordinationi fatte tra sua Maesta Cattolica; et la città d'Anversa* (Florence: Dini, [1585]), EDIT16 80647. For more information on blind booksellers: L. Carnelos, 'Cecità. La percezione di una (dis)abilità nella prima età moderna', in S. Carraro (ed.), *Alter-habilitas. Perception of disability among people* (Verona: Alteritas, 2018), pp. 235–256.

26 *Articoli et condizioni del trattato fatto, & concluso infra l'altezza del Principe di Parma & Piacenza* (Florence: Marescotti, 1585), USTC 763655.

these texts. In his dedication to the general inquisitor of Milan, the printer Tini proudly announced that he had been granted the favour of being the first to translate the conditions of Antwerp's surrender from French into Italian.[27] Tini did not have the official privilege to publish such documents in Milan, but he claimed he had with great diligence obtained the right to publish this specific treaty. As the example of Tini indicates, time was of the essence, as it could help to secure future jobs and privileges.

Some printers included the latest news in other printed works on current events. In the 1572 Florentine re-edition of Luigi Groto's oration celebrating the battle of Lepanto (1571) the title page advertised that it also contained 'newly arrived notices from Flanders' and 'many other beautiful notices coming from different places'.[28] Printers included the latest news in their editions of official ordinances as well. For instance, the Mantuan edition of the general pardon of 1574 contained the latest news coming from Naples on the siege of La Goletta on the North African coast in that same year.[29] The latest news was added as a selling point, as a means to advertise the new edition, probably in the hope that this would attract new buyers.

2   Controlling the Narrative from Oral to Print

The battle of Jemmingen (Jemgum) on 21 July 1568 was the first Habsburg victory in the war of which accounts were printed on the Italian peninsula. Examining this particular case serves to unravel how different means of communication were interwoven in the dissemination of news from the

---

27   Members of the Tini family, active in Milan and Brescia, are mostly known for music printing. See entry by M. Toffetti, 'Tini', in *DBI*, 95 (2019). *Copia delli articoli overo capitol stabiliti, & conclusi per la resa della città d'Anversa, mandate dal Sereniss. Principe di Parma all'Eccellentiss. Sign. Duca di Terranova &c. Governatore del Stato di Milano, & capitano general di Sua Maestà in Italia. Tradotta de Francese in Lingua Italiana* (Milan: Tini, 1585), USTC 805984, A2: 'Ho con molta diligenza, ottenuto gratia d' essere il primo à far tradure di Francese in lingua Italiana, le capitolationi, & articoli, che la città d'Anversa hà con-trattati & stabiliti'. The dedication to Padre frate Gio Battista Borgo Bolognese is dated 13 September 1585.

28   Luigi Groto, *Orazione* [...] *Et la partita dell'armata da Messina, con la relazione di quanto e seguito à Castel nuouo, et gli auuisi di Fiandra di nuouo venuti, col numero delle vele che ha il gran turcho in essere quest'anno 1572* (Florence: Celonaio, 1572), USTC 834753.

29   *Il perdono generale che il re Filippo concede a tutti paesi, stati, et luoghi di Fiandra che voranno ritornare alla solita, & antica obedienza* [...] *Et li auisi venuti da Napoli il 24. d'agosto. Doue s'intente gli assalti dati in la goletta, & il gran tradimento scoperto in detta fortezza, & la giustitia conseguita fra gli detti traditori* (Mantua: s.n., 1574) in BNCF.

battlefield. From the rumours and oral communication about the details of the battle, over the personal letters by the Duke of Alba, to the printed reports, the narrative was shaped by Alba's own account of his victory. On 21 July 1568, the royal army defeated the troops of Louis of Nassau in East Frisia. Just a day later, Alba wrote a letter to Philip II, reporting that some 7,000 enemy soldiers had been killed, but only seven or eight soldiers of his own army.[30] At this stage, it was still unknown what had happened to Louis of Nassau. Seven days later, in a letter to the Council of State, Alba reported that Louis of Nassau had barely escaped his death by swimming across the river; soldiers had apparently found his clothes lying on the bank.[31] Many loyalist contemporaries hoped this crushing defeat would be a decisive blow to the rebel forces. While Alba's victory at Jemmingen was celebrated with public ceremonies in cities throughout the Low Countries, a narrative account of the battle does not seem to have been printed.[32] Scholars have often remarked that the Duke of Alba relied on ceremonial and was reluctant to use the medium of print in the Netherlands.[33] On the international stage, however, he found eager propagators, especially in papal Rome. The papacy was keen to capitalise on this Catholic victory: on 10 August, Pope Pius V declared three days of thanksgiving processions in Rome. News reports of the battle appeared both in Rome and in Bologna.[34]

Oral communication was considered the most reliable way to receive news in early modern Europe and messengers were still dispatched to recount battles in person. After personally writing to Pope Pius V, Alba sent the Spanish captain Cariglio de Melo as a personal messenger to deliver a full and detailed account of the battle to the pope. His arrival was highly anticipated in Rome: an anonymous correspondent reported to Alfonso II d'Este, Duke of Ferrara and Modena, that de Melo had arrived in the city in the middle of the night on 13 August 1568.[35] By this time, rumours, handwritten newsletters and more

---

30   Fagel, *Protagonists of War*, p. 336, and also R. Fagel, B. Santiago Belmonte, L. Alvarez Frances, 'Eer en Schuld. Heiligerlee en Jemmingen in Spaanse ogen', in S. van der Hoek (ed.), *Heiligerlee. Strijd in een landschap van glorie en nederlaag* (Gorredijk, Uitgeverij Noordboek, 2021) pp. 84–88.

31   Stensland, *Habsburg Communication*, p. 34.

32   A news pamphlet describing an earlier victory of 15 July 1568 was printed in Antwerp: *Discours du succes des affaires passez en Phrise. Depuis le septiesme de juillet, jusques au quinziesme dudict moys, que fut le jour de la routte & defaicte de ceux de la Religion pretendue reformee* (Antwerp: s.n., 1568), USTC 11365.

33   Stensland, *Habsburg Communication*, pp. 33–44.

34   Decree by Pope Pius V of 10 August 1568, in G. Brom, A.H.L. Hensen (eds.), *Romeinse bronnen voor de Kerkelijk-Staatkundigen toestand der Nederlanden in de 16de eeuw* (The Hague: Nijhoff, 1922), p. 211.

35   ASMo, CD, Avvisi 6, fol 902: *Di Roma alli 13 d'Ag[osto]*.

detailed anonymous manuscript accounts were already circulating in many
Italian cities. The number of enemy soldiers reported dead varied between
1,500 and 8,000. Some *avvisi* even redrafted the story of the escape of Louis
of Nassau, who was said to have escaped by using a little boat.[36] The anonymous Este correspondent promised to send a printed account of the battle as
soon as it was available. In the meantime, he appended a copy of a detailed
handwritten account of the victory at Jemmingen.[37] The enclosed account was
an Italian translation of a Spanish anonymous report, which almost certainly
originated from the circles around the Duke of Alba; a similar anonymous
account in Spanish was sent to Cosimo I in Florence.[38] This example is typical: it was a customary practice for military commanders to attach such narrative accounts to their correspondence, and these were often circulated in
anonymised copies.[39]

It was so common to copy correspondence and disseminate it further, that
by writing letters to his peers, Alba immediately shaped the narrative of his
victory for a wider international audience. The first account printed in Bologna
consisted entirely of a compilation of copied letters sent by the Alba to
Cardinal Francisco Pacheco de Toledo and to Juan de Zúñiga y Requesens, the
Spanish ambassador in Rome, as well as an anonymous letter sent to Cardinal
Granvelle, who also resided in Rome at that time.[40] David Randall has argued
for English military news that the publication of letters was a way for printers
to provide readers of news with a standard of credibility.[41] While it is certainly

36 BAV, Urb Lat 1040, fol 586v: *Di Anversa di 25 d'luglio a mezza note* (5000 dead); fol 588v:
    D'Anversa li 25 di luglio (2000 dead), fol 590r: *D'Anversa li 28 luglio* with news of the letter
    by the Duke of Alba. See also ASF, MdP 4254, fol 339: A copy of letter sent to the Strozzi
    firm in Venice reported 1500 dead.
37 ASMo, CD, Avvisi 6, fol 838–844: *Relatione di quello che successi in yemecon alli 21 di luglio
    nella battaglia che si guadagnò dalli nimici 1568*, ASMo, CD, Avvisi 6, fol 886–892: *Di Roma
    a xj d'agosto 1568*; fol 902: *Di Roma alli 13 d'Ag[osto]*.
38 *Copia de la relacion de lo subcedido an Yemecon à los 21 de julio de 1568*, edited in *Colección
    de documentos inéditos para la historia de España*, XXXI (Madrid: Real Academia de la
    Historia, 1857), pp. 19–24; See also: ASF, MdP 4253, fol 38–39; and a Spanish account of the
    battle on 15 July 1568, ASF MdP 4254, fol 335–337: *Copia del sucedido en la tornado de frisa
    alo 15 de Julio 1568*.
39 For other examples see Rodríguez-Salgado, 'Diplomatic correspondence, news and narra-
    tives', pp. 24–27.
40 *I felici successi del sereniss. re catholico in Fiandra, & della vittoria hauuta per l'eccell. sig.
    duca d'Alua luogotenente generale di s.m. catholica in quelle contra gli Vgonotti suoi ribelli.
    Et dell'allegrezza che ne fece tre di la santita di n.s. papa Pio quinto. Referendo gratie a Dio
    benedetto di cosi gran benefici* (Bologna: s.n., 1568), USTC 801186. The publication is dated:
    'In Bologna, alli 20 d'agosto 1568'.
41 David Randall, *Credibility in Elizabethan and Early Stuart Military News* (London: Pickering
    & Chatto, 2008).

the case that honour codes embedded in correspondence would render the content more trustworthy, it is critical to note that printed accounts were at this stage entirely based on material emanating from government circles.

Soon after the arrival of de Melo in Rome, another updated account followed suit: the news report entitled *Primi et secondi avvisi della fellicissima vittoria hauuta in Fiandra contra gli heretici, per l'Eccellentissimo S. Duca D'Alva* (First and second notices of the most successful victory obtained in the Netherlands against the heretics by the Most Excellent Duke of Alba) was printed by the heirs of Antonio Blado, the official printer of the Holy See and reprinted in Bologna by Benacci.[42] This publication consisted of two accounts. The first one was a reconstruction of the battle based on the same letters sent by Alba. The second report was the written version of de Melo's oral testimony given to Pius V. At the end of the account, a certain Antonio Barua confirmed the account was a faithful copy of their original sources. This news account provides us with a good example of how the oral transmission of battle news could eventually be rendered into a printed account and the 'authenticity code' that regulated its dissemination across media.

While such testimonials were a means for the authorities to control what was being published, they also provided a way for the public to establish the veracity of such publications. By transferring rumours from oral form to the printed word, these accounts confirmed some of these rumours as facts and present an official and trustworthy account of the events. The news pamphlets describing Alba's victory at Jemmingen show important patterns in Italian news publishing during the second half of the sixteenth century: most war news reports were based on letters or reports sent from high-ranking officials from the battlefield to other members of the ruling elite. In this early phase of the Revolt in the Netherlands, accounts were often faithful translations from Spanish into Italian, demonstrating how Spanish commanders, such as Alba, shaped their own fame as military commanders.[43] Publishers, then, brought the news on current events to an audience wider than the restricted group

---

42   *Primi et secondi avvisi della fellicissima vittoria hauuta in Fiandra contra gli Heretici, per l'Eccellentissimo S. Duca D'Alva* (Rome: Blado, 1568), USTC 804611. See F. Barberi, 'Antonio Blado', *DBI*, 10 (1968) and *Primi et secondi avvisi della fellicissima vittoria hauuta in Fiandra contra gli Heretici, per l'Eccellentissimo S. Duca D'Alva* (Bologna: Benacci, 1568). See A. Cioni, 'Benacci', *DBI*, 8 (1966).

43   The next one dedicated entirely to events in the Netherlands was an account of the battle of Mook in April 1574, where Louis of Nassau was defeated and killed: *Vera relatione della rotta che e stata data in Fiandra al Conte Lodovico di Nansao* (Bologna: Benacci, 1574), Kn 221. It was published in Milan according to the title page of the Bologna edition, but so far no Milanese edition has been found. It is a faithful translation of an anonymous Spanish manuscript account written in Brussels on 17 April 1574 in ASMo, CD, Avvisi 8, unfoliated: *relazione della rotta que se dio al Conde Ludovico de Nassau*. Another example

to whom these original letters were addressed. These news pamphlets celebrated the battle as a decisive victory of the Catholic and Habsburg forces over
the enemy.

3   Selective Narratives of Violence

News of defeats of the Habsburg troops by the rebel forces of William of
Orange was not published in Italian cities, yet an emphasis on good news was
not unique to Italian news culture. News publishers in other European cities
generally refrained from printing accounts of defeats. It is not easy to determine whether this was because printers did not dare to publish unfavourable
news, or whether readers did not buy or keep reports of defeat. It is hard to
discern a consistent publishing policy for the specific case study at hand, as
Alba's other military victories were not promoted in printed accounts on the
Italian peninsula. For several years, from 1568 until 1574, not a single report
on battles or sieges in the Netherlands seems to have been printed.[44] Some of
Alba's military successes, however, did circulate in anonymised separate handwritten reports, as is the case with the defeat of the relief forces of almost 6000
French Huguenots at Quiévrain, in July 1572, or with the conquest of the city of
Haarlem in 1573.[45] It is significant that a rare illustrated news print of the latter
siege was published in Rome in 1573 by Antoine Lafréry, but that no printed
account has.[46] The manuscript relations recounting the siege of Haarlem

---

is *La grande vittoria havuta dall'Altezza del Sereniss. Don Giovanni d'Austria in Fiandra contra ribelli di sua maestà* (Milan: da Ponte, 1578), only surviving copy in ASMo, Avvisi, 142.

44   News of the war appeared alongside other news reports coming from different European
        cities in the few news pamphlets which copied manuscript *avvisi* using the typical place
        and date heading. This type of printed *avvisi* are very rare, and in most cases only one copy
        has survived: *Noui auisi venuti di Leuante nelli quali si intende la difesa di Famagosta [...].
        Con altri avisi di Roma, Napoli, Anversa, Viena, & Costantinopoli, & altri luoghi.* (Modena:
        s.n., s.d. [1571?]), USTC 804904. For more examples see the first chapter.

45   Accounts of the battle of Quiévrain near Mons in ASF, MdP 4254, fol 410–411; ASMn, AG,
        1988, fol 455: *Discorso della rotta delle comp. del S. di Genlis uscito di Francia il Martedi
        sera alli 15 luglio 1572*; ASMn, AG, Fiandra, 574. For a manuscript account on the siege
        of Haarlem and a letter written by Alva to Guglielmo Gonzaga, Duke of Mantua and
        Monferrato, describing the siege: BV, N22, fol 14–18: *Dall Assedio di Arlem suo acquista et
        della honorata vittoria ottenuta dall Illustrissimo d. Federico di Toledo contro ribelli*, with
        the letter starting on fol 16: 'Del qual successo il Signor Duca d'Alva diede avviso al Signor
        Duca di Mantova con una sua lettera la copia della quale ho voluto porre qui sotto'. A copy
        of the same account in BAV, Vat Lat 7080, fol 262–275r.

46   For more information on Antoine Lafréry see Witcombe, *Copyright in the Renaissance*,
        pp. 129–134. In 1602 Giovanni Orlandi re-issued the print of this siege, a handcoloured

circulating on the Italian peninsula certainly emerged from the circles around Alba and do not mention the great difficulties the army had faced in regaining the city.[47] In these accounts, the Duke of Alba was presented as a valorous and prudent army general who had fought in the name of God against stubborn rebels and heretics.[48] In one account, he was even portrayed as a clement leader, since he had offered a pardon to most of the Haarlem citizens.[49] Considering the bibliographic profile of some unique surviving pamphlets, it seems likely that some of these manuscript reports might have been printed, but are now lost.[50]

The respective sacks of Mechelen, Zutphen, and Naarden in 1572 by the Habsburg troops did not receive special coverage in separate manuscript or printed accounts.[51] The silence on these violent episodes, which would become symbols of Spanish cruelty, indicates that these events, although successful in bringing the cities back into the Habsburg rule, were not seen as victories worth publicising. On the Italian peninsula Alba was already associated with cruelty, so portraying him as a merciful leader in handwritten news accounts was aimed at constructing a very different public persona for an Italian audience. While extreme violence did not fit the political agenda of celebration, it was of course eagerly instrumentalised when perpetrated by the other side. Atrocities committed by the troops of William of Orange appeared in printed accounts in Rome and Venice.[52] One news pamphlet, significantly entitled *L'inaudite et monstruose crudeltà usate da gli heretici contra i religiosi* (Unheard-of monstrous cruelty used by the heretics against the friars) may suffice to illustrate how the

---

      version in Rijksmuseum Amtsterdam, RP-P-1952-92 and another one in Bibliothèque Nationale de France, GE D-17027, available via Gallica.

47   Compare to the account by Vitelli in his letter to Concino from Brussels on 17 February 1573: ASF, MdP 651, fol 159: 'ne costa danari, homini et brevi, et reputatione, que di dentro mostrano più anomo che mai e i nostri rebuttati due volte puo giudicar come stanno: la villa alla fin si piegliarà, ma ne sarà costata cara, et haveremo guadagnato niente'.

48   BV, N22, fol 14: 'havendo il duca d'Alva il valore et prudenza quale è stata sempre da rara felicità accompagnata'.

49   BV, N22, fol 18: 'usando in cio non crudeltà, ma soma clementia'; 'havuta il Duca una vittoria cosi importante, et havendo con molti usata la clemenza, et con pochi la giustitia'.

50   On issues of loss: Ugo Rozzo, *La strage ignorata. I fogli volanti a stampa nell' Italia dei secoli XV e XVI* (Udine: Forum, 2008); F. Bruni, A. Pettegree (eds.), *Lost Books: Reconstructing the Print World of Pre-Industrial Europe* (Leiden: Brill, 2016).

51   On the importance of these violent episodes: Peter Arnade, *Iconoclasts and Civic Patriots: The Political Culture of the Dutch Revolt* (New York: Ithaca, 2008), pp. 212–250.

52   *L'inaudite et monstruose crudeltà usate da gli heretici contra i religiosi, nella espugnatione della città di Ruremonda di Fiandra* (Rome: Blado, 1572), USTC 805014 and *L'inaudite et horrende crudeltà usate da gli heretici contra i religiosi, nella espugnatione della città di Ruremonda di Fiandra, il dì 23. di luglio 1572* (Venice: Farri, 1572), USTC 805007.

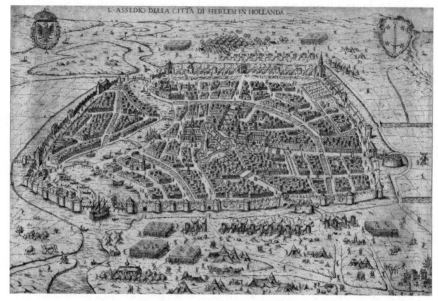

FIGURE 3.2 News print entitled 'L'assedio della città di Herlem in Hollanda', published by
Antoine Lafréry in Rome in 1573, 270 × 399 mm, Rijksmuseum Amsterdam,
RP-P-OB-79.236

reputation of the enemy was blackened. This anonymous author described the
violent attack on the city of Roermond by William of Orange's German troops
in July 1572 and took pains to emphasize their barbarity. Beginning his account
with the destruction of the house and library of the Bishop of Roermond, he
continued to stress the desacralization of churches and monasteries in the city.
Most attention, however, was reserved for the events in the Carthusian monastery where twelve monks were brutally murdered.

This particular letter was not written by a military commander, but probably by a Catholic friar.[53] The different provenance certainly influenced the
tone of the report, which was mainly intended to shock a Catholic audience. In
the Italian battlefield reports, the opponents were simply described as heretics
and rebels, but not demonized to a very great extent. Throughout this text, the

---

53 The letter was written 'dalla Zopa di Mosa alli 28 de luglio 1572'. Another anonymous letter
in Latin, which emanated from the circles around William Lindanus, was sent to Leuven.
For a comparison of the two letters: Gijsbert Hesse, 'De Martelaren van Roermond',
Limburg's Jaarboek, 17 (1911), pp. 170–209 and J. Meerbergen, B.A. Vermaseren, 'De martelaren van Roermond in 1572', in M.J.K. Smeets, A. Van Rijswijck, B.A. Vermaseren (eds.),
Historische opstellen over Roermond en omgeving (Roermond: Bisschoppelijk college,
1951), pp. 257–287.

barbarity and cruelty of the Calvinist troops were constantly emphasised. It included a few horrendous stories to capture their extreme cruelty. After several friars had been brutally murdered, some of the Calvinist soldiers started to rip their bodies apart; other friars were boiled and some were roasted. These soldiers then went into the streets and shouted they had some 'friars fat' for sale.[54] The account devoted ample attention to how these religious men had been martyred, demonstrating they had been singled out because of their faith and not just caught up in a war. Rome played a crucial role as the city hosted a flourishing market for this type of publication combining news accounts with Catholic martyrologies.[55] These first news accounts presented a Catholic readership with the atrocities committed by Calvinist rebels.

4   Promoting Habsburg Pacification and Policy

If narratives of violence were instrumentalised for political purposes and only saw the light through a selective process, Habsburg governmental discourse was subject to similar patterns: news of pacification appears to have been regulated by a defined strategy and a conscious attempt to shape opinion on the Italian peninsula. Several of the edicts promulgated in the Low Countries were translated into Italian and first printed in Milan, mostly by one man: Giovanni Battista da Ponte. Da Ponte, originally from the Low Countries, was one of the most important and active publishers in the city. Crucially, he had close ties to government officials and held the privilege to publish all the edicts and ordinances of the governors of the Duchy of Milan.[56]

---

54   *L'inaudite et monstruose crudeltà*, p. 4: 'alcuni dicono de haver visto due Cartusiani cotti in una caldera tre arrosti in spiedi & pigliando i loro grosso gridavano per la città songia fratesca'.

55   For Low Countries see f.i. printed accounts of cruelties committed in 1572 against the franciscan friars, first printed in 1584 and reprinted in 1594: Agostino Castello, *Trionfo glorioso de frati minori martirizzati dalli heretici nella fiandra & nella Francia* (Rome: heredi Blado, 1584) in BAV Stamp. Cappon. V686 (int 63) and in 1594 printed by heirs of Gigliotti in Rome, copy in Biblioteca Vallicelliana in Rome. See also Nina Lamal, 'De belichaming van christelijke liefde. Gevoelens en lichamelijkheid in zestiende-eeuwse fransciscaanse martelaarsverhalen', *Tijdschrift voor geschiedenis*, 126 (2013), pp. 505–508.

56   See L. Baldacchini, 'Gottardo da Ponte', *DBI*, 32 (1986). For more on his privileges see Massimo Petta, *In Milano, per li Malatesti, stampatori regij e camerali. Una impresa editoriale al servizio delle istituzioni nella Milano spagnola: le botteghe dei primi Malatesta (1594–1664)* (Unpublished PhD thesis, Università degli studi di Milano, 2010), pp. 239–260. I would like to thank Massimo Petta for allowing me to read his work.

While Monica Stensland in her study on Habsburg communication in the Low Countries has characterised government publications as ineffective, Vincent van Zuilen has argued that the publication of edicts by Philip II in the Low Countries was an important means of promotion for the Habsburg regime.[57] Following Van Zuilen, I suggest that the publication of government decisions related to matters in the Low Countries in Milan by the official printer was critical to promoting Habsburg policy both in and beyond Habsburg territory. Milan was a vital diplomatic centre: most other Italian rulers or states had a resident diplomat and agents stationed in the city. The Medici, for example, received news from the Low Countries, from an unknown agent in Milan, who also frequently attached printed texts to his letters. This, presumably, is how two remarkable printed edicts from 1574 have ended up in the Medici archive.[58]

The lucky survival of these two edicts allows a unique insight into the reasons why such official texts were translated into Italian and printed in Milan, where they had no legal status or practical repercussions for the public. Printed by Da Ponte, both edicts had originally been promulgated by Luis de Requesens, the new governor-general in the Netherlands. The first one was an Italian translation of Plantin's Spanish printed 'notification' to the mutinous Spanish soldiers in Antwerp.[59] The second one was Requesens's general pardon of the inhabitants of the Netherlands on 6 June. To appreciate the significance of these translations for a Milan audience, we should know that Requesens had only left Milan less than a year earlier, in the autumn of 1573. Closely aligned to Cardinal Granvelle, he had been in favour of the reconciliation strategy and advocated for a more encompassing general pardon than the first one proclaimed by Alba in 1570.[60] He had been unable to grant such a

57   V. Van Zuilen, 'Les Placards de Philippe II en Flandres et Brabants', pp. 113–129 in B. Ertlé, B., M. Gosman (eds.), *Les écrits courts à vocation polémique* (Frankfurt am Main: Peter Lang, 2006), pp. 113–129.

58   ASF, MdP 3254, fol 55: *Di Milano alli 6 maggio 1574*: 'Di Fiandra non sia altra nova, se non la alligata messa in stampa'. The attached printed copy is no longer present, but given the date it presumably was a copy of the printed report on battle of Mookerheide.

59   The only known surviving copies in ASF, MdP 4254, fol 469: *Don Luis de Requesens commendatore maggiore, notifica il seguente à soldati spagnuoli che stanno al presente con alteratione in questa villa d'Anversa impresso per ordine di S. Eccell. nella stampa Reale di S. Maestà per Christoforo Piantino in Anversa, alli 8. Di Maggio 1574* (Milan: Da Ponte, 1574). The Spanish edition (USTC 440671) printed by Plantin is present on folio 478. The other edict follows on fol 484: *Il perdono generale che il re Filippo concede a tutti paesi, stati, et luochi di Fiandra che voranno ritornare alla solita, & antica obedienza. Con il numero de personaggi che sono esclusi dal sudetto perdono fuori. Et con la restitutione de beni, honori, & gradi, a coloro che lo accettaranno. Publicato dal signor comendator maggiore capitano generale, & luogotenente per detta m. in quelle parti di Fiandra* (Milan: Da Ponte, 1574).

60   See Janssens, *Brabant in het verweer*, pp. 213–221.

pardon upon his arrival in Brussels due to Philip II's hesitancy and the worsening military situation. After the victory of his troops at Mookerheide, Spanish mutineers seized control of Antwerp. In the notification printed by Plantin on 8 May, Requesens requested the soldiers to leave the city and promised to settle the outstanding payments in three months. The general pardon was eventually proclaimed on 6 June and intended to show the regime's clemency. It offered forgiveness to all citizens who returned to the Catholic faith, excluding 296 individuals, and it allowed the restoration of confiscated property.[61] It is likely that Requesens's successor as governor in Milan, his relative Antonio de Zúñiga y Sotomayor, initiated the translation to publicize his decisiveness and clemency.[62] Subsequently, the general pardon was reprinted in other cities on the Italian peninsula including Bologna, Venice and Mantua, to promote the Habsburg reconciliation strategy.[63]

The publication history of the general pardon seems to have been typical of many official publications published in the Low Countries and translated into Italian. Like the general pardon, a translation printed in Milan would serve as the model for reprints in other Italian cities. For instance, the capitulation treaty of the city of Antwerp in 1585, was sent by Alexander Farnese to Charles of Aragon, Duke of Terranova, then governor of Milan, where it was published by Pietro Tini within one month after its conclusion.[64] Tini's Milanese edition was then republished in no fewer than six different cities, including Brescia, Bologna, Genoa and Ferrara.[65]

---

61   See Soen, *Geen Pardon zonder paus*.

62   For his role in the Habsburg administration: Vittorio Ricci, *La Monarchia Cattolica nel governo degli Stati Italiani. Il ruolo dei fratelli Luis de Requesens e Juan de Zúñiga, cavalieri di Santiago* (Cassino: Francesco Ciolfi Editore, 2011).

63   *Il perdono generale che il re Filippo concede a tutti paesi, stati, et luoghi di Fiandra che voranno ritornare alla solita, et antica obedienza* (Venice: Viani, 1574), USTC 828981; *Il perdono generale che il re Filippo concede a tutti paesi, stati, et luochi di Fiandra che voranno ritornare alla solita, & antica obedienza.* (Bologna: Benacci, 1574), USTC 828980 and for Mantua, see footnote 29.

64   *Copia delli articoli overo capitol stabiliti, & conclusi per la resa della città d'Anversa* (Milan: Tini, 1585), USTC 805984.

65   *Copia delli articoli, overo capitoli stabiliti, & conclusi per la resa della città di Anversa* (Bologna: Benacci, 1585), USTC 801388; *Copia delli articoli, overo capitoli stabiliti, & conclusi per la resa della citta di Anversa* (Genoa: s.n., 1585), USTC 805986; *Conditioni, et capitoli fatti, et conclusi in Anuersa* (Ferrara: Buoncompagni, 1585), USTC 857155; *Copia delli articoli, overo capitoli stabiliti, & conclusi per la resa della citta di Anversa* (Brescia: Sabbio, 1585), USTC 805985; *Copia delli articoli, overo capitoli stabiliti, & conclusi per la resa della citta di Anversa* (Piacenza: Bazachi, 1585), USTC 805987; *Copia delli articoli overo capitoli, stabiliti & conclusi per la resa della città di Anversa* (Reggio: Bartoli, 1585), USTC 805983.

These translated edicts offered Italian readers some insight into the current state of events in the Low Countries. Many printed versions had introductions in which the past troubles were briefly explained so that a wider audience could understand the significance of a specific pardon or peace treaty. The underlying message of these documents was always very clear as they announced a way of appeasing the conflict. This was the case with the notification to the Spanish mutineers, the General Pardon of 1574 and with the Perpetual Edict in 1577. The publication of the Perpetual Edict, concluded between Don John and the States, in Milan and Turin had a practical purpose.[66] One of its stipulations was that the Spanish soldiers would leave the Netherlands and return, via Savoy, to Milan where they would be garrisoned. It provided vital information to the local inhabitants and administrators as the arrival and lodging of a large number of soldiers was an issue which greatly alarmed local people during the early modern period. In Milan, the distant conflict was never far away. As one of the central gateways for the Spanish road, the population in Lombardy was used to troop movements and levies to support the war effort.

From Milan Spanish-Habsburg policy and governors were defended. A very specific publication of royalist supporters in defence of Don John, for example, was translated into Italian and reprinted in Milan by Da Ponte.[67] The actors involved in this publication process highlight the close connections and patronage relationships between governors, secretaries and Italian military commanders in service of the Spanish-Habsburg dynasty. In 1578 Da Ponte printed the Italian translation of the *Véritable récit des choses passés aux Pays- Bas depuis la venue du Siegneur Don Jehan d'austriche* (Veritable narrative of the past events in the Low Countries since the arrival of Sir Don John of Austria) written by Hannard Van Gameren, humanist and secretary of Don John.[68] It was translated into Italian by Giuliano Gosellini, the former first

66   *Editto Perpetuo qual viene a trattare dell'accordio, patto et conventione, novamente fatta, della pace universale nelli paesi di Fiandra &c* (Milan: Da Ponte, 1577), USTC 857152; *Editto perpetuo sopra l'accordo fatto tra l'illustre signor don Giovanni d'Austria cavagliero, dell'ordine del Toson d'oro de la parte, & al nome de Re Catholico di Spagna d'una parte e li stati generali di questi paesi di qua d'altra parte: per aquetar li rumori suscitati in essi paesi, per le genti d'arme straniere* (Turin: s.n., 1577), USTC 857153.
67   Stensland, *Habsburg Communication*, pp. 85–88.
68   *Véritable récit des choses passees es Pays-Bas depuis la venue du Siegneur Don Jehan d'Austriche Lieutenant, Gouverneur et Capitaine general pour le Roy en iceulx* (Luxemburg: Marchand, 1577), USTC 4085. The privilege to print this pamphlet dates 11 December 1577. Martin Marchand was granted permission to publish the pamphlet 'en langue Françoise, et Thioyse, qu'autre'.

secretary of the Milanese governor Ferrante Gonzaga-Guastalla.[69] Gosellini still had contact with various members of this branch of the Gonzaga family, including Ferrante's son, Ottavio who was in the Netherlands with Don John and actively defended Don John in his correspondence with various Italian princes. It might well have been Ottavio Gonzaga who provided him with a copy of the French edition of Van Gameren's pamphlet.[70]

Van Gameren's defence was a direct reaction to the States General's justification for taking up arms against Don John, entitled *Sommier discours des iustes causes et raisons, qu'ont constrainct les Estats Generaulx des Païs bas, de pourvoir à leur deffence contre le seigneur Don Iehan d'Austriche* (Short discourse on the just causes and reasons that have constrained the States General of the Low Countries to provide their defence against the Lord Don John of Austria).[71] This latter pamphlet, which has been ascribed to Marnix of St-Aldegonde, was a compilation of intercepted and deciphered correspondence of Don John and his advisors designed to reveal their treacherous nature. This compilation was immediately republished in several languages.[72] The States General were very active in explaining and propagating their motives: they dispatched delegations with this publication to the English and French courts.[73] To counter these initiatives, Van Gameren had published a collection of letters sent by Don John to the States General. The loyalist camp immediately copied the States General dissemination strategies. In December 1577, Maximilien de Longueval, Don John's representative in Paris, received numerous copies to spread at the French court.[74]

That Van Gameren's pamphlet reached the Italian peninsula was due to a deliberate effort coordinated by loyalists. They may well have been galvanised by the rumours that the States General would translate their writings

---

69   For a biography see the entry by M. Giannini, 'Giuliano Gosellini', in *DBI*, 58 (2002).

70   In a letter of 25 December 1577, which was probably written by Ottavio Gonzaga, 'a book of justification that his Highness had published' was included. BAV, Urb Lat 1045, fol 550.

71   Printed in Antwerp by Silvius in 1577, USTC 4078 and 4079.

72   The printer Silvius requested a privilege for seven languages and the pamphlet was printed in three: French, German and Dutch, see Pieter A.M. Geurts, *De Nederlandse opstand in pamfletten 1566–1584* (Nijmegen: Centrale drukkerij, 1956), pp. 66–67.

73   Letter by Longueval on 6 November 1577 from Paris to Don John: *Correspondance du Cardinal Granvelle* 6, pp. 570–574: 'Quant aux depputés des Estatz, ilz ont eu par tout audience ichi, et dict-on qu'ilz viennent pour faire entre leur justification, comme ilz ont faict par quelques livres qu'ilz ont présenté.'

74   Further letters by De Longueval from Paris *Correspondance du Cardinal Granvelle* 6, pp. 577–582, 583–589, 603–605 and the replies by Don John in December 1577 regarding the pamphlet on pp. 597–602.

into Italian and send it to the Italian princes as well.[75] While this specific text does not seem to have reached Italian courts, other rebel pamphlets in French have survived in the princely archives.[76] Gosellini dedicated his translation to Antonio de Zúñiga y Sotomayor, the Spanish governor of Milan. The translation was not only directed at a local market in Habsburg Milan and the wider Italian peninsula but targeted a wider Italian reading audience: it was available at the Frankfurt Book Fair.[77] The goal was to re-establish Don John's reputation on an international level.[78] Milan, as the key centre of Habsburg power in Italy, played a crucial role in the dissemination of these edicts, and thus provided news to an Italian audience as well as promoted the Habsburg pacification strategies and policy on the Italian peninsula.

5 'Greater than Alexander the Great'

The Italian news production on the revolt in the Low Countries received a significant boost with the series of conquests under the leadership of Alexander Farnese, prince of Parma and Piacenza. His military campaigns were immortalized in printed reports almost every year. By comparison, in Spanish cities, news coverage of Farnese's various victories was markedly less enthusiastic, and no accounts appeared in print.[79] It certainly underlines the advanced

---

75   ASF, MdP 4254, fol 559r: 'Di tutte questi cose dicono essersi dato ordine che in piu lingue si stampino i capi più importanti, et che gli stati manderanno a tutti i principi a darne conto etiam in Italia'.

76   See for instance ASF, MdP 4254, fol 612–623 contains Marnix van St Aldegonde, *Response a un petit livret n'agveres publié et intitulé Declaration de l'intention du Seig. Don Iehan d'Austrice en laquelle la vraye intention dudit S. Don Iehan esta manifestement descouverte, & l'origine des presentes guerres & troubles de pardeça bien clairement & la verité exposee* (Antwerp: Plantin, 1578), USTC 4172.

77   Hannard van Gameren, Giuliano Gosellini (trans.), *Vera narratione de le cose passate ne' paesi bassi dopò la giunta del ser. mo s. or Don Giovanni d'Austria con la risolutione de gli obietti contenuti del discorso non vero, mandato in luce da gli Stati d'essi paesi, intorno à la rottura per loro fatta de la ultima pace* (Milan: Da Ponte, 1578), USTC 831760 and USTC 831761. A handwritten copy of Gosellini's text is present in ASMo, Manoscritti della biblioteca, 60, fol 125–693: *Giustificazione di don Giovanni d'Austria* and see *Collectio in unum corpus. Omnium librorum Hebraeorum Graecorum Latinorum necnon germanice italice* (Frankfurt: Bassai, 1592), USTC 623058.

78   For the popularity of Italian in early modern Europe, see Eric R. Dursteler, 'Speaking in Tongues: Language and Communication in the Early Modern Mediterranean', *Past & Present*, 217 (2012), p. 69.

79   A. Martínez Pereira, 'Alejandro Farnese en las relaciones de sucesos españolas', in *D. Maria de Portugal, Princesa de Parma (1565–1577) e o seu tempo* (Porto: University of Porto, 1999), pp. 98–99.

news infrastructure and industry of Italian cities, as Spanish news production would gain momentum in the early seventeenth century. The comparison, nevertheless, highlights that there were different strategies at play to circulate favourable news accounts in different parts of the Spanish-Habsburg empire and its allies. The interest in the actions of Farnese, as an 'Italian' prince, and the larger contingents of soldiers from various Italian states and cities may have led to a larger interested audience. Crucially, news writers, printers and publishers had clearer incentives to devote attention to his victories as it might offer several opportunities for patronage.

Alexander Farnese had been appointed as governor-general after Don John's unexpected death in October 1578.[80] His first military victory followed suit: in June 1579, he conquered the strategically important city of Maastricht. In Bologna, two different news accounts on the successful capture of the city were printed.[81] Importantly, these accounts were only printed when it was certain that the Spanish-Habsburg army had been victorious. Neither of those two news pamphlets offered a description of the city or a comprehensive narrative account of the siege. Readers entered the story in *medias res*: through the letters of Hercole Magno, they could follow the last attacks of the siege with a rather detailed description of the conquest of ravelin at one of the city gates. As such the letters selected for printing presented a far more positive picture of the siege: the strong defence and numerous casualties in the Spanish-Habsburg army due to the heavy fighting were not mentioned. The best example of how these news accounts distorted reality is how one narrated the end of the siege. On 29 June, Farnese's troops were able to enter the city and started to sack the city for three days. Whereas some handwritten newsletters compared these events to the sack of Antwerp by Spanish troops in 1576, one of the printed accounts significantly downplayed the violence claiming the sack happened without any bloodshed.[82] By reprinting the letters sent by

---

80   News on Don John's death in 1578 was printed: *Il Sucesso de l'essequie fatte nella morte del Serniss. S. Don Giovanni d'Austria, qual fu il primo giorno d'Ottobre 1578. Et altri avisi particolari dell' Essercito di S. Maestà nella Fiandra* (Bologna: Bonardo, 1578), USTC 805452. For more on Farnese's campaigns see: Léon van der Essen, *Alexandre Farnèse, prince de parme, gouverneur général des Pays-Bas (1545–1592)* (5 vols., Brussels: Librairie nationale d'art et d'histoire, 1933–1937).

81   *Copia de gli ultimi avisi venuti di Fiandra* (Bologna, Benacci, 1579), UTSC 805472; *Raguaglio della citta di Mastrich assediata, & presa, per il Principe di Parma* (Bologna: Bonardo, 1579), USTC 805508.

82   BAV, Urb lat 1047, fol 244: *Di Roma li 25 luglio 1579*: 'per essersi posta la città a sacco, come segui à quanto in Anversa'. Compare to *Copia degli ultimi auisi*, [A4]: 'sachegiato senza sangue'.

captain Hercole Magno to Farnese's father, the printer portrayed Alexander as a prudent, vigilant, devoted and already experienced army general.[83]

Farnese's success at Maastricht was also immediately captured in printed engravings. In 1580, two engravers active in Rome, Mario Cartaro and Natale Bonifazio, each produced a map depicting the siege of Maastricht.[84] The siege was noteworthy to many contemporaries because the besieging army, under the guidance of the military engineer Gabrio Serbelloni, had constructed an entire defensive line with forts around the city, including a pontoon bridge across the river Meuse, to block counterattacks.[85] The various forts as well as the pontoon bridge are identified on both the siege maps. Bonifazio's map offers a good example of how sieges were translated into a visual report: the city and the surrounding countryside were depicted from a bird's eye view allowing to distil all the siege operations into a single scene. The legend with numbers underneath the image guides the viewer to read the different military actions. These visual representations adhered to the same principles of reliability as news pamphlets: the prose caption reinforced the design was 'truthful' and was based on the one made by the engineer of Farnese, who had been present at the siege.

Hitherto, accounts of a specific siege had been printed once the city had surrendered to the besieging army. This pattern changed when Farnese besieged Antwerp in 1584, one of the largest and most prosperous cities in the Low Countries and a Calvinist stronghold. Printers now started to cover an ongoing siege, the outcome of which was as yet uncertain. Thus in December 1584, a Latin poem circulated in Rome exalting Farnese's heroic virtues in tense

---

83   In *Copia degli ultimi auisi*, [A4]: 'con la gloria singolare del nostro Illustrissimo Signore Prencipe di Parma, e Piacenza Generale di Sua Maestà Cattolica, il quale constanza prudenza, valore, & vigilantia, & con tante continue fatiche che mai Capitano espertissimo ci arrivo'.

84   *Mastrih Fortezza in Fiandra presa dall' Ecc.mo S.or Prencipe di Parma per Re Catolico MDLXXIX alli XXVIIII di Givgno* engraved by Mario Cataro in Universitätsbibliothek Salzburg, Wolf-Dietrich-Klebeband Städtebilder G 34 III; Natale Bonifazio, *Il vero dissegno della città de Mastrich nella Galia Belgica, assediata dall' Ecc.mo Sr Prencipe di Parma, General de sua Mta Catolica, nel quale si vede con ogni diligentia il sito de essa citta, con li suoi forti, è beloardi, in riparo, similmente i luochi doue è accampato il campo de sua Magesta Catholica, con le batterie, assalti,& minere, fatte, & alter cose notabile, come legend alli numeri vederete con li ponti fatti per poter trascorrere di qua et di la dal fiume, el tutto fatto dal disegno del Ingegniero de S Eccelentia* (Rome: Vaccaria, 1580), in Universitätsbibliothek Salzburg, G31 III and in RCT, RCIN 721073.

85   Serbelloni was one of the most important engineers during this siege. For a biography consult entry by F. Biferali in *DBI*, 92 (2018) and Van den Heuvel, *'Papiere bolwercken'*, pp. 157–158.

anticipation of his projected success.[86] Around the same time, Bonifazio produced a siege map, which was published early in 1585.[87] This map, representing the situation on 15 December 1584, focused on the surrounding area showing how Farnese was encircling the city and trying to cut off potential relief sailing in from the river Scheldt. It depicted which forts Farnese had captured and constructed (identified with the letter R in a little flag) and those still under control by the enemy (identified by the letter F). This time, Bonifazio dedicated the print to Cardinal Alexander Farnese, who was an active promoter of his nephew's success in the Eternal City. From Rome, this specific map spread throughout Europe: a copy is also kept in the collection of handwritten newsletters of the Fugger brothers.[88]

Printed narrative accounts provided the public with updates on various spectacular episodes during the siege. Conforming to the pattern noted above, these accounts were printed in Milan and based almost entirely on Farnese's letters to its governor, the Duke of Terranova. In a letter written from Beveren on 10 March 1585, Farnese described the successful construction of his pontoon bridge across the Scheldt, which had been completed to cut off any potential relief into the city. In these same letters, he also reported on the surrender of Brussels, another important Calvinist stronghold in the southern Netherlands.[89] In another lengthy account, Farnese described the attacks of the States fleet on the *Kouwensteinse Dijk* on 26 May 1585.[90] By attacking this

---

86   ASMn, AG, 1988: 'Vinceret ut Belgam, quot misi Iberia quantis, Munitos opibus presidijs que duces. Pace loquar vestra, nil dux tuus Alba nibilque. Quariga et Austricae profuit ira manus, Vincit Alexander tamen hos, imitator et ausus, Sive tuas Caesar seu bone druse tuos, Hic est romanus fatalis laurea binci. Non nisi Roma robore belga potest'.

87   Natale Bonifazio, *Vero et nuovo disegno della pianta della cita di Anversa con tvtti gli svoi forti assediata al presente dal Serenis.o Sig.r Principe di Parma et alla gata dal fivme schelda nello stato si trovava il di xv di Decembre MDLXXXIIII* (Rome: Rasciotti, 1585) in Universitätsbibliothek Salzburg, G30 III and Royal Trust Collection, RCIN 721075.

88   Austrian National Library, Fuggerzeitungen, cod. 8958, fol 114–116. Prints and a drawing of the siege of Antwerp in between newsletters from March 1585.

89   *Copia d'vna lettera scritta dal sig. prencipe di Parma generale in Fiandra per la maestà del re, nostro signore, all'illustrissimo, & eccellentiss. sign. duca di Terranoua, nella quale gli dà conto della resa di Bruselle, con le capitulationi, & di gran parte della Frisia, con altri successi* (Milan: Cologno, 1585), USTC 828815.

90   *Copia della vera relatione mandata all'ilustriss. & Eccellentiss. Sig. Duca di Terranova, Governatore in questo stato & capitano generale in italia, per la maestà del Rè N.S. dal Sereniss. Sig. Prencipe di Parma, dell'ultima notabil vittoria havuta contra li rebelli heretici di Fiandra* (Milan: Da Ponte, 1585), USTC 805982. This is an Italian translation of an anonymous account, possibly redacted by Cosimo Massi, and sent to Philip II's secretary Idiaquez, now in Farnese archives in Naples, C. Piot (ed.), *Correspondance du Cardinal de Granvelle, 12: 1585–1586* (Brussels: Hayez, 1896), pp. 287–297.

FIGURE 3.3   News print entitled 'Vero et Nuovo Disegno della Pianta della Cita di Anversa con
tutti gli suoi forti', published by Natale Bonifazio in Rome in 1585, 243 × 344 mm,
Austrian National Library, Fuggerzeitungen, cod. 8985, fol 115

particular dike near Stabroek, the States General together with Antwerp leadership wanted to regain control over the river. The battle lasted for hours, in the
end, Farnese's troops had been able to repel this attempt. It was presented as
an important and glorious victory, soldiers and officers alike had shown 'their
determination to offer their own blood and life to defend the laws of Our Lord
God and their king'.[91]

Unsurprisingly, after such an extended period of carefully nourished anticipation, the eventual surrender of Antwerp on 17 August 1585, after more than
a year of siege, gave rise to enthusiastic news reports and laudatory poems
in Italian cities.[92] A news print entitled *Il vero disegno del mirabile assedio
della fortissima cita d'Anversa* (The true drawing of the admirable siege of the
strong city of Antwerp), dedicated to Cardinal Farnese, was printed in Rome.

---

91   *Copia della vera relatione mandata*, USTC 805982, p. Biii, 'pronta determination con che
si havevano deliberato di offerire il suo proprio sangue, & la propria vita per diffendere la
legge del Sign. Iddio, & del suo Rè'.

92   For instance Alessandro Guarnelli, *Canzoni et sonetti al serenissimo principe di Parma et
Piacenza* (Rome: Heirs of Blado, 1585), USTC 835035.

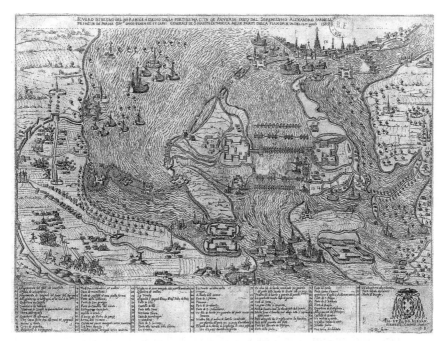

FIGURE 3.4 News print entitled 'Il vero Disegno del mirabile assedio della fortissima cita
de Anversa, fatto dal serenissimo Alexandro Farnese, principe de Parma, govte
luocotenente et capp. generale de S. Maesta Catholica nelle parti della Fiandra
del 27 agosto 1585', printed by Giuseppe Rosi in Rome in 1585, 376 × 497 mm,
Gallica.bnf.fr / Bibliothèque nationale de France, GED-1562 (RES)

This map offers a view of the area surrounding the city of Antwerp at the
end of the siege: showing large parts that have been flooded, the new fortress,
and the pontoon bridge, considered to be Alexander's military and tactical
masterpiece.

In conquering the Calvinist Republic of Antwerp, Farnese as governor-general
offered a full pardon and was willing to restore old privileges. Farnese framed
the capitulation as a treaty of reconciliation as he wanted to be seen also as
a clement leader. In Milan, the ambitious printer Tini was quick to print the
capitulation agreements, claiming he wanted 'to add a sparkle to the bright
light' of Alexander Farnese. Tini also published a news pamphlet on the siege
written by Lorenzo Pontirolo. From Milan, just like the edicts and peace treaties, this account was reprinted in various other cities, such as Brescia, Bologna
and Verona.[93] In his dedication to Gaspare Visconti, Archbishop of Milan,

---

93   *Nuouo auiso, e particolar discorso, della mirabile espugnatione d'Anuersa, con le capitu-
      lationi, & trattati di essa. Ottenuta, dal serenissimo inuittissimo & massimo Alessandro*

Pontirolo claimed he decided to publish an account on the siege of Antwerp which 'had fallen into his hands' to promote 'the great fame, generosity, virtues, valour and glory of Farnese', who was greater than Alexander the Great.[94] Farnese was thus inscribed among the great military leaders of classical antiquity, an element which would be further elaborated upon in the histories commissioned by the Farnese dynasty. The epic, almost providential tones of the news narrative serve to establish a parallel with the well-known historic forerunners of Farnese. This news pamphlet did not offer a chronological overview of this long siege but instead lauded Alexander for taking this impregnable and powerful city.

> Behold Antwerp, behold the biggest fortress of Europe, or even in the whole universe, being conquered, against the opinion of the majority of the Northern population who knew the fortress and the geography of the surrounding area inside out. Those in Antwerp have not spared any effort or money, and they have zealously deployed their talents to free themselves from this siege, they have sought and received help, secret and open favours, money, munitions, vessels, and armed troops, from all surrounding and even far-away princes, and as such [they] have been put at the centre of those uncatholic nations and enemies of the Christian religion.[95]

This opening passage is illustrative of the tone of this entire account. In a very general way, it described how citizens of Antwerp had done their utmost to

---

Farnese. Con le solennità, e trionfi fatti mentre S.A. Sereniss. prese l'ordine del Tosone, di S.M. Catholica (Milan: Tini, 1585), USTC 806036; Nuovo aviso, e particolar discorso della mirabile espugnatione d'Anversa (Brescia: Tini, 1585), UTSC 806038; Nuovo aviso, e particolar discorso, della mirabile espugnatione d'Anversa (Bologna: Benacci, 1585), USTC 806037; Nuouo auiso et particolar discorso della mirabile espugnatione d'Anuersa (Verona: Fantuzzi, 1585), USTC 806039; Nuouo auiso, e particolar discorso, della mirabile espugnatione d'Anuersa (Reggio Emilia: Bartoli, 1585), USTC 763956.

94   Pontirolo, Nuouo auiso, e particolar discorso, A2. The account was dedicated to Gasparo Visconte, Archbishop of Milan, dated 10 September 1585.

95   Pontirolo, Nuouo auiso, e particolar discorso, A2: 'Eccovi Anversa, eccovi espugnata la maggior fortezza d'Europa, & forse dell'universo, et contra all' opinione della maggior parte di popoli di questi paesi settentrionali, che sanno, quel che e gl'è conoscendo il sito di fuora, et la fortezza di dentro. Hanno quei d'Anversa fatto ogni sforzo, et spesa, messo ogni industria, & assotigliato i loro ingegni per liberarsi da questo assedio, havendo subornato, & riceputo aiuto, e favori secreti, & palesi, di danari, monitioni, vaselli, & gente armate, dà tutti i Prencipi convicini, & da molti altri lontani, sendo proprio posti questi stati nelle viscere delle nationi incatholiche, & inimiche della Christiana Religione'.

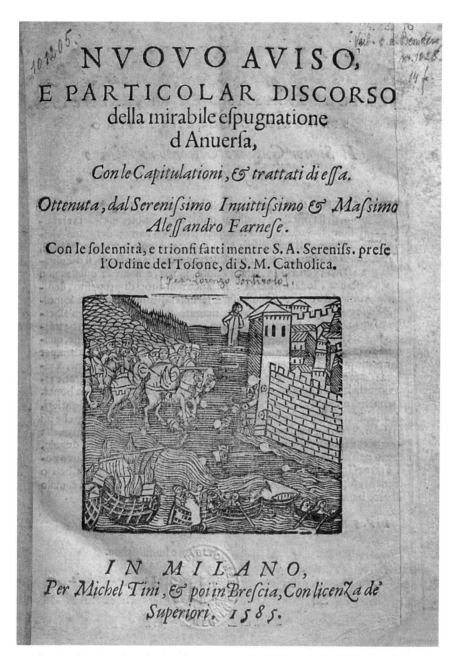

NVOVO AVISO,
E PARTICOLAR DISCORSO
della mirabile espugnatione
d Anuersa,

Con le Capitulationi, & trattati di essa.

Ottenuta, dal Serenissimo Inuittissimo & Massimo Alessandro Farnese.

Con le solennità, e trionfi fatti mentre S. A. Serenis. prese l'Ordine del Tosone, di S. M. Catholica.

IN MILANO,
Per Michel Tini, & poi in Brescia, Con licenza de' Superiori. 1585.

FIGURE 3.5 Lorenzo Pontirolo, *Nuovo aviso e particolar discorso della mirabile espugnatione d'Anversa* (Brescia: Tini, 1585), USTC 806038, Hendrik Conscience Library Antwerpen, K 33888 [C2-542 c]

keep their city out of Farnese's hands. Not just by building bomb ships, and flooding parts of the area around Antwerp but also by soliciting help from Elizabeth I, who is described as one of the main enemies of the true Christian religion. According to Pontirolo it was one of the most notable sieges ever undertaken and won, impossible and unbelievable that Farnese had been able to do so with so few people, so little money and so few provisions. Hence Pontirolo described Farnese's action as miraculous. Most of all, Farnese's actions were glorious because he had brought numerous cities in the Low Countries back into the fold of the Catholic Church. This account stands out as it does not reprint letters written by commanding generals to their peers. It differs significantly in tone and style from earlier battle reports: Pontirolo does not dwell on the various battles in considerable detail, instead he draws attention to the significance of Antwerp and presents Farnese as the defender of Catholicism. Pontirolo's account is an early examples of more interpretative news accounts which would become far more common at the beginning of the seventeenth century.

The publication of news pamphlets, official edicts, and news prints describing or depicting events during the war was shaped by complex interactions between printers and governments in Italian cities. It is difficult to discern a well-thought-out or planned publicity campaign by the Habsburg or papal authorities to promote Habsburg military victories, by tracing the sources of these printed news accounts it becomes clear how the process worked. In writing letters to Spanish ambassadors in Rome or to royal governors in Milan, both Alba and Farnese controlled, to a large extent, their messages from the very start. Printers relied on these official letters and battlefield reports as the raw material for their news pamphlets. For printers copying governmental documents proclaiming good news was beneficial. It was a relatively safe and cheap way to cater to the growing demand for news. It offered oppurtinities to establish relationship with those in power, while at the same time providing reliable news to their readers and eliminating the additional cost of hiring a writer to compose a specific account.

Circumstantial evidence suggests that Milanese governors and official printers cooperated to promote Habsburg power and authority on the Italian peninsula. Milan does not figure prominently in Italian histories of news, and in terms of printed output, it was certainly not as vibrant as Venice or Rome. Yet in this case, Venice and its printers did not even play an active role. In case of news pamphlets on the war in the Low Countries, news was primarily printed in Milan, Bologna and Rome. Milan increasingly played a leading role: news pamphlets and edicts printed in the city were often reprinted in other cities. Reprinting was common on the peninsula as it was an easy, quick, and cheap way for printers to earn money. Some may have (re-)printed news pamphlets or produced news prints to curry favour with powerful members of society, as was the case for promoting Farnese's military victories. As a result, printers contributed to disseminating a uniform pro-Habsburg and pro-Catholic narrative of the events in the Low Countries as numerous readers read the same reports. It also established Farnese's fame and provided the first building blocks to craft a narrative of an Italian hero which would be fully exploited by the first history writers.

Crafting Histories

Information on current events became increasingly and quickly available in contemporary histories as well as world histories or chronicles. Just six months after the battle at Jemmingen in 1568, a history of the Duke of Alba's military campaign against William of Orange was printed in Turin and Venice.[1] The author, Alfonso de Ulloa, explained that the true *relationi* (reports) of Alba's victories in the Low Countries a year earlier had fallen into his hands and that he had decided to write a historical account. In the second half of the sixteenth century authors increasingly relied on 'true accounts, handwritten documents and oral stories' to demonstrate that their historical texts were as up to date as possible.[2]

In this period these contemporary histories and chronicles became a popular genre, especially so in Venice, home to a flourishing book industry.[3] Despite their popularity in the sixteenth century, scholars have dismissed these histories for abandoning humanist prose and principles and adopting a more colloquial factual style, typical of the manuscript newsletters.[4] While this may be the case, the increased reliance and inclusion of information taken from handwritten newsletters, letters as well as other news reports by a variety of history writers on the Italian peninsula is a fascinating phenomenon worthy of scholarly attention. It shows the impact of news stories beyond their own genre and immediate purposes, expanding into the recording of historic events and their

---

1 Alfonso Ulloa, *Commentari del sig. Alfonso Ulloa, della guerra, che il sig. don Fernando Avarez di Toledo duca d'Alua et capitano generale del serenissimo re catolico ha fatto contra Giglielmo di Nansau principe di Oranges* (Turin: Crieger, 1569), USTC 861581 and *Commentari* (Venice: Zaltieri, 1570), USTC 861583.

2 For example: Gio Nicolo Doglioni, *Compendio historico universale di tutte le cose notabili già successe nel Mondo, dal principio della sua creazione, fino all' anno di Christo 1594* (Venice: Zenaro, 1595), USTC 827032, A7: 'scrittori stampati, fuori che alcune poche cose ne gli ultimi tempi, ne' quali mi son servito delle veridiche relatione, & scritture à penna, & à boccha scritte'. See: M. Roello, 'Gio Nicolo Doglioni', in *DBI*, 40 (1990).

3 Grendler, 'Francesco Sansovino', pp. 139–180; D. Frigo, 'Pubblicistica e storiografia nella cultura veneta del primo seicento', in E. Fasano Guarini (ed.), *Informazione politica in Italia (secoli XVI–XVIII)* (Pisa: Scuola Normale Superiore, 2001), pp. 83–136.

4 Eric Cochrane, *Historians and Historiography in Renaissance Italy* (Chicago: Chicago University Press, 1985) pp. 382–387; 487–493. A similar judgment has been expressed more recently by William Bouwsma, *The Waning of the Renaissance 1550–1640* (New Haven: Yale University Press, 2000), pp. 198–214, also see footnote 18.

canonisation into more fixed narratives. Through their contemporary reconfiguration into histories, the news reports transformed from standalone sources of information into the constituents of historical discourse. This included the interpretation of recent events. Although these histories might seem at first an endless enumeration of skirmishes and battles, without an organizing principle, they also offered interpretations as well as political and moral lessons.

Through the examination of key examples and themes, this chapter explores the typology of news used as sources in the first historical accounts of the Revolt in the Low Countries, analysing their textual transformations and reworking them into narratives. It provides a comparative study of the fluidity of news as it was transposed into histories, demonstrating the pervasiveness of news across other print categories than their immediate domain, their impact on other genres, and their role in shaping new textual categories.

1   **Defending Contemporary History**

Delineating the difference between early modern news and history is a difficult issue which brings us back to an already much-debated, yet important question, of what history actually is. From the second half of the sixteenth century to the middle of the seventeenth century this was also a subject of reflection and matter of debate in several contemporary treatises on history writing.[5] The renowned Neoplatonic philosopher, Francesco Patrizi, touched upon this issue in his *Della historia diece dialoghi* (Ten dialogues on history) published in 1560 in Venice.[6] In the third dialogue, Patrizi, together with Giorgio and Paolo Contarini, discussed the question of what constituted history.[7] One of the definitions of history they debated was that of Cicero: history is the memory of events remote from our own memory. Patrizi found this definition quite problematic: he argued one could write a history of events that happened only one or two years ago, or even of the present day.[8] His assertion that history could be a narration of current events is key to this chapter. By including the narration

5   For an overview see G. Spini, 'Historiography: The Art of History in the Italian Counter Reformation', in E. Cochrane (ed.), *The Late Italian Renaissance* (London: Macmillan, 1970), pp. 92–133 and Anthony Grafton, *What was History? The Art of History in Early Modern Europe* (Cambridge: Cambridge University Press, 2007).

6   *Della historia diece dialoghi di m. Francesco Patritio ne' quali si ragiona di tutte le cose appartenenti all'historia, et allo scriverla, et all'osservarla* (Venice: Arrivabene, 1560), USTC 847039.

7   *Della historia diece dialoghi*, pp. 12–19; for more on Patrizi's dialogues, consult Grafton, *What was History?*, pp. 125–141.

8   Patrizi, *Della historia*, p. 13b: 'ch'io posso far historia delle cose, che si fanno hoggi'.

of current events within history as a textual category, Patrizi described what has been called 'instant histories', histories which were written and published so close to the actual events that they blurred the lines between the present and the past.[9] Effectively, this amounted to a reconfiguration of history as a literary genre.

Writers of contemporary histories and world chronicles encountered several obstacles. In his *Della Guerra di Fiandra*, Cesare Campana, a private tutor in Vicenza as well as a prolific author, remarked that it was difficult to write a history of recent events because so many eyewitnesses were still alive.[10] The lack of distance between the event described and their retelling meant that contemporary histories could easily cause offence and sometimes drastic action was taken. In February 1573, the Venetian Council of Ten tried to prevent the publication and circulation of Emiliano Manolesso's contemporary history.[11] The account supposedly contained libellous revelations against dignitaries and princes.[12] They ordered the authorities in Padua to confiscate the manuscript, burn the printing press to avoid further printing and locate potential copies in the bookshops to be confiscated. Despite these rather drastic measures, they were unsuccessful in their attempt to halt its circulation; forty-two copies have survived to the present day.

In a theoretical discourse on historical writing, Campana further elaborated upon the pitfalls of writing contemporary history.[13] He defended his position as a historian of present events and spoke in favour of the genre against the

9   Philip Benedict, *Graphic History: The Wars, Massacres and Troubles of Tortorel and Perrissin* (Geneva: Droz, 2007), pp. 127–128.

10   The famous martyrologist John Foxe experienced difficulties describing recent martyrs and received letters from eyewitnesses to correct him: Elizabeth Evenden and Thomas S. Freeman, *Religion and the Book in Early Modern England: The Making of John Foxe's 'Book of Martyrs'* (Cambridge: Cambridge University Press, 2011), pp. 138–148. For a biography see G. Benzoni, 'Cesare Campana', in *DBI*, 17 (1974); Cesare Campana, *Della Guerra di Fiandra, Fatta per difesa di Religione dalla Maestà di Don Filippo Secondo Re di Spagna* (Vicenza: Greco, 1602), USTC 4034222: 'all' molto illustre et eccellentissimo signore, il signor Gioseppe Rustici'.

11   Emilo Maria Manolesso, *Historia nova nella quale si contengono tutti i successi della guerra Turchesca, la congiura del duca de Norfolch, contra la Regina d'Inhilterra, la guerra di Fiandra, Flisinga, Zelanda & Holanda, l'uccisione d'Ugonotti, le morti de Prencipe, l'elettioni de novi, e finalmente tutto quello che nel mondo è occorso da l'anno MDLXX fin all' hora presente* (Padua: Pasquati, 1572), USTC 840139.

12   See Ioanna Iordanou, *Venice's Secret Service. Organizing Intelligence in the Renaissance* (Oxford: Oxford University Press, 2019), p. 178.

13   Cesare Campana, *Delle historie del mondo. Volume secondo che contiene libri sedici: nei quali diffusamente si narrano le cose avvenute dall' anno 1580 fino al 1596, con un Discorso intorno allo scrivere Historie* (Venice: Angelieri, 1597), USTC 818157.

commonly held views of what constituted good history. It was generally thought that only courtiers or men practiced in the art of government could write histories because of their access to state documents and secrets. According to Campana, it was better to use news accounts, as well as talking to the different participants, and when there were many variations within their accounts, one should stick to the 'common opinion'.[14] In other words, Campana suggested that the telling of contemporary histories should be a 'democratic' process that included the voices of those involved in the actual events. He claimed that it was possible to get hold of *relationi* even when one was outside the environment of the court. Before this time, most writers of histories needed access to archives to compile histories, now, at least according to men like Campana, it was possible to write history through publicly available information. Being a good friend of the Paduan scholar Gian Vincenzo Pinelli, a well-known collector of *avvisi* and political writings, Campana had access to a substantial collection of such documents.[15] He defended his own position as a history writer by claiming that his access to different sources enabled him to avoid bias and strive for the truth. Access to diplomatic reports and other secret information was used as an argument by many authors to prove their impartiality and the veracity of their accounts.[16] Of course, this was in no way a guarantee that these writers would stick purely to the facts and avoid the flattery of people who held positions of power.

2 Crafting a Pro-Habsburg Narrative

Power dynamics and personal networks shaped the content of many instant histories produced in the sixteenth century and continued to influence their circulation across borders, too. The example of Pietro Bizzarri's history of current events in Europe from 1564–68 serves as a good example, demonstrating at various points the prominence of power structures even though at first sight it would seem a rather insipid recounting of recent events. Its textual

---

14   Campana, *Discorso intorno allo scrivere historie*, A7: 'e dove nel racconto gli ho veduti variare, e poco esser concordi, mi son accostato, come soglion fare i Legisti, all'opinion commune'.

15   For more on Pinelli's library: Anna Maria Raugei, *Gian Vincenzo Pinelli e la sua biblioteca* (Geneva: Droz, 2018).

16   Dooley, *Social History of Skepticism*, pp. 98–99. See for example: Bartholomeo Dionigi da Fano, *Giardino di tutte l'historie piu notabili del mondo* (Venice: Varisco, 1606), USTC 4033536 advertising on its title page that it was based on 'true and faithful reports of our times'.

transformations are even more subject to power dynamics. This section identifies such trends through a comparative study of the various versions of
Bizzarri's history.

The Italian Protestant Pietro Bizzarri's history of current events in Europe
from 1564 to 1568 was first published in Lyon in 1568.[17] In the first part, Bizzarri
described the war against the Ottomans in Hungary, whilst the second part
offered a wide panorama of events in Europe, dealing mainly with the recent
religious upheavals in the Low Countries and France. Firpo has dismissed
Bizzarri's history as nothing more than a series of disconnected *avvisi*, yet
it is highly significant in showing Bizzarri's role as a manager of political
information.[18] Bizzarri was born in 1525, after his conversion to Protestantism
around 1543, he travelled to England and was part of a vibrant intellectual scene
of foreign protestants.[19] Having been in religious exile at the English court, he
continued to work as an intelligencer for the English government. During his
brief return to Venice between 1564 and 1568, he had gathered the necessary
information to write his history. Following the *avviso* style, Bizzarri strove for
impartiality, taking no position in the description of the events he narrated. He
neither condemned nor celebrated the iconoclastic fury that ravaged the city of
Antwerp in 1566.[20] If Bizzarri's own take on the events recounted here remains
unspoken, his text is revealing of the network of connections which enabled
his collection of information. For instance, he openly declared: 'I received true
information from Mario Cardoini, who from Antwerp told me all the details
in his letters'.[21] The Neapolitan Cardoini, just like Bizzarri had been an exile at
the English court under Edward's reign where the two had met and become
friends.[22] Cardoini subsequently left England and later fought in service of
Philip II at Saint-Quentin (1557), and Gravelingen (1558). As a military officer
stationed in Antwerp, with the outbreak of the Revolt, Cardoini continued to
supply his old friend Bizzarri, a well-known Protestant, with first-hand information on the events in the Low Countries. In these early days of the revolt, he

---

17   Pietro Bizzari, *Historia della guerra fatta in Ungheria dall'invittissimo imperatore de chris-
      tiani, contra quello de turchi: con la narratione di tutte quelle cose che sono avvenute in
      Europa dall'anno 1564, infino all'anno 1568* (Lyon: Rouillé, 1568), USTC 116065 and another
      edition in 1569 in Lyon (USTC 116068).
18   Massimo Firpo, *Pietro Bizzarri. Esule italiano del Cinquecento* (Turin: G. Giappichelli, 1971),
      p. 462.
19   Information about his life in Firpo, *Pietro Bizzarri*, pp. 15–96.
20   Bizzari, *Historia della guerra*, pp. 140–150.
21   Bizzari, *Historia della guerra*, p. 187: 'ho io havuto vera & indutia informatione dall'illustre
      S. Mario Cardoini il quale d'Anversa me ne dette per sue lettere pieno ragguaglio'.
22   Firpo, *Pietro Bizzarri*, p. 32, 50–52. Cardoini would continue to serve in the Spanish-
      Habsburg army in the Low Countries, in 1583 he was appointed governor of Lier.

was even further involved in the transmission of Bizzarri's newsletters to the English secretary of state, Sir William Cecil.

In 1570 Bizzarri's work was pirated by Alfonso de Ulloa and published under a new title *Le Historie di Europa* (The histories of Europe).[23] Like Bizzarri, Ulloa is a fascinating and multifaceted character with close ties to government circles.[24] Originally from Spain, Ulloa had moved to Venice in the service of Spanish ambassador Diego Hurtado de Mendoza around 1546, and after briefly joining the army of Ferrante Gonzaga, governor of Milan, in 1551, he started his career as a professional writer and translator for several major Venetian publishers such as Gabriele Giolito.[25] At the same time, he continued to work for the Spanish ambassadors in Venice and Genoa as a spy. In 1568, he ran into trouble with the Venetian Inquisition and despite interventions, even by Philip II, he was convicted to life in prison, where he died on 16 June 1570.[26]

In Ulloa's hands, Bizzarri's narrative was transformed from a text that strove for impartiality into a highly politicized account. This entailed a significant shift in the power dynamics underlying the text, which became overtly pro-Catholic and pro-Habsburg. Ulloa dedicated the book to Francesco Lomellini, a powerful Genoese banker, who financed the war efforts of the Habsburg crown. Ulloa skilfully omitted all possible references to Bizzari as an author and made some significant alterations to the text.[27] These changes were made especially concerning the two protagonists of the early conflict in the Netherlands: William of Orange and the Duke of Alba. According to Ulloa, William 'allowed himself to be deceived by the devil' and he abandoned his loyalty to the king.[28] Alba became the hero by eradicating heresy and rebellion.

This change is not surprising as Ulloa had already in 1569 celebrated the Duke of Alba's victories in the Low Countries in another work entitled

---

23   *Le historie di Europa del sig. Alfonso Ulloa, nuovamente mandate in luce. Nelle quali principalmente si contiene la guerra ultimamente fatta in Ungheria tra Massimiliano imperatore de' christiani, & sultan Solimano re de' turchi* (Venice: Zaltieri, 1570), USTC 861583.

24   Most biographical information is based on her monograph Anne Marie Lievens, *Il caso Ulloa: uno spagnolo "irregolare" nella editoria veneziana del Cinquecento* (Rome: A. Pellicani, 2002) and see her entry in *DBI*, 97 (2020).

25   On the *poligrafi* as a group see Claudio di Filippo Bareggi, *Il mestiere di scrivere: lavoro intelletuale e mercato librari a Venezia nel Cinquecento* (Rome: Bulzoni, 1988) also Angela Nuovo and Christian Coppens, *I Giolito e la stampa: nell'Italia del XVI secolo* (Geneva: Droz, 2005).

26   See Magdaleno, *Papeles de Estado de Venecia,* p. 73.

27   Firpo, *Pietro Bizzari,* pp. 191–195.

28   Ulloa, *Le historie di Europa,* pp. 137–138: 'lasciandosi ingannare dal demonio', and on Alva 'destrutti ribelli, et quietato compiutamente il paese, stirpando gli eretici, onde tutti vivono ora catolicamente et in grandissima ubidienza come prima'.

Commentari.[29] With this historical account, Ulloa continued to promote Alba's successes on the Italian peninsula from where it spread to other European cities. The ties of Ulloa to powerful patrons are likely to have also influenced the dissemination of his work. Within a year, this history, first published in Turin and later in Venice, was available to a wider European audience with translations into French, Spanish and German.[30] The French translation by the well-known French writer François de Belleforest was published in Paris, but also in Antwerp and Brussels.[31]

Ulloa promised his readers to describe the war 'with brevity, truthfulness and sincerity so that you hear the truth about the present.'[32] He claimed that he used the true *relationi* of the Duke of Alba's victories.[33] Through close comparison, it becomes clear that Ulloa indeed used some manuscript news reports which had circulated earlier in Italian cities. For his description of the battle of Jemmingen in 1568, Ulloa relied on a manuscript account emanating from the circles of the Duke of Alba.[34] Ulloa likely received these accounts

---

29   Ulloa, *Commentari* (Turin: Crieger, 1569), USTC 861581; *Commentari* (Venice: Zaltieri, 1570), USTC 861583. The Venetian edition was dedicated to the count Giulio Capra, a nobleman from Vicenza.

30   Alfonso de Ulloa, *Comentarios (primero, segundo, tercero) de la guerra, que el illustriss, principe don Hernando Alvarez, duque de Alva, ha hecho contra Guillermo de Nasau, principe de Oranges, y otros rebeldes* (Venice: de Farris, 1569), USTC 340645; *Guerre des Pais Bas entre le duc d'Albe et le prince d'Orange* (s.l.: s.n., 1569), USTC 14102; *Gründliche beschreibung inn zwen thail verfast. Des Niderlaendischen kriegs so Herr don Fernando Alvares von Toledo, Hertzog von Alba kriegs obrister des durchleuchtigsten Catholischen Künigs Philippi gefuert hat wider Wilhalmen von Nassaw, Printzen von Oranien und Graven Ludwigen seinen bruder im Niderland des 1568. Jars* (Dillingen: Mayer, 1570), USTC 660875.

31   *Commentaire premier contenant le voyage du duc d'Albe en Flandres* (Paris: Dallier, 1570), USTC 10003; *Commentaire premier contenant le voyage du duc d'Albe en Flandres* (Antwerp: Marcelin, 1570), USTC 16271; *Le commentaire touchant les troubles advenuz en Flandres* (Brussels: s.n., 1570), USTC 94599. For more on the activities of Belleforest see Michel Simonin, *Vivre de sa plume au XVIe siècle ou la carrière de François de Belleforest* (Geneva: Droz, 1992).

32   Ulloa, *Commentari*, p. 5: 'la qual guerra io prometto di scrivere sotto brevità, con quella verità, e sincerità, che potrò, accioche s'intenda il vero, da' presenti'. Quotations are from Venetian edition of 1570 (USTC 861583).

33   Ulloa, *Commentari*, p. 3.

34   For more on the battle of Jemmingen, see the previous chapter. The most striking example of this copying is the description of the Italian cavalry companies of Don Cesare Gonzaga and Count Curtio Martinengo's attack upon Louis of Nassau's troops at the end of the battle. Compare for instance: ASMo, CD, Avvisi 6, fol 843: 'Con tanta furia, che in un momento si populo la campagna di morti, d'arme, picche et archibuggi, che non vi era loco per dove si potesse passare ne innanzi ne indietro, la gente di conto gli teneva dietro oltra allo scanarli gli tagliavano e li facevano ascondere nelli pantani, e nelli fosfati' with Ulloa, *Commentari*, p. 51: 'Con tanta furia, che in un subito fu coperta la campagna di corpi

from Guzmán de Silva, who was very active in anonymising and distributing official correspondence from Venice.[35] Ulloa copied large parts of this official account of the battle with only occasional alterations.

In the popular brief historical accounts, Ulloa continued the active promotion of Alba's military victories. He applauded the duke's achievement in bringing the Low Countries back to a state of obedience in such a way that 'in our times there will be no more sedition'.[36] The transformations of Bizzari's text by the hand of Alfonso de Ulloa may appear as mere plagiarism by the inattentive reader, but close examination shows that the changes were meaningful and spoke to the power structures to which Ulloa himself reported as an 'instant historian'. The account was no longer an impartial text, but it took a clear turn into propagandistic history.

3   Understanding the Present

Histories of current or recent events were generally written by men who were actively involved in the business of news gathering. Their closeness to news sources was an asset to compiling their contemporary histories. Emiliano Manolesso's history of the recent wars against the Ottomans, and the reigniting of civil strife in the Low Countries and France was published in Padua in 1572. Manolesso had served at the Este court in Ferrara, and, like Bizzari, seems to have been active as a news writer.[37] The last part of Manolesso's history was devoted to the outbreak of new civil unrest in the Low Countries in 1572 and he included some of the latest news in his history published in that same year. He described in great detail the sack of Roermond in July 1572 by William of Orange's troops and their subsequent attack on the Carthusian monastery. His account shows many similarities to the news pamphlets published in Rome and Venice around the same time.[38] Manolesso stressed that the Calvinists

---

morti, di arme, picche, archibuggi che non v'era per dove si passasse innazi né indietro. La gente principale, che seguiva lo incalzo, oltre quelli che ammazzavano, gli molestava, percoteva fieramente facendogli saltare ne' pantani, & ne' fossi'.

35   On his activities Rodríguez-Salgado, 'Diplomatic correspondence, news and narratives', pp. 18–35.

36   Ulloa, *Commentari*, p. 95: 'che a' tempi nostri non sarà piu seditione'.

37   For a biography see R. Zago, 'Emiliano Manolesso', in *DBI*, 69 (2007). He presented an ambassadorial report on Ferrara to the Venetian senate in 1578, but he was not officially appointed as ambassador. In the d'Este archive in Modena, I came across some of his *avvisi*: ASMo, CD, Avvisi 8, fol 404–410.

38   Manolesso, *Historia nova*, p.85: 'ne contenti d'haverlo ucciso li cavorono le interiora, e tagliatili i membri genitali gli li posero in bocca'. Compare this to the pamphlet *L'inaudite*

attacked 'poor friars, whose lives the Turks had spared in the horrendous and bloody loss of Nicosia'.[39] His conclusion was crystal clear: 'they [the Calvinists] exceed the cruelty of the Assyrians, the Egyptians, the Huns, the Goths, the Scythians, the Langobards, and those nations which are considered savage and inhumane such as the Tartars and the Turks'.[40] In Italian cities, where the image of the barbarous Ottomans was omnipresent, such comparisons were frequently used to stress the cruelty of the Calvinists in the Low Countries, and as a good way to emphasise how bad the situation was in the Netherlands.[41] These comparisons were all the more powerful in Manolesso's history because he described the wars against the Ottomans as well. In this way, he created a narrative of Catholicism being under threat from infidels and heretics. The tone and language are a far cry from the more balanced style of *avvisi* and Bizzarri's account.

This linkage between the Dutch Calvinists and the Ottomans was present in many contemporary histories and world chronicles. The connection was explicitly made by the Florentine history writer Giovanni Battista Adriani in his *Istoria dei suoi tempi* (History of his own time) when he summarized the year 1566:

Not only this year was the Christian religion and the Christian rulers affected by the Turks in Hungary, but even more so by Christians of various and perverse divisive confessions, since in parts of the Low Countries [...] a great movement followed with infinite scorn against the divine cult, the good and holy religion, which lasts publicly until this time.[42]

---

et horrende crudeltà usate da gli heretici, p.3: 'li cavoro le viscere & sparsero tutte l'interioa, & havendo tagliati le parti dishoneste gli l'attacorno in bocca'. For more on this episode see the previous chapter.

39   Manolesso, *Historia nova*, pp. 84–85: 'poveri sacerdoti, alla vita de i quali i Turchi hanno nella horenda e sanguinosa perdita di Nicosia perdonato'.

40   Manolesso, *Historia nova*, pp. 86–87: 'superorono la crudeltà delli Assirii, Egitii, Hunni, Gotti, Sciti, Longobardi, e de quelle nationi, che sono tenute fiersissimi, e inhumnissime Tartari e Turchi'; for this well-established trope of comparing Scythians and Ottomans: Sean Roberts, *Printing a Mediterranean World: Florence, Constantinople and Geography* (Harvard: Harvard University Press, 2013), pp. 133–148.

41   Marina Formica, *Lo Specchio Turco. Immagini dell'altro e riflessi del sé nella cultura italiana d'età moderna* (Rome: Donzelli, 2012), pp. 52–63. *Le historie de' successi de' nostri tempi, del R.P. Faustino Tasso vinitiano de' minori osseruanti, diuise in tredici libri* (Venice: Guerra, 1583), USTC 858273, p. 30: 'Come fossero peggio che i Turchi'.

42   Giovanni Battista Adriani, *Istoria dei suoi tempi* (Florence: i Giunti, 1583), USTC 807801, p. 767: 'Non solamente fu quest'anno la religion Cristiana, & I Principi di essa infestata nell'Ungheria da i Turchi, ma molto più da I Cristiani medesimi di diverse, e di perverse religioni lacerate, imperoche nelle parti de' paesi bassi [...] seguì gran movimento con

Adriani presented a Christianity under threat, a conflict which was still ongoing in 1583 when his history was posthumously published in Florence.

Adriani had started to write this history at the request of Duke Cosimo I.[43]
He began with the idea of writing just a history of Florence, but he broad-
ened his scope as the international connections of the city and its rulers were
all-important to explaining its internal matters. In his capacity as an official
historiographer, Adriani had access to the archives of the Medici, and this sets
him apart from history writers discussed earlier such as Bizzari, Manolesso
and Ulloa.[44] Rather than relying on news accounts, Adriani used the letters
sent to the Medici by their trusted correspondents in the Low Countries. He
recounted specific events, details of which he could only have read in these
letters. A particularly telling example is Adriani's description of the citizens,
students and professors in Leuven who defended the churches against iconoclasm in 1566.[45] This same episode had been described in some detail in two
letters sent by Giovanni Battista Guicciardini to Francesco de' Medici (see
Chapter 1).[46] Since Guicciardini was the only one who described this event
in detail (no *avviso* mentioned this alliance to keep Calvinists out of the university town), Adriani must have learned from it from his dispatches in the
Medici archives.[47] Adriani also used Vitelli's letters for some of his sections on

dispregio infinito del culto divino, e della buona, e santa religione infino a questo tempo
pubblicamente duratavi'.

43   G. Miccoli, 'Giovan Battista Adriani', in *DBI*, 1 (1960); his history was reprinted in Venice by
Giunti in 1587 (USTC 807802). For more on his history: Elena Fasano Guarini, *Repubbliche
e principi. Istituzioni e pratiche di potere nella Toscana granducale del '500–'600* (Bologna:
Il Mulino, 2010), pp. 268–269; E. Fasano Guarini, 'Committenza del principe e storiografia
pubblica: Benedetto Varchi e Giovan Battista Adriani', in E. Fasano Guarini, F. Angiolini
(eds.), *La pratica della Storia in Toscana. Continuità e mutamenti tra la fine del '400 e la
fine del '700* (Milan: FrancoAngeli 2009), pp. 79–100 and for history writing in Florence:
Caroline Callard, *Le prince et la république: histoire, pouvoir et société dans la Florence des
Médicis au XVIIe siècle* (Paris: Presses de l'Université Paris-Sorbonne, 2007).

44   Adriani, *Istoria dei suoi tempi*, p. 2: 'ne ho ancora voluto i riscontri delle scritture pubbliche,
dalle queli molto meglio, che da alcun'altra parte (come hò conosciuto per esperzienza) si
puo il vero retirarre'. See.

45   Adriani, *Istoria dei suoi tempi*, p. 768.

46   In one letter on 11 September 1566 and the other on 5 October 1566 written from Leuven.
In the latter Guicciardini wrote: 'Questi cittadini si sono congiunti con quelli della
Università et giurato volere vivere et morire insieme, et guardare le chiese, et che non sia
predicato dalli Calvinisti o altri settarij, nè in la villa né fuori e tutto sta in pace e ci si fa
strettissime guardie di e notte', see *Lettere di Giovan Battista*, pp. 273–276.

47   In a letter from 31 August 1566, the Jesuit Schipman wrote that iconoclasm had been
prevented by the authorities in Leuven and that the Jesuits patrolled the city's defenses
during night shifts see Jozef Andriessen, *De Jezuïeten en het Samenhorigheidsbesef der
Nederlanden 1585–1648* (Antwerp: De Nederlandsche boekhandel, 1957), p. 4.

the events in the Low Countries, at the same time chronicling Vitelli's role in the war. He mentioned Vitelli's involvement in the imprisonment of Egmont and Horne in September 1567, as well as his leading role in the negotiations with the Spanish mutineers at Haarlem in 1572.[48]

Ulloa, Manolesso, and Adriani all relied on letters, manuscript accounts and news reports to compile their histories, but did not stick to just listing the facts. They added comments for readers to understand the unfolding events. Giovanni Battista Adriani used the examples of the Low Countries and France to demonstrate the dangers to secular princes that the spread of new religious movements among the population could mean the loss of their sovereignty over a state.[49] Overtly pro-Catholic language was used in all three of the histories. Ulloa's *commentari* had a clear polemical tone right from the start when he wrote that with the treaty of Cateau-Cambrésis in 1559, peace had been established in Europe, but that the devil once again sought to sow discord. The devil was not yet satisfied with the spread of 'the false doctrine of the wicked Luther' in many parts of Europe and he decided to turn his attention to the Low Countries.[50] As we have already seen, this kind of language was largely absent from handwritten newsletters. These history writers offered a Catholic view of events by using a repertoire of terms to condemn heresy and rebellion.

4   Claiming 'Italian Virtue': The First Italian History

In the contemporary histories discussed so far, the conflict in the Netherlands was placed within a broader European context chronicling ongoing events. The first history entirely dedicated to the Revolt and printed on the Italian peninsula was Pedro Cornejo's *Origen de la civil dissension in Flandres* (Origin of the civil dissension in the Low Countries). Cornejo, a Spanish Carmelite, had been in the Low Countries from 1567 until 1577. His history was first published in Spanish in Lyon in 1577, and then reprinted twice in Turin in 1579 and 1580.[51] Two years later, the Italian translation by Camillo Camilli, was

---

48   Adriani, *Istoria*, pp. 1401–1402, parte due, p. 76, 84.
49   Adriani, *Istoria*, p. 755.
50   Ulloa, *Commentari*, p. 1.
51   Pedro Cornejo, *Origen de la civil disension de Flandes con lo a la buelta de esta hoja en dos partes contenido* (Turin: Belvicqua, 1579), USTC 824097, and the edition in 1580 by Belvicqua (USTC 344172). The two Turin editions contained a dedication to the Duke of Savoy. For more on his history see: Rodríguez Pérez, *De Tachtigjarige Oorlog in Spaanse ogen*, pp. 51–57; 62–64.

printed in Brescia.[52] Interestingly, Camilli dedicated the work to the Venetian *condottiere* Scipio Costanzo, whose son Giovanni Tomaso had recently died on the battlefield in the Low Countries.[53] Giovanni Tomaso embodied the ideal devout Catholic soldier who fought against the enemies of the Catholic faith.[54] In 1571 he was at Lepanto where he had been captured by the Ottomans. After three years of imprisonment, he was exchanged with other prisoners. Upon his release, according to an *aviso*, he wrote a letter to the Venetian government asking them for permission to fight as a volunteer in the Low Countries.[55] By 1577, he had joined the Habsburg forces in their fight against the Calvinists, where he died in 1581, prompting Torquato Tasso, the famous Italian poet, to compose two rhymes celebrating Costanza as a defender of the Catholic faith.[56] Camilli's dedication cleverly used this exemplary career of an Italian soldier's service and sacrifice for the Catholic faith to link the two struggles against the infidels and the heretics in the Low Countries. It also highlights the 'Italianification' of texts, a growing emphasis in historical texts on the role Italian soldiers and generals played in the wars in the Low Countries.

This phenomenon comes to the fore in *Historia della ribellione della Fiandra*, the first history solely dedicated to conflict written by an Italian author.[57] The Florentine citizen Francesco Bocchi made extensive use of Ulloa's and Cornejo's histories, two pro-Habsburg accounts of the revolt.[58] Ulloa, in his

---

52   Pedro Cornejo, *Della historia di fiandra di pietro cornelio libri x. Nella quale si vede l'origine delle civili dissensioni, & guerre universali dal principio fin a questi tempi; con la descrittione di tutto quel paese, in quante provincie sia diviso, la qualità de' Fiamenghi, i Stati generali, & come pervenisse nella casa d'Austria.* (Brescia: Marchetti, 1582), USTC 824099. This Italian translation was reprinted in 1583 (USTC 824100).

53   Cornejo, *Della historia di Fiandra libri x*, p. 2. References are to 1582 edition (USTC 824099).

54   Based on Antonio Possevino's ideas in *Il soldato christiano*, first published in 1569. See Vincenzo Lavenia, *Il catechismo dei soldati. Guerra e cura d'anime in età moderna* (Bologna: edb, 2014).

55   ASMn, AG, 1982, fol 254r–255r: *Di Venetia alli 22 febraro 1577*.

56   *Rime di Torquato Tasso* (Pisa: Capurro, 1822), p. 117: In morte di Gian Tomaso di Costanzo: 'Non pianga alcun, ma lodi la tua morte, che felice è colui che per difesa di nostra fede s'arma, e more in guerra'.

57   ASF, CS I, f. CCLXXV n. 494: *Historia della ribellione della Fiandra avvenuta sotto la corona del Re Cattolico Filippo Secondo di Spagna*. See also: Cees Reijner, 'Het eerste Italiaanse geschiedwerk over de Opstand: Francesco Bocchi's kroniek van een oorlog of biografie van een Italiaanse oorlogsheld?', *Belgisch tijdschrift voor filologie en geschiedenis*, 95 (2017), pp. 297–320.

58   For Bocchi's use of Ulloa compare the speeches by the Duke of Alba and Oranges to their soldiers in 1568 near Maastricht (fol 62r–v and pp. 57–58). For some examples of intertextuality between Bocchi and Cornejo, see the story of a Spanish soldier protecting churches in Brussels in 1566 (fol 25v–26r and p. 31); for the descriptions of prodigy during the siege of Zierikzee as a 'corono di fuoco' (fol 114 and p.108); also see the description of

turn, had already relied heavily upon reports emanating from the circles around the Duke of Alba. This process of re-elaboration illustrates how news was processed, reused and reworked. The extensive rewriting and reframing of histories were not done for their own sake but also serve a purpose in the intellectual and personal agenda of the authors. Bocchi did not just copy and paste; by contrast, as we will see, his glorification of Italian military talent would become a dominant feature of Italian history writing on the conflict.

Between 1572 and 1582, Bocchi lived in Rome, probably serving in the household of Cardinal Ferdinand de' Medici.[59] Back in Florence, he tried to earn a living as a private tutor. He was also a prolific writer and worked as a corrector in the printing house of Marescotti.[60] In 1585, he completed his manuscript covering the events in the Netherlands from 1566 to 1579. In sharp contrast to the polygraphs working in Venice, Bocchi intended to write a humanist history of the civil wars in the Low Countries claiming that he decided to do so because of the great misfortunes that sprang from this war, which he hoped would provide material for political and moral lessons.[61]

His history was, however, never printed although the surviving manuscript copy, now in state archives of Florence, suggests that it was being prepared for printed publication. The last page of the manuscript includes pre-approval by two censors.[62] In the manuscript, words are sometimes crossed out and extra comments are added in the margins; these interpellations were quite probably made by the censors. Their most clear intervention is when the name of the controversial Florentine political thinker Machiavelli is crossed out in the manuscript.[63] It is difficult to assess why this work was not eventually published. A court case from 1587 between Bocchi and the publisher Giorgio

---

the pacification of Ghent as 'Lega Santa' (fol 127 and p. 123), its placement before the sack of Antwerp (whilst chronologically the sack preceded the conclusion of the pacification) and of the prodigies during the sack of Antwerp (fol 140 and p. 129).

59   S. Seidel Menchi, 'Francesco Bocchi', in *DBI*, 11 (1969).

60   For an overview of Bocchi's work: Rodolfo de Mattei, 'Una inedita "risposta" al Machiavelli di Francesco Bocchi', *Archivio Storico Italiano*, 124 (1966), pp. 22–30.

61   *Historia della ribellione*, fol 13. He referred to ancient authors quite frequently in the margins of the text, especially to Livy. For popularity of Livy see Peter Burke, 'A Survey of Popularity of Ancient Historians, 1450–1700', *History and Theory*, 5 (1966), pp. 146–147 and the evaluation with new data by Freyja Cox Jensen, 'The Popularity of Ancient Historians 1450–1600', *The Historical Journal*, 61 (2018), pp. 561–595.

62   *Historia della ribellione*, fol 143. On the organization of censorship in Tuscany see Sandro Landi, *Il governo delle opinioni: censura e formazione del consenso nella Toscana del Settecento* (Bologna: il Mulino, 2000), pp. 34–40.

63   *Historia della ribellione*, fol 126. For another example where Machiavelli's name was expunged from a Florentine manuscript see Bryce, *Cosimo Bartoli*, p. 281.

Marescotti offers some clues.[64] Bocchi claimed he had not received payment for his work as a corrector in Marescotti's publishing firm. The records of this trial show that it was quite common for authors in Florence to finance, at least partially, the publication of their work with Marescotti.[65] His deteriorating relationship with one of the most important publishers in Florence was a serious problem; Bocchi probably did not have the necessary funds to finance the publication himself.

Silvia Seidel Menchi claims that Bocchi was encouraged to write this history by Gian Vincenzo Vitelli, son of Chiappino Vitelli, to exalt the military virtues of his father, who had fought for so many years in the Low Countries.[66] While Vitelli is the main protagonist in Bocchi's history, as we will see, it is still unclear whether Bocchi wrote the history on the demand of Gian Vincenzo or to gain his patronage. If Bocchi wrote the history on the commission of Gian Vincenzo, one might suppose that he would have had access to Vitelli's letters. There is, however, no evidence that Bocchi was granted permission to work in the archive of the Medici family whilst he was writing his history. Moreover, there is scant textual evidence that he read or used Vitelli's letters.[67] Rather than using these letters or other news reports, he seems to have relied on printed contemporary chronicles. Bocchi did not mention which of these recent histories he used, whereas he did refer to older chronicles such as the fourteenth-century Florentine humanist and diplomat Giovanni Villani in his marginal notes.[68] Close reading and comparative analysis indicate that Bocchi

---

64   Gustavo Bertoli, 'Autori ed editori a Firenze nella seconda metà del sedicesimo secolo: il "caso" Marescotti', *Annali di storia di Firenze*, 2 (2007), pp. 77–93.

65   Bertoli, 'Autori ed editori a Firenze', pp. 89–91.

66   Seidel Menchi in *DBI*: 'scritta su incoraggiamento di Giovan Vincenzo Vitelli per celebrare il padre Chiappino Vitelli, che aveva combattuto in Fiandra come condottiero'.

67   For example, in his description of the imprisonment of Egmont and Horne, he did not mention Vitelli's presence, whilst in his letters Vitelli claimed he witnessed the event. Instead, Bocchi's description of this episode closely followed Cornejo's account see fol 34v–35 and p. 36. Nor did he use Adriani's history, who did mention Vitelli's presence. He also does not mention the role of Giovanni Battista del Monte, a nephew of Vitelli, in the battle of Mookerheide in 1574, who according to Vitelli's letters was responsible for the victory (Antwerp 10 May 1574, ASF, MdP 651, fol 269v: 'Ogni giorni s'è piu verificato che l'honor della vittoria che s'hebbe contra nemici a giorno passati si deve in maggior parte à Gio battista del Monte mio nepote et cosi lo confermano tutti i capitano che vi si trovorno'). In later Italian histories, as we will see in the last chapter, Del Monte's crucial role would be highlighted.

68   *Historia della ribellione*, fol 3,5. Villani's chronicle was published several times in the sixteenth century both in Venice and in Florence. On the importance of Villani's chronicle see P. Clarke, 'The Villani Chronicles', in S. Dale, A. Williams Lewin, D.J. Osheim

used Ulloa's *Commentari* and Cornejo's *Origen*.[69] Bocchi's use of both these histories, instead of the Medici archive, suggests that he probably did not write the history on the demand of Gian Vincenzo, but that he hoped to gain his favour.

Bocchi placed Chiappino Vitelli at the centre of the narrative. In describing the gathering of Alba's troops for their march to the Low Countries in 1567, Vitelli is introduced as one of the most honourable and virtuous soldiers in this army.[70]

> He was not superior to the Duke of Alba in dignity, but his virtues were in high esteem in the army [...] and from his leadership many successes and victories were expected.[71]

Whereas Ulloa had presented Alba as the virtuous captain, in Bocchi's account Alba did not get much of the glory. Bocchi even claimed that Alba bestowed all the credit for the victory at Jemmingen in 1568 upon Vitelli.[72] At various points in the history, Vitelli is presented as the embodiment of military prudence; as the perfect military commander adopting many of the tropes we have seen developed in descriptions of heroic military feats in other earlier treatises on the wars.[73] Bocchi seized on any trope of military excellence he could find. The lack of sleep, for instance, was a commonplace in military literature which

---

(eds.), *Chronicling History: Chroniclers and Historians in Medieval and Renaissance Italy* (Pennsylvania: Pennsylvania State University Press, 2007), pp. 113–143.

69   For Bocchi's use of Ulloa compare the speeches by the Duke of Alba and Orange to their soldiers in 1568 near Maastricht (fol 62r–v and pp. 57–58). For some examples of inter-textuality between Bocchi and Cornejo, see the story of a Spanish soldier protecting churches in Brussels in 1566 (f25v–26r and p. 31); for the descriptions of prodigy during the siege of Zierichzee as a 'corono di fuoco' (f114 and p.108); also see the description of the pacification of Ghent as 'Lega Santa' (fol 127 and p. 123), its placement before the sack of Antwerp (whilst chronologically the sack preceded the conclusion of the pacification) and of the prodigies during the sack of Antwerp (fol 140 and p. 129).

70   *Historia della ribellione*, fol 30v–31r.

71   *Historia della ribellione*, fol 31v–r: 'Egli non era maggiore del duca d'Alva per dignità, ma il nome di sua virtù tanto era in pregio nell'esercito, (...), et per lo suo consiglio si aspet-tavano felici avvenimenti et vittorie'.

72   *Historia della ribellione*, fol 52.

73   *Historia della ribellione*, fol 47, 61v. Bocchi had written a discourse on military virtues of ancient and modern warriors: *Discorso di Francesco Bocchi fiorentino a chi de' maggiori guerrieri, che insino à questo tempo sono stati, si dee la maggioranza attribuire* (Florence: Marescotti, 1573), USTC 815009. On this genre see M. Fantoni, 'Il "Perfetto Capitano": storia e mitografia', in M. Fantoni (ed.), *Il "Perfetto Capitano": immagini e realtà (secoli XV–XVII)* (Rome: Bulzoni, 2001), pp. 15–67 and Vincenzo Caputo, *La 'bella maniera di scrivere vita': biografie di uomini d'arme e di stato nel secondo cinquecento* (Naples: Edizioni Scientifiche Italiane, 2009).

became equivalent to military valour.[74] This helps to understand Bocchi's comment that Vitelli, when he was on campaign in 1568, was on his horse for more than eighteen hours. Bocchi also stresses that Vitelli hardly slept and always went to bed with his clothes on, prepared for a possible attack.[75]

The description of Vitelli's death in 1575 was the occasion for Bocchi to glorify his deeds. Vitelli showed Italian virtues and valour on the battlefield, he was the modern embodiment of ancient Roman military discipline bringing glory upon the whole of Italy.[76] His conclusion about Vitelli was clear: 'Never did an army have a man of more valour than Vitelli, neither amongst the Italians, nor amongst the Spanish'.[77] He immortalized Vitelli as a remarkable and talented Italian commander. Bocchi's work marks the beginning of long tradition: it places Italian generals at the centre of the narrative and even downplays the role of Spanish commanders.

5   The Farnese Quest for a Suitable History Begins

Perhaps the best and most eloquent example to discuss the repurposing of news into histories is that of Alexander Farnese. In the previous chapter, I examined the campaign of persuasive news devoted to creating Farnese's public persona, including his military talent and clemency. As well as using widely disseminated news reports, the information capacity of the Farnese powerhouse fed extensively into the histories of the revolt in the Low Countries. This section considers the case study of Campana's history devoted to Alexander Farnese's siege of Antwerp and the relevance to narratives of power and politics both in Italy and across borders.

Following Alexander Farnese's death in 1592, the relationship between the house of Farnese and the Spanish monarchy was very strained.[78] After the failure of the Armada in 1588 and Alexander's reluctance to support the Catholic

---

74 On this aspect see Fréderique Verrier, *Les Armes de Minerve. L'humanisme militaire dans l'Italie du XVIᵉ siècle* (Paris: Presses de l'université de Paris-Sorbonne, 1997), pp. 202–206.

75 *Historia della ribellione,* fol 61v: 'Era breve il suo sonno, et quesi sempre indosso con le sue vesti, peroche per provedere il tutto quando si travagliava in campagna, stava à cavalla diciotto hore'. On 26 August 1568, Vitelli wrote the following: 'Io stando della mattina fin a menza notte à cavallo per riconoscere I luoghi suddetti'. ASF, MdP 649, fol 217.

76 *Historia della ribellione*, fol 117-v: 'Valore Italiano', 'la virtù italiana' 'Rinnovare il costume lodevole della disciplina militare, che à Romani così gran prove partoriva , [...] che con tanta gloria si dice dell' Italia.'

77 *Historia della ribellione*, fol 117v: 'Non ci havea homai nell'esercito huomo di maggior valore del vitelli, ne tra gli italiani, ne tra gli spagnuoli'.

78 For an overview of the various problems: S. Derks, 'Le ricompense della guerra: giustificazione e rappresentazione di Alessandro Farnese nel *Liber relationum* di Paolo Rinaldi',

League in France, he had fallen out of favour in Madrid. His sons, Duke
Ranuccio I and Cardinal Odoardo, both actively started to promote the deeds
of their father as a way to re-establish the dynasty's prestige.[79] Their prestigious
projects have received attention from scholars, the most famous one being
Annibale Carracci's paintings in Palazzo Farnese in Rome.[80] Accompanying
the visual memorialisation campaign, Duke Ranuccio wanted a history about
his father's exploits. In 1595, the task was assigned to Antonio Querenghi, who
did not complete this commission, because of his deteriorating relationship
with the Farnese.[81] The task passed to a former member of Alexander's household, Paolo Rinaldi, who had been in the Low Countries during Alexander's
governorship.[82] Sebastiaan Derks has argued Rinaldi's work should be seen as
part of this wider campaign to rehabilitate Alexander Farnese.[83] Rinaldi's history was not intended to be printed, and presumably circulated in manuscript
within the Parmesan and Roman court circles.

The only Italian history promoting Alexander's deeds reaching a considerable audience on the Italian peninsula and in other parts of Europe, including the Dutch Republic, was Cesare Campana's *Assedio et Racquisto d'Anversa*
(Siege and Conquest of Antwerp).[84] It was printed in 1595 by the entrepre-
neurial Venetian printer-publisher Ciotti, and republished in the same year in
Cremona by Pellizari and by Zanni.[85] Campana did not write the history on

in G. Bertini (ed.), *Militari italiani dell'esercito di Alessandro Farnese* (Guastalla: Mattioli, 2013), pp. 211–219.

79   B. de Groof, 'Alexander Farnese and the origins of modern Belgium', in B. de Groof, E. Galdieri (eds.), *La dimensione europea dei Farnese* (Rome/Brussels: Belgisch Historisch Instituut te Rome, 1993), pp. 195–219; R. Sabbadini, 'L'uso della memoria. I Farnese e le immagini di Alessandro, duca e capitano', in M. Fantoni (ed.), *Il "Perfetto Capitano": immagini e realtà (secoli XV–XVII)* (Rome: Bulzoni, 2001), pp. 155–182.

80   Literature on this project is vast, see Roberto Zapperi, 'Annibale Carracci e Odoardo Farnese', *Bollettino d'arte*, 84 (1999), pp. 87–102.

81   Uberto Motta, *Antonio Querenghi (1546–1633): Un letterato padovano nella Roma del tardo Rinascimento* (Milan: Vita e Pensiero, 1997), pp. 111–150.

82   The manuscript survives in two copies: one in KBR, Ms II. 1155: *Liber relationum* and another one in BNCF, Fondo Magliabechiano, II, I, 235: *Historia di Fiandra del tempo che comandò l'armata il Duca Alessandro Farnese, composta da Paolo Rinaldi nel 1599.*

83   Derks, 'Le Ricompense', pp. 228–229.

84   The Antwerp-born merchant Daniel van der Meulen owned a copy of this work, see N. Lamal, 'The circulation and collections of Italian books in the Low Countries at the beginning of the seventeenth century', in R. Adam, C. Lastraioli (eds.), *Itineraires du livre italien a la Renaissance Suisse romande, anciens Pays-Bas et Liege* (Paris: Garnier, 2019), pp. 103–126.

85   Cesare Campana, *Assedio e racquisto d'Anversa, fatto dal serenissimo Alessandro Farnese prencipe di Parma, &c.* (Vicenza: Ciotti, 1595), USTC 818152. For more on Ciotti see David E. Rhodes, 'Some Neglected Aspects of the Career of Giovanni Battista Ciotti', *The*

the request of the Farnese family, but his narrative was clearly intended to fit their attempts to rehabilitate Alexander. He dedicated his work to Alexander's heir, Ranuccio I Farnese, hoping for a reward or compensation. He chose the siege of Antwerp as a subject since it offered him an excellent opportunity to immortalise Farnese's deeds. Already during his lifetime, as we have seen in the previous chapter, conquering this impregnable city had become the prime example of Alexander's military genius: his victory immediately inspired writers, poets and sculptors.[86] Giovanni Botero described Farnese in his *Ragion di stato* (1589) as the best and vivid example of a perfect military commander: he had shown all his virtue, prowess, valour, military skills in conquering the city of Antwerp.[87] His triumph at Antwerp was crucial to the Farnese family for another reason. After bringing Antwerp back into the Habsburg and Catholic orbit, Alexander achieved one of the family's long standing goals: Philip II withdrew his troops from Piacenza. The restitution of this strategically important city had been one of the main aims of the Farnese family for several decades.[88] In addition, Alexander also became a member of the prestigious Order of the Golden Fleece in 1585.

Library, IX (1987), pp. 225–239. Reprinted under a new title: Cesare Campana, *Imprese nella Fiandra del serenissimo Alessandro Farnese* (Cremona: Pellizari, 1595), USTC 818154; (Cremona: Zanni, 1595), USTC 818153.

86   *De bello Belgico Ad Alexandrum Farnesium serenissimum Parmæ, & Placentiæ principem* (Perugia: Bresciano, 1586), USTC 845503. For more information see F. Pignatti, 'Aurelio Orsi', in *DBI*, 79 (2013). It was also the topic of a poem written by the Spanish soldier Miguel Giner's *El sitio y toma de Anvers*, first published in Zaragoza in 1586 (USTC 348807), and reprinted in Milan by Da Ponte in 1587 (USTC 345626) and one year later in Antwerp by Plantin (USTC 440548). Eckhard Leuschner, 'Francesco Villamena's "apotheosis of Alessandro Farnese" and Engraved Reproductions of Contemporary Sculpture around 1600', *Simiolus: Netherlands Quarterly for the History of Art*, 27 (1999), pp. 144–167.

87   See comments by Giovanni Botero (1589) in C. Continisio (ed.), *La Ragion di Stato* (Rome: Donzelli, 1997), p. 171: 'Alessandro Farnese Duca di Parma rappresenta oggi al mondo un esempio così chiaro e vivo di perfetto condottiere d'eserciti [...] mannegiando sempre l'arme sotto un clementissimo e giustissimo Re, in servizio della Chiesa e di Dio, ha vino e domato, or con le maniere di Fabia, or con quelle di Marcello, la ribellione e l'eresia, superato le difficoltà de' siti e la natura de' luoghi, espugnato piazze inespugnabili, vinto popoli invincibili: e, per non dir d'altro, non è virtù di Capitano, non arte di milizia, non prodezza, non valore, ch'egli non abbia mostrato nell'assedio della incomparabile città di Anversa'.

88   On the importance of Piacenza: see D. Parrott, 'The Role of Fortifications in Early Modern Europe; the Farnese and the Security of the Duchies of Parma and Piacenza', in C. Mozzarelli (ed.), *I Farnese. Corte, guerra e nobiltà in antico regime* (Rome: Bulzoni, 1997), pp. 243–311.

To Campana, Alexander Farnese was 'the light and splendour of Italy and the whole Christian military'.[89] He characterised Farnese's decision to capture Antwerp as follows:

> It was an excellent idea to move all the troops to defeat the malicious humours of the rebels, as a place, that is without doubt the heart of this infected body, from which these corrupt spirits flew to other limbs that fed the obstinate persistence of this plague.[90]

This depiction of Antwerp as a hotbed of heresy was a recurrent image in Catholic discourse.[91] Campana's references to the obstinacy and ferocity of the inhabitants of Antwerp, a theme that had, as we have seen, become a commonplace in Italian accounts of the conflict, it only served to add further lustre to his achievement in recovering Antwerp, the jewel of the Netherlands.[92]

To obtain the necessary information for his history, Campana was in contact with crucial figures in the Parmesan court. He corresponded with Count Pomponio Torelli, an important nobleman in the Duchy of Parma, who was in charge of the negotiation for the restitution of Piacenza in 1585. Campana copied almost word for word the information he received from Torelli on the siege of Antwerp and the restitution of Piacenza.[93] Campana was equally in contact with Cosimo Masi, secretary of Alexander Farnese, who probably also supplied him with first-hand information.[94] Masi had an in-depth knowledge

---

89   Campana, *Assedio et racquisto*, p. 65: 'lume, e splendore, non pur d'Italia, ma di tutta la militia Christiana'.

90   Campana, *Assedio e Racquisto*, pp. 15–16: 'Era dunque ottimo consiglio, il voltar quivi tutte le forze, per opprimere i maligni humori de' ribelli, come luogo, ch'era senza dubbio il cuore di tutto quel corpo infetto, e donde scorrevano per gli altri membri quei corrotti spiriti, che nodrivano l'ostinata malvagità di cotal pestilenza.'

91   See especially Giovanni Botero's description in his *Relazioni Universale. Terza Parte* (Brecia: compagnia Bresciana, 1599), USTC 816588, p. 112: 'un campo di zizania, e di confusione, una schola di bestemmie, uno stecca di desperatione e di furore, una lerna d'errori: una Hidra d'Heresie'.

92   For this aspect of clemency see BA I 230 inf, fol 63–69v: *Lettera di Pomponio Casteno Auditor Generale dell'Infanteria Italiana ad Alessandro Farnese d. di Parma sopra la pietà verso dio, e clemenza che deve usarsi vinte*, on fol 66: 'Percio v. Alt sotto quel nome di Allessandro meritamento non sollo immita i detti ma supera Allessandro magno in pietà e misericordia'.

93   Gabriele Nori, 'Una biografie parallela di Alessandro Farnese: Pomponio Torelli e Cesare Campana', *Aurea Parma*, 62 (1978), pp. 34–35; Marzio Dall'Acqua, *Pomponio Torelli tra assolutismo e controriforma. Mostra documentaria e bibliografica* (Parma: Baroni e Villani, 1976), p. 16.

94   Arnaldo Barilli, 'Nuovi documenti su Alessandro Farnese', *Archivio storico per le province parmensi*, 15 (1938), pp. 91–92.

of these events and had access to many documents. After Alexander's death, he was in charge of organizing the transfer of Alexander's archive from the Low Countries to Parma.[95] Campana never mentioned these sources in his account, but he sometimes inserted phrases to reassure his reader of the veracity of his narrative.[96]

From the outset of Campana's account, the influence of both Torelli and Masi is noticeable. Campana wrote that the Duke of Alba 'imposed great iniquitous taxes on these people, levying them with so much rigour, that it caused new tumults and new wars'.[97] By this time, it had become commonplace in Italian discourse, and certainly in pro-Farnesian discourse, to blame the Duke of Alba for igniting the civil war with his taxation policy.[98] Campana repeated the difficulties faced by Alexander: his lack of money and soldiers and the slowness of deliberation in Spanish councils.[99] By stressing the obstacles Alexander encountered, Campana strengthened his prudence and valour. Farnese's ingeniousness was demonstrated by his building a pontoon bridge over the river Scheldt to prevent any rebel ships from supplying Antwerp. According to Campana, many members of the prince's war council doubted the success of such an undertaking. He commented that the bridge was superior to any bridge in antiquity and that no one in their time had dared to dream of such a marvellous achievement.[100]

This comparison with antiquity already occurred in news pamphlets and serves to highlight how news reports and histories became bound together as part of a single discourse. Classical examples were important at a time when many writers were discussing the superiority of antiquity over modern military practices.[101] Alexander's bridge over the Scheldt, however, was favourably compared to Julius Caesar's bridge over the Rhine. In 1594 the famous

95   G. Bertini, 'Cosimo Masi', in *DBI*, 71 (2008).

96   Campana, *Assedio et racquisto*, p. 49: 'mi hanno riferito persone, che n'hebbero buona certezza, essere stato tale'.

97   Campana, *Assedio et racquisto*, p. 5: 'ch'impose grossi balzelli à quelle genti, e riscosseli con tanto rigore, che se ne cagionarono nuovi tumulti, e nuove guerre'.

98   Exemplary for such a discourse is the manuscript account on the causes of the Revolt written around 1586 in BAV, Urb Lat 817, Pars II, fol 240–286: *Cause per le quale la Fiandra tumultuò et si ribellò al re Cattolico, con una breve descrittione di costumi, ricchezze, feste, qualità, sito et modo di governo di essi Paesi Bassi.*

99   Léon van der Essen, 'Correspondance de Cosimo Masi, secrétaire d'Alexander Farnèse, concernant le gouvernement de Mansfeld, de Fuentes et de l'Archiduc Ernest aux Pays-Bas, 1593–1594', *Bulletin de l'Institut historique Belge de Rome*, 27 (1952), pp. 357–390.

100   Campana, *Assedio et racquisto*, p. 23.

101   Orsi had already compared this bridge to Caesar's bridge over the Rhine-river and in funerary orations for Farnese similar comparisons were made: Sabbadini, 'L'uso della memoria. I Farnese', pp. 162–163.

FIGURE 4.1 'Ponte d'Alessandro Farnese duca di Parma sula Schelda' by Antonio Tempesta,
part of Francesco Patrizi, *Paralleli militari, ne'quali si fa paragone delle milizie
antiche* (Rome: Zannetti, 1594), USTC 847058, pp. 371–373. Rijksmuseum
Amsterdam, RP-P-OB-79.978

painter and engraver Antonio Tempesta made a drawing of Farnese's bridge for
Francesco Patrizi's work comparing ancient and modern military practices.[102]
Two years later, the famous humanist Justus Lipsius also included the bridge
in his *Poliorceticon*.[103] In a similar fashion, Campana compared the obstacles
Farnese encountered with those faced by the ancient military commanders.[104]

---

102   Eckhard Leuschner, *Antonio Tempesta. Ein Bahnbrecher des römischen Barock und seine
europäische Wirkung* (Petersberg: Michael Imhof, 2005), pp. 374–375.

103   On Lipsius' poliorceticon, see J. de Landtsheer, 'Justus Lipsius' *De militia romana*. Polybius
revived, or How an ancient historian was turned into a manual of early modern warfare',
in K. Enenkel, J.L. De Jong, J. de Landtsheer (eds.), *Recreating Ancient History: Episodes
from the Greek and Roman Past in the Arts and Literature of the Early Modern Period*
(Leiden: Brill, 2001), pp. 101–122.

104   Campana, *Assedio et racquisto*, p. 39: 'perche non si legge mai, ch'alcun di quegli antichi
tanto celebrati, si trovasse à guerreggiar contra popoli ferocissimi, armiggeri, ostinati à
difendere una imaginata libertà, & con persuasione, benche facilissima, di conservar'
insieme la propria religione; il qual non havendo forze di genti da difendersi, nonche
d'assaltare, non denari, non altre provisioni bastanti à tentar grandi imprese, con le proprie arme nemiche, con le proprie loro forze li vincesse'. This recalls one of Torelli's letters quoted in Lucia Denarosi, *L'accademia degli Innominati di Parma: teorie letterarie e
progetti di scrittura (1574–1608)* (Florence: Società Editrice Fiorentina, 2003), p. 176: 'Onde
pare a me che il Principe in ciò si possi preporre a molti generali antichi, perché essi

Campana's account shows how his reliance on information from Parmesan nobles helped to shape a distinctly pro-Farnesian narrative which would have a lasting impact. His history was used to compose two epic poems celebrating Alexander's victory in Antwerp: an unfinished manuscript *Anversa Liberata* (Antwerp Delivered) and Sanvitale's *Anversa Conquistata* (Antwerp Conquered) printed in Parma in 1609.[105] Since both poems, obviously, were inspired by Torquato Tasso's literary masterpieces *Gerusalemme Liberata* (Jerusalem Delivered) and *Gerusalemme Conquistata* (Jerusalem Conquered), these poems implicitly compared Farnese to Tasso's epic hero, Godfrey of Bouillon, who had conquered Jerusalem during the first crusade.[106]

Campana's account and the subsequent poems indicate that these various authors were conscious of the Farnese desire to commemorate this most illustrious member of the dynasty. The Farnese family still did not have a full account of Farnese's actions in the Low Countries and would continue to search for a suitable author. They understood that history was a powerful tool to craft a specific image during a period where they needed to reassert the credit of their house.

This chapter's analysis of historical accounts and their authors reveals how narratives were constructed soon after the events had taken place. The groups of writers discussed so far, with the exception of Rinaldi, had a common denominator: they did not have in-depth knowledge of the Low Countries. They had not (yet) travelled to the Netherlands, lived there or actively participated in the war. Therefore these history writers relied on earlier reports, copied other chronicles, and re-used already existing imagery. The chronicles illustrate a Catholic fervour that permeated large sections of Italian society. The Calvinist rebels were presented, together with the Ottomans, as the barbarous 'other'.

---

combatterono con nemici potenti, ma questo superò prima le difficoltà, et ci comprò col valore il potere et l'armi da vincere, non essendoli somministrate le privisioni in tempo'.

105   Fernando Salsano (ed.), *Anversa Liberata, tre canti inediti. De' Capelli di Sta Maria Maddalena, due odi inediti* (Bologna: Commissione per i testi di lingua, 1956). Salsano ascribed the poem to Marino, for a brief overview of the discussion on authorship, see Denarosi, *L'accademia degli Innominati di Parma*, pp. 165–166. Fortuniano Sanvitale, *Anversa Conquistata* (Parma: Viotto, 1609), USTC 4030232. For more on Sanvitale, see Fernando Salsano, 'Fortuniano Sanvitale', *Studi Secenteschi*, 5 (1964), pp. 69–72.

106   This parallel between Alexander Farnese and Godfrey of Bouillon was already present in the first edition of Tasso's *Gerusalemme liberata* in 1581 published in Parma by Viotti: see Denarosi, *L'accademia degli Innominati di Parma*, pp. 80–81, 240–254; Emma Grootveld and Nina Lamal, 'Impious heretics or simple Birds? Alexander Farnese and Dutch rebels in Post-Tassian Italian poems', *Quaderni d'Italianistica*, 35 (2014), pp. 63–97.

Instant historians took it upon themselves to arrange matters that were very often still in progress; this required a significant perceptiveness and a good deal of luck when it came to understand or guess longer-term consequences of the events that were being recounted. The example of Bizzarri's history and Ulloa's 're-elaborations' appeared at a time when many contemporaries indeed believed that the war was definitely over.[107] These accounts reflect the wishful thinking expressed in letters and *avvisi*, rather than offering a thorough analysis of past events that informed their understanding of what the near future may bring. While some scholars have dismissed these chronicles for their lack of organizing principle, they offered interpretations and added more commentary than the *avvisi*.

The first histories specifically dedicated to describing the revolt were clearly meant to glorify Italian military commanders in the case of Vitelli, and to cultivate Italian heroism and dedication to the Catholic cause. Both Bocchi and Campana show a certain fervour to foster the braveness of the actions of the Italian military commanders. Both authors were hoping to receive some kind of reward for their efforts. The case of Alexander Farnese demonstrates the function of historical texts within a specific political context. Alexander's status as a military hero was crafted by the Farnese family both during and after his lifetime for political and dynastic reasons.

---

107   See the remark made in Manolesso, *Historia nova*, p. 97: 'Questo fu il fine della presente guerre di Fiandra, la quale se bene nel principio riempi il mondo de gravissimo spavento, pure come il foco mancandoli il nutrimento tosto se estingue, cosi mancate le forze nel mezzo del suo corso s'amorzo, ne in se apportò alcun danno al Christianesmo'.

'Nothing more than a Flea': Debating and Describing New States (1598–1609)

It is a great wonder that a poor Hollander, who is nothing more than a flea next to the Monarch of Spain and the Indies, dared to besiege the city of Rheinberg.[1]

∴

The opening lines of this *avviso* of 28 September 1601 expressed the widespread amazement at the Dutch capture of Rheinberg, a strategic town on the Rhine, while at the same time a Dutch garrison was defending the coastal city of Ostend. How was it possible that the Dutch were able to challenge the most powerful monarch on the planet? This question both puzzled and captivated many contemporaries. In *Ragguagli di Parnaso* (news reports from Parnassus), printed in Venice between 1612 and 1613, the political satirist Traiano Boccalini described the dogged resistance of the Dutch Republic against the 'iron and the gold of the valorous and wealthy Spanish nation' as a miracle.[2] It is the beginning of the myth of 'the little Republic that could', which has since dominated historiography.[3]

In this tradition, scholars have focused almost exclusively on the emergence of this new republican state, its *de facto* recognition with the conclusion of the Twelve Years' Truce in 1609, and have ignored the arrival of a new ruling branch of the Habsburg dynasty in the Southern Netherlands. Strongly influenced by the paradigm of republicanism, Italian and Dutch scholars have privileged Guido Bentivoglio's *Relatione delle Province Unite di Fiandra* (Report on

---

1 ASF, MdP 4256, fol 99, *Copia d'avvisi venuti da Paesi bassi de 28 settembre 1601*: 'È maraviglia grande che un povero holandese che non è altro ch'una mosca paragonato con un Monarcha di Spagna et delle Indie habbia hauto ardimento di assediare la città di Berch'.

2 Traiano Boccalini, *Ragguagli di Parnaso. Centuria Seconda* (Venice: Farri, 1613), USTC 4029076, p. 16. On Boccalini see entry by L. Firpo in *DBI*, 11 (1969).

3 L. Cruz, 'The Epic Story of the Little Republic that could: The Role of Patriotic Myths in the Dutch Golden Age', in L. Cruz, W. Frijhoff (eds.), *Myth in History, History in Myth* (Leiden: Brill, 2009), pp. 159–173.

© KONINKLIJKE BRILL NV, LEIDEN, 2023 | DOI:10.1163/9789004538078_007

the United Provinces of the Low Countries) as the sole source to argue that
Italian commentators admired the Dutch Republic.[4] According to Mastellone,
the Seven United Provinces became an inspiring political model for Italian
states aiming for political independence from Habsburg Spain during the
seventeenth century.[5] It is time to move beyond this reductive republican
interpretation of this crucial moment in the reconfiguration of the complex
relationship between Italian states, the Netherlands and the Habsburg empire.
Italian rulers, intelligencers and diplomats were as interested in the dynastic
experiment in the southern Netherlands. In the last effort to appease the conflict, Philip II in 1598 decided to cede sovereignty of the Low Countries to his
daughter, Infanta Isabella Clara Eugenia, and her future husband Archduke
Albert of Austria.[6] News of the transfer of sovereignty and its potential to
establish a new ruling branch of the Austrian Habsburgs reignited the debate
about Spanish policy in the Low Countries.

This chapter traces these renewed discussions in Italian political circles for
or against appeasement as well as their reflections on the emergence of new
states between 1598 and 1610. It argues that the ability of the Dutch Republic
to resist the Habsburg monarchy for a sustained period was not simply celebrated as a Dutch success, instead, it created much more nuanced reflections
upon the Habsburg power, the nature of peace in Europe, economic realities
and geopolitical alliances. As Philip III and Lerma were trying to conclude
peace with their chief enemies in Europe, the situation on the Italian peninsula was increasingly less stable due to the growing anti-Spanish sentiments.[7]

---

4   Bentivoglio, *Relationi* (Antwerp: Meerbeeck, 1629), USTC 1001516. Fascimile edition by
    S. Mastellone and E.O.G. Haitsma Mulier (eds.), *Relatione delle Provincie Unite. Facsimile
    dell'edizione "Elzeviriana" Brusselles 1632* (Florence: Centro Editoriale Toscano, 1983). See
    Clerici, 'Ragion di Stato e politica internazionale', pp. 188–223; V.I. Comparato, 'From Crisis
    to Civil Culture to the Neapolitan Republic of 1647: Republicanism in Italy between the
    Sixteenth and Seventeenth Centuries', in M. Van Gelder, Q. Skinner (eds.), *Republicanism
    and Constitutionalism in Early Modern Europe* (Cambridge: Cambridge University Press,
    2002), pp. 169–194 and Cees Reijner, 'Gesprekken in Genua over het Twaalfjarig Bestand', *De
    Zeventiende Eeuw*, 30 (2014), pp. 76–96.
5   Salvo Mastellone, 'Holland as a Political Model in Italy in the Seventeenth Century', *Bijdragen
    en Mededelingen betreffende de Geschiedenis der Nederlanden*, 98 (1983), pp. 568–582 and
    Salvo Mastellone, 'I Republicani del Seicento ed il Modello Politico Olandese', *Il Pensiero
    Politico*, 18 (1985), pp. 145–163.
6   Luc Duerloo, *Dynasty and Piety. Archduke Albert (1598–1621) and Habsburg Political Culture in
    an Age of Religious Wars* (Burlington: Ashgate, 2012), pp. 36–57.
7   Bernardo García García, *La Pax Hispánica: política exterior del Duque de Lerma* (Leuven:
    Leuven University Press, 1996), pp. 22–30 and Paul C. Allen, *Philip III and the Pax Hispanica,
    1598–1621. The Failure of a Grand Strategy* (London/New Haven: Yale, 2000).

According to one anonymous political observer, the question of whether peace would be beneficial to the Habsburg empire agitated many in Italy.[8] One of the guiding principles of Spanish policy, based on Botero's and Lipsius's ideas, was the importance of maintaining reputation.[9] As we have seen, whereas most Italian political commentators in 1577 had refrained from questioning the Habsburg king's reputation and resources, this certainly changed by 1600. In political tracts and memorials, Italian political intelligencers and theorists reflected if and how it would be possible for the king to conclude a peace or a truce with the Dutch without losing his reputation.

In their diagnosis, the different authors referred to the classical past pointed to the experiences of this long war and developed the ferocious nature of the inhabitants to reflect on the right course of action. Their reflections reveal a change in the perception of the inhabitants of the Low Countries, which had begun in 1577, and offer evidence that more than republican ideals played a role in these debates. The discussions reveal the centrality of the Low Countries in Italian thinking about the preservation of the different realms of the composite Habsburg empire and its dominion over the rest of Europe, while at the same time recognising the economic opportunities lying ahead. In chronologically outlining the debates and key arguments, from the Act of Cession in 1598 to the arrival of the first Venetian diplomat in the Dutch Republic in 1610, the variety of reasons for Italian engagement with the long war in the Low Countries will become clear.

1 Debating the Dynastic Solution

In the final decade of Philip II's reign, the almost permanent state of war in the Low Countries, with little significant territorial gains, was a continuous burden on the crown's treasury and threatened the preservation of the composite monarchy. The need to find a peaceful resolution to the conflict was urgent and several important political thinkers in the Habsburg empire, including the Dominican friar and philosopher Tommaso Campanella, weighed in

---

8 BV, N22, fol 59–65: *Se la Pace di Fiandra sia riuscibile, se sia utile al Re Cattolico, se riuscendo pur debba da S.M. licentiarsi gli esercito, e sio segua la pace o non possa la Maesta far impresa contra il Turco e dove.*

9 John H. Elliott, *Spain and Its World 1500–1700: Selected Essays* (New Haven/London: Yale University Press, 1989), pp. 162–188 and also see: F. Pommier Vincelli, 'Il concetto di reputazione e i giudizi sulla monarchia spagnola', in L. Lotti, R. Villari (eds.), *Filippo II e il Mediterraneo* (Rome: Laterza, 2003), pp. 289–324.

on this discussion.[10] In his treatise *Discorso sui paesi bassi*, written between 1593 and 1594, Campanella revived the old solution that a member of the Habsburg family would be able to restore the ancient, natural obedience that the Netherlandish inhabitants once had towards a just prince.[11] He considered it a necessary step, as the new ruler might then be able to negotiate a truce with the Dutch. At this stage in his life, Campanella was still a proponent of a Habsburg providential universal monarchy: reconquering the Low Countries was crucial for the conservation of the empire and its dominion over the rest of Europe.

In 1598, Philip II opted for a dynastic solution by agreeing to the marriage of his daughter Isabella to the archduke Albert of Austria, governor-general of the Low Countries.[12] The Act of Cession, reprinted in numerous Italian cities, presented the decision as 'the true way forward to reach a good and honest peace to liberate the country from the long and bloody wars that have been going on for a long time'.[13] Various Italian political writers started to speculate as to why Philip II had taken this decision, and indeed whether it was a good one. One of

---

10   L. Firpo, 'Tommaso Campanella', in *DBI*, 17 (1974) and L. Firpo (ed.), *Discorsi ai principi d'Italia ed altri scritti filo-ispanici* (Turin: Chiantore, 1945), pp. 28–29.

11   Manuscript copies in BAV, Barb Lat 5242, fol 109–118: *Discorso circa il modo, col quale i Paesi Bassi, volgarmente dette i Fiandre, si possino ridurre sotto l'obedienza del Re Cattolico*; and in Biblioteca Corsiana e Lincei 469, fol 145–161. In 1600 the text was incorporated in his important political tract *Monarchia di Spagna*, for more see J-L. Fournel, 'La pensée politique de Campanella', in M. Blanco-Morel, M-F. Piéjus (eds.), *Les Flandres et la culture espagnole et italienne aux XVIᵉ et XVIIᵉ siècles* (Lille: Travaux et Recherche, 1998), pp. 124–128. See also V. Frajese, 'Campanella e la monarchia di Spagna', in *Filippo e il Mediterraneo*, pp. 357–386.

12   Isabel and her future husband Archduke Albert of Austria were not given full sovereign powers, even though their authority was reasonably extensive. The Habsburg crown continued to control military and foreign affairs of the Southern Netherlands. If the couple did not have any legitimate heirs, the Low Countries would revert to Spain. See: W. Thomas, 'Andromeda Unbound, the Reign of Albert and Isabella in the Southern Netherlands, 1598–1621', in W. Thomas, L. Duerloo (eds.), *Albrecht en Isabella 1598–1621: Essays* (Turnhout: Brepols, 1998), pp. 2–3; B. de Ridder, V. Soen, 'The Act of Cession, the 1598 and 1600 States General in Brussels and the Peace Negotiations during the Dutch Revolt', in R. Lesaffer (ed.), *The Twelve Years Truce (1609). Peace, Truce, War and Law in the Low Countries at the Turn of the 17th Century* (Leiden/Boston: Brill, Nijhoff, 2014), pp. 48–68.

13   *Dichiaratione et nota dei capitoli publicati nella Congregatione de' stati de Brabanti* (Rome: Bonfadino, 1598), USTC 812790, A1: 'esser il vero camino per pervenire ad una buona, & fedel Pace, e liberarsi da una dura e sanguinosa guerra dalla quale sono stati travagliati per un longo spatio d'anni'. Other editions in Bologna, (USTC 764288); Ferrara (USTC 812789); Cremona (USTC 812792), and under a different title: *Copia dell'assegnatione fatta dal re cattolico, per dote della serenissima infanta Isabella, Clara, Eugenia sua figliola maritata al serenissimo Alberto arciduca d'austria. Delli stati di Brabantia, & Paesi Bassi. Con*

them was Francesco Maria Vialardi, just like Scipio di Castro, another obscure and fascinating character. Originally from Vercelli, this humanist and intelligencer started his career in the service of Savoy and archduke Ernst of Austria, and moved a fair bit between different Italian courts and academies, before he was active in Rome at the end of the sixteenth century.[14] Vialardi held firmly pro-French sentiments and ran into trouble for his views: he was condemned to six years in prison by the Holy Office in 1592. Using various pseudonyms, he supplied a range of princely rulers with weekly political newsletters including Gonzaga, Medici, Della Rovere and d'Este. He was known and praised for his ability to inform and offer shrewd political analysis.[15]

He probably wrote the treatise *Discorso della cessione dei Paesi Bassi fatta da Filippo re di Spagna a Isabella Clara Eugenia sua figliola del 1598* (Discourse on the cession of the Low Countries by Philip, king of Spain, to his daughter Isabel Clara Eugenia in 1598) at the behest of the ambitious Ferdinand de' Medici, Grand Duke of Tuscany.[16] His treatise was quickly copied as the different surviving copies in Italian archives and libraries attest.[17] In the eyes of several Italian ruling dynasties, such as the Medici and Savoy, this transfer of power and territory represented an interesting case. These ducal families had royal ambitions of their own, and even considered the Act of Cession as an important precedent.[18] Charles Emanuel I, Duke of Savoy, for instance, had married the Spanish infanta Caterina in 1585, with the hope of acquiring a

---

le conditioni di essa, & altre dichiaratione dignissime da doversi sapere (Vicenza: Greco, 1599), USTC 812791.

14   Luigi Firpo, 'In margine al processo di Giordano Bruno. Francesco Maria Vialardi', *Rivista Storica Italiana*, 68 (1956), pp. 325–364; Tomaso Vialardi di Sandigliano, 'Un cortigiano e letterato piemontese del cinquecento: Francesco Maria Vialardi', *Studi Piemontesi*, 34 (2005), pp. 299–312; for the latest overview see entry by L. Vaccaro in *DBI*, 99 (2020).

15   See the comment by his learned friend Angelo Grillo: 'sa trovar gli uomini fuor del mappamondo e spia quel che si fa nel globo della luna', in his *Delle lettere* (Venice: Ciotti, 1604), USTC 4036040, p. 549.

16   Vialardi to Ferdinand I from Rome on 22 October 1597, in ASF, MdP 3623, fol 36r: 'Dicasi quello si vuole di questa investitura di Fiandra, io non la credo: che conosco gl'artifici spagnuoli, e però non voglio fare un discorso, e una fatica inutile: ma se sarà vera, che il tutto può essere i' vo ben farlo come va'. For Ferdinand's relationship with Spain consult Paola Volpini, *Los Medici y España: príncipes, embajadores y agentes en la Edad Moderna* (Madrid: silex, 2017).

17   His treatise in VA, R55, fol 74–80: *Discorso della cessione dei Paesi Bassi fatta da Filippo re di Spagna a Isabella Clara Eugenia sua figliola del 1598*; ASTo, Corte Esterni, Spagna, 4, nr 6: *Discorso di Francesco Maria Vialardo della cessione dei Paesi Bassi fatta da Filippo II Re di Spagna, ad Isabella Clara Eugenia sua figliuola l'anno 1598*. Other copies in BNCF, Cod G. Capponi 58 and in Biblioteca Angelica Rome, 1792, fol 200–220.

18   Spagnoletti, *Le dinastie italiane*, pp. 41–44.

significant part of the Habsburg empire, such as Milan or Portugal.[19] In 1603, at a time when Philip III had no heir to the throne, he sent his two sons to Madrid, accompanied by ex-Jesuit and political thinker Giovanni Botero, to present them as possible candidates for the throne.[20] The Act of Cession, at least according to the Savoyard interpretation, made it possible for Charles Emanuel's sons to inherit the Low Countries if the Archdukes should die without a legitimate heir.[21]

Vialardi's *Discorso* presented useful arguments to princes such as Ferdinand I and Charles Emanuel I to make their cases. He provided many historical examples of how states can be acquired and by enumerating these cases, he presented a legitimate basis for ceding territory. He relied on historical precedents to unravel structures, understand the world and learn political lessons. His treatise, at the same time, stands out for the very realistic and vivid analysis of the situation by stressing the devastation in the Netherlands and the enormous drain of Spanish resources in this war.

> the Low Countries can be called a colony of death: after an intolerable amount of gold spent during more than thirty years of continuous warfare, after the destruction of more than a thousand places, and after the loss of more than a hundred men of rank, more than fifty thousand soldiers, and an incredible number of horses, the result is the loss of Holland, Zeeland, Friesland, Utrecht, Zutphen, Guelders, and the island of Vlissingen, [...] and the transfer of the much praised trade from Antwerp to Amsterdam.[22]

---

19   For Savoy's quest for a royal title consult R. Oresko, 'The House of Savoy in search for a Royal crown in the seventeenth century', in R. Oresko, G.C. Gibbs, H.M. Scott (eds.), *Royal and Republican Sovereignity in Early Modern Europe: Essays in Memory of Ragnhild Hatton* (Cambridge: Cambridge University Press, 1997), pp. 272–350.

20   Vittorio Ansaldi, 'Giovanni Botero coi principi sabaudi in Spagna', *Bollettino storico-bibliografico Subalpino*, 25 (1933), pp. 322–328.

21   The documents written and collected to prove this claim in ASTo, Corte Esterni, Spagna, 4: Scritture riguardanti il dritto del duca di Savoia sopra la Fiandra per la successione all'Infanta Isabella Chiara Eugenia.

22   VA, R55, fol 76v: 'che i paesi bassi si possono chiamare colonia della Morti, doppo una intollerabil somma d'ora, spesa doppo trenta e più anni di continua guerra, e la ruina di più di mille luoghi, e doppo la perdita di più di cento huomini signalati, e più de 50 m di soldati, et un numero incredibile di cavalli, il frutto che se n' e cavato, et il guadagno, che sen' e fatto, e che si sono alienati Olanda, Zelanda, Frisia, Utrecht, Zucfu (sic.), parte di Gheldria, l'isola Flesinghen, [...], et se e levato il celebratissimo traffico a Anversa e ridotto a Amsterdam'.

This war had been a bottomless pit, or a black hole in which men and money, as well as horses just disappeared, without any significant gain. Despite all this effort, Philip II had lost seven provinces and trade had moved to Amsterdam. He added that Philip II could no longer continue the war without risking the loss of control in Italy or sustaining damage to Spanish commercial interests in the Indies. The enormous cost of the war for the Spanish empire would become, as we shall see, a recurrent theme in both pro- and anti-Spanish discourse in Italy during the early seventeenth century.

Vialardi concluded that Philip II had made the right decision in ceding these lands to Isabel and in marrying her to Albert. In his eyes, Albert, a religious man, who also had an admirable military record, was the best available candidate. His recent military victories against France between 1596 and 1597 even had forced Henry IV to make peace with Spain in 1598 at Vervins.[23] The Act of Cession, according to Vialardi, was the best way to reach universal peace in Europe. With this assessment, Vialardi moved away from the idea of a universal monarchy, which was very prominent in Campanella's reasoning, and promulgated the idea of a balance of power which would be able to maintain peace and stability.

Not everybody agreed with Vialardi's assessment. One of his opponents was Girolamo Frachetta, author of various printed works on reason of state, who was also active as an intelligencer and political commentator in Rome in the service of the Spanish ambassador.[24] Frachetta saw Philip II as a pious warrior, who had to continue his battle against heresy.[25] In his treatise discussing the Act of Cession, Frachetta argued it damaged the king's reputation to alienate the Netherlandish provinces, especially since so much effort had been put into winning this war. He was extremely worried about the intentions of France, so he argued the king needed to have control over the Netherlands as it was an active school for military discipline and it would allow him to pre-empt any French attack on Spain or Italy.[26] As large sums of money would be needed to preserve the state and defend it on two fronts, Frachetta expressed his worries

---

23   For printed news on the Italian peninsula on these victories consult the bibliography for the relevant years.

24   E. Baldini, 'Girolamo Frachetta informatore politico al servizio della Spagna', in C. Continisio, C. Mozzarelli, (eds.), *Repubblica e virtù: Pensiero politico e monarchia Cattolica fra XVI e XVII secolo* (Rome: Bulzoni, 1995), pp. 465–482.

25   Vincelli, 'Il concetto di reputazione', pp. 293–295.

26   ASF, CS I, fol 261–266v: *Se il Re Cattholico habbia ben fatto a dare i Paesi Bassi et la Borgogna in dote alla Serenissima Infanta Donna Isabella di Girolamo Frachetta* and BAV, Urb Lat 859, fol 433–439v.

over Albert's capabilities to pacify the Low Countries considering his recent failure to keep control of the city of Amiens.[27]

A year later, Minuccio Minucci, Bishop of Zadar and papal expert in German affairs, pursued this sceptical line about Albert, in a treatise written for Pietro Aldobrandini, the papal secretary of state.[28] After having served multiple years as a papal diplomat in the German lands and as an agent for Duke of Bavaria at the Spanish court, he was considered extremely knowledgeable in matters of state. He warned Aldobrandini that the Dutch Republic would not be impressed by Albert given how advantageous the war has been especially for the provinces of Holland and Zeeland, which was most clearly visible when looking at Amsterdam, which he described as a prosperous city, full of people, with great wealth and beautiful buildings.[29] Minucci elaborated on the scope of the Dutch trade network: the rebel provinces conducted business with Danzig, Lubeck, Hamburg, and other Baltic ports, and became rich by importing spices and other precious goods from the Indies.[30] In his treatise, Minucci recalled that a merchant from Amsterdam had told him that these two provinces, and particularly the city of Amsterdam, would always choose to wage war against the Habsburg empire, rather than conclude a peace deal. In short, the Dutch Republic was capable of continuing the war effort thanks to its flourishing trade.

The enormous cost of the war for Spanish crown was used by proponents and opponents of Philip's decision to argue their case. Frachetta and Minucci, both more pro-Spanish oriented commentators, were realistic in their assessment of the difficulties laying ahead of the archducal couple. Frachetta, for

---

27   Frachetta continued to write treatises on the conflict in the following years, see for example several texts in Urb Lat 821, fol 404r–406v: *Discorso del modo di guerreggiare contro i ribelli de Paesi Bassi, scritto a dì 22 novembre 1605*.

28   The text was published anonymously as 'Discorso intorno la Guerra di Fiandra' in *Tesoro Politico* (Vicenza: Ventura, 1605), USTC 4034267, pp. 320–331. The exact same version in manuscript in the Vatican Library reveals the identity of its author: BAV, Urb Lat 857, fol 335–338: *Lettera o discorso di mons. Minutio Munitii, arcivescovo di Zara, sopra quello che potesse partorire l'investitura della Fiandra nell' Infante di Spagna*. For a biography see A. Kohler, 'Minucci', in *DBI*, 74 (2010). In 1584 he had already written *Parare sopra le cose di Fiandra*, which he had presented to Philip II in *I codici Minucciani*, p. 152, 154.

29   *Discorso intorno la Guerra di Fiandra*, p. 322: 'sono accresciute mirabilmente d'edificij di popolo di splendore, e di potenza, & gli habitanti sono riempiti di ricchezze'.

30   Amsterdam had become one of the main trading ports importing grain from the Baltic: Milja van Tielhof, *The 'Mother of All Trades': The Baltic Grain Trade in Amsterdam from the Late Sixteenth to the Early Nineteenth Century* (Leiden: Brill, 2002) and Maartje van Gelder, 'Supplying the *Serenissima*. The role of Flemish merchants in the Venetian grain trade during the first phase of the Straatvaart', *International Journal of Maritime History*, 16 (2004), pp. 39–60.

instance, was not convinced that the Dutch were altogether tired of waging
war, he predicted that prince Maurice will have little effort to convince them to
continue fighting in defence of their liberty. Minucci offered a realistic understanding of the growing economic importance of the United Provinces, and
of the potential stumbling blocks in the upcoming peace negotiations in 1608.

2   The Issue of Free Trade

After several attempts at brokering peace by the archducal couple, the Dutch
Republic, the archducal Netherlands and Spanish monarchy agreed to a temporary armistice in 1607 for eight months.[31] In 1608, a large international peace
conference was organized in The Hague, where those parties, and several other
foreign ambassadors, met to discuss the terms of a peace treaty. Gio Gaulberto
Paoli, the agent of Francesco Colonna in Brussels, commented: 'this long war,
and now the peace negotiations keep the whole of Europe in suspense'.[32] It
was an important moment for the war-torn Low Countries, and crucial for
maintaining peace in the rest of Europe. Bentivoglio, the newly arrived papal
representative in Brussels, was therefore instructed to advocate a peaceful
solution, safeguard the Catholic religion, and crucially keep a close eye on the
relationship between France and the Dutch Republic, as the papacy wanted to
guarantee the recently concluded peace between France and Spain.[33]

Trade interests were another reason why Italian statesmen and observers
were paying close attention to the peace negotiations. Since 1590 large parts
of the Italian peninsula, and especially the Northern regions, were hit by bad
weather, causing crop failure and famine. These Italian states, amongst others
Tuscany and Venice, tried to obtain more steady grain supplies from the Baltic
area and due to the importance of Amsterdam as a grain trade centre, they had
turned towards establishing contact with the Dutch Republic. Ferdinand I de'
Medici had designated Livorno to be a free port and a trading city to attract,
amongst others, Dutch merchants. Already during the peace negotiations, in

---

31   Willem J.M. Eysinga, *De wording van het Twaalfjarig Bestand van 9 april 1609* (Amsterdam:
     Noord-Hollandsche Uitgevers Maatschappij, 1959) and Simon Groenveld, *Het Twaalfjarig
     Bestand 1609–1621. De Jongelingsjaren van de Republiek der Verenigde Nederlanden* (The
     Hague: Haags Historisch Museum, 2009).
32   Letter from Brussels on 5 January 1608 in ASF, Urbino I, 199, fol 595r: 'La lunga guerra che
     qui è stata, et la negotiatione che hora si fa di pace tiene sospesa tutta Europa'.
33   Belvederi, *Guido Bentivoglio e la politica europea*, pp. 49–60. For the instruction see
     S. Giordano (ed.), *Le istruzioni generali di Paolo V ai diplomatici pontifici 1605–1621*
     (Tübingen: Max Niemeyer, 2003) I, pp. 496–506.

summer 1608, Vincenzo I Gonzaga, Duke of Mantua and Monferrato travelled
to Amsterdam (with the permission of Philip III) to meet with some Protestant
Lucchese merchants, such as Giovanni Calandrini, to discuss shipments of rice
and grain to Mantua.[34] Peace between the Dutch and Habsburg monarchy
would create economic opportunities and make trade with the Dutch a less
complicated matter for Italian states.

The Dutch insistence on free trade and navigation with the Indies during
the peace negotiations was of particular interest to Italian merchants and rulers. In a few Dutch pamphlets the Republic's right to navigate the seas and
trade with the Indies was fiercely defended.[35] Several Italian agents and correspondents in Brussels tried to get hold of these pamphlets and had them
translated into Italian.[36] One pamphlet in particular was dispatched by most
Italian correspondents: *Memorie vande gewichtige redenen die de Heeren Staten
genereal behoren te bewegen om gheenszins te wijcken vande handelinghe ende
vaert van Indien* (Memorandum of the important reasons that should induce
the States General not to withdraw trade and navigation from the Indies).[37]

---

34   F. Luzzati Laganà, 'Giovanni Calandrini', *DBI*, 16 (1973). In the years after the truce,
      Calandrini shipped rice and cereals to Venice, goods which were ultimately destined for
      Mantua, his letters from 1608 and 1609 in ASMn, AG 575, fol 921–927. See also: Antonella
      Bicci, 'Italiani ad Amsterdam nel Seicento', *Rivista Storica Italiana*, 102 (1990), pp. 907–914;
      Ole Peter Grell, *Brethren in Christ: A Calvinist Network in Reformation Europe* (Cambridge:
      Cambridge University Press, 2011), pp. 19–64.

35   Craig Harline, *Pamphlets, Printing and Political Culture in the Early Dutch Republic*
      (Dordrecht: Martinus Nijhoff, 1987), p. 8; Nina Lamal, *'Beter een oprechten crijgh dan een
      geveynsden peys'. Pamfletten en publieke opinie in de aanloop naar het Twaalfjarig Bestand
      (1607–1609)* (Unpublished MA thesis, KU Leuven, 2010).

36   Letter by Paoli from Brussels 12 April 1608 in ASF, Urbino I, 199, fol 598r: 'L'esser questa
      scrittura stata fatta in lingua fiaminga è capitata qua in settimana santa, non potetti farla
      tradurre et inviarla l'ordinario passato à V. Alt. Ser.ma è parto di gran maestro contiene
      la sostantia di questo accordo et da questa depende la conservatione de gli stati'. Letter
      by Aurelio Alciati from Brussels on 19 April 1608 to Virginio II Orsini in ASC, Archivio
      Orsini, I, 118, fol 513r: 'Mando a VE qui allegata una scrittura fata e stampata in Olanda
      circa l'articolo delle navigationi dell'Indie, che fra i punti più importanti e'l principale, Io
      l'ho dopo ch'estata tradotta dalla lingua fiammengha nell'Italiana accomodata in molti
      luoghi, e riduttala a maggior chiarezza'.

37   *Memorie vande gewichtige redenen die de Heeren Staten genereal behoren te bewegen
      om gheenszins te wijcken vande handelinghe ende vaert van Indien* (s.l.: s.n., 1608), USTC
      1033257, 1033258, 1033259, 1014428, and two translations into French (USTC 6026038;
      6803742). The papal nuncio Guido Bentivoglio translated and sent it to Rome (Clerici,
      'Ragion di Stato e politica internazionale', pp. 202, 220). For manuscript copies see ASF,
      MdP 4259, fasc 4, fol 71–72v: *Ragioni più importanti che dovrebbe indurre i stati generali a
      non cedere la navigatione e traffico dell'indie* (an incomplete translation of the *Memorie*
      pamphlet); fol 73–76: *Breve compendio delle ragioni più importanti, perle quali gli stati gen-
      erali delle Provincie Unite non debbon acconsentire in alcuna maniera nel presente trattato*

All these different agents, ranging from soldiers to the papal nuncio, seemed to recognize the importance of *Memorie* pamphlet: it was an attack upon the supposed rights of the Habsburg monarchy to trade exclusively with the overseas territories based on international law. Martine van Ittersum has suggested the anonymous writer of this pamphlet knew Hugo Grotius' memorandum on the issue for the Dutch East India Company (VOC) in 1607.[38] In this influential text, the humanist and jurist Grotius had made a strong case for freedom of trade and navigation.[39] The members of the VOC wanted to safeguard the trade with the Indies and therefore probably sponsored pamphlets which directly defended the United Provinces' right to this trade.[40] This can explain why Grotius' conception of free trade based on natural law was propagated by the *Memorie*. So before the publication of Grotius's treatise in 1609, Italian rulers were already well aware of his arguments.

Ferdinand had been very active to find different ways to get involved in overseas trade from Livorno.[41] Spain and Portugal, however, held the monopoly and kept to their monopolistic policies. The Medici were well informed about the overseas activities of the Dutch: they had received numerous reports from a variety of agents about the establishment of the VOC in 1602 as well as detailed information about their operations.[42] From several memoranda in the Medici archive, it seems Ferdinand in 1608 entertained the possibility he would be able to participate in the trade with the Indies through the VOC. The *Memorie* pamphlet played a crucial part in spreading these ideas on the Italian peninsula

---

di pace di cedere, e lasciare la navigatione et il traffico dell'Indie. Stampata in Olanda tradotto della lingua fiammenga, nell'italiana, e ridotto à maggior chiarezza et in miglior forma. Another copy in the Biblioteca Moreniani in Florence and in BAV, Urb Lat 861, fol-155v, with a summary of the main arguments on fol 157–159; two more copies in VA, N22, fol 122–125, 130–137.

38   Grotius only published this text as *Mare Liberum* (Free Sea) after the conclusion of the Truce in April 1609 (USTC 1028212), see Martine Van Ittersum, *Profit and Principle: Hugo Grotius, Natural Rights Theories and the Rise of Dutch Power in the East Indies (1595–1615)* (Leiden: Brill, 2006), pp. 284, 302–310.

39   Van Ittersum, *Profit and Principle*, p. 233.

40   Van Ittersum, *Profit and Principle*, pp. 283–284; 289–295.

41   For these initiatives: Brian Brege, *Tuscany in the Age of Empire* (Cambridge Mass: Harvard University Press, 2021).

42   The Medici-agent Jan van der Neesen, originally from the Southern Netherlands, sent detailed information on the VOC to Florence: ASF, MdP 4259, fol 9: *Raguaglio nel modo gl'olandesi negoziano nell'America*, ASF, MdP 4256, fol 116; 163. See also Marie-Christine Engels, *Merchants, Interlopers, Seamen and Corsairs. The Flemish community in Livorno and Genoa (1615–1635)* (Hilversum: Verloren, 1997) and Brege, *Tuscany in the Age of Empire*, pp. 88–106.

and was of importance to other European and Italian states, such as the Grand
Duchy of Tuscany, and the Genoese state.[43]

3   The Roman Past: Untameable Subjects

In the unfolding Italian debates on war and peace from 1607 to 1609, the image
of the people of the Low Countries continued to play an important role. In
1577 several political commentators had first used the nature of the inhabitants of the Low Countries as an argument to advocate a peaceful solution to
the conflict. The image of the warlike people in the Low Countries, who might
be difficult to conquer, began to develop. Two decades later, partly owing to a
resurgent interest in Tacitus, this image of ferocious fighters had only gained
more traction, although it now tended to be applied exclusively to the inhabitants of the Seven United Provinces in the north. Several treatises argued that
it was better for the king to conclude a peace deal by presenting the Dutch as
wild and indomitable creatures.[44] One anonymous author's starting point was
that 'the Dutch were the most rebellious of all the other rebels' as they had
been seditious since Roman times.[45]

Based on Tacitus, the idea that the Batavians were direct ancestors of the
Hollanders had gained ground in humanist circles.[46] Tommaso Contarini, the
first Venetian diplomat in the Dutch Republic, mentioned the importance of
the Batavian Revolt to the Dutch, in his report to the Venetian senators upon
his return in 1610:

---

43   Later, the Genoese launched numerous initiatives to establish their own company, mod-
      elled on the Dutch example of the VOC: E.O.G. Haitsma Mulier, 'Genova e l'Olanda nel
      Seicento: contatti mercantili e ispirazione politica', in R. Belvederi (ed.), *Atti del Congresso
      internazionale di studi Rapporti Genova-Mediterraneo-Atlantico nell'età moderna* (Genoa:
      Istituto di scienze storiche, 1983), pp. 431–444.

44   BV, N22, fol 59–65: *Se la Pace di Fiandra sia riuscibile, se sia utile al Re Cattolico, se riuscendo
      pur debba da S.M. licentiarsi gli esercito, e sio segua la pace o non possa la Maesta far
      impresa contra il Turco e dove.*

45   BV, N22, fol 59v–60r: 'gl'olandesi in parte furono i più ribelli di tutti gli altri, ribelli come
      coloro che fino al tempo delli antichi Rom. Eccitarono sempre seditiosi e riccolto contra
      il lor Principe'.

46   In the Vatican archives a sixteenth-century manuscript on the history of Holland up
      until Charles V's reign is still extant, Miscell. II, vol 76: *De Hollandia seu Hotlandia, quon-
      dam Batavia appellata.* For the ideas in humanist circles in Holland see Karen Tilmans,
      *Aurelius en de Divisiekroniek van 1517. Historiografie en humanisme in Holland in de tijd
      van Erasmus* (Hilversum: Verloren, 1988) and Sandra Langereis, *Geschiedenis als Ambacht.
      Oudheidkunde in de Gouden Eeuw: Arnoldus Buchelius en Petrus Scriverius* (Hilversum:
      Verloren, 2001).

[the Dutch] affirm they have been part of this nation since the time of Gaius Caesar, they boast that they have never been subjects, but rather allies and friends of the Roman Empire, and that in the course of one thousand seven hundred years, they have maintained this Republican state form, which has been left largely unchanged.[47]

Contarini saw that the Dutch used the Batavian Revolt against the Romans under Claudius Civilis (68–70 AD) to justify their revolt and to defend the organization of their government and state. With Hugo Grotius's 1610 treatise on the antiquity of the Batavian Republic, the 'Batavian myth' became instrumental in Dutch political culture.[48] The Batavians had cherished and defended their freedom, and the States General was presented by Grotius as the guardians of this ancient freedom.[49]

In contrast to Grotius, most Italian treatises interpreted the Batavian past to demonstrate the ferocious, but above all perfidious nature of the Dutch. At the same time, they also used it to legitimate a peaceful solution. If the powerful Roman army had not been able to conquer these people, they concluded, the king could honourably make peace with them. The treatise entitled *Discorso o parere con il quale si mostra, che complischi al re di Spagna di lasciare i Paesi Bassi in loro libertà* (Discourse or opinion in which it is demonstrated that the Spanish king should leave the Low Countries in their freedom) serves as a good example to understand this line of reasoning.[50] The anonymous author stated that the Habsburg empire was without a doubt far greater than the Roman

---

47   P.-J. Blok (ed.), *Relazioni Veneziane. Venetiaansche Berichten over de Verenigde Nederlanden* (The Hague: Martinus Nijhoff, 1909), p. 29: 'Affermano essere stata propria di quella natione sino a tempi di Caio Cesare, gloriandosi di non essere mai stati sudditi, ma si bene confederati et amici dell' Imperio Romano, et per il corso di mille settecent' anni essersi mantenuta la forma della loro Republica poco disimile dal governo presente'.

48   I. Schöffer, 'The Batavian Myth during the Sixteenth and Seventeenth Centuries', in E.H. Kossmann, J.S. Bromley (eds.), *Britain and the Netherlands. Volume 5: Some Political Mythologies* (The Hague: Martinus Nijhoff, 1975), pp. 78–101 and Eco Haitsma Mulier, 'De Bataafse mythe opnieuw bekeken', *Bijdragen en Mededelingen betreffende de Geschiedenis der Nederlanden*, 111 (1996), pp. 344–367.

49   J. Blanc, 'Hugo Grotius, Historiographe des Bataves au XVIIe siècle', in C. Grell (ed.), *Les Historiographes en Europe de la fin du Moyen Âge à la Révolution* (Paris: Presses de l'université Paris-Sorbonne, 2006), pp. 297–311 and N. de Brézé, 'L'histoire des Bataves et des Romains dans la peinture des Pays-Bas aux XVII et XVIIe siècles', in V. Soen, Y. Junot (eds.), *Les Identités aux pluriel. Jeux et enjeux des appartenances autour des anciens Pays-Bas* (Lille: Revue du Nord, 2014), pp. 95–112.

50   I have found three copies of this discourse in different Roman libraries: BAV, Urb lat 860, fol 296–298v: *Discorso o parare, con il quale si mostra, che complischi al re di Spagna di lasciare i Paesi Bassi in loro libertà*; BV, N22; fol 102–105: *Discorso sopra la tregua di Fiandra,*

empire had ever been, but that the time had now come to preserve this empire instead of seeking to enlarge it.[51] The Romans had not tried to keep hold of the most remote regions of their empire, so the king should no longer try to incorporate those northern parts of the Low Countries which objected to his rule. Moreover, it was better not to keep these lands, because the king knew very well that its inhabitants had an untameable and even barbarous nature. It is an image which is far removed from an admiration of the Dutch republican ideals and state.

While various Italian authors used the comparison between the Roman past and the Habsburg present in this manner to argue that the Habsburg king was not weak in offering peace; others employed it as a specious pretext for a harsher analysis. The *Discorso o parere*, for example, forcefully stated the reasons for peace.

> Spain has been sucked dry by the Flemish leeches, [...] and finally Spain has been used almost as a gateway, through which all the treasures of Peru and Mexico have been shipped into those states, so that the whole of Spain is left without money or men.[52]

The unflattering image of the Low Countries as bloodsucking leeches here emphasises the point that this long war had completely drained Spanish resources and finances. This more realistic analysis of the situation had already been made by Vialardi in 1598, and it became an important and recurrent theme in anti-Spanish discourse during the first decades of the seventeenth century. In Boccalini's anti-Spanish political satire, posthumously published in 1614, the Spanish monarchy arrived at Parnassus to ask Apollo to cauterise the festering wound of Flanders on her left arm.[53] Apollo consulted his politi-

---

Biblioteca Corsiana e dei Lincei: *Discorso delle ragioni et avvantaggi della pace e tregua di Fiandra per il Re Cattolico*.

51   This idea was inspired by the political theory of Giovanni Botero, which argued that a ruler should first try to maintain his state before expanding it: Viroli, *From Politics to Reason of State*, p. 253.

52   *Disorso sopra la tregua in Fiandra*, fol 103: 'È stata succhiata da sanguisughe Fiaminghe [...] e finalmente ha servitor quasi di ponte, per dove tutti i thesori del Perù et Megixgo (sic.) traghettino in questi stati, si che restando del tutto la Spagna priva e di danari e d'huomi'.

53   Traiano Boccalini, *Cetra d'Italia. Sopplimento de' ragguagli di Parnaso* (s.l.: s.n., 1614), USTC 4026743, pp. 3–21: 'La Monarchia di Spagna entra in Parnaso con gran pompa e chiede ad Apollo, che gli si ferri il cauterio della Fiandra, è non l'ottiene'. See Jan J. Poelhekke, 'Het thema "Nederlanden" bij Trajano Boccalini', *Tijdschrift voor Geschiedenis*, 62 (1949), pp. 262–272.

cal doctors on this issue, and they decided that Spain's desire to dominate the whole world, helped by the precious metals coming from Peru, could have serious repercussions for Italy. Therefore, they decided it was better to leave this wound open so that 'the pernicious humours from Peru' were confined to the Low Countries.

While the doctors in Boccalini's text dreaded the Habsburg monarchy's desire to dominate the entire Italian peninsula and world, the authors of these anonymous manuscript treatises feared that Spain's preoccupation with the Low Countries might jeopardize the peace in Italy in another way. The war had diverted Spanish attention from other strategic theatres in the Mediterranean; they could neither fortify nor supply Sicily, Naples and Lombardy.[54] This neglect of their own territories in Italy made these parts vulnerable to attacks, as shown very recently by the Venetian interdict crisis. The Venetians, according to this author, clearly had not feared the military strength of Lombardy, and neither had the French as they declared their support for Venice. Interestingly, this author pointed to the Spanish preoccupation with the Low Countries as the main reason for the Italian princes' apparent lack of respect for the Spanish king's interests.[55] These remarks point to a growing awareness that anti-Spanish sentiments were brewing in various Italian states. In this view, it was better to use all the Spanish king's resources to rebuild their strong and formidable empire, which would consequently be feared once more by all the other states. Hence it was not damaging to the king's reputation to conclude a peace with the Dutch; it was necessary for him to do so, to rebuild the reputation of his empire.[56]

These accounts were written by authors favourable to the Spanish-Habsburg monarchy. They used the past and political aphorisms to demonstrate that the Spanish monarchy was devastated and losing its reputation. The Boterian notion that it was better to conserve a state, rather than to expand it, is an example of such a maxim; but its use ignored the fact that the seven provinces in the North had been part of the Spanish-Habsburg empire, and had in effect been lost. The imagery of the uncontrollable, uncivilized and even

---

54   *Discorso sopra la tregua*, fol 103r. Scipione Ammirato earlier had promoted the idea to focus on the war theatre in the Mediterranean in *Orazione di Scipione Ammirato al serenissimo e potentissantissimo re cattolico suo signore Filippo re di Spagna &c; intorno il pacificar la cristianità, e gli prender unitamente l'arme contra gli infedeli* (Florence: Giunti, 1594), USTC 809114.

55   *Discorso sopra la tregua*, fol 103v.

56   For more on 'necessity' in political discourse consult Lisa Kattenberg, *The Power of Necessity. Reason of State in the Spanish Monarchy ca. 1590–1650* (Unpublished PhD, University of Amsterdam, 2018).

bloodsucking Dutch people was used to justify the conclusion of peace and to safeguard the reputation of the Habsburg monarchy.

4   Debating the Truce

The peace negotiations in 1608 between the archducal Netherlands, Habsburg Spain and the Dutch Republic at The Hague almost failed. The French diplomat, Pierre Jeannin, salvaged the negotiations with the proposal of a temporary truce, which was concluded in April 1609 for twelve years. According to soldier and astute political observer, Aurelio Alciati, it was concluded 'to the amazement of all, the joy of a few, and the sorrow of many'.[57] Philip III and several ministers realized the truce was problematic for Spain's reputation as its key demands had not been met.[58] Most importantly the rights of Catholics in the United Provinces were not guaranteed, and the Dutch did not promise to stop trading with the Indies. While Philip III did not recognise the United Provinces as a sovereign state, the Truce was a *de facto* acknowledgment of their independence.[59]

For various Italian participants and observers, it was clear that the Truce was a sign of Spanish weakness. Various Italian correspondents in the Low Countries confirmed the treaty had been concluded without any advantages for the Spanish, but recognized that they did not have any other option than to agree.[60] Alciati, for example, concluded that the treaty was an absolute necessity for the Spanish.[61] Frachetta, the pro-Spanish political intelligencer in Rome, worried about the dangerous repercussions of this treaty.[62] The conclusion of this temporary truce did not end the debates as political theorists

---

57   ASRC, Orsini I, 120, fol 661r: 'con meraviglia de tutti, allegrezza de pochi, e dolor de molti'.
      For more information on Alciati, see Lamal, 'Communicating Conflict', pp. 18–19, 24.
58   Allen, *Philip III and the Pax Hispanica*, pp. 232–233, 236.
59   The French text of the temporary truce stated that the Archdukes recognized the Dutch
      Republic 'as if they were free states', see: Simon Groenveld, *Unie- Bestand- Vrede. Drie fundamentele wetten van de Republiek der Verenigde Nederlanden* (Hilversum: Verloren, 2009),
      p. 106. The Dutch representatives had protested against this choice of words, because of
      the inherent duplicity of this formulation. It was also apparent to the Venetian ambassador, Giorgio Giustiniani, who travelled through the Dutch Republic in 1608, *Relazioni Veneziane*, pp. 10–11: 'Io concludo perciò, che bisogna che i Signori Stati pensino a clausolare meglio la lor sovranità o che le dette parole non serviranno loro di niente'.
60   VA, N22, fol 258.
61   ASRC, Orsini I, 120, fol 661v.
62   BAV, Urb Lat 821, fol 418r–422r: *Discorso sopra la tregua di Spagna con li stati di Zelanda, scritto àdi primo luglio 1609*.

pondered whether the king and the archdukes had made the right decision to conclude a treaty with the United Provinces.

This question came to be particularly urgent in Genoa, where it was discussed in a fictional dialogue of several Genoese men called *Ragionamento sopra la tregua dei Paesi Bassi* (Discussion on the truce of the Low Countries). The text was not without status: it was written by the Genoese nobleman Giovanni Costa and printed in 1610 by Giuseppe Pavoni, the official printer of the Genoese Senate.[63] Costa's contribution to Italian publications on the Revolt in the Low Countries is unique: it was a printed political discourse, whereas, it was far more common for such texts to circulate in manuscript form and it was the only printed text on the conflict in the Low Countries in a dialogue form.[64] As such, but also for its content, it merits attention.

Cees Reijner has recently argued that although at first sight Costa's *Ragionamento* seems to be a pro-Habsburg text, Costa's sympathies lay firmly with the United Provinces.[65] With his analysis, Reijner follows in the footsteps of republican historiographical tradition, wherein the United Provinces became the example for other Italian states to follow, and especially for other republics, like Genoa. Genoa had a complex relationship with the Spanish crown: it claimed neutrality, though, in practice, many of its merchant bankers financed the Habsburg war effort, creating a powerful synergy of mutual interests.[66] Early seventeenth century, there was criticism in Genoa of its close relationship with Madrid and the organization of the Genoese senate, but it is too easy to equate the growing mistrust and anti-Spanish feelings in various Italian states with sympathies for the Dutch Republic.[67] Costa's fictitious discussion

---

63   Giovanni Costa, *Ragionamento di Giovanni Costa, gentil'huomo genovese, sopra la triegua de' Paesi bassi, conchiusa in Anuersa l'anno 1609* (Genoa: Pavoni, 1610), USTC 4026637. On Pavoni see Maria Maira Niri, *La tipografia a Genova e in Liguria nel XVII secolo* (Florence: Olschki, 1998), pp. 79–89. For a biography of Costa: G. Nuti, 'Giovanni Costa', in *DBI*, 30 (1981) and R. Belvederi, 'Il "Ragionamento di Giovanni Costa, Gentil'Huomo Genovese", in R. Belvederi (ed.), *Genova, la Liguria e l'Oltremare tra Medioevo ed età moderna: studi e ricerche d'archivio* (Genoa: Fratelli Bozzi, 1981), pp. 175–360.

64   Dialogues were often used in Genoese political culture: A. Pacini, '"Pignatte di vetro". Being a Republic in Philip II's Empire', in T. Dandelet, J. Marino (eds.), *Spain in Italy: Politics, Society, and Religion 1500–1700* (Leiden: Brill, 2007), pp. 197–225.

65   Reijner, 'Gesprekken in Genua', pp. 84–85.

66   C. Bitossi, 'Le vicissitudini di una simbiosi: Genova e la Spagna nell'età di Filippo II', in G. di Stefano, E. Fasano Guarini, A. Martinengo (eds.), *Italia non spagnola e monarchia spagnola tra '500 e '600. Politica, cultura e letterature* (Florence: Olschki, 2009), pp. 83–103, for changes in early seventeenth century: Kirk, *Genoa and the Sea*, pp. 84–99.

67   A well-known critic was Andrea Spinola. For his analysis of the relationships between Madrid and Genoa consult C. Bitossi (ed.), *Andrea Spinola. Scritti Scelti* (Genoa: Sagep, 1981), pp. 89–103.

is primarily a defence of universal peace promoted by the archdukes. Paying particular attention to the specific Genoese context, this text also reflected the wider debate in Italian political circles on the desirability of peace.[68]

In the dialogue, the host of this noble company opened the discussion by outlining the causes of the wars in the Low Countries, referring to the common stereotype that the Netherlandish nobles were 'already rebellious in their heart'.[69] Rebelliousness was, as we have already seen, an inherent characteristic attributed to the inhabitants of these lands. Despite this natural inclination to rebel, the Duke of Alba was blamed for starting such a cruel war, an analysis which was by now rather commonplace in Italian texts.[70] To the host, only the archdukes had been able to turn the tide, because they strove for peace in the Christian world by concluding a truce with the United Provinces. Other authors such as Vialardi had earlier expressed similar hopes for such a universal peace. The idea that the archdukes were inspired by Christian devotion in their aim for universal peace is a recurrent theme throughout this text.

The rest of the *Ragionamento* consists of two long speeches held by an opponent (second speaker) and a proponent of the truce (third speaker). In the way the text is structured, the proponent has the advantage to react and rebut the arguments put forward by the opponent. The opponent of the truce argued, based on the rules of reason of state, that starting negotiations with the rebels was dishonourable and a clear sign of weakness. The proponent contradicted this idea, arguing that it was honourable and prudent of the archdukes to negotiate with the rebels since it showed that they had learned from past wars. Peace, and not war, was necessary to regain control over the Dutch territories. It was the only way to cure the 'Dutch wound' and to reach a universal Christian peace.[71] Moreover, when a state is of no use to a prince and causes damage to his other states, it is necessary to abandon that state. The metaphor of the healthy body was used to illustrate this point.

> Just like the wise doctor, who in order to save a human body, cuts and
> separates the infected parts likely to contaminate other [healthy] parts.[72]

---

68 In 1615, during the war of Monferrato, Costa wrote another treatise reflecting on expansionism of Savoy as a threat to Italy's peace, see *Trattato della pace e della libertà d'Italia e de' modi di conservarle* (Genoa: Pavoni, 1615), USTC 4027144.

69 Costa, *Il Ragionamento*, p. 12: 'già ribelli nell'animo'.

70 Costa, *Il Ragionamento*, p. 14.

71 Costa, *Ragionamento*, p. 25: 'la piaga de gli Holandesi'.

72 Costa, *Ragionamento*, p. 31: 'che fa il savio medico, che per la salvezza d'un corpo humano, taglia, e separa alcuna parte corrotta di esso, & atta a contaminar l'altre'. For a similar analogy see Vialardi's discourse: VA, R55, f75: 'che si tenghino con tanta spesa, danno, ch'

This argument, as we have seen, was commonplace in manuscript treatises in the years before the conclusion of the truce. This speaker provided many historical examples from Roman history and more recent times of emperors and kings concluding peace treaties and losing a part of their territories. The inference was that Philip III and the archdukes did not lose their reputation, but that this decision instead enhanced their reputation.

The opponent of the truce referred to the first article of the treaty, in which the Archdukes and Philip III had agreed to regard the Dutch Republic as a free state over which they had no rightful claim.[73] It was not an official recognition of the existence of the Dutch Republic nor of their sovereignty. However, to this speaker, this formulation was more than one step too far: Philip III and the Archdukes had lost their natural and sovereign claims. It might, he stated, inspire the other obedient provinces to join the Dutch Republic, enthused by their freedom and the right to trade with the Indies. The fact that 'these heretics' could now trade with Catholic subjects of the Spanish king was also problematic to this proponent of war.

These arguments were again countered by the third speaker, who argued that the conclusion of the truce did not imply that this territory was lost forever to the Habsburg crown. He rather saw it as a temporary matter, because he thought that the archdukes in the end would be able to recover these states through 'gentleness and fatherly love'.[74] While this idea seems, with the advantage of hindsight, a somewhat naïve assessment of the situation, from their perspective it was an understandable one. Campanella had already argued, that the Dutch embraced Calvinism because of their insatiable desire to be

---

e meglio lasciarli, che tenerli, perche dove l'havere stati accresce potenza, tenerli con dispendi la deminuisce, cosi come nell nostro corpo gli humori, che sono fomiti della vita, si trappo si riducevo a una parte, alle quale sia bisogno che la natura somministi li spiriti, et il calore, che sono le sue forze, et devon essere distribuiti all' altri parti, sono piu presto viscere di morte che di vita'.

73   *Articoli del trattato della tregua fatta, et conchiusa nella citta di Anuersa adi 9. d'aprile 1609* (Florence: Grinieri, 1609), USTC 4025525 which claims to be based on the French edition published by Hillebrant van Wouw in The Hague: *Articles du traicté de trefve faict et conclu en la ville et cité d'Anvers, le neufiesme d'avril 1609* (The Hague: Van Wouw, 1609), USTC 1032151. Manuscript copies: ASF, MdP 4256, fol 470–472; 480–483: *Articoli della tregua del Re di Spagna e del Arciduc con i paesi bassi*. Despite its Italian title, the document contained the French text of the treaty; VA, N22, fol 253–257: *Articoli della tregua di 12 anni conchiusa in Anversa*, translated from French into Italian. Bentivoglio sent a printed edition: AAV, Fondo Borghese II, 98, fol 83: 'S'e stampato qui ultimamente in francese il trattato della tregua et a gli articoli (...) s'e stampata queste scrittura dalla parte di qua per haver fatto il medesimo gli stati. Manda una di queste scritture stampate a vs Ill.ma'.

74   Costa, *Ragionamento*, p. 33: 'con dolcezza, & amor paterno'.

free, rather than out of religious convictions.[75] The religious aspect was thus not seen as a major obstacle in bringing those provinces back under Habsburg Catholic rule. A clear proponent of peace, this speaker further contested the idea that the Dutch would be able to infect the lands of the Habsburg king with their heretical beliefs. He argued that the Dutch merchants were 'ignorant and uncouth' in matters of religion.[76] They were already present in all the Mediterranean trading ports, such as Marseille, Genoa, Livorno and Venice, and there they had never tried to introduce Calvinism. A remark which attests to the growing numbers of Dutch merchants in the Mediterranean. The second speaker's arguments against the truce were very much in line with some of the Spanish ministers' opposition to its conclusion.[77] The war against the Dutch Republic needed to continue since it was the only way to contain the spread of heresy, and thus a defensive war would have been better than stopping it altogether. His conclusion was clear: 'when the war stops, the strong Spanish nation will become womanish and soft, so that in a few years, order and military discipline will be lost'.[78]

The proponent of peace instead argues that the Spanish Habsburg empire would benefit from this pause: the king could first repay the money he owed to foreign nations, and then reorganise his finances. This list of priorities was clearly influenced by the Genoese preoccupations, where numerous merchants were in trouble after the bankruptcy of the crown in 1607.[79] As the last point to prove the necessity of the truce, and to prove a truce would not affect Spanish morale, this speaker referred to the numerous problems in the Habsburg army. Due to a lack of pay, the soldiers had mutinied many times, but luckily this had been remedied by the Genoese patrician and officer Pompeo Giustiniani, Ambrogio Spinola's right-hand man in the Habsburg army.[80] Both Genoese men were presented as the keepers of order and discipline. This speaker used

---

75   Campanella further elaborated upon this idea in *Monarchia di Spagna*: see Fournel, 'La pensée politique de Campanella', p. 125.

76   Costa, *Ragionamento*, p. 50: 'sono indotti e rozzi, e lontani da queste contemplationi di religione'.

77   Those opposed to pacification are known as *reputacionistas*: García García, *La Pax Hispanica*, pp. 86–88.

78   Costa, *Ragionamento*, p. 22: 'cessando la guerra si renderà effemminata, e mollo la fortissima nation spagnola'.

79   Kirk, *Genoa and the Sea*, pp. 88–91.

80   Costa, *Ragionamento*, p. 53. For a biography of Spinola see Antonio Rodriguez Villa, *Ambrosio Spínola, primer marqués de los Balbases* (Madrid: Fortanet, 1905). Pompeo Giustiniani's history of the war between 1601 and 1609, published in 1609 in Antwerp, devoted ample attention to these mutinies. For more information on Giustiniani's history see chapter 7.

Spinola's positive judgement on the truce to add authority to his argument that the decision to conclude a truce should be applauded.[81] As a final comment, he referred to the peace in Italy: Philip III and the archdukes followed in the footsteps of their illustrious ancestors, who had established peace in Italy. In bringing temporary peace to the Low Countries, a war which had divided the Christian world, they furthered peace between the Christian princes. The conclusion was clear: the truce was to be lauded.

Genoese interests appear throughout this text. Given those interests, it is no surprise that the text leaned towards peace and that Genoese patricians such as Spinola, the main broker of the Truce, received praise. The Genoese pro-peace argument should not be equated with political or ideological support for the Dutch Republic. While Costa was indeed appreciative of the new Republic in the North and its many trade fortunes, at the same time, many Genoese merchants were dependent on the Habsburg crown and trade. It was for this reason, and not for Republican sisterhood, that Costa considered peace to be desired above all other things. In arguing so, moreover, his text echoed longstanding Italian debates on the issue both in manuscript and print.

5   'A New Power in the World': Describing a New State

After the indirect recognition of the sovereignty of their state, the United Provinces were quick to send their first official diplomatic representatives to several of the most important courts in Europe in search of allies. This search also led them to the Italian peninsula: in 1609, Cornelis van der Mijle, was sent to Venice to inform the Venetian Senate of the conclusion of the Twelve Years' Truce.[82] In 1610, the Venetians reciprocated this visit and sent Tommaso Contarini as an ambassador to The Hague as a courtesy. The Republic remained cautious and was at this stage not prepared to establish more formal relations. Contarini's *relazione* (report), presented to the Senate at the end of his visit, was one of the first overviews of this new state written by an Italian visitor, which was all the more unique because travelling to Amsterdam or other cities in the Dutch Republic had been extremely difficult for most (Catholic) Italians before the conclusion of the Truce.[83]

---

81   Costa, *Ragionamento*, p. 56.

82   The instructions given to Van der Mijle are published in Johannes C. de Jonge, *Nederland en Venetië* (The Hague: Van Cleef, 1852), pp. 410–411.

83   Brussels 30 August 1608, AAV, Fondo Borghese II, III, fol 76: 'Da i bagni di Spa e venuta qua S.A. [Vincenzo Gonzaga] per andar in Anversa e quindi in Ollanda per curiosità di veder

The Truce, then, both necessitated and allowed Italian agents to collect intelligence on the new state of the United Provinces and its institutions at a time when up-to-date information was scarce. This was certainly one of the reasons why Guido Bentivoglio, the papal nuncio in Brussels wrote his *Relatione delle Province Unite di Fiandra* (Report on the United Provinces of the Low Countries). Crucially, even after the conclusion of the Truce, Bentivoglio was not allowed by the pope to travel and visit the United Provinces. Upon finishing his *Relazione* in August 1611, he remarked in a letter to his learned friend Antonio Querenghi:

> But I have at least seen it, and likewise, I have uncovered the most hidden secrets of this new Republic of the United Provinces through an exquisite piece of information that I have tried to obtain from many places.[84]

Unfortunately, we do not know which text or texts helped Bentivoglio to understand and to write about this new Republic without first-hand experience.[85]

His *Relatione* is considered by several scholars to be a formative text in the Italian conception of this new state as Bentivoglio expressed a positive judgement on this new Republic.[86] Partly because the first edition of his reports in 1629 was seized by the order of Council of Brabant and its immediate publishing success, scholars have failed to study the original context and form of this text.[87] It was a diplomatic report written to supply the papal curia with up-to-date information about this new state and accompanied by a similar report on the archducal Netherlands. Nuncios were expected to write realistic political accounts and analyses, and Bentivoglio's texts are comparable to those written by his fellow diplomats in Venice.[88] While the Venetian *Relazioni*

---

quel paese'; 'che questo viaggio d'Ollanda lo faceva con la participatione e consenso di S.M.tà Cattolica'.

84   Bentivoglio, *Raccolta di Lettere*, p. 18: 'Ma l'ho veduta almeno, ed hò penetrate insieme i più occulti arcani di questa nuova Republica delle Provincie Unite per via d'una esquisita notitia, che da mille parti hò procurato d'haverne'.

85   A possible candidate is the French translation of Guicciardini's *Descrittione*, published in 1609 in Amsterdam, which was expanded considerably to reflect more accurately the new political realities: *Description des touts les pays-bas autrement appellez la Germanie Inferieure ou Basse Allemagne* (Amsterdam: Claesz, 1609), USTC 1033146. For a description of the new form of government, together with substantial information on the Batavians, see pp. 33–34, 40–47.

86   *Relatione delle Provincie Unite*, pp. 13–14.

87   Bernard Vermaseren, *De Katholieke Nederlandsche geschiedschrijving in de XVIᵉ en XVIIᵉ eeuw over den Opstand* (Maastricht: Van Aelst, 1941), pp. 213–214.

88   On these reports A. Koller (ed.), *Kurie und Politik, Stand und Perspektiven der Nunziaturberichtsforschung* (Tübingen: Max Niemeyer Verlag, 1998). On Venetian *Relazioni* see A. Contini, 'L'informazione politica sugli stati italiani non spagnoli nelle relazioni veneziane a

are much better known, the aim of these compositions was the same: to provide an overview of a given country's geography and history, state institutions,
economic and military strength, key political figures and diplomatic relationships with neighbouring states. Since these documents often contained sensitive information, they were not meant to be copied or published, but many
nevertheless did. They were actively sought after by other ambassadors, intelligence agents and collectors. Hence, Scipio Borghese, the papal secretary of
state, repeatedly advised Bentivoglio to keep his text out of the public eye.[89]

Throughout his report on the United Provinces, Bentivoglio used the monarchy as a point of reference to explain the institutions of this new republican government.[90] In a thorough analysis of their form of government, he
concluded that the Dutch had changed as little as possible in how the state
worked.[91] Before the outbreak of the revolt, the state had been, according to
Bentivoglio, a mix between monarchy, aristocracy and democracy.[92] Now, it
only had a little touch of monarchy, referring to Maurice of Nassau's position as
stadtholder within the Republic. He conventionally described the government
of the United Provinces as a human body, of which the States General was the
head, the provinces its members, and the cities and nobles its muscles.

The notion that the system was designed in order to strike a balance between
unity and local autonomy was also apparent to the first Venetian representative
in 1610.[93] Contarini concluded that this was not a single republic, but one of
seven republics which had been united for their security.[94] While Bentivoglio's
point of reference was the monarchy, to the Venetian ambassadors, their own

---

metà cinquecento (1558–1566)', in E. Fasano Guarini (ed.), *Informazione politica in Italia*
(*secoli XVI–XVIII*) (Pisa: Scuola Normale Superiore, 2001), pp. 1–10.

89   For manuscript copy see AAV, Pio vol 85. For the cited letter by Borghese to Bentivoglio,
Rome 13 August 1611, see *Archivalia in Italië*, III, p. 6: 'onde ella ha da restar quieta et di
questo et del giuditio che si fa dell'opera'. On their circulation consult De Vivo, *Information
& Communication*, pp. 57–70.

90   Bentivoglio, *Relationi*, pp. 10–11. This was also the case in Guicciardini, *Description*, p. 47.

91   Bentivoglio, *Relationi*, p. 20.

92   Compare to Guicciardini, *Description*, p. 57: 'peut ester nommé un gouvernement mesté,
participant de la Monarchie, Aristocratie, & Democratie'. Koenigsberger described this
system as 'Dominium politicum et regale': Helmut Koenigsberger, *Monarchies, States
Generals and Parliaments. The Netherlands in the Fifteenth and Sixteenth Centuries*
(Cambridge: Cambridge University press, 2001), pp. 220–340.

93   On the importance of the Union of Utrecht as a constitutional basis, see Groenveld, *Unie-
Bestand- Vrede*, p. 17; A. Van Deursen, 'Tussen eenheid en zelfstandigheid. De toepassing
van de unie als fundamentele wet', in A. Van Deursen (ed.), *De hartslag van het leven, studies over de republiek der Verenigde Nederlanden* (Amsterdam: Bert Bakker, 1996), p. 308.

94   *Relazioni Veneziane*, p. 42: 'Alle quali si può dar nome non di una Republica sola, ma più
tosto di sette Republiche congionte e unite insieme nella uniformità del governo per la
lor sicurezza'.

state was an obvious point of reference to describe this new republic. Contarini noted the similarities between Venice and the Dutch Republic: '[they] shared similar interests, had the same form of government and had a similar relationship with the sea'.[95] One of the specific goals of these *relazioni* was to reinforce the 'myth of Venice', the idea of Venice as a uniquely stable republican state.[96] The Venetians saw in the Dutch Republic a confirmation of the superiority of their own form of government as the mixed government of the Dutch Republic mirrored their governmental system.[97]

This first envoy already recognised that this new state outstripped Venice both in commercial trade and military affairs.[98] Contarini expressed admiration for the quality of the soldiers and the organisation of Maurice's army. Bentivoglio gave a rather positive sketch of Maurice of Nassau's capacities, writing:

> Maurice has resisted the attacks of many nations, that for the Spanish crown have gone to fight in the Low Countries, [he] has depleted the inexhaustible gold of the Indies, has benefited from so many mutinies in the Spanish army, and with his cautious and confident warfare, has in the end achieved a truce, which has culminated in the founding of the United Provinces.[99]

He further described Maurice as a man of great military reputation and compared his military competence to that of his Habsburg opponent, Ambrogio Spinola.[100]

---

95   *Relazioni Veneziane*, p. 26: 'possono riputarsi nondimeno cosi congionte con esso per conformità degl'interessi, per la forma del loro governo et per la commodità del mare'.

96   A good starting point is Edward Muir, *Civic Ritual in Renaissance Venice* (New Jersey: Princeton University Press, 1986), pp. 13–61.

97   *Relazioni Veneziane*, p. 44 ; A. Fontana, 'Les Provinces Unies dans les relations des ambassadeurs vénitiens au XVIIᵉ siècle', in M. Blanco-Morel, M-F. Piéjus (eds.), *Les Flandres et la culture espagnole et italienne aux XVIᵉ et XVIIᵉ siècles* (Lille: Travaux et Recherche, 1998), p. 141.

98   *Relazione Veneziane*, p. 104: 'con mia mortificazione confesso che non solo gareggia ma vince di grandezza e di sito l'istessa Venetia, ma nel traffic grande di mercantile et di numero del popolo di gran lunga la supera'. Another example is their admiration for the Dutch and their navigational skills: *Relazione Veneziane*, p. 39 and Bentivoglio, *Relationi*, p. 30.

99   Bentivoglio, *Relationi*, p. 80: 'ha sostenuto i torrenti di tante natione, che per la corona di spagna son calate a combattere in Fiandra, ha fatto consumar l'oro inesausto dell'Indie, ha goduto il benefitio di tanti ammutinamenti dalla parte de gli spagnoli, e co'l suo guerreggiar circonspetto, e sicuro, ha fatta conseguire in ultimo alla Provincie unite una tregua, ch'è tornato in lor gran vantaggio e stabilimento'.

100 Bentivoglio, *Relationi*, p. 82.

For the papal curia, it was important to know exactly what might happen in the future. Bentivoglio addressed the question as to whether this new state would be sustainable.[101] As we have already seen some observers had presented the truce as the ideal way for the Habsburg empire to regain strength. Many saw the truce as a temporary matter, and some thought that soon the states in the North would be reunited under Habsburg rule. Bentivoglio first considered the reasons why the state might be durable and then evaluated the reasons why it might not be. In his argument for the durability of the new Dutch state, Bentivoglio referred to their ancient love of liberty, largely following the Grotian interpretation of the Batavian myth.[102] Already in his letters addressed to the papal secretary in 1608, Bentivoglio had stressed that the Dutch were driven by a strong need to preserve their freedom together with an infinite hatred of the Spanish yoke.[103] Secondly, as Bentivoglio had explained, the Dutch had not drastically changed their governmental institutions since they had become a republic. They had merely adapted some of the rules along the way, which made their government a stable one. These two elements could make this new state as durable as the Swiss republic.[104]

Typical of this type of *discorsi*, Bentivoglio weighed his arguments and continued that, on the other hand, one could argue that obedience of a people toward a prince is equally common, even in these Northern provinces. These people had been just as used to being ruled by one person, as they had been to liberty. It was thus perfectly possible that they might return to their 'original reverence and respect towards the prince'.[105] The papal nuncio spotted many possible problems in their state which might disrupt their concord, one of them being that the province of Holland was too dominant in the government.

Another potential problem was the differences in religion in one state, an issue that might divide the inhabitants. Campanella had suggested that the diversity of opinion among the inhabitants of the Dutch Republic could offer an ideal opportunity to re-establish the king's authority. He had already referenced the theological conflict between Arminius and Gomarus, two

---

101   Bentivoglio, *Relationi*, p. 98–110: 'Se questa nuova Republica delle Provincie Unite sara durabile'.

102   Bentivoglio, *Relationi*, p. 98.

103   Bentivoglio to Borghese, Brussels 10 May 1608, AAV, Fondo Borghese II, 115, fol 181: 'il rispetto di conservarla libertà, e l'odio, et abborrimento, infinito contro il giogo spagnolo.'

104   On this subject see A. Holenstein, T. Maissen, M. Prak, (eds.), *The Republican Alternative. The Netherlands and Switzerland Compared* (Amsterdam: Amsterdam University Press, 2008).

105   Bentivoglio, *Relationi*, pp. 104: 'pristina riverenza, & ossequio verso quel principe'.

theology professors at the university of Leiden, on the issue of predestination in Calvinism.[106] The argument that the variety of beliefs would offer the opportunity for the king ultimately to recover these lands was not completely far-fetched. Around the same time as Campanella wrote his treatise, the famous humanist Justus Lipsius made similar observations in a letter to Francisco de San Víctores de la Portilla, a Spanish nobleman and captain.[107] Lipsius thought it was best to opt for peace or at least for a truce. Like Campanella, he expressed the hope that this would enable the Spanish to sow discord in the Northern Netherlands and finally reconquer them.[108] In his conclusion, Bentivoglio was quite clear: he did not think this state would last long and might soon return under the leadership of one person.

Bentivoglio thought that the Republic could return to the Habsburg fold and proposed as the most likely scenario the establishment of a new princely dynasty in the Low Countries. He praised the Archdukes in his other *relatione* for establishing peace. Bentivoglio then saw the Act of Cession as a sign that the king also realised this was the only way to recover the United Provinces. Like many of his contemporaries, Bentivoglio reasoned that the need for a strong leader would in the end be more powerful than any innate desire for liberty.

Bentivoglio recognized the Dutch desire for liberty, as we have seen, other Italian political observers and thinkers, including more Spanish hardliners such Frachetta, had done that before him. Recognising that the revolt had been driven by a desire for freedom was part of their analysis. The emphasis on the love of liberty of the people, thus should not lead scholars to conclude that authors such as Costa and Bentivoglio unequivocally expressed their admiration for this new state. In the analysis of both parties, the conclusion that other nations could no longer be intimidated by Habsburg power was implicitly present.

The war in the Low Countries had seriously damaged the Spanish empire's power and authority, as Bentivoglio concluded: 'it had left the body of such a

---

106   On these problems see Arie Th. Van Deursen, *Bavianen en slijkgeuzen, Kerk en kerkvolk ten tijde van Maurits en Oldenbarnevelt* (Assen: Van Gorcum, 1974).

107   N. Mout, 'Justus Lipsius between war and peace', in J. Pollmann, A. Spicer (eds.), *Public Opinion and Changing Identities in the Early Modern Netherlands: Essays in Honour of Alastair Duke* (Leiden: Brill, 2007), pp. 141–162.

108   His letter very quickly circulated in manuscript and was in 1608 printed in the Dutch Republic to prove the deceitful nature of the Spanish: *Ivsti Lipsii sent-brief, in welcke hy antwoorde gheeft aen een seker groot heer, op de vraghe, welck van dryen den coning van Hispaengien best gheraden ware, oorloghe oft peys, oft liever bestant met den Fransman, Engelsche ende Hollander* (Dusseldorf: Horst, 1608), USTC 1033024, 1033026, 1033560. The Dutch translations had been prohibited by the States General on 17 September 1608, therefore the text was published under a false imprint.

powerful and great Monarchy, weak and exhausted'.[109] To some, there was no other option open to Philip III and the Archdukes than to conclude a peace or a truce with the Dutch Republic. In their eyes, peace was the only way to safeguard the Habsburg reputation and empire. To others, concluding a peace exposed its weakness. These political tracts often offered realistic assessments of the situation and provided the necessary information on the constellation of the new states. This chapter has challenged the existing republican paradigm to argue that the reactions to Dutch success in challenging the Habsburg monarchy in Italian states opened far broader questions about war and peace, the potential prospect of a new princely dynasty, as well as overseas trade in Italian discourse.

---

109   Bentivoglio, *Relationi*, p. 127: 'hanno fatto consumar i tesori del Rè di Spagna, e lasciato esausto e languido il corpo di quella sì potente e sì gran Monarchia'.

The Rise of Confessional and Polemical News Pamphlets

This chapter explores the emergence of different types of occasional printed news pamphlets on the Italian information market. Until the 1590s, the majority of the printed news reports publicising Spanish Habsburg military victories in the Low Countries were based on letters and separate accounts military commanders sent to their superiors or peers on the Italian peninsula.[1] The practice of printing copies of (anonymised) letters from the battlefield continued well into the seventeenth century, but increasingly these initial reports were accompanied by more interpretative news accounts. For example, in 1625 the Milanese printer Melchior Malatesta published a *ragguaglio* on the siege of Breda, explaining he hoped this account would satisfy:

> the reasonable curiosity, not so much of the common people, but of those readers who love histories, who are experienced in military arts, and acquainted with the Low Countries, because they wanted to receive a precise account of the surroundings of this city, of the way the Nassau family gained it.[2]

Before chronicling the events during the siege of Breda, the city's geographical and strategic position, its symbolic importance as it was a personal possession

---

1   *Raguaglio dell'assedio et espugnatione della terra di Cales et fortezza di essa* (Viterbo: [Colaldi], 1596), USTC 807099 was a printed copy of 'lettere di xxvi d'aprile 1596 d'Anversa'. Another news pamphlet on the siege of Calais was based entirely on a letter sent to the governor of Milan: *Vera et compita relatione dell'impresa di Cales fatta dal Serissimo Principe Cardinale Alberto d'Austria cavata da una lettera scritta da persona principale che si trovò sul fatto all' eccelletissimo signore contestabile di Cassigli essendo governatore del stato di Milano del 1596*, it is preserved solely as a manuscript copy in BA G286 inf, fol 467r–472v and as a printed edition in Turin (USTC 807111), based on a Milan printed edition which has not survived.

2   *Breve Ragguaglio del sito, e positura della villa di bredà et in che modo, e quando divennero Padroni di essa gli Conti di Nassau, detti poi Prencipe d'Orange; e quante volte in che maniera, ed in che tempo l'hanno persa, e recuperata, e come ultimamente s'è resa all'Eccellentissimo Sig. Marchese Spinola, con l'inventario delle monitioni, e stromenti militari trovati in essa nella sudetta resa* (Milan: Malatesta, 1625), USTC 4005875, A2: 'alla ragionevole curiosità non tanto del popolo, quanto delle persone amiche delle storie, esperimentate nell'arte militare, e pratiche de' Paesi di Fiandra, perche desideravano havere minuta contezza del sito di questa villa'.

of the Nassau family, and a very brief historical overview of when the Nassaus acquired the city, were explained to the reader. With this news pamphlet, Malatesta specifically addressed the needs of the educated audience of Habsburg administrators, the local Milanese elite and high-ranking soldiers who wanted to know more and understand the importance of this victory. He did so, however, in a way that was distinctly different from the sixteenth-century accounts.

The appearance of more contextualised accounts, such as the one printed by Malatesta in 1625, was a crucial development in the provision of printed news on the Italian peninsula in the seventeenth century. Typically, news pamphlets now offered their readers an overview of the history and geographical position of a particular city before launching into the details of a specific siege or battle. Crucially, these more narrative news pamphlets also presented an ideological framework guiding the interpretation of his readers as they were increasingly permeated with distinctly pro-Habsburg and confessional Baroque rhetoric. In the sixteenth century, the Netherlandish rebels were described as enemies in Italian news publications, but not blackened to the degree they were in the first half of the seventeenth century. The way enemies and events were portrayed changed, and a highly militant Catholic tone and pro-Habsburg narrative developed. This chapter will outline the emergence of the new narrative framework in Italian news pamphlets, and discuss its effect on how Spinola, the most famous Italian general of the seventeenth century, was portrayed.

During this period, Milan's official printers, such as the Malatesta family, continued to play a crucial role in publishing and disseminating news accounts on events in the Low Countries.[3] Naples, the other centre of Habsburg power on the Italian peninsula, emerged as a new player publicising Habsburg victories. Naples was one of the largest and most populated cities in early modern Europe but had been only a printing centre of minor importance throughout the sixteenth century.[4] In the seventeenth century, this would change significantly, and several printers became involved in the production of news

---

3   The current data on the numbers of news pamphlets printed in Italian cities during the seventeenth century is far from complete. Numerous news pamphlets are not recorded in the online collective catalogue of the National Library Service in Italy (OPAC SBN), which makes it, at times, a real challenge to find news pamphlets and locate existing copies. For Venice, researchers can use bibliographies such as Caterina Griffante (ed.), *Le edizioni veneziane del seicento. Censimento* (2 vols., Milan: Ed. Bibliografica, 2003–2006).

4   For Naples see T. Astarita (ed.), *A Companion to Early Modern Naples* (Leiden: Brill, 2013). In this volume, there is no chapter dedicated to printing and the print industry in the city, which has received very little attention in comparison to other large cities such as Venice and Rome. During the sixteenth century just 33 news pamphlets were printed in Naples, compared to 123 news pamphlets in Milan (data USTC). From 1600–1650 the number increased

pamphlets.[5] The printers started to reissue the same news reports as their Milanese counterparts, turning the city into a hub for pro-Habsburg news publications both in Italian and Spanish in Southern Italy.

In both Milan and Naples, defending the Spanish Habsburg power became more urgent as the century progressed and the first cracks in the *Pax Hispanica* started to appear. At the start of the seventeenth century, some Italian states, chief amongst them the Duchy of Savoy and the Venetian Republic, were looking for new potential allies. In 1619, the Venetian Republic concluded an alliance with the Dutch Republic, a change which, as we shall see, had a major impact on the news production in the city.[6] The changes in political alliances started to fragment the uniform narrative of Habsburg success with the circulation of conflicting narratives. In 1635, with the official entry of France into the Thirty Years' War, news reports became part of the polemic between the pro-Spanish and pro-French parties, which was a crucial change in Italian news culture. This chapter demonstrates how printed news reports from Low Countries became more ideologically charged in the seventeenth century.

1   The Emergence of a Narrative Framework

At the end of the sixteenth century, narrative news pamphlets started to appear across the Italian peninsula. Bernardino Beccari, a somewhat obscure news writer active in Rome between 1593 and 1600, played an important role in this development.[7] His news reports describing specific episodes from the war in the Low Countries exemplify this trend. Beccari publicised the same minor military victories as major successes as the loyalist Habsburg publishers in Brussels and Antwerp, but he was not satisfied with simply translating their

---

slightly to 47 news pamphlets. A comprehensive study of the printed news production in Naples during this period is still missing.

5   For the increase in production consult S. Sbordone, 'Editori e tipografi a Napoli nel 600', *Quaderni dell'Accademia Pontaniana*, 12 (1990), pp. 5–93, and for more on printing in early modern Naples: Giovanni Lombardi, *Tra le pagine di San Biagio. L'economia della stampa a Napoli in età moderna* (Naples: Edizioni Scientifiche Italiane, 2000).

6   See de Jonge, *Nederland en Venetië*, pp. 104–114.

7   Little is known about his life, he disappears from view in 1600. In a handwritten newsletter, I came across a reference to 'a Bernardin Beccaro' who had died in a fight (BAV, Urb Lat 1068, fol 204: *Supplica di Venetia del primo aprile* [1600]). For an brief overview of Beccari's career: Tullio Bulgarelli, 'Bernardino Beccari da Sacile antesignano dei giornalisti italiani', *Accademie e Biblioteche d'Italia*, 34 (1966), pp. 123–126. Bulgarelli recorded 45 news pamphlets in his bibliography; the USTC has doubled this number to 90 (last checked on 4/02/2021).

news reports.[8] Instead of republishing copies of letters or manuscript *avvisi*, he created his accounts from a variety of sources and shaped them into a straightforward narrative which was geared toward a Roman Catholic readership. Beccari provided his readers with necessary background information on the events he was describing and a moral framework to interpret these events. For instance, he began his report on the siege of Hulst in 1596 with a description of the town's geographical location and an explanation of its importance.[9] Apart from this contextual information, Beccari interpreted the events in a distinctly Catholic and Habsburg fashion. The following, for example, are the opening lines of Beccari's report on the recapture of the fortress of Rheinberg in 1599 by the Spanish-Habsburg army:

> It seems that in these times God, Our Lord, favours the matters of the true Christians, the Catholics and especially of the Serene house of Austria, that because of its piety, was granted an empire with so many kingdoms and dominions. At the same time that the soldiers of the Emperor are winning in Hungary, likewise in the Low Countries, the army of Archduke Albert is fighting the heretical rebels successfully.[10]

---

8   Bernardino Beccari, *La maravigliosa vittoria ottenuta dalle Genti del Rè Cattolico contra i ribelli heretici che havevano sorpresa la città di Lira in Brabantia a dì 14 d'ottobre 1595* (Rome: Mutio, 1595), USTC 813028; *Discours ende warachtich verhael van het inne nemen van de stadt van Liere door den vyant* (Brussels: Velpius, 1595), USTC 402347; *Cort Verhael van den Aenslach, ende veroveren der stadt Liere* (Antwerp: Ballo, 1595), USTC 415575. For reprinting of pamphlets by the Malatesta's: *Vera, et compita relatione della battaglia, assedio, et presa della citta, & Castello di Dorlens Stampata in Arras in lingua francese; et ristampata in Milano in lingua italiana* (Milan: Malatesta, 1595), in BUA. The news on the siege of Amiens in 1597 was also based upon the Arras-edition *Breve et vero discorso delli particolari successi occorsi sotto la città d'Amiens, tra gli assediati, & gli inimici. Dopoi il martedi 15. mercoledì 16 & la giobba 17. di luglio fino il lunedì seguente alli 21* (Milan: Malatesta, 1597), USTC 807118 – *conforme la copia stampata in Aras*. See *Discours touchant la prise admirable de la grande et puissante ville d'Amiens* (Arras: De La Rivière, 1597), USTC 13462.

9   Bernardino Beccari, *L'assedio, et presa di Hulst fortezza principale della Fiandra, occupata da gli heretici ribelli de Re cattolico l'anno 1591 a di 25 di settembre* (Rome: Mutio, 1596), USTC 812969: 'Hulst, terra del contado di fiandra, provincia della Gallia Belgica, la quale ha steso il suo nome à tutte l'altre provincie de' paesi bassi, è capo di una picciola Regione, che si chiama li quattro uffici, continua al paese di Vuaes, & una delle più forti, & delle più munite piazze che sieno in quella provincia'. He probably used Guicciardini's *Descrittione* for the general descriptions, compare to p. 246: 'al picolo paese di Waes, & altri villaggi, li quattro uffici. (...) le quali sono in una piccola regione (...) Hulst è la principale d'esse, che veramente è terra ragionevole'.

10 Bernardino Beccari, *Aviso della presa di Berck Fortezza Principale posta su'l rheno, & di Vvesel Piazza siuata sù'l medesimo fiume* (Milan: Malatesta, 1600), USTC 813022, A2: 'Pare che'l N.S. Iddio voglio in questo tempo prosperare da tutte le parti le cose de' veri

By equating the successes of Emperor Rudolf II against the Ottomans in Hungary and those of his brother Albert in the Netherlands, Beccari presented the (Austrian) Habsburgs as sole defenders of the Catholic faith against infidels and heretics. Furthermore, he propagated the idea of *Pietas Austriaca*, namely the idea that God had granted them all this prosperity as a reward for their piety.[11]

For each event he described, Beccari presented a clear narrative framework guiding the interpretation of his readers. Thus, he even turned the defeat of Habsburg troops under the leadership of Albert of Austria by Maurice of Nassau's army at Nieuwpoort in 1600 into a victory.[12] Beccari's report of the event, the only Italian example I have encountered that describes this defeat of the Habsburg army in the Netherlands, describes the confrontation between the two forces in general terms and claims that the Habsburg troops fought valorously even in their retreat. In doing so, it paints the complete opposite picture that emerges from the manuscript reports and letters written by numerous Italian soldiers directly after this ferocious battle.[13] These soldiers all described the retreat as disorderly and chaotic and recognised that they had fought a lost battle and a very bloody one indeed.

Beccari's version of the battle of Nieuwpoort was more in line with official accounts by Archduke Albert and the papacy. Albert, wounded in battle, had immediately attempted to put a positive spin on his defeat in his letter to the Council of State in Brussels, in which he claimed that he had not lost courage, and ordered more troops to confront Maurice of Nassau.[14] Frangipani, the papal nuncio in Brussels, sent a copy of Albert's letter to the papal secretary

Christiani, et Cattolici, et spetialmente quelle della Serenissima casa d'Austria, per la pietà sua, che fu causa che S.D.M. le desse l'imperio, et le habbia poi conceduti contanti Regni et dominij; poiche mentre le genti dell'imperatore fanno progressi notabilissimi in Ungheria, etiando ne' Paesi Bassi si combatte felicemente dall' essercito del Ser.mo Arciduca Alberto contra i ribelli heretici'.

11   Beccari, *Avviso della presa*, A2: 'per la pietà sua, che fu cause che S.D.M. le desse l'imperio, et le habbia poi conceduti contanti Regni, et dominij'.

12   Bernardino Beccari, *Relatione del seguito dell'armata hollandese in Fiandra, da che arrivò in detta Provincia, che fù alla fine di giugno fin che è partita di là, che segui al primo d'agosto* (Rome: Mutio, 1600), USTC 813024.

13   Lamal, 'Communicating Conflict', pp. 22–24; BAV Urb Lat 1068, fol 454–455: *Relatione della fattione seguita alli 2 luglio fra l'ess.to catholico et il nemico fra Neuporte et Ostendem*: 'Non e dubbio che il nemico sendo stato Signore della campagna puo realmente chiarmarsi vittorioso'; ASF, MdP 4256, fol 31–34r: *Relatione di quanto e successo ne gl'esserciti di Fiandra* and another account on fol 37–41bis; VA, N22, fol 92–93; ASF, DU I, 198, fol 492–495; ASMn, AG, 575, fol 28–35 by Mario Stivivi, house steward of Philip of Croy, who wrote a similar account for d'Este in ASMo, CD, Ambasciatore Germania, 66.

14   Letter published in M. Gachard (ed.), *Actes des États Généraux de 1600* (Brussels: Deltombe, 1849), pp. 561–562.

in Rome.[15] The official report influenced Beccari, as he also focussed on these reinforcements and presented Maurice's whole enterprise as a complete failure, writing that Maurice had left 'without having gained any honour'.[16] He concluded on a positive note with a brief description of the courageous actions of the Genoese captain Frederick Spinola against the retreating Dutch naval fleet. Here he followed the preferred version of the events within the papal curia and the archducal regime. Contemporaries, such as the political intelligencer Vialardi in Rome, commented on the positive spin the papal curia had given to the defeat at Nieuwpoort. He wrote to Ferdinand de' Medici that he was awaiting further particulars from Maurice's letters to arrive at the French ambassador in Rome, but that it was laughable to see how they 'console themselves' by drawing attention to the success of Frederick Spinola.[17] Vialardi's letter offers evidence that it was necessary to control the narrative early on, as the information from the Dutch side was arriving in Rome via other routes.

Beccari was highly gifted at composing these interpretative and narrative news accounts, they were incredibly popular: they were reprinted in various cities on the Italian peninsula (Milan, Naples, Bologna, Ferrara), and published in Seville as well as in Brussels in Spanish and French translations.[18] Their wide reach across different Habsburg territories illustrates the emergence of a more uniform, transnational pro-Habsburg news production.

Two decades later, another little-known news writer in Rome, Johannes Bergh followed in Beccari's footsteps, publishing comparable news reports. Bergh was active as a translator and news writer between 1622 and 1626.[19]

---

15   A. Louant (ed.), *Nonciature de Flandre, Correspondance d'O.M.F., premier nonce de Flandre*, III, (Brussels/Rome/Paris: Belgisch Historisch Instituut te Rome, 1942), p. 154. Similary Beccari wrote that Albert 'non essendo punto perduto d'animo più vigoroso, & più forte', raising a 'più grosso & più poderoso essercito'. BNCF, II, I 107, fol 39–42: *Successi di Finadra e rotta di Neuport*, emphazised the huge losses in Maurice's army.

16   Beccari, *Relatione del seguito*, A4.

17   ASF, MdP 3623, unfoliated, letter written on 4 august 1600: 'per consolargli vogliono dire che dal conto di Maurizio sia morte Ernesto di Nassau suo fratello, e tanti soldati, e affondati tanti vascelli da lo spinola, e cosa da ridere'; 'ma per consolersi dicono, che spinola ha messo a fondo la nave, sopra la quale erano tutte le ricurezze di Mauritio'.

18   *Marauigliosa vittoria ottenuta dalle genti de re catolico contra i ribelli heretici che havevano sorpresa la città di Lira in Brabantia* (Verona: Discepolo, 1596), USTC 812987; *Relacion nueva y muy verdadera de los sucessos del archiduque cardenal Alberto de austria en los estados de Flandes en este Anno de 1596* (Seville: Cabrera, 1596), USTC 338860. See: Carmen Espejo, 'The Prince of Transylvania: Spanish News of the War against the Turks, 1595–1600', in J. Raymond, N. Moxham (eds.), *News Networks in Early Modern Europe* (Leiden: Brill, 2016), pp. 512–541.

19   He translated, wrote and published other news pamphlets between 1622 and 1626: Giovanni Bergh (trans.), *Verissima relatione nella quale si narra la gran rotta che l'essercito di sua maesta cesarea ha dato nuouamente a quello del marchese di Baden ouero Durlach*

Originally from the Low Countries, he was presumably a member of the Catholic Netherlandish community in Rome.[20] Bergh referred to his accounts as a 'narrativa istoriale' or 'historical narrative', a description which exemplifies that these more narrative reports were considered to be both news and history at the same time.[21] Like Beccari's pamphlets, they gave an overview of sieges or battles, embedding the news in a larger narrative and providing a moral framework for the reader to interpret events. His accounts represent how news reports printed in Rome became imbued with a specific counter-reformation rhetoric. For example, Bergh started his lengthy account of the siege of Breda published in 1625 with a brief description of the state of Europe from 1619 onwards, the year in which the progress of 'heretics' made Catholics tremble as they started to threaten the whole of Europe:

> with the steady hope of the final extermination of the mighty house of Austria: then also threatening the Apostolic See, attempting to dominate Italy, attack Spain, promoting the French Huguenots, trying to introduce a Huguenot republic with La Rochelle as its capital city, and finally allying themselves with the Turks and other enemies of Christians.[22]

Even more, than Beccari had done before him, Bergh provided a providential reading of current events and placed the struggle in the Low Countries in a broader perspective with the idea that across Europe, Catholics were threatened by the Protestants. At the end of his account, he stated that every faithful Catholic must be delighted that so many Catholics had been freed from the Calvinists and therefore render thanks to God and Mary for this victory.

---

nel Palatinato doppo vna battaglia sanguinosa (Milan: Malatesta, 1622), USTC 4002889; Giovanni Bergh, Relatione verissima della presa fatta per forza d'Assalti dal sig. Conte di Tilli (Rome: Fei, 1622), USTC 4042331.

20   In his dedication of the pamphlet to Gerardo Meys, he described himself as a compatriot. Meys was originally from Maastricht, and played a role in the fraternity of Santa Maria in Campo Santo dei Tedeschi. See Giovanni Bergh, Ragguaglio delli principali successi nell'assedio della città di Breda. Postovi dall'Eccellentiss. Sig. Marchese Spinola, Generalissimo dell'Armi di Sua Maestà Cattolica nelli Paesi bassi (Rome: Grignani, 1625), USTC 4000037, A1.

21   Bergh, Ragguaglio, p. 15. For more on the blurry lines between news and history see chapter 4.

22   Bergh, Ragguaglio, A2: 'Con esperanza ferma del final' esterminio dell'Augustissima casa d'Austria. Minacciavano poi anco alla Sede Apostolica, insidiavano d'opprimer l'Italia assaltar la Spagna, suppeditar fomenti all'ugonotti della Francia, introdur la Republica di questi in essa, con far capo la Rocella, & finalmente confederarsi col Turco, & con altri nemici del nome Christiano'.

The tone of Bergh's pamphlets is distinctly post-Tridentine and divine intervention is omnipresent.[23] In case of his news pamphlet on the siege of Breda, Bergh devoted an entire page to the story of Charles Lambert, who had been part of the crew on the peat barge responsible for capturing Breda by surprise in 1590 and had been appointed as governor of Nijmegen as a reward for his services. In January 1625, during the siege of Breda, Lambert decided to conquer the small city of Goch by surprise as a diversion strategy. His troops desecrated altars, crucifixes, and holy images. Bergh focuses on Lambert's actions: he wanted to burn the last remaining image of Our Lady, and suddenly, he could not speak a word, became furious and died after a few days, leaving Bergh to conclude: 'a great prodigal shown against this impious heretic'.[24] In these Catholic news reports, God's wrath was omnipresent.

The militant tone and the presence of divine punishment developed by the news writers Beccari and Bergh in Rome would become a core characteristic of news reports publicising Habsburg victories in other cities for the remainder of the war in the Low Countries. For instance, in 1638, one Neapolitan news pamphlet on the failed Dutch attack on Kallo, a fort near Antwerp, also dwelt extensively on the death of Maurice of Nassau-Siegen, son of William of Nassau-Siegen, the commander of the Dutch troops, as a vindication of God because he had burnt the image of the Holy Virgin and Saint Anthony in the fort of Kallo 'with great scorn'.[25] According to this report, Maurice was wounded more than fourteen times, and his body no longer looked human.

Italian news reports in the early seventeenth century, then, became a blend of facts and miracles, as readers received historical and geographical information about specific towns or cities to understand the significance of a Habsburg victory. The insertion of stories showcasing divine retribution against the Protestant heretics clearly illustrated God's favouring of the Habsburg cause and His support for the near-universal Catholic struggle against the infidels.

---

23   In his account of the defeat of a Dutch fleet by the pirates of Dunkirk in 1626, he attributed their victory to the image of the Holy Virgin from Scottish Catholic refugees: Giovanni Bergh, *Vera relatione del maraviglioso successo della perdita dell'armata Olandese appresso Donchirchen* (Milan: Malatesta, 1626) in BNMV. For reporting on Dunkirk pirates in Verhoeven's newspaper: P. Arblaster, 'Our Valiant Dunkirk Romans': Glorifying the Habsburg War at Sea, 1622–1629', in J. Raymond, N. Moxham (eds.), *News Networks in Early Modern Europe* (Leiden: Brill, 2016), pp. 583–596.

24   Bergh, *Ragguaglio*, [A3]: 'Prodigio grande mostrato contro questo empio heretico'.

25   *Recit de la descente des Hollandois a Calloo et de la victoire que Dieu a donnée sur eux aux armes du Roy Catholique, au mois de Iuin de l'année* M.DC.XXXVIII (Brussels: Velpius, 1638), 6: 'con gran vilipendio'. Copy in ASF, MdP 4878.

2   **Making Spinola?**

The changing discourse in news reports affected how Italian generals were represented in news pamphlets. In the previous chapter on printed news pamphlets, we have seen that the Italian printed news production received a boost with the military successes of Alexander Farnese. In those publications, Farnese was presented as a genius military commander and a clement leader. The various military successes of the Genoese patrician Ambrogio Spinola, who arrived in the Netherlands in 1603 with a large contingent of Italian troops, were also publicized on the Italian peninsula.[26] However, his actions were not glorified to a similar extent as Farnese's in Italian news pamphlets. This sharply contrasts with historians' observation that Spinola was acutely aware of his reputation and tried to shape it by using the possibilities of the printing press.[27] In the archducal Netherlands, for instance, the Antwerp-based publisher Abraham Verhoeven, was instrumental in making Spinola a well-known figure.[28] Verhoeven's numerous news publications and prints dedicated to Spinola's victories, starting with his campaigns of 1605 and 1606, promoted his fame and reputation.[29] But this did not translate into similar levels of celebration and glorification in the different news pamphlets published in Italian cities.

The reasons why Spinola did not obtain an equal status as an Italian hero compared to Farnese, not even after his conquest of Breda in 1625, are two folded. Firstly, while the Spinola family was a prominent Genoese aristocratic banking family closely aligned with Madrid, they did not have extensive networks of patronage on the Italian peninsula. Secondly, the changing discourse established a more unifying narrative of Habsburg power. The ultimate praise for victories is bestowed upon the Spanish Habsburg king and God, rather than on Spinola as the military commander.

---

26   For more on Spinola: Asunción Retortillo Atienza, *Ambrosio Spínola, de Génova a Ostende (1569–1604)* (Madrid: Ministerio de Defensa, 2017).

27   See for instance B. De Groof, 'A Noble Courtier and a Gentleman Warrior. Some Aspects of the Creation of the Spinola Image', in J. Fenoulhet, L. Gilbert (eds.), *Narrative of Low Countries History and Culture. Reframing the Past* (London: UCL Press, 2016), pp. 26–34.

28   For more information on Verhoeven: Paul Arblaster, *From Ghent to Aix. How They Brought the News in the Habsburg Netherlands, 1550–1700* (Leiden: Brill, 2014), pp. 74–121.

29   For a more general overview consult N. Lamal and P. Arblaster, 'Spinola's fame in the news press', in S. Mostaccio, B.J. García García, L. Lo Basso (eds.), *Ambrosio Spinola between Genoa, Flanders and Spain* (Leuven: Leuven University Press, 2022), pp. 213–250.

Spinola's first military success was to end the protracted siege of Ostend, a coastal city in Flanders, in 1604.[30] This siege had been one of truly epic proportions: around 20,000 Habsburg troops had attacked this last Dutch stronghold in the southern Netherlands for more than three years. It became a media event in large parts of Europe: in the German lands, England, France, and the Dutch Republic, numerous news reports and contemporary chronicles offering an overview of the actions during the siege were available to a wide audience in 1604 before the city surrendered to Spinola.

In Italian cities, only a very brief and hastily produced account appeared, approved by Don Pedro de Toledo, the archducal resident in Rome.[31] On the title page and throughout the text, Ambrogio Spinola was referred to as 'Francesco', simply mentioning that he had brought the necessary funds to finance the war and had been able to encourage the soldiers to fight. The lack of extensive coverage of Spinola's actions and the error in this news pamphlet can be partly explained by his status. Compared to Alexander Farnese, he was not the heir to a duchy on the Italian peninsula and a member of an influential dynasty with powerful connections in Rome. The Spinola family could not rely on an extensive network of patronage and did not have a similar influence and position in papal Rome as the Farnese's had with their cardinals. At this stage, as a Genoese patrician without any previous military experience, he was not well-known outside of his native city of Genoa. The military engineer Pompeo Targone, was much better known throughout Italy, and especially in Rome, than Ambrogio. Targone had been in service of the papacy before going to Ostend, where he constructed various siege machines. His inventions had received ample coverage in the *avvisi*, manuscript and printed accounts of the siege of Ostend.[32]

---

30 W. Thomas (ed.), *De Val van het Nieuwe Troje. Het beleg van Oostende (1601–1604)* (Leuven: Davidfonds, 2004), pp. 173–175; Anna E.C. Simoni, *The Ostend Story: Early Tales of the Great Siege and the Mediating Role of Henrick Haestens* ('t Goy-Houten: HES & De Graaf, 2003).

31 *Relatione dell'assedio della fortezza d'Ostenden posto nella Fiandra* (Siena: s.n., 1604), USTC 4025524: 'Ego Corn. Camerarius Secretarius Don Petri de Toledo Belgicae hanc relationem iuxta fidem historia veram esse, ac probamtestor signo manuali. Roma 18. Octobris 1604'.

32 For a far more detailed description of the siege, see the anonymous handwritten account in Vallicelliana, N22, fol 178–190: *Breve relatione de' successi seguiti in Fiandra, dal principio dell'assedio d'Ostenden fino alla fine del'espugnazione*; the same account is present in the military papers of Giovanni di Raffaelo de Medici in BL, AD Ms 48.769A. Various *avvisi* in ASF, MdP 4256. A selection is now available via the online exhibition of euronews project: 'The Exciting News of Ostend (1601–04): How Florentines Seized the Siege' <http://omeka .euronewsproject.org/omeka/neatline/fullscreen/the-exciting-news-of-ostende>.

In the next years, the absence of active promotors in Rome and strong patronage networks had a noticeable effect on the content of news prints and reports. It is visible in a Roman news print on Spinola's successful siege of Rheinberg in 1606, which presented the military engineer Pompeo Targone, who was prominently depicted on horseback together with his invention of the field milling machine, instead of the general.[33] Targone's close ties to the Borghese papacy may help to explain the Roman print maker's decision to heap praise on the engineer rather than on Spinola. The printed news reports of Spinola's victories at Oldenzaal and Lingen, by and large, lacked a celebratory tone as they were based on anonymous handwritten reports offering predominantly detailed, almost day-by-day, dry factual accounts of military manoeuvres and operations.[34] In the case of Alexander Farnese, the news accounts had been based on copies of the letters by members of his entourage or himself giving great prominence to his actions. This was not the case for Spinola, it seems that the absence of his own 'voice' in print resulted in a promotional gap, where instead the anonymous authors of these accounts celebrated the actions of other Italian military commanders, such as the Milanese veteran Carlo Emanuele Teodoro Trivulzio.[35]

The importance of patronage for the production of news is best illustrated by the Genoese edition of the news report of Spinola's victories at Oldenzaal and Lingen, printed by Pavoni.[36] Pavoni reprinted the same factual account, as

---

33   *Berges svl reno assediata et presa a pati il di 2 de ottobre 1606 dal sig.re Marchese Spinola*, engraved by Giovanni Maggi and published by Hendrik van Schoel in Rome, dedicated to Juan Fernandez Pacheco, the Spanish ambassador in Rome in RCT, RCIN 721129.

34   *Relatione dell'impresa di Oldensel e di Linghen fatta dall'illusstiss & eccellentiss. signore marchese Spinola nella prouincia di Frisia quest'anno 1605. alli 10. e 18. Agosto* (Florence: Caneo, 1605), USTC 4031155; *Relatione del seguito in Fiandra per opera dell'illustrissimo & Eccellentissimo Signor Marchese Spinola dalla presa di Linghen, & d'Oldensel fino al presente* (Viterbo: Discepolo, 1606) USTC 4043090. BAV, Cappon. 164, fol 196r–199r: *Compendio dei successi seguiti in questi stati di Fiandra nella campagna dell'anno 1605*; BV, N22, fol 165–168v: *Compedio delli successi seguiti in questi stati di Fiandra nella campagna nell'anno 1605*, fol 169–172v: *Relazione di quanto è seguito sotto Rhinberg li 12. sett. 1606*; Same two accounts in BL, AD MS 48.769A, fol 34–39v and fol 40. Also in ASMn, AG, Fiandra, Scritture Diverse: *Compendio de successi seguiti in fiandra nella campagna del 1606*.

35   See for example: 'in buon ordine del conte Theodoro, ch'inanimando continuamente i suoi et con le parole et con l'essempio del suo valore, non mancò in cosa alcuna all'officio di savio et prudente capitano', in BAV, Cappon. 164, fol 196r–199r.

36   *Relatione del seguito in Fiandra per opera dell'Illustrissimo & Eccellentissimo Signor Marchese Spinola dalla presa di Linghen, & d'Oldensel fino al presente* (Genoa: Pavoni, 1606). Pavoni's dedication is dated 25 January 1606. The only surviving copy is now kept in the Biblioteca Civica A.G. Barrili in Savona. I would like to thank the Director Marco Genzone for sending me pictures of this copy. Francesco Pico from Savona owned this publication in 1608.

had appeared in other Italian cities, but he turned it into a laudatory publication through the addition of poems by the Ligurian poets Gabriello Chiabrera and Ambrosio Salinero.[37] Very few news reports were printed in Genoa in the early seventeenth century and no other news reports of Spinola's victories seem to have appeared in his native city.[38] Its appearance might be explained by Ambrogio brief return to Genoa in April 1606, on his way from Madrid to Brussels. Before leaving for the Low Countries, Ambrogio already had the reputation as a patron for poets in the Genoese republic.[39] It may have spurred the printer into action. Spinola's military feats provided an excellent opportunity for Pavoni to show his allegiance to the Genoese Republic and to seek favours from various members of the Genoese literary scene. As Pavoni explained, in his dedication to the Genoese painter Bernardo Castello, he had published this news of Spinola's campaign so that everyone:

> will enjoy the glories and honours of the citizens and their homeland, like I felt the infinite delight that this Most Serene Republic of Genoa is renowned because of its children of great esteem and inestimable reputation in the arts of war and peace.[40]

In several of the poems, there is a first attempt at glorifying Spinola's deeds. In a longer poem, dedicated to Paolo Agostino Spinola, Ambrogio is celebrated as a great warrior for his victory at Ostend, as even Alexander Farnese had been unable to conquer this city.[41] The comparison with the Farnese highlighted Spinola's qualities as a military commander. Yet in contrast to Farnese, Spinola was above all presented as a Genoese hero, rather than an Italian one. Spinola's

---

37   *Relatione del seguito in Fiandra*, pp. 16–17.

38   The USTC records only eight news books printed in Genoa for the sixteenth century. Pavoni mostly printed literary works: Graziano Ruffini, *Sotto il segno del Pavone. Annali di Giuseppe Pavoni e dei suoi eredi 1598–1642* (Rome: FrancoAngeli, 1995) and Niri, *La tipografia a Genova*, pp. 79–89. Another example of a printed news report in Genoa: *Nuovo aviso della presa della città chiamata la maometta in Barbaria* (Genoa: Pavoni, 1602), USTC 4043988.

39   E. Zucchi, 'Contesting the Spanish Myth. Republican Shaping of Ambrogio Spinola's image in Genoese literature', in S. Mostaccio, B.J. García García, L. Lo Basso (eds.), *Ambrogio Spinola between Genoa, Flanders and Spain* (Leuven: Leuven University Press, 2022), pp. 251–270.

40   *Relatione del seguito in Fiandra*, p. 5: 'godirà delle glorie, e de gli onori de' cittadini, e della patria commune, com'io fra me stesso sento infinito gusto che questa Serenissima Republica di Genova vada sì felicemente crescendo ne suoi figli di credito, & riputazione inestimabile nell' arti della guerra e della pace'.

41   The author is poem is unknown, see *Relatione del seguito in Fiandra*, pp. 18–22.

victories were a manifestation of the magnificence of the Genoese Republic and Genoese identity.

Spinola's greatest moment of glory was the conquest of Breda, after eleven months of siege.[42] The victory was celebrated throughout the Habsburg territories. Milan was decorated with allegorical scenes related to the war. Milanese printers, chief amongst them the official printer Melchior Malatesta, produced accounts of the siege and the Milanese celebrations, which included a solemn mass, public festivities and fireworks.[43] The Malatestas had a privileged relationship with various governors and even established a printing office in court. By this time, the Malatesta firm had become the most important publisher of news in Milan. The circulation of his news pamphlets was based on a network connecting the Malatestas in Milan to Marco Antonio Benvenuti in Rome and Secondino Roncagliolo in Naples.[44] In the case of the siege of Breda, his initial account, which reprinted a letter written on 5 June from the battlefield, was quickly reprinted in these cities, including in Bologna and Piacenza.[45] Due to this network, the same version of the events was read in several Italian cities. In those accounts, the siege was described as heroic, but in neither of the publications did Spinola receive particular praise for his actions.[46] Only in Rome,

---

42   On the publicity surrounding the siege of Breda, see: S.A. Vosters, *Het beleg van Breda in het wereldnieuws* (Delft: Eburon, 1987); S.A. Vosters, *Het beleg en de overgave van Breda in geschiedenis, literatuur en kunst* (Breda: Gemeentelijke archiefdienst, 1993).

43   *Dichiaratione delle allegrezze fatte nel solenne apparato fato nella chiesa di Santo Eustorgio di Milano per ringraziare Iddio nell'occasione della resa di Breda* (Milan: Colonna, 1625), USTC 4007652 and the verses in Lombard dialect recounting the festivities in the city by Andrea da Milano, *Ragionamento fatto in lode di Bredà di Porta Noua, doue si contengono tutti i Bredà feste, giuochi, e fuochi fatti nella città di Milano per l'allegrezza della presa di detto Bredà* (Milan: Malatesta, 1625), USTC 4002785.

44   See M. Petta, 'Networks of Printers and the Dissemination of News: the case of Milan in the sixteenth and seventeenth Centuries', in R. Kirwan, S. Mullins (eds.), *Specialist Markets in the Early Modern Book World* (Leiden: Brill, 2015), pp. 64–84.

45   *Copia d'vna lettera scritta dal campo sotto Breda adi 5. giugno 1625. Quale racconta la resa di quella piazza, con le capitulationi stabilite trà l'eccellentiss. Sign. Marchese Spinola Generalissimo delli Esserciti intrati per S.M. in Alemagna, e Governatore Generale nelli Stati di Fiandra. Et altri felici successi occorsi innanzi à questa resa* (Milan: Malatesta, 1625), USTC 4004822. *Copia d'una lettera scritta dal campo sotto Bredá. Adì 5. di Giugno 1625* (Rome: Grignani, 1625), USTC 4004796 ; *Copia duna lettera scritta dal campo sotto Breda adi 5. giugno 1625* (Piacenza: Ardizzoni, 1625), USTC 4007806; *Copia d'una lettera scritta dal campo sotto Breda a 5. di giugno 1625* (Naples: Roncagliolo, 1625), USTC 4002675; *Copia d'vna lettera scritta dal campo sotto Breda. Alli 5. di Giugno 1625* (Bologna: Tebaldini, 1625) in Biblioteca Comunale dell'Archiginnasio.

46   Malatesta dedicated *Breve Ragguaglio del sito, e positura della villa di bredà et in che modo* to Gerolama Doria Spinola, Duchess of Sesto, she was the daughter in law of Ambrogio Spinola, but even here specific praise for Ambrogio was lacking.

did the Roman bookseller Benvenuti finance the publication of Bergh's more elaborate news account by Lodovico Grignani. Bergh presented Spinola as 'gran guerriero', who had shown to the world:

> his valour, his singular prudence and shrewdness, his intrepid spirit, in the clamour of arms, with which he has no regard for heat, nor for cold, nor for the firing of muskets or cannon in any danger, of his mature judgement and well-considered deliberations, and of his readiness to execute them.[47]

This brief enumeration of his qualities was as much praise as Spinola received. As in other publications, the emphasis in Bergh's narrative was fully on the importance of the victory for the Habsburg dynasty. The development of highly militant Catholic rhetoric and the official Habsburg narrative influenced the extent to which Spinola was presented as a hero. It is perhaps most clearly captured by the Florentine soldier Pieri who in his day-by-day factual account of the siege, first printed in 1626 in Bologna, Milan, and Venice, wrote:

> But God, who was the protector of this enterprise, thwarted all the hopes of the enemy, and Marquis Spinola, zealous for the service of God and his King, did not feel any discomfort, did not know any fatigue and did not estimate any danger [...] Divine help was never mistrusted.[48]

Spinola then was only able to withstand various attempts by the Dutch to relieve the city because he was acting with the help of God to preserve the Catholic religion and Habsburg power.

---

47   C. Casetti Brach and M. Carmela di Cesare, 'Lodovico Grignani', *DBI*, 50 (2003). Bergh, *Ragguaglio*, p. 15: 'del suo valore, della singolar prudenza, & accortezza, dell'animo suo intrepido, nello strepito dell'arme, col quale non ha riguardo al caldo, nè al fredoo, nè colpi de moschetti, o cannoni in qual si voglia pericolo, del maturo conseglio e deliberationi ben ponderate e della prontezza di metterle in essecutione'.

48   Pier Francesco Pieri, *Diario del seguito in Fiandra dalli xxi luglio mdcxxlv sino alli 25 d'agosto del 25 con l'assedio, e resa di Bredà col seguito del campo cattolio e dell'olandese* (Bologna: Mascheroni, 1626), USTC 4006135; Printed in Milan with new title: *Nove gverre di Fiandra dalli XXI. Lvglio M.DC.XXIV. sino alli 25. d'Agosto del 1625. con l'assedio, e resa di Bredà, col seguito del campo cattolico, e dell'olandese*, (Milan: Besozzo, 1626), USTC 4002937 and Venetian edition in 1626 by Ciotti (USTC 4007181), p. 34: 'Ma Iddio, che fù protettore di questa impresa, fece sortire vane tutte le speranze del nemico, & il Marchese Spinola zelante del servitio di Dio, e del suo Rè non sentiva disagi, non conosceva fatiche, e non stimava pericoli, [...]. Mai si diffidò dell'aiuto Divino.'

Ambrogio Spinola had a publicity disadvantage on the Italian peninsula compared to Alexander Farnese. It was partly because the Farnese family, as a ruling dynasty on the Italian peninsula, had a large patronage network to promote the success of Alexander. In Spinola's case, it seems that his entourage, and family, were not as actively involved when it came to promoting his military successes in Italian cities. Crucially, they may have had fewer opportunities to undertake such actions as the changing ideological discourse in news pamphlets worked against promoting Spinola. Compared to Farnese, neither Spinola's letters and accounts, nor those of his entourage, appeared on the Milanese printing presses. These news accounts now presented a unified narrative of Habsburg power supported by God with little room to cultivate a new Italian hero.

3   Growing Divisions

Due to several Italian states' shifts in international alliances, the uniformity of news publishing on the Italian peninsula started to fragment. Venice, never a wholehearted supporter of the Habsburg dynasty, concluded a formal defensive alliance with the Dutch Republic in 1619. Their involvement in anti-Habsburg collaborations impacted the news production in the Venetian Republic.[49] For instance, in 1624, Antonio Pinelli, the official printer of the Venetian state, printed an account describing the Dutch capture of Salvador da Bahia, the capital of colonial Brazil.[50] According to Michiel van Groesen, this victory had been 'the most lavishly celebrated military victory in the war against Spain until that point' in the Dutch Republic itself, where pamphlets had presented it as a major blow to Habsburg power in the Indies.[51] It is therefore significant that an Italian news account of this Dutch success appeared in Venice not long after the news had reached the Dutch Republic.

---

49   Significantly Bartolomé de Las Casas' account on the Spanish atrocities in the Indies, first published in Seville in 1552, was translated into Italian by Giacomo Castellani for the first time and printed in 1626 in Venice: *Istoria, o brevissima relatione della distrutione dell'Indie occidentali di monsig. reverendiss. don Bartolomeo dalle Case, o Casaus; conforme al suo vero originale spagnuolo stampato in Siviglia* (Venice: Ginammi, 1626), USTC 4006104.

50   *Relatione dell'acquisto fatto dall'armata holandese della Citta di S. Saluadore nella Baia di tutti i Santi* (Venice: Pinelli, 1624), USTC 4004828. Pinelli was appointed as 'stampatore ducale' in 1617, see the entry by A. Giachery in *DBI*, 83 (2015).

51   Michiel van Groesen, *Amsterdam's Atlantic: Print Culture and the Making of Dutch Brazil* (Philadelphia: University of Pennsylvania Press, 2016), pp. 44–71.

In the opening lines of this Venetian account, the Protestant Dutch soldiers were described as valorous, prudent, brave, and courageous, which
was exactly the opposite of what audiences were reading in other Italian cities. Minor details in the text illustrate that Pinelli's news account was geared
toward a Venetian audience. For example, the reference that Piet Heyn, the
vice-admiral of the Dutch fleet, had already served the Venetian Republic during its war against the Austrian Habsburgs in Gradisca, is highly significant in
this respect.[52] As such this news account reinforced the idea of a long-standing
friendship between these two republics. The subsequent Spanish-Habsburg
victories in 1625 including the conquest of Breda, where Venetian soldiers were
fighting alongside the Dutch troops, and the recapture of Salvador da Bahia
were not publicised in Venice.[53] Political alliances shaped the printed production of news in Italian cities to a considerable degree.

At the start of 1625, French troops had crossed the Alps and joined forces
with the Duke of Savoy, who moved his army towards the Genoese Republic.[54]
Several of the news pamphlets on the success at Breda in 1625 contained references to the escalating situation on the Italian peninsula.[55] One news report
warned that the success in Breda was a great consolation to the Catholics, but
that the rage of the heretics and their supporters would now be even greater
not only outside, but also within Italy.[56] The divisions between the pro-French
and the pro-Spanish party became apparent in popular genres. In Milan a
Navarineida was printed, a poetic composition in Lombard dialect on the
Navarin, a reference to the pro-French factions in the city.[57] Such compositions
were often recited by pedlars and posted in public places throughout the city.[58]

---

52 In 1617 he had left Dutch Republic as captain of Neptunus and was in 1618 forced to serve
the Republic of Venice until 1621, see H.C.H. Moquette, 'Rotterdammers in dienst van
Venetië', *Rotterdams Jaarboekje*, (1914), p. 44.

53 BNM, Cl. VII, cod. 1093/5, fol 52v: 'Italiani sudditi della Ser.ma Republica che militano nelli
esserciti di questi Signori'. The recapture by Bahia under the command of Don Fadrique
de Toledo were publicised in Milan, Rome and Naples, see the separate entries in the
bibliography.

54 For an overview of the situation on the peninsula: D. Parrott, R. Oresko, 'The House of
Savoy and the Thirty Years War', in H. Schilling, K. Busmann (eds.), *1648, War and Peace in
Europe: Politics, Religion, Law and Society* (Münster: Veranstaltungsgesellschaft 350 Jahre
Westfälischer Friede, 1998), pp. 141–160.

55 Bergh, *Ragguaglio delli principali successi*, [A1v], 'Massimamente in queste turbolenze
d'Italia'.

56 *Relatione della solenne entrata in Breda della Serenis. Infante D. Isabella Clara Eugenia arciduchessa d'austria. Adi 12. Giugno 1625* (Milan: Malatesta, 1625), USTC 4005876.

57 *Descors intorna a la resa de Brada in despresij di Navarin Nostrans Dà in lus da Battista da
Miran* (Milan: s.n., 1625).

58 Pedlars have been studied mainly in the Venetian context and for the sixteenth century,
see Rospocher and Salzberg, 'Street Singers in the Italian Renaissance', pp. 628–653.

The poem claimed that the *Navarin* was very displeased with the success of Spinola at Breda, which was seen as a showcase for Spanish-Habsburg military strength. It ended with the motto: 'Long Live Spain, and long live the wine, so shrink all the *Navarin*'.[59] In the following years, France re-entered the scene as a significant player in Italian politics with the second war of succession of Mantua and Monferrato (1627–1631).[60] It pitted France against Spain for control of northern Italy. During this war, Turin, as the capital city of the duchy of Savoy, developed into a centre producing anti-Spanish polemics.[61]

One final reason for a change occurring in Italian reporting in the mid-1620s was the fact that Spain ever more ran out of steam. The siege of Breda in 1625 was the last great battle won by the Habsburg troops in the Low Countries. For almost ten years after Breda, almost no news pamphlets on the war against the United Provinces were published in Italian cities for the simple reason that there was no good news to report. The Spanish-Habsburg crown lost significant amounts of territory to the Dutch; especially the losses of 's Hertogenbosch in 1629 and Maastricht in 1632 were humiliating.[62] While Spanish publishers of *Relaciones* reported on minor victories during these sieges, Italian publishers seem to have by and large refrained from doing so, presumably because other information was available, and instead turned their attention to the military advances of the German Catholic league in the Holy Roman Empire.[63]

---

59   *Descors intorno a la resa de Brada*, p. 7: 'Viva Spagna e viva el vin, e crepen tugg i Navarin'.

60   For more information see David Parrott, 'The Mantuan succession crisis 1627–1631: A Sovereignty Dispute in Early Modern Europe', *The English Historical Review*, 112 (1997), pp. 20–65; S. Externbrink, 'The Thirty Years' War in Italy 1628–1659', in O. Asbach, P. Schröder (eds.), *Ashgate Research Companion to the Thirty Years' War* (Farnham: Ashgate, 2014), pp. 177–190. *Insinuatione di un compendioso discorso delle giuste ragioni, che hà la casa di Nevers, unita hoggi con quella di Mantova, sopra li ducati di Brabant, Lothier, Limburgh et signoria di Anvers, ne' Paesi Bassi della Fiandra, dalla corona di Spagna occupati* (Paris: s.n., 1628), USTC 6020580. On the claims of the Duke of Nevers see D. Parrott, 'A prince souverain and the French Crown: Charles de Nevers 1580–1637', in *Royal and Republican Sovereignty in Early Modern Europe*, pp. 149–187.

61   See for instance *Giustificatione delle attioni di Spagna & manifestazione delle violenze di Francia* (s.l.: s.n., s.d.), *Risposta per la riputazione spagnuola al finto conseglio di stato sopra la fuga* (s.l.: s.n., s.d.), USTC 4000722 and *alla maestà del Re d'un buono e fedele Francesce circa le turbulenze d'Italia* (Turin: Stampator ducal, 1628), USTC 4005893. For a Sabaudian perspective consult: A. Blythe Raviola, 'Sabaudian Propaganda and the Wars of Succession of Mantua and Monferrato, 1613–1631', in S. Alyn Stacey (ed.), *Political, Religious and Social Conflict in the States of Savoy, 1400–1700* (Bern: Lang, 2014), pp. 53–76.

62   For a handwritten report on the loss of 's Hertogenbosch, presumably written by Baldassare Nardi, see AAV, Miscellanea Arm II, vol 139, fol 355–364v: *Relatione del assedio di Bolduch*. For more information on these military campaigns: Olaf van Nimwegen, *The Dutch Army and the Military Revolutions 1588–1688* (Woodbridge: Boydell, 2010), pp. 219–234.

63   See for instance *Vitoria que el governador de Bolduque tuvo contra el principe de Orange* (Seville: de Lyra, 1629), USTC 5013772. For more on the Spanish *relaciones*, see Henry

4   Polemical Instruments

France's unilateral declaration of war against Spain in 1635 marks the beginning of an intense propaganda war between the two major powers.[64] On the
Italian peninsula, the duke of Savoy and the duke of Parma had concluded an
alliance with France; together they aimed to attack Lombardy.[65] News reports
of French victories were often printed in Turin and Casale Monferrato in the
next decade.[66] The French declaration of war and a first account of the French
army of 26,000 men defeating the Habsburg forces of Prince Thomas of Savoy
near Les Avins were published anonymously in Italian. The existence of anonymous pro-French news pamphlets in Italian was until now not known; the copies in the Medici Archive are unique survivors.[67]

The offensive to counter a French narrative on the Italian peninsula was
undertaken by printers in Milan and Naples, the two most important Habsburg
cities. Rome, where news favourable to Habsburgs had always appeared,
under Urban VIII during this period no longer contributed to producing such
accounts. The occasional news pamphlets now became a polemical instru-
ment in this war of words. Due to the news publications in favour of the

---

Ettinghausen, 'The News in Spain: Relaciones de sucesos in the Reigns of Philip III and
IV', *European History Quaerterly*, 14 (1984), pp. 1–20; H. Ettinghausen, 'The Golden Age
of Single Event Printed Newsletter: *Relaciones de sucesos*, 1601–1650', A.S. Wilkinson,
A. Ulla Lorenzo (eds.), *A Maturing Market: The Iberian Book World in the first half of the
Seventeenth Century* (Leiden: Brill, 2017), pp. 241–258. For Italian publications consult:
*Relatione della gran vittoria ottenuta dal generale conte di Tilli, con l'essercito della Lega
cattolica, contro il re di Danimarca* (Rome: Grignani, 1626), USTC 4004721; *Relatione della
vittoria havuta dalli cattolici contro li Protestanti d'Alemagna & Svedesi sotto la città di
Norlinghen* (Milan: Malatesta, 1634), USTC 4012081.

64   On this topic: Jose M. Jover, *1635: Historia di una polémica y semblanza de una gene-
       ración* (Madrid: Consejo superior de investigaciones científicas, 1947). For a more liter-
       ary approach: Maria Soledad Arrendondo, *Literatura y propaganda en tiempo de Quevedo:
       guerras y plumas contra Francia, Cataluña y Portugal* (Madrid/Frankfurt am Main:
       Iberoamericana/Vervuert, 2011).

65   For the military campaigns in Italy: Gregory Hanlon, *The Hero of Italy: Odoardo Farnese,
       Duke of Parma and his Soldiers and his Subjects in the Thirty Years' War* (Oxford: Oxford
       University Pres, 2014) and his *Italy 1636: Cemeteries of Armies* (Oxford: Oxford University
       Press, 2016).

66   *I felici progressi dell'armi del Re Christianissimo nelle provincie di Spagna, Fiandra,
       Borgogna, & Alsatia, occorsi nelli mesi di Giugno, Luglio, & Agosto del 1638: descritti in
       lingua Francese, e tradotti nell'Italiana* (Casale Monferrato: s.n., 1638), USTC 4046167;
       Seconda e compita relatione della segnalata vittoria ottenuta dalle armi francesi in Fiandra
       (Piombino: s.n., 1648), USTC 4020043.

67   These two pamphlets are in ASF, MdP 4878. *Ordine del Re Christianissimo al suo residente
       in Bruselles di chieder in suo nome la liberatione dell'arcivescovo di Trevari, con ciò che è
       seguito dappoi, tradotto dal Francese* (s.l.: s.n., [1635]).

French, the need for reliable and trustworthy news became more of a priority in Italian printed news culture. That is to say, publishers stressed the reliability of their reports more forcefully and showed an increasing awareness of the existence of pro-French news publications. In the editorial address of *Auuisi certissimi della rotta di molte troppe francesi* (Certain notices of the defeat of many French troops) Filippo Ghisolfi, Milanese publisher and competitor to the Malatestas, referred to the false reports of the French, and at the same time stressed the reliability of the news he printed.[68]

> If we were so eager to publish the true progress that God gives us over those, who have declared war against Our Catholic Majesty, and are engaged in disseminating false reports in their gazettes, which eventually have discredited the authors, and ridiculed them publicly, we would have enough material to satisfy the curious and to promote success on more solid grounds.[69]

In this account, Ghisolfi reprinted and translated the manuscript *avvisi* from August, coming from Luxemburg, Rome, Brussels and many other places. The news pamphlet has been described by the Italian historian Valerio Castronovo as the first printed newspaper, while it relied upon *avvisi* just as many news pamphlets in the sixteenth century had done.[70] The way news was reported and presented had not significantly changed. However, the polemical undertone of the editorial address to the reader was a new element of Milanese news culture.

The authorities and printers reacted as pro-French narratives started to appear in Italian. Not long after the French invasion of the Low Countries, an anonymous pro-French account of the conquest of the Brabantine town by the

---

68   *Auuisi certissimi della rotta di molte troppe francesi seguita nella Lorena, Fiandra, Lucemburg, & altri luoghi. Tradotti in italiano da fidelissimo originale. Con aggiunta delle cose più vicine* (Milan: Ghisolfi, 1635), USTC 4012085. The Malatesta's briefly faced competition in production of news from Ghisolfi who had started his news publishing activities after the devastating plague of 1631, for more on Ghisolfi see Paola Arrigoni, *Filippo Ghisolfi: Tipografo, editore e calcografo* (Milan/Udine: Mimesis, 2022), pp. 75–77.

69   *Auuisi certissimi della rotta di molte troppe francesi*, A1: 'Se noi fossimo si pronti à publicar gli avantaggi verissimi, che Iddio ci dona sopra quelli, che havendo dicharata la Guerra à S.M. Cattolica, s'ingegnano di seminar falsi rapporti nelle loro gazette: le quali alla fine hanno discreditati gli auttori, & resili ridicoli appresso al Mondo: Noi havressimo ben sovento materia da contentari i curiosi e fabricar trofei sopra fondamento più sodi'.

70   V. Castronovo, 'La stampa periodica fra Cinque e Seicento', in V. Castronovo, C. Capra, G. Ricuperati (eds.), *La stampa italiana dal Cinquecento all'Ottocento* (Rome: Laterza, 1980), pp. 25–26.

French and Dutch forces was printed in Italian. It presented the French-Dutch army in a very favourable light, as it did not mention the violent sack by the investing army.[71] The sack of Tienen on 9 June 1635 by the French-Dutch army became a critical event in news pamphlets printed in the Habsburg Netherlands, as well as in Milan and Naples.[72] In a series of compendia containing the latest news printed during 1635, one could follow the progress of the Spanish Habsburg army.[73] In all these compilations, the events in Tienen were mentioned: the first one in the series stated that the French and Dutch 'did the most abominable cruelties that have never been heard of by barbarous armies'.[74] Their acts of iconoclasm and the rape of nuns received ample attention and by focusing on this event, the impiety and unreliability of the French could be shown to an Italian audience. In one of the last compiled news pamphlet printed in 1635, the sack of Tienen was described as a 'miserable spectacle' and the barbarity and impiety of the French were stressed throughout. The anonymous author expressed the amazement of the Habsburg soldiers to discover that the French army had dared to despise the Catholic religion, and he stated that the Habsburg troops all hoped that a vengeful God would come to their aid. Once again, the Habsburg troops were presented as the true defenders of Catholicism.

This kind of narrative build-up helped to show that God was indeed on the side of the Habsburg forces because the reader would soon find out that the Cardinal-Infant had successfully taken Schenkenschans, a strategical

---

71 *Breve relatione della vittoria ottenuta dall' armi di* S.M. *sotto il commando del Sig. Prencipe d'Oranges, & Signori marescialli di Sciattiglion & Bressè. Sopra l'armata del Serenissimo Caridanl Infante a Tirlemont in Fiandra* (s.l.: s.n., 1635) in ASF, MdP 4878.

72 Jover, *1635: Historia di una polémica,* pp. 293–305. For Habsburg Netherlands consult Arblaster, *From Ghent to Aix,* pp. 177–183.

73 *Relatione delli successi di fiandra dal di che l'eserciti di Francia & Olanda vniti entrorono nelli stati obedienti di sua maesta cattolica sin alli dodeci di lugio, e della vittoria, ch'hebbe in questo giorno sua real altezza il signor infante cardinale contro gli esserciti inmici* (Naples: Longo, 1635), USTC 4009368. At the end of the account, the reader was told that the *relatione* was based on several letters sent by ministers and other official of the Spanish crown. An overview was also given of all the letters that had been used to compile the account. *Seconda relatione del seguito in Fiandra et in diverse parti di Germania nel presente anno 1635* (Naples: Longo, 1635), USTC 4008481; the title page mentions it is based on Milanese edition: *Distinta e vera relatione di quanto è successo al Serenissimo Cardinal Infante di Spagna et alle sue armi nella fiandra doppo la sopresa di treveri sino à Novembre 1635* (Milan: Malatesta, 1635), USTC 4010427.

74 *Relatione delli successi di Fiandra dal di che l'eserciti di Francia & Olanda entrorono nelli stati obedienti di Sua Maestà Cattolica fin alli dodeci di Luglio* (Naples: Longo, 1635), USTC 4009368, p. 1: 'facendo le più abominevoli crudeltati, che già mai da eserciti Barbari si sentirono'.

170

river fortress on the Rhine, on 28 July 1635. It was a significant success for the
Habsburg army, as it offered the possibility of launching an attack on the Dutch
Republic itself. In Milan, Ghisolfi produced a news print depicting the fortress
copying Bonaventura Peeters' bird's eye view.[75] The text beneath recounted in
detail the successful nightly attack. Two days after it was captured, the Dutch
army started to lay siege to the place. The painter and engraver Giovanni Paolo
Bianchi followed suit and created another news print detailing the first attacks
by the Dutch troops.[76] The Count-Duke of Olivares had instructed the Cardinal
to defend the fort at any cost.[77] However, it would be a short-lived success for
the Habsburg forces, as Frederick Henry retrieved this fortress in April 1636.
Again, as had been the case in the first phases of the Revolt in the Netherlands,
losses and defeats of Habsburg forces were not publicized.

From 1635 onwards, Naples emerged as an important centre for the defence
of Spanish-Habsburg interests. Egidio Longo, royal printer, produced numerous
polemical texts and news pamphlets in both Italian and Spanish.[78] He cultivated important connections by dedicating many of his news reports to members of Neapolitan nobility close to Habsburg power. He choose his dedicatees
carefully: two of his news accounts in 1635 were dedicated to Don Frabritio
Lanario, the son of Francesco Lanario, who had been to the Low Countries and
written a short and popular history of the Revolt. In the same year, Longo also

75   *Discritione [sic] del sito è positura della gran fortezza di Schinhen e del modo con la quale la
     Guarnigione de Gheler commandata dal Luogotenente Colonello Anholt del Regimento del
     Conte di Embden ne fece la sopresa la notte de 27 di Luglio 1635* (Milan: Ghisolfi, 1635) in RCT
     (RCIN 722089).
76   *Vera Descrittione del famoso Forte di Schench, importato alli 28. Luglio 1635. Sotto gli Auspicij
     della Real Altezza del Sig. Cardinal Infante* (Milan: Gariboldi, 1635) in RCT (RCIN 722090).
     This news print was decicated to Antonio Ronchio, the Grand Chancellor of the State of
     Milan. On function of Grand Chancellor see Antonio Álvarez-Ossorio Alvariño, 'La som-
     bre del gobernador y cuello de la República: el Gran Canciller del Estado de Milán', in
     G. Mazzocchi (ed.), *El corazón de la Monarquía. La Lombardia in età spagnola* (Como: Ibis,
     2010), pp. 15–41.
77   Jonathan Israel, *The Dutch Republic. Its Rise, Greatness, and Fall 1477–1806* (Oxford: Oxford
     University Press, 1998), pp. 529–530.
78   See for instance *Auuisi di diuerse parti mandati alla Francia da un suo affettionato, tradotti
     di francese in italiano* (Naples: Longo, 1635), USTC 4008471 and *Manifesto delle giustificate
     attioni della Corona di Spagna, e delle violenze della Corona di Francia. Tradotto dalla lin-
     gua castigliana nell'italiano* (Naples: Longo, 1636), USTC 4011105. For a brief biography:
     Giampiero di Marco, 'Librai, editori e tipografi a Napoli nel XVII secolo (Parte II)', *La
     Bibliofilía*, 112 (2010), pp. 143–144. Identified by Encarnación Sánchez García as one of the
     few publishers who specialised in printing Spanish books in Napels, see his *Imprenta y
     cultura en la Nápoles virreinal: los signos de la presencia Española* (Florence: Alinea, 2007),
     pp. 67–74.

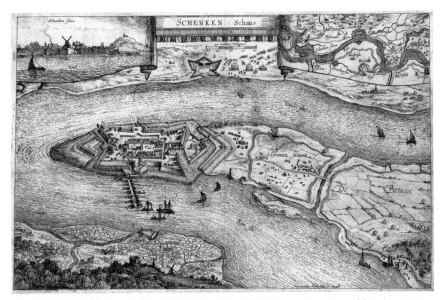

FIGURE 6.1   'Gezicht op de vesting Schenkenschans' by Bonaventura Peeters (1) in Antwerp
between 1624–1652. Rijksmuseum Amsterdam, RP-P-1933-300

published Lanario's Spanish translation of famous *Romulo* written by Virgilio
Malvezzi.[79]

Longo kept his news publications as up-to-date as possible. For instance,
in 1638, he publicized Frederick Henry's failed attempt to take the city of
Antwerp using the account printed by his counterpart Velpius in Brussels.[80] He
quickly produced a second edition which also included the latest news from
the French front: where the Spanish-Habsburg and imperial troops under the
command of Ottavio Piccolomini and Prince Thomas of Savoy had successfully taken Saint-Omer on the French border.[81] In the next couple of years, the

---

79   See Alexandra Danet, 'El Rómulo del Fabricio Lanario de Aragón (Naples, 1635): notes sur
une traduction espagnole méconnue du Romulo de Virgilio Malvezzi', *Studi secenteschi*,
50 (2009), pp. 63–87.

80   *Relatione del gran rotta data dall'armi spagnuole all'olandesi, sotto il forte di Calò vicino
Anversa, con la ricuperatione del medesimo forte, acquisto de vascelli, e di quanto haueuano
i medisimi olandesi portato in capo, seguita a 21. Di Giugno 1638* (Naples: Longo, 1638), USTC
4008488. The Italian account was a partial translation from the French edition printed in
Brussels by Velpius, *Recit de la descente des Hollandois a Calloo*.

81   *Relatione del gran rotta data dall'armi spagnuole all'olandesi […] E delle fattioni fatte da
s.a. il principe Tommaso di Sauoia, e dal Conte Piccolomini contra l'arme francesi in soccorso di Sant'Omer, con hauergli fatto leuar l'assedio da quella piazza* (Naples: Longo, 1638),
USTC 4010711.

official printers in Milan and Naples continued to focus on the few military success stories for the remainder of the war in the Low Countries.[82]

Until the beginning of the seventeenth century, news of Catholic and Habsburg defeats was not printed in Italian cities. As divisions within Italy started to emerge, the uniform news market fractured, now news accounts favourable to the Dutch and the French were distributed and printed mainly from Venice and Turin. The legitimacy of Habsburg rule was even more fiercely defended in printed news pamphlets from Milan and Naples. The distribution of these texts was aided by networks which connected Milan to Rome and Naples. In the early seventeenth century, authors and printers had made editorial interventions in the information arriving from the Low Countries. In their news pamphlets, they presented a uniform framework to read and interpret the ongoing events. Readers received more factual information about specific places, these details helped to emphasize the importance of a siege or battle in the Low Countries. A highly militant Catholic tone started to permeate reports of military battles and the Habsburg monarchy was presented as the bulwark of the Catholic religion in Europe. The paramount importance of the Habsburg dynasty had an impact on the portrayal of military commanders serving the dynasty. In news pamphlets, Spinola was not glorified to the same extent as Farnese and even a remarkable absence of Spinola in news prints. This difference between the two generals, as we will see in the next chapter, was only partly rectified by some members of Spinola's entourage in their contemporary histories exalting Spinola's achievements in the war.

---

82   War efforts in the southern Low Countries were mostly concentrated on the French border and after 1638 large confrontations with the Dutch army did no longer occur.

CHAPTER 7

The Development of Italian Historical Narratives

Prominent American and Italian scholars have expressed negative judgement of the histories written by Italian authors in the seventeenth century. Chief amongst them is Eric Cochrane, who detected a 'crisis of content' as Italian history writers allegedly witnessed a period in which events worthy of their attention on the Italian peninsula were lacking, and therefore had to turn their attention to foreign conflicts.[1] Giorgio Spini presented a similar argument stating that the Italian attention for foreign conflicts was superficial.[2] While these scholars primarily claimed to regret the decline of the *ars historica*, their statements are nonetheless illustrative of the profound influence of the anticlerical and anti-Spanish ideas of nineteenth-century Italian nationalists such as Benedetto Croce. These ideas continue to hold sway: Italian histories on the Revolt characterised as pro-Spanish or too overtly Catholic have not been deemed worthy of scholarly attention.[3] Scholars instead prefer to analyse historical accounts by Italian authors, such as Bentivoglio or Conestaggio, whom they champion as objective or critical observers of the Revolt in the Low Countries.[4] It reduces the complexities of Italian history writing to binary positions, being either pro-Spanish or anti-Spanish. This point of view has obscured the original context and reasons why different Italian authors wrote and published their accounts, and so far scholars have failed to appreciate and trace some of the similarities in Italian historical accounts on the Revolt in the Low Countries.

This chapter explores the similarities of Italian histories on the Revolt in the Low Countries written and published during the first half of the seventeenth century. In doing so I argue that Italian attention for foreign wars was not superficial. This war was perhaps fought in a distant place, but it was not a foreign conflict to a large group of people. In this period, the history of this war was written by merchants, diplomats and soldiers who had spent a part of their

---

1 Eric Cochrane, 'The Transition from Renaissance to Baroque Historiography: the Case of Italian Historiography', *History and Theory*, 19 (1980), pp. 21–38; Cochrane, *Historians and Historiography*, pp. 382–387; pp. 487–493. See also Bouwsma, *The Waning of the Renaissance*, pp. 198–214.

2 Spini, 'Historiography: The Art of History in the Italian Counter Reformation', pp. 91–133. For negative judgments of the period see Sergio Bertelli, *Ribelli, libertine e ortodossi nella storiografia barocca* (Florence: La Nuova Italia, 1973).

3 See for instance: Reijner, *Italiaanse geschiedschrijvers over de Nederlandse Opstand*, pp. 30–33.

4 Reijner, *Italiaanse geschiedschrijvers over de Nederlandse Opstand*, pp. 137–138, 143–184; On the impartiality of Bentivoglio, see also Belvederi, *Guido Bentivoglio e la politica europea*, p. 45.

careers in the Low Countries. Whereas most histories previously had been written by news agents or polygraphs, now most authors had more in-depth knowledge of the Low Countries. Having been an eyewitness or participant, as we will see, had an impact on how some of these authors interpreted and described the war, which as decades passed and interpretations started to shift could lead to criticism from the Habsburg authorities.

In writing histories about the war, Italians wrote about their involvement and achievements and crafted their own narratives of past events. In chronicling the numerous battles and sieges, military men included themselves in the storyline and were keen to showcase Italian military prowess. Highlighting the achievement of the Italian nation was not the sole preserve of Italian commanders, crucially, all Italian authors continued to a considerable degree to write about courageous Italians. Some weaved short biographies of Italian soldiers subtly into their accounts, perhaps to please a specific patron or ruler, others wrote a history on commission.

The historical accounts were the result of Italians' fascination for the Revolt in the Low Countries. Throughout the conflict, letters, news reports, and political analysis had shaped Italian contemporaries' perceptions. These reports and tracts left a lasting impression on the Italian historical interpretations of the war. A war full of events which 'have held many in suspense, and awakened curiosity', in the words of the young Neapolitan Francesco Lanario.[5] It was one of the reasons why he compiled the first short Italian history of the Revolt.[6] Just like political theorists and commentators, these history writers wanted to understand the nature and the consequences of this devastating war. Or to quote the Jesuit Famiano Strada, author of *De Bello Belgico*: 'how it happened that on the shores of Holland with a few fishing boats, a new republic suddenly reared its head and every day became more ponderous'.[7] Analysing the

---

5   Francesco Lanario, *Le gverre di Fiandra brevemente narrate* (Antwerp: Hieronymus Verdussen, 1615), USTC 1003607, p. 4: 'Le turbulenze, c'hanno aggitata la Fiandra nel corso d'una guera di piu di 40. Anni continuoi, sono state sì grandi, e piene d' accidenti sì diversi, et tanto gravi, che si come il presente secolo non ha veduti, nell' incertezza delle cose humane, avvenimenti, che piu di questi habbian tenuti sospensi gli animi, e svegliata la curiosità, cosi pare, che possa credersi, ch'alla posterità non siano per esser mai rappresentati altri successi di maggior ammiratione'.

6   For more on Lanario's carreer and his history: N. Lamal and H. Cools, 'An Italian Voice on the Dutch Revolt: The work of Francesco Lanario in a European perspective', in A-L. Van Bruaene, M. Kavaler (eds.), *Urban Perspectives on sixteenth-century Netherlandish Art & Culture* (Brepols: Turnhout, 2018), pp. 375–388.

7   I use the contemporary Italian translation of Strada's work by the Jesuit Carlo Papini: *Della Guerra di Fiandra deca prima* (Rome: Scheuss, 1638), USTC 4011323, p. 1: 'Donde sia accaduto, che ne i lidi dell'Ollanda da poche barche di pescatori habbia una nuova Republica in un tratto alzata la testa, che ogni giorno più ponderosa nell'armi […]'.

past could offer practical and valuable lessons for current and future crises. As most authors set out to explain why the war had been able to rage for more than forty years, to varying degrees, they laid bare some of the mistakes of Spanish-Habsburg policy in the Low Countries. Increasingly, as we will see, on some specific issues, their interpretations were subject to criticism or changed voluntarily as they started to diverge from Spanish ones.

1   The Authors and their Histories

This chapter analyses five different Italian histories printed between 1609 and 1648 which were often reprinted and translated in Italian cities and in major European publishing centres. These five accounts were available to a wider European audience and shaped contemporaries' understanding of the conflict. With the cessation of hostilities in 1609, the first published account was a war chronicle: *Delle guerre di Fiandra* (On the wars of the Low Countries) by Pompeo Giustiniani.[8] The Genoese military commander described the most recent military campaign in which he fought from 1601 to 1606. Giustiniani was a war veteran: he had arrived under Farnese's leadership in 1587 and had stayed until 1597, before returning in 1601 and being promoted by Spinola as maestro di campo in 1603.[9] Giustiniani is presented as the author, but his account was presumably ghost-written by Giuseppe Gamurini. The Tuscan military engineer was responsible for designing the twenty-nine engravings of towns, encampments and war machines in the accounts.[10] Thanks to an unidentified (Italian) merchant-investor, who was probably confident there would be an interested public both in the Low Countries and in Italian cities, the Antwerp printer Joachim Trognaesius was able to take on this rather ambitious publication project as the book contained several large double folded engravings.[11]

---

8   Pompeo Giustiniani, *Delle guerre di Fiandra libri VI di Pompeo Givstiniano del consiglio di guerra di s. m. c. e suo maestro di campo d'infanteria italiana. Posti in luce da Gioseppe Gamvrini gentil'huomo aretino con le figure delle cose piu notabili* (Antwerp: Trognesius, 1609), USTC 1003522.

9   D. Busolini, 'Pompeo Giustiniani', in *DBI*, 57 (2001).

10   Giustiniani, *Delle guerre di Fiandra*, p. 78 for more on Targone's military experiments during the siege and their inefficiency. Many of these images, especially the one containing the various inventions of Roman military engineer Pompeo Targone, became very popular and were often reused in other history works. For the popularity of these images see Simoni, *The Ostend Story*, pp. 163–172.

11   This information is based on a letter written by Aurelio Alciati to the Duke of Mantua and Monferrato on 9 November 1609 in ASMn, AG, Fiandra, 576, fol 610.

A Roman *aviso* in 1610 even reported on the publication of the book in Antwerp describing it as 'molto curiosa'.[12]

The subsequent publication trajectory demonstrates the wider interest for this military account on the Italian peninsula.[13] Already one year after its publication in Antwerp, it was printed in Venice by Ciotti and Giunta.[14] This Venetian firm reprinted the text in 1612, and three years later, the Milanese printer Bidelli reprinted the account.[15] In these three editions, the engravings were not reproduced, as they all focussed far more on easily readable accounts. In 1611, a Latin translation had already been published in Cologne, together with an updated version of Aubertus Miraeus' *Gentis Spinulae illustrium elogia*, listing all Spinola's victories.[16] This specific edition, with the engravings, was aimed at a learned international audience.

The soldier Francesco Lanario wrote a very different history: he was the first Italian author to offer a full overview of the entire conflict from 1559 to 1609. The young Neapolitan nobleman had arrived in Antwerp as peace negotiations with Dutch were already underway, and subsequently, instead of attaining glory on the battlefield, spent his time in the city's garrison reading histories before he decided to write one.[17] His account was first published in Antwerp in 1615. He condensed the history of conflict to less than 200 pages, as he claimed a short account could be useful for those who did not have the time to read long histories. He compensated for his lack of personal fighting experience by interviewing veteran soldiers.[18] His short narrative, just like Giustiniani's war chronicle, was quickly republished on the Italian peninsula: in Venice, Milan and Naples.[19] In 1623, Lanario translated his own account

---

12   BAV, Urb. Lat. 1078, fol 268v: Roman newsletter (21 April 1610).

13   For more information: N. Lamal, 'Publishing Military Books in the Low Countries and in Italy in the Early Seventeenth Century', in R. Kirwan, S. Mullins (eds.), *Specialist Markets in the Early Modern Book World* (Leiden: Brill, 2015), pp. 223–240.

14   Pompeo Giustiniani, *Delle guerre di Fiandra libri VI* (Venice: Giunta e Ciotti, 1610), USTC 4026708.

15   The Venetian edition in 1612 (USTC 4028432); Pompeo Giustiniani, *Delle guerre di Fiandra libri VI* (Milan: Bidelli, 1615), USTC 4022169.

16   Pompeo Giustiniani, *Bellvm Belgicvm siue Belgicarvm rervm, e commentariis* (Cologne: Kinckius, 1611), USTC 2120047, 2041789, 2107014, 2081051.

17   Lanario, *Le gverre di Fiandra*, p. 1. 'Non havend' io havuto fortuna di venir in Fiandra in tempo, che vi s'adoprassero l' armi, ho procurato di temperar' il dispiacevol' otio delle guarnigioni con l' honesto trattenimento del legger gli autori, c'hanno scritte le guerre de i Paesi Bassi'.

18   Lanario, *Le gverre di Fiandra*, p. 5: 'con maggior sicurezza poter credere alla relatione d'alcuni soldati vecchi ch'anchor sopravivono'.

19   Francesco Lanario, *Le guerre di Fiandra dal principio de' primi motivi in quelle parti, sino al presente breve, e diligentemente narrate* (Venezia: Baglioni, 1616), USTC 4021781; *Le guerre*

into Spanish, whereas in Paris and Cologne respectively a French and German translation were published.[20] His short history proved to be quite a success in Catholic Europe.[21]

In terms of reprinted editions and translations, Gerolamo Conestaggio's *Delle Guerre della Germania inferior* (On the Wars of the Low Countries), printed posthumously in Venice in 1614, was less successful. However, it was a bit of a sensation as several tracts attacked the work and it became the subject of intense debate.[22] Conestaggio covered the conflict from 1566 to 1577, roughly corresponding to the period he had lived in Antwerp as a member of the Genoese trading nation.[23] Conestaggio's presence in the Low Countries is important to understand how he described the events. Immediately before or after the sack of Antwerp in November 1576, he left the city for Lisbon. Following his stay in Lisbon, he wrote a history of Philip II's conquest of Portugal, which was first published in Genoa in 1585 and had been well-received.[24] After a short stay in his hometown, he was active as a consul for the Genoese nation in Venice, where he remained firmly connected to the commercial networks of the Low Countries, as he married Isabella Perez, sister of Nicolò Perez, a merchant from Antwerp active in Venice.[25] He returned to Genoa, where he probably started writing his history.

In 1605 he was in contact with Juan Vivas Cañamás, the Spanish representative in Genoa, to obtain a pension and information from the king and

---

di Fiandra brevemente narrate (Milan: Bidelli, 1616), USTC 4022150; *Le guerre di Fiandra brevemente narrate. Con l'agiunta de i successi dell'illustriss. et eccell. Sig. D. Pietro Girone duca d'Ossuna vicerè, e capitan generale in questo regno* (Naples: Rocagliolo, 1617), USTC 4025948.

20   Francesco Lanario, *Las guerras de Flandes, desde el año de mil y quinientos y cincuenta y nueve hasta el seiscientos y neuve* (Madrid: Sánchez, 1623), USTC 5008178.

21   On these different translations: Lamal and Cools, 'An Italian Voice on the Dutch Revolt', pp. 375–388.

22   Gerolamo Conestaggio, *Historia delle guerre della Germania inferiore, divisa in dieci libri* (Venice: Pinelli, 1614), USTC 4026677.

23   For biographical details see: M. Cavanna Ciappina, 'Gerolamo de Franchi Conestagio', in *DBI*, 27 (1982).

24   Montserrat Casas Nadal, 'Sobre la difusión de l'unione del Regno di Portogallo alla corona di Castiglia de Conestaggio (1585)', *EPOS*, 23 (2007), pp. 197–220; S. Andretta, 'Scrivere di altri paesi: il Portogallo e le Fiandre nell'opera di Girolamo Conestagio de' Franchi', in M. Firpo (ed.), *"Nunc Alia tempora alli mores" Storici e storia in età posttridentinà: atti del convengo internazionale* (Florence: Olschki, 2005), pp. 479–489.

25   Maartje van Gelder, 'In liefde en werk met de Lage Landen verbonden: de Genuese koopman en literator Girolamo Conestaggio (ca. 1530–1614/1615)', in M. Van Gelder, E. Meijers (eds.), *Internationale handelsnetwerken en culturele contacten in de vroegmoderne Nederlanden* (Maastricht: Shaker, 2009), pp. 43–53.

the Council of State in Madrid for his project.[26] The Council, as was customary, checked the manuscript before it would be printed. At the start of 1609,
Conestaggio complained in a letter to secretary of the council that he had
not received his pension and had been waiting for his revised manuscript for
more than a year.[27] After his complaint, Conestaggio received a large sum of
money (1.200 ducats), but the communication between the two parties seems
to stop.[28] It makes it difficult to establish the edition printed posthumously by
Pinelli in Venice in 1614 had been altered or whether it is the more uncensored
version. The fierce criticism orchestrated from Spanish court suggests that The
work became the subject of intense criticism as Conestaggio did not deliver
on his own promise to praise the king and his forebearers.[29] In 1632 it would
appear on the Index of Forbidden books in Spain. Two years later, the Elsevier
firm in Leiden republished his histories.[30]

Each of these three authors had different first-hand experiences of the
Revolt in Low Countries, yet in highlighting their knowledge and access to other
trusted sources, they all tried to reinforce the reliability and trustworthiness
of their accounts. None other than Cardinal Guido Bentivoglio put so much
emphasis on his knowledge of these wars. He was fascinated by the war Low
Countries from an early age and spent a few years as a papal representative at
the archducal court in Brussels (1607–1616). By the time Bentivoglio's first part
of his history was printed in 1632, his reputation as an expert was already firmly
established in diplomatic and learned circles thanks to the publication of his
diplomatic reports in 1629 which also included a brief history of the revolt. The
printer of his 1632 edition stressed Bentivoglio's familiarity with the conflict
as a selling point.[31] Throughout his three-part history, Bentivoglio reminded
his readers of his close ties to the conflict through the various members of his

26   Cees Reijner, 'Een Italiaanse verdediger van de Opstand? De internationale controverse
      rond het werk van Gerolamo Conestaggio', *Tijdschrift voor Geschiedenis*, 2 (2013), p. 177.
27   His letter to Andrés de Prada from Genoa on 16 January 1609 in AGS, Estado, Legajo
      1433, 246.
28   Minute of letter from council on 6 april 1609 to Cañamás in Genoa (AGS, Estado, Legajo
      1932, 330) with the instruction to settle the outstanding payments for the pensions
      granted to Conestaggio.
29   See his letter to Philip III on 20 October 1605 'de servir a la fama y a la Gloria de V. Mag.,
      de su Padre y Abuelo', AGS, Estado, Legajo 1433, 130.
30   Gerolamo Conestaggio, *Historia delle guerre della Germania inferiore, divisa in dieci libri*
      (s.l., s.n., 1634) [Leiden: Elzevier, 1634], USTC 1011778. The title-page bore their printers
      mark of the palm tree with the motto 'Assur go pressa'.
31   Guido Bentivoglio, *Della guerra di Fiandra* (Cologne: s.n., 1632), USTC 4044867: 'perch'egli
      sia nato a questi di Fiandra havendone havuta per iscuola, si puo dire la propria casa sua'.

family involved in the action, as well as to his privileged access to personal tes-timonies, and first-hand accounts of protagonists such as Ambrogio Spinola.[32] Bentivoglio's monumental history appeared in three volumes between 1632 and 1639.[33] Together with Lanario's brief account, it was one of the few on the Italian book market to cover the entire conflict from 1559 to 1609. This history was almost immediately reprinted in Leiden by the Elsevier firm and Baba in Venice.[34] It was translated into French, Spanish, English and Dutch.[35]

In the same year as Bentivoglio's history, the first volume of Famiano Strada's *De Bello Belgico* was published in Rome by Francesco Corbelleti.[36] Compared to the other authors, the Jesuit Famiano Strada had spent no time in the Low Countries, but instead, he reminded his readers throughout his history of his access to 'state secrets'. His history was divided into two decades: the first one covered the war from 1559 to 1578, with the second one, printed only in 1647, covered Farnese's governorship until 1590.[37] He did not succeed to reach the year 1592, the year in which his main protagonist Alexander Farnese died. Some members of the republic of letters speculated that the Spanish king had prevented the last two years' of Alexander's life to be included in this history,

32   References to his family, in second part: Bentivoglio, *Della Guerra di Fiandra* (Cologne: s.n., 1636), USTC 2522659, p. 202, 516, 518, 527 and in the third part: *Della Guerra di Fiandra* (Cologne: s.n., 1639), USTC 2036098, p. 415.

33   Guido Bentivoglio, *Della guerra di Fiandra, descritta dal cardinal Bentivoglio* (Cologne: s.n., 1632–1639), USTC 2522659. The first edition published in 1632 only consisted of eight 'books' or chapters; in the subsequent edition of the first volume in 1633 the ninth and tenth books were added.

34   Guido Bentivoglio, *Della guerra di Fiandra* (Leiden: Elzevier, 1635–1640), USTC 2514084, 1024205, 1011879; *Della guerra di Fiandra* (Venice: Baba, 1637–1640), USTC 4012526; *Della guerra di Fiandra* (Venice: Giunta and Baba, 1645), USTC 4018089.

35   For more see N. Lamal, '"Translated and Often Printed in Most Languages of Europe": Movement and Translation of Italian Histories on the Dutch Revolt across Europe', in M. McLean, S. Barker (eds.), *International Exchange in the Early Modern Book World* (Leiden: Brill, 2016), pp. 124–146.

36   Original manuscript in BAV, Vat. Lat. 7067 containing corrections and the imprimatur; Famiano Strada, *De bello belgico decas prima ab excessu Caroli v. imp. Usque ad initia prae-fecturae Alexandri Farnesii Parmae, ac Placentiae Ducis III* (Rome: Corbelletti, 1632), USTC 4011524.

37   Famiano Strada, *De bello belgico decas secunda ab initio praefecturae Alexandri Farnesii Parmae Placentiaeque ducis III anno 1578 usque ad annum 1590* (Rome: Corbelletti, 1647), USTC 4033994. For a first overview of the editions of Strada's work, see Ferdinand Vanderhaeghen, 'Fam. Strada De bello Belgico decas prima et decas secunda : description des diverses éditions de cet ouvrage', in *Extrait des livraisons de la Bibliotheca Belgica ou Bibliographie générale des Pays-Bas* (Ghent: Vyt, 1881).

as it contained the accusation that Philip II had poisoned his cousin.[38] The fact that Strada wrote his history on behalf of the Farnese family certainly has tainted his reputation and the later reception of his work.[39] Bentivoglio and Strada have been studied in opposition to each other by some scholars, more recently Florian Neumann has rehabilitated arguing he was equally writing a political history.[40] Together with Bentivoglio's monumental history, Strada's extensive account would also become one of the bestsellers on the Revolt with numerous re-editions, and translations in Italian, French, Spanish, English and Dutch.[41]

2   Italian Military Prowess

Some histories written by Italian professional veteran commanders in the Spanish-Habsburg army, above all, showcased Italian military prowess. This tendency was not unique to the Italians fighting in the conflict, English soldiers wrote about their own actions and involvement as well.[42] The arrival of Ambrogio Spinola and his subsequent major victory at Ostend in 1604 offered Italian officers again ample material to publicize their role as main protagonists in the war in both military treatises and contemporary histories.[43] After having missed the opportunity to exalt Spinola's achievements in printed news

---

38   Letters by Guy Patin to Nicolaas Heinsius on 20 June 1647 and to Chales Spon on 22 march 1648: L. Capron (ed.), *Correspondance complete et autres écrits de Guy Patin* (Paris: Bibliothèque interuniversitatire de santé, 2018). Available online: https://www .biusante.parisdescartes.fr/patin/?do=pg&let=1045 and https://www.biusante.parisdes cartes.fr/patin/?do=pg&let=0152.

39   His work was anticipated by members of the Republic of letters, as for example, Guy Patin wrote to Nicolaas Heinsius on 8 January 1647 to visit Strada whilst he was in Rome and ask him when they would be able to read the second part of his history. In Capron, *Correspondance complete*, online: https://www.biusante.parisdescartes.fr/patin /?do=pg&let=1043.

40   See Rengenier C. Rittersma, 'Le orrecchie si piene di Fiandra. Famiano Strada (1572–1649) und Guido Bentivoglio (1577–1644) und ihr Interesse am niederländischen Aufstand', *Quellen und Forschungen aus italienischen Archiven und Bibliotheken*, 89 (2009), pp. 263–284; Florian Neumann, *Geschichtsschreibung Als Kunst: Famiano Strada s.i. (1572–1649) und die Ars Historica in Italien* (Berlin: Walter de Gruyter, 2013). An earlier positive judgment see: J. Ijsewijn, 'Cardinal Granvelle and the prince of Orange in Strada's De Bello Belgico', in *Les Granvelles*, pp. 177–183.

41   Lamal, 'Movement and Translation of Italian Histories', pp. 124–146.

42   Dunthorne, *Britain and the Dutch Revolt*, pp. 13, 79.

43   Examples of military treatises by Italian military commanders include Lelio Brancaccio, *I carichi militari* (Antwerp: Trognesius, 1610), USTC 1003548; Lodovico Melzo, *Regole Militari* (Antwerp: Trognesius, 1611), USTC 1003563 and Flaminio della Croce, *Teatro militare* (Antwerp: Aertssen, 1617), USTC 1035391 with ample attention for their own actions,

pamphlets immediately following the conquest of Ostend in 1604, plans to write and publish a history of his military campaign between 1601 and 1606 seem to have materialised quickly.

Spinola had a hand in propagating his successful military campaigns. Already at the end of 1608, Spinola solicited the help of the Milanese foot soldier Aurelio Alciati to revise Giustiniani's entire manuscript.[44] Alciati was highly educated and a close friend of the Tuscan military engineer Giuseppe Gamurini.[45] In a letter to the Duke of Mantua and Monferrato, Alciati expressed his reluctance in writing contemporary history, a recurring problem in this period, as he claimed that some matters have to remain unaddressed to avoid offending powerful people. Alciati commented that the content of the book is 'very true', but that some details have been omitted, concluding that the history treats 'very often the Marquis Spinola, and often Giustiniano'.[46]

Giustiniani and Spinola are the main protagonists in this account, the actions of other Italian and also Spanish commanders are mentioned, but not in a very detailed way. Throughout the text, Giustiniani promoted himself by inserting passages demonstrating his courage. For instance, when a fire erupted in a military machine constructed by Targone he and his men ignoring the danger to his life managed to extinguish it.[47] Other passages illustrated that Spinola trusted and valued him as well as highlighting his service and dedication to the Spanish-Habsburg crown.[48] For instance, when he got severely wounded in his right arm in 1604, Giustiniani added that he had shown his honour and reputation when facing many dangers in the service of his prince.[49]

---

those of other Italian commanders. For their international success consult: Lamal, 'Publishing Military Books in the Low Countries and in Italy', pp. 223–240.

44   Alciati, Brussels 20 december 1608 in ASMn, AG, 575, fol 764: 'il Marchese m'ha commandato ch'io la rivede, il che faccio per obedirlo solamente, del resto conosco che l'anima dell'historia è la verita, ne veggio modo di poterla dire trattandosi di persone vive'.

45   Gamurini to Cioli, Brussels 2 May 1615, ASF, MdP 1817, fol 55v: described Alciati as 'mio grande amico'.

46   Alciati, Brussels November 1609 in ASMn, AG, 575, fol 786: 'Si tratta spessissimo del Marchese Spinola, e spesso del Giustiniano'.

47   Giustiniani, Delle guerre di Fiandra, pp. 75–76: 'destarono grandissimo incendio in qualla machina, che molto difficilmente si poteva estinguere, perche nel medesimo tempo facevano gl'assediati batteria con i sette pezzi nella parte ove abbrusciava, à fine ch'alcuno non se vi potesse accostare per ammorzarlo: ma Giustiniano non guardando il pericolo, con la suagente l'estinse.'

48   Giustiniani, Delle guerre di Fiandra, p. 68: 'vi mandò ancho separatamente (si che l'uno non sapesse dell'altro) il Colonello Giacomo Franceschi, e Pompeo Giustiniano, de' i quali molto si fidava, per haver trovato buoni i loro pareri'.

49   Giustiniani, Delle guerre di Fiandra, p. 127: 'Di qui si vede à quanto gravi pericoli possa e debba l''honore e la reputatione esporre un Capitano in servitio del suo Prencipe'.

The largest share of the praise goes to Spinola, who just like Alexander at Antwerp, had faced numerous obstacles during the long siege of Ostend. These obstacles are a crucial theme in the text, as Spinola had been able to prove the experts and soldiers wrong by conquering the city.[50] Despite the many difficulties Spinola 'never lost his courage, but made necessity a virtue; with a fearless heart and a cheerful face, he provided everything, not resting neither during the day nor the night'.[51] The picture emerging from this history is that of a military commander partaking in the action, who was able to encourage and inspire his men into battle.[52]

As Vitelli and Farnese before him, Spinola was presented as an ideal military commander, but he was, however, not glorified through a comparison with ancient military commanders, which had been the case for both Vitelli and Farnese. Bentivoglio presented Spinola as someone who was able to animate and reward his soldiers but did not bestow him any other significant praise.[53] It was nearly half a century later, Spinola was compared to heroes from antiquity in Italian histories. For instance, in 1673 the Jesuit Angelo Gallucci praised Spinola as 'the Genoese Achilles' and 'Ligurian Hercules', but equally described him as another Alexander Farnese.[54] In Gallucci's retelling of the siege of Ostend, Giustiniani convinces Spinola to accept the general command to emulate Farnese and obtain a similar level of glory.[55] Such a comparison was still absent in Giustiniani's original version of these events.

Giustiniani presented Spinola as a celebrity.[56] He described that huge crowds had gathered in The Hague to see Spinola in person, adding many travelled

---

50   Giustiniani, *Delle guerre di Fiandra*, p. 145: 'poiche un anno avanti era tenuta per inespugnabile da i piu esperti e valorosi soldati che fossero nell'esercito Cattholico [...] vi concorreva anchora la commune opinione, che quella Città, ò Terre, alle quali non si può torre il soccorso, e che sono in forte e capace sito, non si passino espugnare: e qual Città e piu forte d'Ostende?'

51   Giustiniani, *Delle guerre di Fiandra*, p. 139: 'Non si perdè d'animo lo Spinola, ma facendo di necessità virtù, con animo intrépido e faccia allegra provedeva ad ogni cosa, non posando ne giorno ne notte'.

52   Giustiniani, *Delle guerre di Fiandra*, pp. 82–83, 278.

53   See for instance, Bentivoglio, *Della guerra di Fiandra*, III, p. 460 and p. 516.

54   He had continued the work of Strada, it was printed in Rome in two parts as *De Bello Belgico ab anno Christi 1593 ad inducias annorum 12 an 1609 pactas* by Corbelleti. Translated by Jacopo Cellesi and printed as *Historia della Guerra di Fiandra. Parte Prima* (Rome: Lazari, 1673), pp. 5–6.

55   Angelo Gallucci, Jacopo Cellesi (trans.), *Historia della Guerra di Fiandra. Parte Seconda* (Rome: Lazari, 1673), pp. 275–277.

56   It was thanks to Spinola's valour and diligence that the Dutch had wanted to negotiate a peace: Giustiniani, *Delle guerre di Fiandra*, p. 328.

from the most remote places and island 'so formidable was the name Spinola'.[57] This description of Spinola's visit to the Dutch political capital echoed the positive reports in manuscript newsletters, claiming that people in the streets had shouted that Spinola was a good and beautiful man.[58] The subsequent difficult peace negotiations in The Hague between the United Provinces and Spain are not discussed in any detail, the history simply ends with the treaty conditions of the Twelve Years' Truce. It was not Giustiniani's intention to delve into the difficult peace negotiations and other sensitive political issues related to the Truce, but rather to focus on descriptions of military skirmishes and victories. Italian military expertise, valour, as well as magnanimousness, were once again at the forefront of contemporary history of the wars in the Low Countries.

This tendency to praise their achievements, irritated several Spanish generals, exacerbating the already intense rivalries between the two 'nations' in the Spanish-Habsburg army.[59] In the prologue of his *Las guerras de los Estados Baxos* (1622), Carlos Coloma, one of the most important Spanish military commanders, described Giustiniani as a 'chronicler of himself and his nation'.[60] Coloma also accused Italian authors of 'inventing honours', by which he meant that they neglected achievements and victories obtained by Spanish generals to devote ample attention to their own actions, embellishing their involvement and successes in the war.[61] The worst offender according to Coloma was Gerolamo Conestaggio who highlighted the actions of Chiappino Vitelli instead of Don Fadrique in 1572–1573 and had assigned the victory at Mookerheide in 1574 to the Tuscan soldier Giovanni Battista del Monte, nephew of Vitelli, when the Spanish commanders Sancho Dávila and Bernardino de Mendoza had been credited for this victory.[62]

---

57   Giustiniani, *Delle guerre di Fiandra*, p. 311.

58   BAV, Urb Lat 1076 part I, fol 149–150v: *Relazione del viaggio del marchese Ambrogio Spinola fatto all'Aya per il congresso della pace dell'Aya.*

59   The rivalry between Spanish and Italian nations in the army was well known: see the comments by Guido Bentivoglio in his *Relatione*, p. 147: 'Fra la Spagnuola, e l'Italiana sono state emulation continoue, havendo volute la Spagnuola pretender sempre la superiorità con l'Italiana e l'Italiana l'uguaglianza con la Spagnuola'.

60   Carlos Coloma, *Las guerras de los Estados Baxos, desde el año de* MDLXXXVIII *hasta el de* MDXCIX (Cambrai: De la Rivière, 1622), USTC 1119766. Subsequent editions Antwerp in 1624 (USTC 1508913 and 5029348) in 1635 (USTC 5025894 and 1510983) and Barcelona in 1627 (USTC 5005502), p 4: 'coronista de si mismo, y de su nacion'.

61   Coloma, *Las guerras de los Estados Baxos*, p. 4v: 'en la batalla de Moquen quiere que governasse nuesta cavalleria Iuna Bautista del Monte, porque fue la cavalleria mucha cause de aquella vitoria: sienda verdad que la governava Don Bernardino de Mendoça y con razón, como Capitan Español mas antiguo, y la primera clase de la nobleza de España, [...]'.

62   For passage in Conestaggio see, *Delle guerre*, p. 332–334. For the battle of Mookerheide it is possible that Conestaggio used Campana's *Della Guerra di Fiandra, Parte Prima* (Vicenza:

It is certainly not a coincidence that Francesco Lanario, after having spent time at the court in Madrid, added several short biographies of important Spanish commanders, who had fought in the Low Countries and were still serving in the Council of State, to the Spanish translation of his history printed in 1623.[63] In his 1617 Neapolitan edition, Lanario had praised Pedro Téllez-Giron's, viceroy of Naples at the time, honour, military prudence and fearlessness.[64] In his Spanish translation, he reinforced and highlighted the 'valour and military experience' of all these Spanish commanders at a time when the Spanish-Habsburg empire under royal favourite Olivares, to whom Lanario dedicated his work, increasingly felt the need to defend itself in historical writings.[65]

3   Diverging Narratives

Both Jacob Soll and Richard Kagan have argued respectively for France and Spain that, in this period, histories became a crucial tool for governments to build support among local audiences.[66] The circulation of competing narratives and interpretations of the same events meant that histories were now

Greco, 1602), USTC 4034222, who equally praised Giovanni Battista del Monte, see p. 127. For another example consult the funerary oration, *Oratione funebre dell'aggravato academico Delio in morte dell'illusstrissimo, & Eccellentissimo Sig. Gio Battista del Monte* (Padova: Crivellari, 1615), USTC 4028536, p. 18: 'il nostro glorioso guerriere l'inciminciato corso della vittoria, ne meno si mostrò prudente in prender parito, che valoroso, e forte in condurlo à fine, egli quel giorno vinse la guerra, perche veduta la confusione e disordine de' nemici, solo frà gli altri si spinse innanzi, e facendo stragge d'alcuni pochi, ch'ancora ostinatamente faceano fronte'. A feat celebrated by the family Del Monte in their villa Arrivabene in Florence with a cycle of frescos with various battle scenes from the Low Countries.

63   Lanario, *Las guerras de Flandes*. Short biographies of amongst others: Don Pedro de Toledo (p. 49), Don Enrique de Guzman (p. 68), Don Diego de Ibarra (pp. 80–81), Don Augstio Messia (p. 82), Don Francesco de Mendoza (p. 99).

64   In address to the reader Lanario (USTC 4025948) referred to 'le molte, e diverse relationi, che mi facevano de'memorabili progressi che fece il Duca d'Ossuna in cinque anni di residenza ne'Paesi Bassi', claiming he did not have time and certain news to include it in the earlier edition printed in Antwerp. For a brief overview of these changes, see Sánchez García, *Imprenta y cultura en la Nápoles virreinal*, pp. 106–109.

65   See for instance Lanario, *Las guerras de Flandes*, p. 129: 'valor y experiencia militar'. He shortened the extensive references to Duke of Ossuna's activities in Spanish translation.

66   Richard L. Kagan, *Clio and the Crown. The Politics of History in Medieval and Early Modern Spain* (Baltimore: The John Hopkins University Press, 2009), p. 206 and Jacob Soll, *Publishing the Prince. History, Reading, and the Birth of Political Criticism* (Ann Arbor: University of Michigan Press, 2008).

more often criticized and attacked. Conestaggio's posthumously history became the subject of intense criticism.[67] Examining the criticism levelled against Conestaggio's *Delle Guerre della Germania inferior* will reveal the issues where Italian interpretations started to diverge from the Spanish ones.

Due to this criticism, Conestaggio has been portrayed as an Italian sympathizer of the Revolt in the Low Countries.[68] Conestaggio did not, however, offer radically new or overtly critical interpretations of the Revolt. The various anonymously published critiques in both Italian and Spanish against his history are, I argue, illustrative of how his more observational style and direct testimonies did not fit easily within the now entrenched partisan views of the past. Printed in Venice in 1614, during the first war of Monferrato (1613–1615), the fierce backlash against his history should be understood in light of the tense political climate at a time of growing anti-Spanish sentiments.[69] This case illustrates the process by which the Revolt was memorialized became part of international debates and current political alliances.

In his foreword to the reader, Conestaggio claimed that the moment now seemed right to write a history which would aim to tell the truth instead of flattering or satisfying the powerful. Inspired by the language of reason of state, he used the metaphor of the body politic: the Low Countries were once a strong and healthy body, but this body was affected by a malignant disease, and whilst various of its members were arguing, no doctor could be found who knew the cause of this disease and so no adequate cure could be given.[70] In line with contemporary political tracts, Conestaggio expressed the widespread amazement that a little republic could withstand the might and wealth of the Spanish-Habsburg empire. He outlined what his readers would find in his truthful narration of events in an engaging way.

---

67   *Avertimenti sopra l'istoria delle guerre della Germania inferiore di Geronimo Conestaggio fatti da Adriano Stopenro ad instanza del Sig. Marchese N. Prencipe del Sacro Imperio Tradotti dal Francese in Italiano per T.P.* (s.l.: s.n., 1619), USTC 4041510; Pierre Mathieu, Juan Pablo Mártir Rizo (trans.), *Historia de las guerras de Flandes, contra la de Geronimo de Franqui Conestaggio* (Valencia: Mey, 1627), USTC 5005867. Anonymous manuscript in KBR, M 7023: *Observations sur l'ouvrage de Conestagio, Delle guerre della Germania inferiore.*

68   Reijner, 'Een Italiaanse verdediger van de Opstand?', pp. 173–187.

69   P. Pelizzari, 'Echi letterari della prima guerra del Monferrato: la prosa di Alessandro Tassoni', in P. Merlin, F. Ieva (eds.), *Monferrato 1613. La viglia di una crisi europea* (Rome: Viella, 2016), pp. 179–196 and Francisco Javier Álvarez Garcia, *La Quietud de Italia ante la crisis del Monferrato (1612–1618) Gestión política y rétorica del conflicto* (Unpublished PhD thesis, Universidad Complutense de Madrid, 2019).

70   Conestaggio, *Historia delle guerre della Germania inferiore*, A3.

You can see that a woman [Margaret of Parma] achieved difficult tasks, but a valorous and rigorous captain [the Duke of Alba] lost what she had preserved: that executing justice created injustice, that pardoning caused dissent, that imposing taxes reduced revenue. And in the end, a small, infertile, and poor province contended bravely and for a long time with the power and the richness of a ruler of half the globe, all against the normal course of human things.[71]

In this brief summary, several elements are present that, as we have seen in the previous chapters, were quite commonplace in earlier Italian discourse on the Revolt. In his foreword, Conestaggio pointed to the unjust measure taken by the Duke of Alba, which had caused a further escalation of the conflict, an analysis which was shared by many contemporary politicians, observers and later authors. In political treatises written in 1577 several Italian political thinkers had argued along similar lines. In his history, Conestaggio described how Philip II had realized that the stringent rule of Alba had only caused damage and too late had opted for a softer approach. He even speculated that the course of events might have turned out differently if not for Alba's mismanagement, who had left the affairs of the Low Countries in 1573 more muddled than ever before.[72] According to his critics, with this statement, he failed to mention that heresy had been the main reason for the revolt and Conestaggio instead seemed to lay the blame for the revolt squarely at Alba's feet, without looking at the actions of Orange. For most Italian authors it was, however, possible to recognize that the Duke's decisions had caused popular discontent, which was exploited by William of Orange for his own purposes. Criticism of Alba's policies was a dominant feature of Italian histories.

Criticizing Alba's rule became increasingly controversial in Spain during the early seventeenth century. In his Spanish translation, Lanario removed or adapted a few sentences related to the actions of the Duke of Alba. For instance, he deleted the sentence suggesting that the introduction of new taxes was the strongest cause for the continuation of the conflict.[73] Tellingly as well, Lanario changed the sentence that Alba's government displeased 'both the Catholics and heretics' in the Low Countries to the inhabitants not being content, removing any kind of suggestion of Catholics being actively involved

---

71   Conestaggio, *Historia delle guerre della Germania inferiore*, A3v.
72   Conestaggio, *Historia delle guerre della Germania inferiore*, pp. 320–321.
73   Lanario, *Le guerre di Fiandra*, p. 34: 'Il motivo di queste impositioni fu uno dei piu gagliardi fomenti, che fecero continuare le turbolenze de quei paesi'. Half a century later, similar small changes were made by the Spanish translator of Strada's history in 1681 see Lamal, 'Movement and Translation of Italian Histories', pp. 134–135.

in the revolt.[74] The murkiness of the conflict started to disappear in some historical accounts, and it shows the emergence of a far more fixed narrative of Catholics versus Protestants. These adaptations indicate the interpretation of the conflict and Alba's governorship had become quite different in official Spanish history.

Another bone of contention was Conestaggio's references to Spanish mutinies and atrocities committed after Alva's governorship. Conestaggio explained that it was necessary to devote ample attention to describing the great mutiny in Antwerp of 1574, as it had caused great damage to the cause of the king.[75] It had reinforced to the inhabitants of the Low Countries that they were being torn apart more by their friends than by their enemies, and as a consequence had the mutiny had kindled their disobedience and rebellion. This interpretation was very much in line with contemporaries, the governor-general Requesens had insisted that the Spanish soldiers had made them lose the Low Countries rather than the actions of William of Orange.[76] Acknowledging past mistakes was, however, not always as controversial as in Conestaggio's case.[77] Keen to offer some crucial political lessons, Bentivoglio followed Conestaggio's example in dwelling extensively on the events during the mutiny in Antwerp of 1574.[78] According to the Cardinal, the numerous mutinies following this particular one in Antwerp had been almost more harmful to the king than the armies of the enemy.[79]

---

74 Lanario, *Le guerre di Fiandra*, p. 25: 'Con tali modi cominciò il Duca il suo governo, che ben presto si conobbe, che la sua amministratione era per dispiacere così à, i, Cattolici, come à gli heretici', compare to Lanario, *Las guerras de Flandes*, p. 16: 'no avia de contentar a los Flamencos'.

75 Conestaggio, *Historia delle guerre della Germania inferiore*, p. 327: 'Mi sono forse trattenuto più di quel, che si usa in raccontare i particolari di questo mottino, ma lo ho fatto à studio, per parermi cosa notabile e maggiore di quanto altre simili ne habbia sentite mai, oltre che merita forse scriversi per il danno che fece alle cose del Re.'

76 For full quote see Parker, *The Army of Flanders*, p. 157.

77 Lanario, *Le guerre di Fiandra*, p. 50: 'Alle cose del Re fu dannosissimo questo mottino, si come fu sopra modo favorevole a, i, disegni dell' Oranges e de' suoi fautori, i quali corrotto di già totalmente il popolo & i capi d' esso secero di modo, che gli Spagnuoli furono dichiarati ribelli di s.m. essendosi di quei giorni tumultuato contro di loro in Brusselles, & altrove'.

78 Bentivoglio must have read Conestaggio's account, see BAV, Barb Lat 4934, fol 9–13: *Riposta alla precedente censura che detto il Cardinal Bentivoglio ad un suo familiare in una aggiunta di lettera scritta da Roma al sudetto Signore Henrico Arnò sotto li vi di ottobre 1633.*

79 Bentivoglio, *Della guerra di Fiandra*, p. 380: 'e che per tal rispetto alle cose del Re in Fiandra sono state quasi più dannose l'armi de' suoi soldati, che quelle de' suoi nemici', and on p. 385.

The lack of criticism for Bentivoglio's similar observations highlights how Conestaggio's stark analysis of the situation was not appreciated in a historical account in the lead-up to the Thirty Years' War. Most significant in this respect is Conestaggio's account of the sack of Antwerp in 1576.

> With rage they were entering the houses; how they treated men and women, is not only vicious and inhumane to do, but also sad and painful to describe, because after they had pillaged all they had found in the houses and satiated their beastly desires, killing those who contradicted them. There was no torture, no matter how cruel, that during those three days, they did not use against those poor people to make them confess if they had anything else hidden [...] so that one could say, that one of the happiest, richest cities in the world, was forced into the deepest sorrow, that could be tolerated.[80]

Again, one of Conestaggio's critics attacked his treatment of this violent episode by claiming that there were still many people alive who had witnessed this event and could vouch that his account was false.[81] His critics tried to contradict Conestaggio's status as an eyewitness. Conestaggio's account of the gruesome events in Antwerp is similar to the extensive letter written, a few days after the sack, by the Medici correspondent Giovanni Battista Guicciardini on 4 November 1576. Guicciardini described it as 'an act that surpasses every barbarous cruelty'.[82] He narrated how the streets were covered with dead bodies and how squeaks came from the houses where women and men were being slaughtered or tortured by soldiers for their money.[83] Guicciardini had equally expressed his indignation at the miserable fate this city suffered at the hands of

---

80   Conestaggio, *Historia delle guerre della Germania inferiore*, p. 449: 'Con che rabbia entrassero per le case, come trattassero gli huomini, e le donne di esse, non solamente è cosa fiera & inhumana il farli, ma e lagrimevole il dirsi, perche dopo di haver perdato tutto quello, che havevano trovato nelle case, e satollati mille loro brutti desiderij, uccidendo chi lor contradiceva, non rimase niuna sorte di tormento, per crudele che sia, che in tre giorni, che dirò il sacco, non essercitassero ne' miseri cittadini, per far lor dire se havevano altro di nascosto, [...] di maniera che si pùo dire, che una delle più felice, e più ricca città del mondo, fù ridotta nella maggior infelicità, che sopportar si possa'.

81   KBR, M 7023, *Observations sur l'ouvrage de Conestagio*, fol 57–60.

82   Brussels, 10 November 1576, quotation *Lettere di Giovan Battista*, p. 369: 'Ma quello che ha passato ogni barbara crudeltà è stato l'incendio grande che in più luochi della terra'.

83   *Lettere di Giovan Battista*, p. 369: '[...] del romore grande del sacco, di fuoco, d'occisioni, et le strade coperte di corpi morti, et di feriti miseramente di ferro et di archibusate, che con urla et lamenti inauditi finivano o meno propinqui a finire miseramente la lor vità, ne mancavano per le case le strida di donne et huomini, che erano occisi dai soldati, o tormentati, perche non volevano palesare i lor danari, perché in tal modo dicano esserne periti assai, ma soprattutto pietoso a vedere quelli che ascosi prima alto et in luoghi oscuri

those who called themselves soldiers of the Spanish king, lamenting the loss of such a beautiful and prosperous mercantile city.[84] Neither he nor Conestaggio interpreted the events as God's wrath or punishment. It shows that by now there was a real difference between perceptions of how history should be written and the current letters offering descriptions of the events.

4 Defending Farnese

The divergence between Spanish and Italian narratives of the conflict was particularly clear when it came to Alexander Farnese's governorship. In his chronicle, Francisco Verdugo, Spanish commander and governor of Friesland, had been extremely critical of Alexander Farnese's leadership.[85] Yet, the first printed edition of Verdugo's work had appeared in Italian translation in Naples in 1605, and crucially Girolamo Frachetta, the translator, had removed most of Verdugo's negative judgments of Farnese.[86] Two years later, Duke Ranuccio Farnese received word from his agent in Madrid in 1607 that Antonio de Herrara, the official historiographer at the Spanish court, would include some criticism of Alexander's governorship in the last part of his universal chronicle. He petitioned him, to present a more favourable picture of his father.[87] The continuing contestation reinforced the idea that a pro-Farnesian history was needed, hence Ranuccio turned to the Jesuit order to find a suitable author.

Famiano Strada, professor of rhetoric at the *Collegio Romano*, started to write this history between 1616–1618.[88] Whilst Antonio Querenghi had previously been allocated this task without privileged access to archival material;

---

84   delle case, che poi abrucciarono, non sapendo trovare modo da scampare, arsero vivi, onde alcuni mezi arrostit si gettarono atterra dalle finistre'.
     Lettere di Giovan Battista, p. 369: 'è stata osservantissima et fedelissima, et in ogni bisogno ha posto aiuto di somme eccessive di danari, et obligatasi à quantità non minore, tanto che s'era indebitata grossissimamanete, et la quale di belleza, richeza et superbi edifitij non era inferior ad alcuna altra città di qua (p.370) da i monti, ma di commertio di mercanti d'ogni natione, et di grandeza di negotij di qualunche sorte che sia, superiore a tutte l'altre d'Europa'.

85   For his judgments on Farnese: Jan van den Broek, *Voor God en mijn koning. Het verslag van colonel Francisco Verdugo over zijn jaren als legerleider en gouverneur namens Filips II in Stad en Lande van Groningen, Drenthe, Friesland, Overijssel en Lingen (1581–1595)* (Assen: Van Gorcum, 2009), pp. 43–44, 62 and Raymond Fagel, 'Alexander Farnese and Francisco Verdugo: the War in the North East', *Tiempos Modernos*, 35 (2017), pp. 14–29.

86   *Li Commentari di Francesco Veduro delle cose successe in Frisia. Nel tempo, che egli fù governatore, & capitan generale, in quella provincia* (Naples: Stigliola, 1605), USTC 4036021.

87   See Kagan, *Clio and the Crown*, p. 191. He wrongly identifies Ranuccio as Alexander's nephew.

88   Andriessen refers to letters from 1616 by the General of the Jesuit Order Mutio Vitelleschi to procure manuscripts from Habsburg Netherlands for Strada, see Andriessen, *De*

now letters, accounts and other documents from the Farnesian archive in Parma were dispatched to Strada in Rome, and in the Habsburg Netherlands, Jesuits helped out with translating documents for Strada. Writing a history based on so much archival material was a monumental task: The first volume of Strada's *De Bello Belgico* was only published in Rome in 1632.[89] Both in the 1590s and the 1630s, Alexander Farnese's reputation was used to further the family's political and military goals. This tense political context of the publication of Strada's history has hitherto remained largely unnoticed by scholars. The first volume was dedicated to Odoardo I who had aligned himself with France in these years.[90] Strada compared Odoardo to Alexander Farnese, and predicted similar great deeds. This was rhetorical flattery typical for dedications, but Odoardo was known to be extremely eager to strive for glory. The memory of his forebear's great deeds thus continued to play an important role in Parmesan politics and its relationship with the Habsburg crown.

Strada compensated for the fact he had not been to the Low Countries by frequently reminding his readers of his privileged access to official sources and other histories.[91] His reliance upon a variety of sources shows that history as research was not a dead letter: it was simply used to fit a distinct narrative. His accounts of Alba's and Requesens' governorship, Strada acknowledged, were significantly less well-documented and these sections of his history are much briefer. Strada criticized the Duke of Alba's policies as he relied on letters exchanged between Margaret and Alexander with royal advisors such as Granvelle and Spanish ambassadors such as Guzmán De Silva who had been critical of the Duke of Alba.[92] His source base suited Strada's main purpose rather well. His first volume was, above all, meant to re-habilitate Margaret of Parma's governorship until 1567 and to prepare the ground for a celebration Alexander Farnese's military genius in the second one.[93]

---

jezuïeten en het samenhorigheidsbesef, p. 32 (footnote 37). The date 1618 is based on Strada's dedication.

89   Famiano Strada, *De bello belgico decas prima* (Rome: Corbelletti, 1632), USTC 4011524.

90   For instance, in 1633, Odoardo had removed the Golden Fleece collars of Alexander and Ranuccio from the equestrian statues in Piacenza. On Odoardo's fatal alliance with France: Hanlon, *The Hero of Italy*, pp. 20–41.

91   Strada, Papini (trans.), *Della Guerra di Fiandra deca prima*, USTC 4011323, 'Al lettore'. Strada relied on Rinaldi's manuscript account at various instances in the second volume: Neumann, *Geschichtsschreibung Als Kunst*, pp. 211–213.

92   *Della Guerra di Fiandra deca prima*, p. 301–320.

93   Famiano Strada, Paolo Segnere (trans.), *Della guerra di Fiandra deca seconda* (Rome: Corbelletti Heirs, 1648), USTC 4020566, p. 345: 'da noi è stato veduto un modello del ponte, de' forti & dell'altre moli, di cui habbiamo à parlare, [...], insieme con un quadro, ov'eran dipinti gli argini de' lavoranti, ivi con gran maraviglia di tutti fu contemplato'.

Strada described the numerous battles and sieges in vivid detail, and often mentioned the heavy toll of war for both civilians and soldiers. Just like Lanario had done for Spanish generals, Strada included brief biographies of many military officers, describing and often praising their actions in battle.[94] Interestingly in his description of the battle of Mookerheide (1574), Strada referred to the different opinions of which commander was responsible for this victory, and reiterated that Del Monte deserved to be credited. He concluded this section with the claim that Del Monte would soon receive more applause and praise for his actions under the leadership of Alexander Farnese, 'the defender of Italy'.[95] A passage characteristic of Strada's work as Farnese was the real hero of the story: he expanded upon the earlier comparisons between Farnese and Julius Caesar and Alexander the Great, thus presenting Farnese as both a military genius and a pious warrior.[96] At the same time, he equally praised Farnese for his more reconciliatory approach, forgiving the inhabitants of the Low Countries and restoring their ancient privileges.

In his memoirs, Cardinal Guido Bentivoglio dedicated several pages to reviewing Strada's history and criticized him for glorifying the Farnese too much.[97] He was also critical of his many biographical digressions. Interestingly, Bentivoglio also included a short biography in the first part of his history of Raffaelo Barberini, the merchant who became part of Vitelli's entourage. The reason for this inclusion is illustrative of how histories were used to praise those in power: Raffaelo was the paternal uncle to the sitting Pope Urban VIII in 1632 and thus his actions in the Netherlands had to be included.[98]

The criticism of Strada's work did not halt the contemporary success of this history alongside Bentivoglio's account. It would become one of the bestsellers on the Revolt in Catholic Europe, and more specifically in the Habsburg Low Countries.[99] The Latin editions, mostly in octavo, were immediately reprinted in Antwerp by the Cnobbaert firm which had close ties to the Jesuit order. The first volume was printed in 1635, with a second edition just a year

---

94   Another telling example is his praise for action of Camillo Capizucchi, captain of an Italian *terzo*, during the battle of Kouwendijk during siege of Antwerp: *Della guerra di Fiandra deca seconda*, pp. 394–396, 401.

95   *Della Guerra di Fiandra, deca prima*, pp. 379–380.

96   *Della Guerra di Fiandra, deca prima*, pp. 378–379, translation of term 'Il paladino d'italia'.

97   Guido Bentivoglio, *Memorie del cardinal Bentivoglio, con le quali descriue la sua vita, e non solo le cose a lvi svccesse nel corso di essa* (Venice: Baba and Heir of Giunta, 1648), USTC 4020325, p. 139: 'Giudicato ch'egli habbia ecceduto per qualche particolare affetto verso la casa Farnese'. For other criticism of Strada's portrayal of Farnese see Neumann, *Geschitschreibung als Kunst*, p. 282.

98   Bentivoglio, *Della guerra di Fiandra*, pp. 390–391.

99   Lamal, 'Movement and Translation of Italian Histories', pp. 130–132.

later. In 1648, one year after the original publication of Strada's second volume in Rome, the firm in Antwerp again issued their own edition in octavo format.[100] These numerous octavo editions were aimed at a European-wide Latin reading public.

Crucially, the Cnobbaert firm also published a Dutch translation of the first decade in 1645 by Willem van Aelst, an Antwerp schoolteacher. A year after its appearance in Antwerp, Van Aelst's translation was reprinted in Amsterdam by Nicolaes van Ravesteyn without significant changes. This Dutch translation of the first decade was also republished in other cities in the Dutch Republic: in Rotterdam and Dordrecht (1655). Strada's criticism of Alba resonated in both the Habsburg and the Northern Netherlands, where his history was republished multiple times and recommended reading for school pupils.[101] The memorialisation campaign of the Farnese family thus was incredibly successful in promoting a specific version of the Revolt in the Netherlands.

This chapter has shown that various Italian histories written in the first half of the seventeenth century presented a moderate interpretation of the conflict. Whereas printed Italian news reports became imbued with counter-reformation rhetoric and firmly pro-Habsburg sentiments, the Italian histories of the Revolt in the same period were markedly different in tone. Their descriptions and interpretations of past events were embedded into a clear Catholic framework, the rebels were often labelled as heretics, but equally incorporated decades of reporting and political debates on the war to critique some Spanish policies as well as describe the cruelties of war. Their accounts presented a decidedly Catholic narrative of the conflict in which Italian soldiers and commanders played a starring role. Like in the printed news pamphlets, Alexander Farnese continued to claim the leading role, with Spinola not receiving similar levels of praise. On the Italian peninsula, Alexander Farnese's status as a perfect military commander and clement hero continued to be shaped by the political ambitions of his successors.

100   See for instance the letter by Guy Patin to Charles Spon on 22 March 1648 from Paris that he has received the Antwerp edition (reference footnote 37).
101   Pollmann and Stensland, 'Alba's reputation in the early modern Low Countries', pp. 323–325.

Epilogue

In this place all the news of the world flows, [...] From this country depend all the major revolutions, it cannot only be called the true school of military arts but also of politics, since here one gets to know all the nations of Europe, it is a place where one can observe all the different humours, affects and inclinations. Warfare is conducted more with judgements and strategies than with the weapons themselves; men are of a pleasant nature, easy to pardon but even easier to raise up.[1]

∴

Italians considered the Low Countries a theatre of political and military importance, as can be seen in the fragment of a letter written by the soldier Tomaso Obizzi in 1631. Brussels, and the Low Countries in general, were considered as a prime location for anyone wanting to keep up to date with the most military and political changes in Europe. Brussels and Antwerp were seen as one of the frontiers in Catholic Europe. During the seventeenth century, as the balance of power was shifting both in Italy and in Europe, the need for accurate information became all the more pressing. Italian states continued to recruit the services of experienced observers.

In 1628 the Italian Capuchin Bernardino Sernicoli asked Chrisogono Flacchio, secretary of the papal nuncio in Brussels, to provide the Tuscan Secretary of State, Andrea Cioli, with news every week.[2] For twenty years, Flacchio had been in charge of supplying the papal curia with regular news reports.[3] He sent 'the gazettes from Holland' to Rome and added a translated

---

1 Brussels 2 March 1631, ASF, MdP 4259, fasc 4, fol 163: 'Qui collano tutte le nuove del mondo [...] e di qui dependono la maggior rivoluzioni de principe e si puo non solo chiama la vera scola dell'arte militare ma ancora della Politica, poiche vi conoscono tutte le nazioni dell'Europa, dove si vegono varie sorti d'humori, d'affetti, e d'inclinazione. Il guerreggiare si fa più col giudizio e le statageme che [v] con l'armi Il guerreggiare si fa più col giudizio e le statageme che [v] con l'armi gl'huomini sono di natura piacevole facile al pardonare, ma piu facile al sollevarsi.'

2 To Bernardino Piccolomini in Siena, Brussels 4 September 1628, ASF, MdP 1418, fol 84–85.

3 Flacchio, originally from Rieti, had been secretary of Latin letters in Brussels since 1606–1607: AAV, SdS, NF 14C, fol 224 (letter from Brussels on 17 May 1625): 'sta servendo alla S. Sede Ap. già sotto cinque nunti'. He also acted as internuncio see L. Van Meerbeeck (ed.), *Correspondance*

handwritten copy of Broer Janszoon's Amsterdam-based newspaper *Tydinghe uyt verscheyde quartieren* (Tidings from different quarters) either in Italian or in Latin.[4] His diligence in acquiring news did not go unnoticed by other Italian potentates; the Tuscan government had already approached him for his services.[5] Flacchio had previously refused to serve another ruler than the pope, but in 1628 he agreed to report weekly on events in the Low Countries. He specified that he did not expect an official title or a stipend, but requested the protection of the Grand Duke claiming that informants were not well-regarded at the court in Brussels.[6] Just a few years earlier, in 1625 Giovanni Battista Pasini, a Venetian merchant living in Brussels, was imprisoned on the order of governess Isabel. Pasini supplied information to the Venetian Senate and the Venetian ambassadors in Paris, London and The Hague.[7] He was accused of communicating intelligence with the enemy and was imprisoned for more than one year. To avoid such a scenario, dispatching Flacchio's letters became a complex and secret operation which involved several Capuchin friars. Sernicoli signed Flacchio's letters and posted them to Bernardino Piccolomini, a Capuchin friar in Siena, who forwarded the letters to the secretary of state Cioli in Florence.[8]

This case offers another intriguing example of the complexity of the networks of communication between the Low Countries and Italy. From the start of the Revolt in 1566, Medici rulers had an informational advantage with trusted Florentine correspondents in the political centre, and on or near the battlefield. Their secretaries of state continued to find ways to have access to trusted correspondents on the ground for reliable information. Throughout this book, it has become clear that a lack of official representatives in Brussels certainly did not hinder the Italian rulers from knowing exactly what was happening.

---

    des nonces Gesualdo, Morra, Sanseverino avec la Secrétairerie d'Etat Pontificale (1615–1621) (Brussels/Rome: Belgisch Historisch Instituut te Rome, 1937), p. 419, 424, 515.

4 AAV, SdS, NF 14C, fol 224v–225: 'a mandar a VS Ill. la Gazzetta d'Ollanda [...] Qui giunta dunque mando a VS Ill.ma la detta Gazzetta stampata con la sua traduttione in Italiano'. A copy of Broer Jansz' newspaper issue of 28 June 1625 on fol 287.

5 Bernardino Sernicoli to Bernardino Piccolomini in Siena, Brussels [unknown date] September 1628, ASF, MdP 1418, fol 86.

6 Bernardino Sernicoli to Bernardino Piccolomini in Siena, Brussels 4 September 1628, ASF, MdP 1418, fol 84v: 'scrivere avvisi che questa per se solo è molto male inteso qui'.

7 Various copies of Pasini's letters and other letters related to the matter in Contarini's letter books BMV, Cl. VII, cod. 1093/5, vol II, fol 104–106v, 132, 169–170, 191, 243. Pasini's *avvisi* can be found in ASVe, Avvisi, 4; 13. He started as informer and spy for the first Venetian secretary, see Christofforo Suriano from The Hague on 31 August 1616 in ASVe, Senato, Dispacci, Signori Stati, Filza 2, fol 166r, mentions his name in cypher as someone who keeps an eye on Venetians in service of Spanish in Southern Low Countries.

8 Various letters from 1628 and 1629 in ASF, MdP 1418.

The use of alternative channels of acquiring information had advantages. Compared to early modern official ambassadors, these more informal correspondents were less closely watched and had more freedom in their daily news gathering practices; they were ideal conduits of information.

Within those networks, and in the particular context of the Low Countries, military men acted as crucial suppliers of news. Whilst on campaign, officers were involved in the business of news and intelligence. Experienced war veterans, such as Lodovico Melzo and Lelio Brancaccio, reiterated in their military manuals that diligence in acquiring intelligence was one of the main qualities military commanders needed to master.[9] In letters to their rulers or patrons, military officers described battles at length and they included plans of citadels and sieges. They offered shrewd observation and refined judgements on contemporary events. The role of military men in providing information is a crucial aspect of early modern news culture and one that until this point has been unfairly neglected.

These military officers often enclosed official letters or anonymised manuscript accounts of battles with their correspondence; not infrequently these texts were subsequently printed in different Italian cities. Milan, as the centre of the Habsburg monarchy in northern Italy, was an important centre for the publication of news of the Revolt in the Low Countries. There is no evidence that the Habsburg government in Milan was directly involved in the propagation of news of military victories in the Low Countries.[10] But indirectly, the publishers in Milan must have had access to the authorities for their sources of information; they certainly would not have published information without their tacit approval.

Throughout the sixteenth century Italian news culture presented a uniform pro-Habsburg and Catholic narrative. The anonymity and specific style of reporting news in *avvisi* should not mislead historians to conclude these were impartial sources. Their content was influenced by a variety of actors, some closely affiliated to Spanish-Habsburg power, yet their involvement has become invisible to researchers. To capture the movement of information and how the message was manipulated requires a lot of painstaking research and comparing. Tracing letters exchanged between military commanders and Italian dukes or Spanish ambassadors on the peninsula allows to recover some of the early attempts at crafting a specific narrative.

---

9   Brancaccio, *I carichi militari*, p. 254; Melzo, *Regole Militare*, pp. 211–212.
10   For a similar observation in Habsburg Netherlands during the seventeenth century: Arblaster, *From Ghent to Aix*, pp. 260–262.

The reliance of printers on official accounts written by military commanders celebrating their own successes further illustrates how political affiliation shaped the message. Studying the printed news production in Italian cities, and the changing political realities on the peninsula, are further crucial indications of these mechanisms. During the seventeenth century, the growing importance of France and its renewed ambitions to control Italian states influenced the news production. Anti-Spanish pamphlets, reports of Dutch victories, and pro-French news accounts started to appear in Venice and in Turin. In the pro-Habsburg news accounts, printed in Milan and Naples, the Habsburg forces were presented as the real defenders of the Catholic faith.

In Italian discourse, the Netherlandish enemy was portrayed as rebellious and heretical. The Italians, following Guicciardini's characterization, considered the inhabitants of the Low Countries to be rebellious, stubborn and gullible. As the war progressed, the fierce and warlike qualities of the inhabitants became a dominant trope. Yet whereas in 1577 this image was applied to all the inhabitants of the Low Countries, later this gradually was ascribed only to the Dutch. In crafting the image of the Dutch as a formidable and stubborn opponent, the achievements of Italian commanders such as Alexander Farnese or Ambrogio Spinola in subduing them gained even greater significance and resonance. The glorification of Italian military qualities emerged partly as a counter-image to that of the Netherlandish enemy.

In news pamphlets, fuelled by patronage opportunities, the first writers started to glorify Alexander's achievement in conquering the city of Antwerp in 1585. During and after his lifetime, Alexander's status as a hero was further cultivated by his family for clear political and dynastic objectives. The situation was different for Ambrogio Spinola, who was not glorified on the Italian peninsula to the same extent as Farnese had been. In news pamphlets, victories were assigned to the Habsburg dynasty and it seems that Spinola's family promoted their famous relative's renown less actively in Italy, as they did not have the same urgent dynastic need to do so.

While scholars have claimed that there was no national consciousness during this period in Italy, a sense of Italian identity was cultivated in many histories on the Revolt in the Netherlands.[11] This identity was largely defined by their military abilities and prowess, as well as their clemency and religiosity. A distinct Italian narrative of the Revolt emerged partly from a rivalry with the Spanish nation within the Habsburg army and was shaped by existing news

---

11   See F. Gilbert, 'Italy', in O. Ranum (ed.), *National Consciousness, History and Political Culture in Early Modern Europe* (Baltimore/London: John Hopkins University Press, 1975), pp. 21–42.

and political discourse on the Italian peninsula. Blaming Duke of Alba's policies was not invented by the Farnese family to present Margaret of Parma and
Alexander Farnese in a more favourable light. In newsletters and political treatises, the policies of the Duke of Alba were blamed for the problems in the Low
Countries by most political thinkers and history writers.

The unexpected success of the rebel forces in defying the powerful Spanish-
Habsburg army was very relevant to their own perceptions of Habsburg power
and the likelihood of continued Habsburg hegemony on the Italian peninsula.
In the anonymous pamphlet, *Il cittadino fedele* (The faithful citizen), published
during the Neapolitan Revolt (1647–1648), the readers were reminded how
remarkable was the Dutch achievement: 'from simple fishermen, hardened by
their long practice of war, [they] have made themselves respected amongst
the potentates'.[12] Such references to the myth of the small state that successful resisted Spanish rule has been used by historians to argue that the Dutch
Republic became an inspirational example in early modern Europe.

The evidence presented here, however, suggests, especially with regard to
Italy, this republican tradition has been overemphasized in scholarship. Italian
authors did reflect on constitutional issues and noted the Dutch emphasis
on traditional liberties, but what increasingly fascinated them was the unexpected possibilities opened up by the strength of Dutch resistance. Their interest in this conflict predated the creation of this new republican state. What
the Italian elites were interested in were the dynastic, military and economic
possibilities this war created. At a prosaic level, to many of them the wars
offered the possibility of employment for the aristocratic military officer class;
to acquire military skills, to network and to secure a future position.

These Italian observers and their texts indicate the close ties between Italian
states and the Spanish-Habsburg empire. Political commentators such as di
Castro, Campanella and Frachetta sought to influence Habsburg policy. Many
of these writers supported Habsburg rule on the Italian peninsula because they
saw it as a guarantee of peace between the different Italian states. The fragility
of the *Pax Hispanica* and the political fragmentation of the Italian states is part
and parcel of this story. This difficult balance meant that there was a real need
to defend Habsburg policy and to create a consensus. Attempts to establish a
consensus can be seen in Costa's dialogue on the Twelve Years' Truce, where
the Genoese noblemen were discussing the reputation of the Habsburg monarchy. For pro-Habsburg political writers, it was impossible to avoid mentioning the enormous drain of resources this long war had caused to the Habsburg

---

12   Silvana D'Alessio, *Contagi. La rivolta napoletana del 1647–48: linguaggio e potere politico*
      (Florence: Centro Editoriale Toscana, 2003), p. 78.

monarchy. The majority of these political discourses were, however, not permeated by anti-Spanish rhetoric. But the dangers posed to Habsburg power and empire were very much part of the story.

While Italian writers could not disguise a grudging respect for Dutch fighting spirit, very few Italians reporting from the Netherlands or commenting on events at home actively hoped for the eventual success of the revolt. But increasingly they had to admit the possibility that Habsburg power might be damaged – perhaps even fatally so – by the long, apparently endless, conflict in their Northern dominions. In this respect these Netherlandish narratives, whether print or manuscript, public or more restricted, throw important light on wider historical perceptions of the history of Italy in the period. To historians particularly of the Renaissance, the treaty of Cateau-Cambrésis in 1559 has been seen to settle the question of Italy.[13] For France this was a telling and decisive defeat. The aspirations first raised by the invasion of 1494 were finally dashed. The story told in these pages suggests that this settlement was by no means final. The *Pax Hispanica* was by no means as secure as this neat periodization would imply. Those who chafed under Spanish rule, and those who relied on Spanish arms, both watched the unfolding events in the Netherlands with increasing fascination. A few did so in a spirit of hope, many more with anxiety that the unexpected weakness of Habsburg military force would damage the capacity to protect Italy from the terrible consequences of foreign incursion that the peninsula had endured between 1494 and 1527. For Italians, the Low Countries were never a faraway country of which they knew little. Rather, the Netherlands were an essential part of their international, economic and cultural hinterland. The closeness with which they followed events, exposed here for the first time, and the sophisticated analysis applied to these distant conflicts, pays eloquent tribute to the strength of the bonds that united these separate nations.

---

13   For an overview of these views see Levin, *Agents of Empire*, pp. 2–3.

Bibliography

1 Archival Material

Archivio Apostolico Vaticano

Fondo Borghese
    I: 10, 765, 429–448.
    II: 31–32, 98, 100, 111, 114, 115.
    III: 80.
Fondo Pio: 91, 93.
Misc Arm: 11, 34, 139.
Nuntiature d'Inghilterra: 1.
Nuntiature di Fiandra: 4, 6, 7, 12, 12A, 14B, 14C.

Archivio Storico Capitolina Roma

Archivio Orsini
    Prima Serie, Lettere: 106, 107, 108, 109, 110, 111, 112, 113, 114, 115, 116, 117, 118, 119, 120, 121, 122, 123, 124, 125, 127.
    Prima Serie, Avvisi: 398, 399.

Archivio di Stato di Firenze

Mediceo del Principato
    Avvisi di Fiandra: 4253, 4254, 4255, 4256, 4257, 4258, 4259.
    Avvisi da Milano: 3254.
    Avvisi da Roma: 4025, 4026.
    Avvisi da Venezia: 3079, 3080, 3081, 3082, 3083.
    Stampati, Francia: 4878.
    Carteggio Universale
        Cosimo I: 575, 576, 577, 610, 612, 649, 650, 651.
        Ferdinando I: 716, 895, 915, 916, 924, 960, 961, 988.
    Carteggio dei Segretari
        Serguidi: 1179, 1180, 1193.
        Cioli: 1343, 1368, 1372, 1373, 1379, 1381, 1390, 1392, 1414, 1417, 1418, 1426, 1430, 1434, 1435.
        Gondi: 1471, 1474, 1475, 1477, 1479.
    Lettere Vialardi: 3623, 3624.
Miscellanea Medicea
    14/6: Avvisi dal carteggio del Card. Ferdinando.
    28/27: Lettere del Giovan Battista Guicciardini (1577).

29/2: Rapporti politici al Cardinale Ferdinando de Medici (1572).

251: Collection of avvisi from the Dutch Republic 1629–1643

Urbino

Classe Prima: 100, 198, 199

Archivio General de Simancas

Estado, Legajo: 1433, 1932.

Archivio di Stato di Modena

Cancelleria Ducale, Sezione Estero

Avvisi e notizie: 6, 7, 8, 9, 10, 11, 12, 13, 16, 17, 18, 21, 23, 24, 26, 28, 101, 110, 128.

Ambasciatore, Germania: 43, 44, 50, 60, 66, 72, 87.

Cancelleria Ducale, Raccolte e Miscellanea

Documenti di stati e città: 164

Archivio di Stato di Mantova

Archivio Gonzaga

Avvisi: 1981, 1982, 1983, 1984, 1986, 1988, 1989, 1990, 1998, 1999, 2000, 2001.

Esteri: 564, 565, 574, 575, 576, 577.

Archivio di Stato di Torino

Corti Stranieri

Corte Spagna: 4

Negoziazioni colla Corte di Spagna: 1, 2

Lettere principe forestieri

Alemagna: 3

Parma: 82, 83

Lettere di Ministri Olanda: 1

Materie politiche Negoziazioni con Olanda: 1

Archivio di Stato di Venezia

Avvisi: 4, 9, 13

Senato, Dispacci, Signori Stati, 2.

Biblioteca Ambrosiana

D 188 inf; G276 inf; G286 inf; I 230 inf, S96 sup.

Biblioteca Apostolica Vaticana

Urb Lat: 817, 818, 828, 854 Pars I, 854 II, 1040, 1041, 1042, 1043, 1044, 1045, 1046, 1047, 1048, 1052, 1053, 1068, 1072, 1073.

Barb Lat: 3544, 3546, 4934, 4958, 5321, 5369, 5776, 6789, 6797, 6803.
Boncompagni: D5, D10.
Ottob Lat: 2348.
Cod Vaticano: 6436.

Biblioteca Nazionale Centrale di Firenze
Manuscripts
Capponi: 58, 109.
II, I, 107, fol 39–41: *Successi di Fiandra e rotta di Neuport.*
II, I, 235: *Historia di Fiandra del tempo che comandò l'armata il Duca Alessandro Farnese, composta da Paolo Rinaldi nel 1599.*

Biblioteca Nazionale Marciana
Manuscripts
Cl. VII, cod. 1093/5: Letter books by Contarini from The Hague between 1624–1625.

Biblioteca Vallicelliana
Manuscripts
N22: Relazione e memorie istoriche de costumi, ricchezze, sito, riti e governo de paesi bassi. Con le notizie delle guerre accadute nella fiandra e della tregua fatta tra l'arciduca Alberto d'Austria e li stati d'olanda
N32: Raccolta di scritture spettanti alli negozi della Spagna e delle Indie
R55: Trattati varii di politica e ragione di stato

Biblioteca Nazionale Centrale di Roma
Manuscripts
Fondo Gesuitico: 315, 418

Bibliothek Museum für Kommunikation, Frankfurt
D10: Geschlossene Sammlung von Geschäftsbriefen aus dem Jahr 1585

Koninklijke Bibliotheek van België, Brussel
Manuscripts
II. 1155: Rinaldi, *Liber relatiorum*
II. 5193: Recueils de documents relatifs aux événement politique de l'Europe (XVIᵉ siècle)
6009: Francesco Orsino, *Della Guerre di Fiandria, 1620–1632.*
M 7023: Observations sur l'ouvrage de Conestagio.

2   Ephemeral Publications on the Revolt in the Low Countries

Occassional news pamphlets and edicts printed in Italian or in Italian cities with news on the Revolt in the Low Countries from 1566–1648 in chronological order. During the Twelve Years' Truce (1609–1621) fighting temporarily stopped in the Low Countries, so I have not included printed news pamphlets during this period, but that does not imply that there were none.

1567 *Diversi avisi de le cose piu notabili seguite novamente in Transilvania & Ongaria [...] Et di piu tutto quello che e seguito tra le principe de la Lamagna e sua Cesarea Maesta circa la dieta, e quell'che s'ottenuto in Praga con altre spedition per Fiandra, & novi avisi di Costantinopoli* (Padua: Pasquati, 1567), USTC 804538.

Ordinatione del catolico re Filippo per la pacificatione della villa d'Anversa, sopra il fatto della religione. Publicata in detta villa alli xxviii. di maggio MDLXVII (Bologna: Benacci, 1567), USTC 809779.

Ordinatione et editto provisionale, fatto per sua maesta catolica sopra la pacificatione dell tumulti della citta d'Anuersa, circa il fatto della religione, e quello che ne dipende. Fatto publicare nella detta citta per l'illustrissima signora Margarita duchessa di Parma, e Piacenza regente, e gouernatrice di quel paese a di XXVIII di maggio MDLXVII. (Rome: Accolti, 1567), USTC 809780.

1568 *Copia de una lettera venuta nouamente laquale vi narra tutte le cose successe in Fiandra Vienna & Polonia, dela guerra, & di tutto l'essercito del campo cristiano, dove intenderete una rotta data dal Duca d'Alua a l'esercito nemico con mortalita grande de nemici. Et altri avisi come legendo possete intendere* (s.l.: s.n., [1568]), in BL, Shelf mark General Reference Collection 9314.aa.3.

I feliciss successi del sereniss. re catholico in Fiandra, & della vittoria hauuta per l'eccell. sig. duca d'Alua luogotenente generale di s.m. catholica in quelle contra gli Vgonotti suoi ribelli. Et dell'allegrezza che ne fece tre di la santita di n.s. papa Pio quinto. Referendo gratie a Dio benedetto di cosi gran benefici (Bologna: s.n., 1568), USTC 801186.

Primi et secondi avvisi della fellicissima vittoria hauuta in Fiandra contra gli Heretici, per l'Eccellentissimo S. Duca D'Alva secondo le lettere mandate al cardinal Pacecco, al cardinal Granuela, & al s. ambasciatore di sua maiesta catholica in Roma. E secondo la relation del cap. Cariglio de Melo mandato da sua ecc. a n. signore. Dove si narrano le cose per ordine col numero de morti, & i nomi degli huomini segnalati, & illustri. Et la vittoria havuta in Francia contra gli Ugonotti, & con un epigramma in lode del signor duca d'Alua (Rome: Blado, 1568), USTC 804611.

Primi et secondi avvisi della fellicissima vittoria hauuta in Fiandra contra gli Heretici, per l'Eccellentissimo S. Duca D'Alva (Bologna: Benacci, 1568), in Leiden University Library, PAMFLT 1568:6.

1569 *Copia d'alcuni avisi venuti novamente di Francia, di Oriliens d'inghilterra, & d'Alemagna, d'Amosin, Lione, &Viena. Dove s'intende di molte scaramuccie, & battaglie fatte tra Prencipi Christiani, et Ugonotti, nelle quali il S. Iddio ha concesso Vittoria in favore de' nostri Christiani,. Con la ribellione di certi signori della fiandra, quali sono stati giustitiati, come legende intenderete* (Bologna: Benacci, 1569), USTC 804647.

1570 *Copia de diuersi auisi de Roma, Napoli, e Mesina, Spira, Anuersa, & Cipro* (Venice: s.n., 1570), USTC 762012.

    Copie di avvisi venuti di Anversa, di Spira, di Roma, di Venezia, di Spagna, di Francia, & di Costantinopoli, Ne quali si continiene tutte le cose occorse dal primo di agosto fino a quest'hora presente, tanto di mare, quanto di terra, e specialmente tutti i capitoli, che nostro signore ha mandato al re cattolico intorno alla cruciata (Florence: s.n., 1570), USTC 804715.

    Avisi venutti nuovamente da diversi paesi delle gran rovine e danni de marcantie e altre robe e morte de persone assai che a fatto il mare e fiumi e tempesta grande cioè in Leone di Francia e in Anversa e in Fiandra (s.l.: s.n., [1570]), USTC 804706.

1571 *Noui auisi venuti di Leuante nelli quali si intende la difesa di Famagosta et della presa de due maone è quattro passa cavalli, & cinquanta pezzi d'artiglieria con 10.millia cantara di frumento, dalli 2. ottobre in qua. Con altri avisi di Roma, Napoli, Anversa, Viena, & Costantinopoli, & altri luoghi. Et la venuta de principi, venuti a Venetia con la regina di Polonia* (Modena: s.n., s.d. [1571?]), USTC 804904.

1572 *L'inaudite et monstruose crudeltà usate da gli heretici contra i religiosi, nella espugatione della città di Ruremonda di Fiandra* (Rome: Blado, 1572), USTC 805008.

    L'inaudite et horrende crudeltà usate da gli heretici contra i religiosi, nella espugnatione della città di Ruremonda di Fiandra, il dì 23. di luglio 1572 (Venice: Farri, 1572), USTC 805007.

    Orazione di Luigi Groto cieco di Hadria, fatta al serenissimo principe Luigi Mocenigo, et alla Signoria di Vinezia. Con la lettera di monsignor Cornelio vescouo di Bitonto, al signor Marc'Antonio Colonna doppo la vittoria christiana, contra il turcho. Et la partita dell'armata da Messina, con la relazione di quanto e seguito à Castel nuouo, et gli auuisi di Fiandra di nuouo venuti, col numero delle vele che ha il gran turcho in essere quest'anno 1572 (Florence: Celonaio, 1572), USTC 834753.

    Auuisi venuti da diuerse parti particolarmente da Cattaro e da Castel Nuouo da ventotto di maggio per insino alli venticinque di giugno MDLXXII. Onde si intende tutte le imprese d'importanza fatte per mare e per terra nelle parte di Leuante come nel Ponente d'Inghilterra di Francia d Alemagna di Venetia di Roma, e d'Anuersa e d'altri luoghi (Florence: s.n., 1572), EDIT16 78194.

1573 *L'assedio della città di Herlem in Hollanda* (Rome: Lafréry, 1573). Etched news print 270 × 399 mm, Rijksmuseum Amsterdam, RP-P-OB-79.236.

1574 *Don Luis de Requesens commendatore maggiore, notifica il seguente à soldati spagnuoli che stanno al presente con alteratione in questa villa d'Anversa impresso per ordine di S. Eccell. nella stampa Reale di S. Maestà per Christoforo Piantino in Anversa, alli 8. Di Maggio 1574* (Milan: Da Ponte, 1574), in ASF, MdP 4254.

Il perdono generale che il re Filippo concede a tutti paesi, stati, et luochi di Fiandra che voranno ritornare alla solita, & antica obedienza. Con il numero de personaggi che sono esclusi dal sudetto perdono fuori. Et con la restitutione de beni, honori, & gradi, a coloro che lo accettaranno. Publicato dal signor comendator maggiore capitano generale, & luogotenente per detta m. in quelle parti di Fiandra (Milan: Da Ponte, 1574), in ASF, MdP 4254.

Il perdono generale che il re Filippo concede a tutti paesi, stati, et luoghi di Fiandra che voranno ritornare alla solita, et antica obedienza. Con il numero de personaggi che sono esclusi dal sudetto perdono fuori. Et con la restitutione de beni, honori, et gradi a coloro che lo accettaranno. Publicato dal signor comenda-tor maggiore capitano generale, & luogotenente per detta maestà in quelle parti di Fiandra (Venice: Viani, 1574), USTC 82898.

Il perdono generale che il re Filippo concede a tutti paesi, stati, et luochi di Fiandra che voranno ritornare alla solita, & antica obedienza. Con il numero de personaggi che sono esclusi dal sudetto perdono fuori. Et con la restitutione de beni, honori, & gradi, a coloro che lo accettaranno. Publicato dal signor comendator maggiore capitano generale, & luogotenente per detta m. in quelle parti di Fiandra (Bologna: Benacci, 1574), USTC 828980.

Il perdono generale che il re Filippo concede a tutti paesi, stati, et luoghi di Fiandra che voranno ritornare alla solita, & antica obedienza. Con il numero de personaggi che sono esclusi dal sudetto perdono fuori. Et con la restitutione de beni, honori, et gradi a coloro che lo accettaranno. Publicato dal s. comendator maggiore capitano generale, & luogotenente per detta maesta in quelle parti di Fiandra. Et li auisi venuti da Napoli il 24. d'agosto. Doue s'intente gli assalti dati in la goletta, & il gran tradimento scoperto in detta fortezza, & la giustitia conseguita fra gli detti traditori (Mantua: s.n., 1574), in BNCF V.MIS 1118.11.

Vera relatione della rotta che e stata data in Fiandra al Conte Lodovico di Nansao con molti altri signori che lo seguivano nel giorno 14. d'Aprile 1574 con il numero de prigioni, e della Gente morta, e sbarattata, & altri assai parti colari notabili (Bologna: Benacci, 1574), USTC 804222.

1575 *Tutti gli avisi novi di tutte le parti di Europa, et massime di Roma, di Fiandra, et di Francia. Ne quali s'intende i preparamenti di guerra & ciò che si crede dell'armata turchesca* (Brescia: s.n., 1575), USTC 805264.

1577 *Editto Perpetuo qual viene a trattare dell'accordio, patto et conventione, novamente fatta, della pace universale nelli paesi di Fiandra &c* (Milan: Da Ponte, 1577), USTC 857152.

Editto perpetuo sopra l'accordo fatto tra l'illustre signor don Giovanni d'Austria cavagliero, dell'ordine del Toson d'oro de la parte, & al nome de Re Catholico di Spagna d'una parte e li stati generali di questi paesi di qua d'altra parte: per aquetar li rumori suscitati in essi paesi, per le genti d'arme straniere (Turin: s.n., 1577), USTC 857153.

1578   *Il Sucesso de l'essequie fatte nella morte del Serniss. S. Don Giovanni d'Austria, qual fu il primo giorno d'Ottobre 1578. Et altri Avisi particolari dell' Essercito di S. Maestà nella Fiandra* (Bologna: Bonardo, 1578), USTC 805452.

     La Grande Vittoria havuta dall'Altezza del Sereniss.mo S.or Don Giovanni d'Austria in Fiandra contra ribelli di sua Maesta Catholica, con la morte, e presa di sei milla persone, e de molti standardi, e bandiere, & acquisto d'alcune terre, e capi. Tradotta di Spagnuolo in lingua Italiana (Milan: Da Ponte, [1578]) in ASMo, CD, Avvisi e notizie dall'estero, 142.

     Gosselini, Giuliano (trans.), *Vera narratione de le cose passate ne' paesi bassi dopò la giunta del ser. mo s. or Don Giovanni d'Austria con la risolutione de gli obietti contenuti del discorso non vero, mandato in luce da gli Stati d'essi paesi, intorno à la rottura per loro fatta de la ultima pace* (Milan: Da Ponte, 1578), USTC 831760.

1579   *Copia de gli vltimi auisi venuti di Fiandra all'Illustrissimo & Eccentissimo Signore Duca di Parma & Piasenza &c. doue s'intende minutamente tutti gli assalti, sacaramucie, che sono occorse, sotto la fortezza di Mastrich. Con la presa, & il vero disegno della fortezza* (Bologna: Benacci, 1579), UTSC 805472.

     Copia de gli vltimi avisi venuti di Fiandra all'illustrissimo, & eccellentissimo sig. duca di Parma, Piasenza, &c. doue s'intende minutamente tutti gli assalti, scaramucie, che sono occorse, sotto la fortezza di Mastrich. Et con la presa di detta città (Padua: Pasquato, 1579), Biblioteca Palatina in Parma, Shelfmark Misc Erud 4.351.

     Raguaglio della citta di Mastrich assediata, & presa, per il Principe di Parma. Generale dell'Essercito del Rè Philippo Catholico nella Fiandra (Bologna: Bonardo, 1579), USTC 805508.

1580   *Vero discorso e relatione della battaglia fatta alli 17. di Giugno 1580: tra Hardenberghe et Gramsberghe, paese d'Overysse i sù le 3. hore dopò mezo giorno da i soldati di sua Maestà Cath. Condotti per Martnio Schenck de Nydeggen al soccorso di Groeninghen. Et il Conte d'Hohenloe capo di quelli della nova lega d'Utrecht< Data al campo presso Hardenberge alli 19 di Giugnio 1580* (Bologna: Benacci, 1580), USTC 804161.

     Mastrih Fortezza in Fiandra presa dall' Ecc.mo S.or Prencipe di Parma per Re Catolico MDLXXIX alli XXVIIII di Gìvgno (Rome: Cataro, [1580]). Etched news print, 342 × 438 mm, in Universitätsbibliothek Salzburg, Wolf-Dietrich-Klebeband Städtebilder G 34 III.

     Bonifazio, Natale, *Il vero dissegno della città de Mastrich nella Galia Belgica, assediata dall' Ecc.mo Sr Prencipe di Parma, General de sua Mta Catolica, nel quale si vede con ogni diligentia il sito de essa citta, con li suoi forti, è beloardi, in riparo, similmente i luochi doue è accampato il campo de sua Magesta Catholica, con le batterie, assalti,& minere, fatte, & alter cose notabile, come legend alli numeri vederete con li ponti fatti per poter trascorere di qua et di la dal fiume, el tutto fatto dal disegno del Ingegniero de S Eccelentia* (Rome: Vaccaria, 1580). Etched and engraved news print, 320 × 434 mm, in Universitätsbibliothek Salzburg, G31 III and in RCT, RCIN 721073.

1584 *Avviso dell' aspra et crudel morte data a Baldassare Borgogne in Delfi d' Hollandia & la sua constantia. Per haver ammazato il Principe de Orange inimico della Santa Fede Cattolica* (Rome: Bonfadino, 1584), USTC 805865.

   Avviso dell' aspra et crudel morte data a Baldassare Borgogne in Delfi d' Hollandia & la sua constantia. Per haver ammazato il Principe de Orange inimico della Santa Fede Cattolica (Florence: s.n., 1584), USTC 836285.

   Avviso dell' aspra et crudel morte data a Baldassare Borgogne in Delfi d' Hollandia (Carmagnola: Bellone, 1584), USTC 805867.

   Auuiso dell'aspra e crudel morte data a Baldassarre Borgognone in Defli d'Hollandia, & la sua constantia. Per haver ammazzato il principe de Orange inimico della santa fede cattolica (Bologna: Benacci, 1584), USTC 764237.

   Adviso dell'aspra et crudeli morte data a Baldassare Brogognese in Delfi d'Hollandia et la sua constantia per haver ammazato il principe d'Orange inimico della santa fede catholica (Palermo: Carrara, 1584), USTC 805856.

1585 *Articoli et condizioni del trattato fatto, & concluso infra l'altezza del Principe di Parma & Piacenza e gouernatore, e capitan generale in questi paesi, in nome di sua maestà, come duca di Brabanzia, e marchese del santo imperio da vna parte, et la città d'Anuersa dall'altra parte, addi 17. di agosto 1585 tradotta di lingua Franzese in Toscana da Giorgio Marescotti* (Florence: Marescotti, 1585), USTC 763655.

   Bonifazio, Natale, *Vero et nuovo disegno della pianta della cita di Anversa con tvtti gli svoi forti assediata al presente dal Serenis.o Sig.r Prencipe di Parma et alla gata dal fivme schelda nello stato si trovava il di xv di Decembre MDLXXXIIII* (Rome: Rasciotti, 1585). Etched and engraved news print, 243 × 344 mm, in Universitätsbibliothek Salzburg, G30 III and RCT, RCIN 721075.

   Conditioni, et capitoli fatti, et conclusi in Anuersa dal serenissimo prencipe di Parma, & di Piacenza, &c. Luogotenente, governatore, & capitano generale di sua maesta catolica nella Fiandra, il giorno XVII. d'agosto, l'anno 1585 (Ferrara: Buoncompagni, 1585), USTC 857155.

   Copia della vera relatione mandata all'ilustriss. & Eccellentiss. Sig. Duca di Terranova, Governatore in questo stato & capitano generale in italia, per la maestà del Rè N.S. dal Sereniss. Sig. Prencipe di Parma, dell'ultima notabil vittoria havuta contra li rebelli heretici di Fiandra (Milan: Da Ponte, 1585), USTC 805982.

Copia delli articoli overo capitol stabiliti, & conclusi per la resa della città d'Anversa, mandate dal Sereniss. Principe di Parma all'Eccellentiss. Sign. Duca di Terranova &c. Governatore del Stato di Milano, & capitano general di Sua Maestà in Italia. Tradotta de Francese in Lingua Italiana (Milan: Tini, 1585), USTC 805984.

Copia delli articoli, overo capitoli stabiliti, & conclusi per la resa della città di Anversa (Bologna: Benacci, 1585), USTC 801388.

Copia delli articoli, overo capitoli stabiliti, & conclusi per la resa della citta di Anversa (Genoa: s.n., 1585), USTC 805986.

Copia delli articoli, overo capitoli stabiliti, & conclusi per la resa della citta di Anversa (Brescia: Sabbio, 1585), USTC 805985.

Copia delli articoli, overo capitoli stabiliti, & conclusi per la resa della citta di Anversa (Piacenza: Bazachi, 1585), USTC 805987.

Copia delli articoli overo capitoli, stabiliti & conclusi per la resa della città di Anversa (Reggio: Bartoli, 1585), USTC 805983.

Copia d'una lettera scritta dal sig. prencipe di Parma generale in Fiandra per la maestà del re, nostro signore, all'illustrissimo, & eccellentiss. sign. duca di Terranoua, nella quale gli dà conto della resa di Bruselle, con le capitulationi, & di gran parte della Frisia, con altri successi (Milan: Cologno, 1585), USTC 828815.

Il vero disegno del mirabile assedio della fortissima cita de Anversa, fatto dal serenissimo Alexandro Farnese, principe de Parma, govte luoco tenente et capp. generale de S. Maesta Catholica nelle parti della Fiandra del 27 agosto 1585 (Rome: Rossi, 1585), Etched and engraved news print, 376 × 497 mm, in Universitätsbibliothek Salzburg, Wolf-Dietrich-Klebeband Städtebilder G 35 III; Bibliothèque nationale de France, GED-1562 (RES); RCT, RCIN 721976.

Nuouo auiso, e particolar discorso, della mirabile espugnatione d'Anuersa, con le capitulationi, & trattati di essa. Ottenuta, dal serenissimo inuittissimo & massimo Alessandro Farnese. Con le solennità, e trionfi fatti mentre S.A. Sereniss. prese l'ordine del Tosone, di S.M. Catholica (Milan: Tini, 1585), USTC 806036.

Nuovo aviso, e particolar discorso della mirabile espugnatione d'Anversa, con le capitulationi, & trattati di essa, ottenuta dal serenissimo, invittissimo, & massimo, Alessandro Farnese (Brescia: Tini, 1585), USTC 806038.

Nuovo aviso, e particolar discorso, della mirabile espugnatione d'Anversa, con le capitulationi, & trattati di essa, ottenuta, dal serenissimo invitissimo & massimo Alessandro Farnese. Con le solenità, è trionfi fatti mentre sua altezza serenissima prese l' Ordine del tosone, di sua maestà catholica (Bologna: Benacci, 1585), USTC 806037.

Nuouo auiso et particolar discorso della mirabile espugnatione d'Anuersa, con le capitulationi, & trattati di essa, ottenuta dal serenissimo, inuittissimo, & massimo, Alessandro Farnese, con le solennità, e trionfi fatti mentre s.s. sereniss. prese l'ordine del Tesone di s.m. catolica (Verona: Fantuzzi, 1585), USTC 806039.

Nuouo auiso, e particolar discorso, della mirabile espugnatione d'Anuersa. Con le capitulationi, & trattati di essa. Ottenuta, dal serenissimo, inuitissimo, & massimo Alessandro Farnese. Con le solenità, e trionfi fatti mentre s.a. sereniss. prese l'Ordine del tosone, di s.m. catholica (Reggio Emilia: Bartoli, 1585), USTC 763956.

Ordinationi fatte tra sua Maesta Cattolica; et la città d'Anuersa (Florence: Dini, [1585]), EDIT16 80647.

Ordinationi fatte tra sua Maesta Cattolica et la città d'Anuersa (Florence: scalee di Badia, 1585), USTC 836744.

1586 *Avviso della presa della citta di Nuis vicino a Colonia fatta dall'altezza del serenissimo Alessandro Farnese principe di Parma, capitano generale di sua maestà cattolica, il di XXVI di luglio MDLXXXVI* (Rome: Bonfadino, 1586), USTC 806086.

Lettere del molto Illustre; & Reuer Signor Minuccio Minucci. Consigliero primario del serenissimo signor duca di Bavera. Scitta al Serenissimo Duca Ferdinanda di Bauera sopra l'assalto, & presa di Novesio (Milan: Piccaia, 1586), in BNB.

1587 *Copia di una lettera venuta da Torino. Nella quale si narra la presa di Anclusa fortezza di grandissima importanza, città posta in mare ottenuta dal Serenis. Duca di Parma in Fiandra* (Rimini: Antico, 1587), USTC 806194.

La terza rotta delli hiretici in Francia con la presa dell'Escluse del Serenissimo Signor Duca di Parma, & con altri particolari, come leggendo intenderete (Macerata: Martellini, 1587), USTC 80627.

Avisi del signor duca di Parma capitano generale di S. Maesta cattolica, alle inscluse, nell'isola del Gasante, e qui intenderete l'ordine fatto da S.A.S. per impedire il pasto all'armata, della regina d'Inghilterra, la quale andava in socorso dell'infedeli, e come s'attornò, per voler passare, e al primo assalto vi resto sei vasseli, come leggendo intenderete (Bologna: Bonardo, 1587), USTC 806169.

1588 *Relatione del gran prodigio apparso nouamente sopra la città di Rupelmonde in Fiandra. Doue s'intende quanto tempo sia durato, il terrore che ha posto a que' popoli, & la conuersion di molti heretici* (Venice: Larduccio, 1588), USTC 828505.

Relatione del miracoloso prodigio apparso nell'aria. Nouamente sopra la citta di Rupelmonde in Fiandra. Dove s'intende quanto tempo sia durato il terrore che ha posto a que' popoli & per causa di quello la conversion di molti heretici. Come legendo intenderete (Urbino: Ragusij, 1588), USTC 837719.

1590 Rigone, Girolamo (trans.), *Il vero, e compito raguaglio di quanto hà valorosamente fatto il Sereniss. Duca di Parma e Piacenza in liberara dall'assedio la gran città di Parigi con la minutissima descrittione del suo viaggio* (Milan: Da Ponte, 1590), USTC 806622.

Rigone, Girolamo (trans.), *Il vero, e compito raguaglio di quanto hà valorosamente fatto il Sereniss. Duca di Parma e Piacenza in liberara dall'assedio la gran città di Parigi con la minutissima descrittione del suo viaggio* (Parma: s.n., 1590), USTC 806621.

1595   *Copia d'una relatione venuta dal Campo Catholico governato dal Sig. Conte di
       Fuentes in Picardia sotto Dorlen* (Milan: s.n., 1595), USTC 806931.

       *Vera, et compita relatione della battaglia, assedio, et presa della citta, & Castello
       di Dorlens. Stampata in Arras in lingua francese; et ristampata in Milano in lingua
       italiana* (Milan: Malatesta, 1595), in BUA, XIV b.32 21.

1596   Beccari, Bernardino, *La maravigliosa vittoria ottenuta dalle Genti del Rè Cattolico
       contra i ribelli heretici che havevano sorpresa la città di Lira in Brabantia a dì
       14 d'ottobre 1595* (Rome: Mutio, 1595), USTC 813028.

       Beccari, Bernardino, *L'assedio, et presa di Hulst fortezza principale della
       Fiandra, occupata da gli heretici ribelli de Re cattolico l'anno 1591 a di 25 di settem-
       bre* (Rome: Mutio, 1596), USTC 812969.

       Raguaglio dell'assedio et espugnatione della terra di Cales er [sic] *Fortezza di
       essa* (Viterbo: [Colaldi], 1596), USTC 807099.

       *Vera et compita relatione dell'impresa di Cales, fatta dal serenissimo prencipe
       cardinale Alberto d'Austria. Cauata da una lettera scritta da persona principale,
       che si trovò sul fatto* (Viterbo: [Colaldi], 1596), USTC 807110.

       *Vero raguaglio della feliccisima vittoria havuta dall'Illustrissimo, & Reuerendis-
       simo Cardinale d'Austria, della città, & fortezza di Cales, havuta alli 18. del mese
       d'Aprile 1596* (Turin: s.n., 1596), USTC 807111.

1597   *Breve et vero discorso delli particolari successi occorsi sotto la città d'Amiens, tra gli
       assediati, & gli inimici. Dopoi il martedi 15. mercoledì 16 & la giobba 17. di luglio fino
       il lunedì seguente alli 21* (Milan: Malatesta, 1597), USTC 807118.

1598   *Dichiaratione et nota dei capitoli publicati nella congregatione de' stati de Barbanti,
       sotto il dì 12 d'agosto 1598 per ordine di s.m.c. per li Paesi Bassi, e di Borgogna.
       Donati, & consessi per dote della serenissima infanta maritata nel serenissimo
       Alberto arciduca d'Austriadote delle serenissima infanta* (Ferrara: Baldini, 1598),
       USTC 812789.

       *Dichiaratione et nota dei capitoli publicati nella Congregatione de' stati de
       Barbanti, sotto il dì 12 d'agosto 1598 per ordine di sua m. catt. per li Paesi Bassi, e di
       Borgogna. Donati, & consessi per dote della serenissima infanta, da maritarsi nel
       serenissimo Alberto arciduca d'Austria* (Rome: Bonfadino, 1598), USTC 812790.

       *Dichiaratione et nota dei capitoli publicati nella Congregatione de' stati de
       Barbanti, sotto il dμ 12 d'agosto 1598 per ordine di s.m.c. per li Paesi Bassi, e di
       Borgogna. Donati, & consessi per dote della serenissima infanta, da maritarsi nel
       serenissimo Alberto arciduca d'Austria* (Bologna: Benacci, 1598), USTC 764288.

1599   *Copia dell'assegnatione fatta dal re cattolico, per dote della serenissima infanta
       Isabella, Clara, Eugenia sua figliola maritata al serenissimo Alberto arciduca
       d'austria. Delli stati di Brabantia, & Paesi Paessi. Con le conditioni di essa, & altre
       dichiaratione dignissime da doversi sapere* (Vicenza: Greco, 1599), USTC 812791.

Dichiaratione et nota de capitoli publicati nella congregatione de' stati de Barbanti, per ordine di sua m. cattolica, per li Paesi Bassi, e di Borgogna (Cremona: Zanni, 1599), USTC 812792.

1600 Beccari, Bernardino, *Aviso della presa di Berck Fortezza Principale posta su'l rheno, & di Vvesel Piazza siuata sù'l medesimo fiume. Toltò à ribelli heretici de Paesi Bassi dall'eccellentissimo s. Ammirate d'Aragon* (Milan: Malatesta, 1600) USTC 813022.

     Beccari, Bernardino, *Relatione del seguito dell'armata hollandese in Fiandra, da che arrivò in detta Provincia, che fù alla fine di giugno fin che è partita di là, che segui al primo d'agosto* (Rome: Mutio, 1600), USTC 813024.

1601 *Vero dissegno della fortissima citta di Ostende. Assediata dal Sereniss. Arciduca* ALBERTO D'AVSTRIA *con potentissimo essercito, quest anno* MDCI (s.l.: s.n., [1601]). Etched and engraved map, 265 × 334 mm, in RCT, RCIN 721112.

1604 *Relatione dell'assedio della fortezza d'Ostenden posta nella Fiandra. Assediata del sereniss. arciduca Alberto d'Austria alli cinque di luglio 1601. Et resa all' illustrissimo. & Eccellentissimo Sig. Marchese Francesco Spinola genovese alli 21. Di settembre 1604* (Siena: s.n., 1604), in BUA, XIV b.32 62.

     Relatione dell'assedio della fortezza d'Ostenden posto nella Fiandra; assediata del serenissimo arciduca Alberto d'Austria, alli 5. di luglio 1601. Et resosi all'illustriss. & eccellentiss. sig. marchese Spinola genouese, alli 22. di Settembre 1604 (Rome: Facciotti, 1604), Biblioteca Angelica in Rome, F. ANT TT.1 40/22.

1605 *Relatione dell'impresa di Oldensel e di Linghen fatta dall'illusstiss & eccellentiss. signore marchese Spinola nella prouincia di Frisia quest'anno 1605. alli 10. e 18. Agosto* (Florence: Caneo, 1605), USTC 4031155.

1606 *Relatione del seguito din Fiandra per opera dell'illustrissimo & Eccellentissimo Signor Marchese Spinola dalla presa di Linghen, & d'Oldensel fino al presente* (Genoa: Pavoni, 1606), Biblioteca Biblioteca Civica A.G. Barrili in Savona, Shelfmark IV F 8 30.

     Relatione del seguito din Fiandra per opera dell'illustrissimo & Eccellentissimo Signor Marchese Spinola dalla presa di Linghen, & d'Oldensel fino al presente (Viterbo: Discepolo, 1606), USTC 4043090.

     Magi, Giovanni (engraver), *Berges svl reno assediata et presa a pati il di 2 de ottobre 1606 dal sig.re Marchese Spinola* (Rome: Orlandi and Van Schoel, 1606). News print, 399 × 511 mm, RCT, RCIN 721129.

1609 *Articoli del trattato della tregua fatta, et conchiusa nella citta di Anuersa adi 9. d'aprile 1609* (Florence: Grinieri, 1609), USTC 4025525.

1621 *La presa d'una nave ollandese nel porto di Cet, carica di monitioni di guerra mandata dalli stati d'olanda, dal conte Mauritio per soccorso dei rebelli* (Viterbo: Discepoli, 1621), USTC 4041586.

     La presa d'una nave ollandese nel porto di Cet (Milan: s.n., 1621), USTC 4041588.

La presa d'una nave ollandese nel porto di Cet, carica di monitioni di guerra mandata dalli stati d'olanda, dal conte Mauritio per soccorso dei rebelli (Turin: Cavalleris, 1621), USTC 4002052.

Relatione vera della vittoria hauuta da Don Fedrico di Toledo Osorio Capitano Generale dell'armata, & essercito del mare Oceano, contra 31 nauilio Olandese nel Stretto di Gibilterra alli 10 d'agosto 1621. Giorno di San Lorenzo. Stampata in Madrid, con licenza del Sig D. Gonzalo Perez Valenzuela del Conseglio di S. Maesta in casa di Berardino de Gusman (Rome: Discepolo, 1621), USTC 4004786.

1622 *Assedio di Berges sul fiume zoon* (s.l.: s.n., 1622). Etched news print, 279 × 357 mm, in RCT, RCIN 7722006.

Lo Spaventoso assedio e resa della città di Giulliers, all' esercito delle serenissima arciduchessa di Fiandra (Brancaccio: Fei, 1622), USTC 4042208.

1623 *Maravigliosa e stvpenda vittoria ottenuta dalli Portoghesi contra gl'heretici Olandesi nelle Indie orientali. Cavata dalle lettere venute per via Filippine, & da una relatione stampata in Lisbona nel mese di giugno 1623* (Milan: Malatesta, 1623), in BNM, Shelfmark Misc 2230 056.

Relatione delle cose notabili stabilite nelle corte di S.M. catholica. Delle mutatione di officiali, & mercedi; & di altre curiose novita successe in Spagna, & in altre parti, come nelle Indie, nel mare, in Turchia, in Fiandra, in Alemagna, & in Ungaria (Milan: Malatesta, 1623), USTC 4004690.

1624 *Breue descriptione della citta, & paese di Bredà con l'assedio del Marchese Spinola postoui à 28 d'Agosto di l'anno 1624* (The Hague: Hondius, 1624). Engraved map, in RCT, RCIN 722011.

Relatione dell'acquisto fatto dall'armata holandese della Citta di S. Saluadore nella Baia di tutti i Santi (Venice: Pinelli, 1624), USTC 4004828.

Vera relatione dell'impresa vanamente tentata dalli Ollandesi, co'l mezzo del governatore di Berghes su la Soma, contro il castello d'Anuersa, li 13. di Ottobre 1624. Con la nota di quanto l'inimico ha lasciato nel ritirarsi dal detto castello d'Anuersa (Rome: Fei, 1624), USTC 4005084.

Vero Disegno della Pianta della citta di Breda, con tutte le sue Fortificationi Baluardi, Ridotti, Mezzelune, & alri lauori militari, fatti intorno, & dell' Assedio postogli dal Campo di Sua Maesta Catholica per l'Eccellentissimo Signor Marchese Spinola, alli 27. di Agosto 1624 (Naples: Orlandi, 1624), News print, 385 × 361 mm, RCT, RCIN 722012.

1625 Avendano y Vilella, Francesco de, *Relacione del viaggio e successo dell'armata, che per ordine di S.M. s'ivio al Brasil* (Milan: Malatesta, 1625), USTC 4004829.

Avendano y Vilella, Francesco de, and Pizzuto, Francesco Gio (trans.), *Relatione del viaggio, et successo dell'armata, che per ordine della maestà cattolica andò al Brasil a discacciarne gl'inimici, che l'havevano occupato. Con la capitulatione della resa* (Rome: Grignani, 1625), USTC 4005085.

Bergh, Giovanni, *Ragguaglio delli principali successi nell'assedio della città di Breda. Postovi dall'Eccellentiss. Sig. Marchese Spinola, Generalissimo dell'Armi di Sua Maestà Cattolica nelli Paesi bassi* (Rome: Grignani, 1625), USTC 4000037.

Breve racconto dello stato delle cose di guerra nell'Indie Orientali dell'anno 1623. Cavata da una lettera scritta in Goa li 27. di genaro del 1624. Che poi fu stampata in Lisbona li 11. Novembre dell'istess'anno, & adesso e stata fedelissimamente dalla lingua portoghese nella nostra italiana trasportata (Milan: Malatesta, 1625), USTC 4002891.

Breve Ragguaglio del sito, e positura della villa di bredà et in che modo, e quando divennero Padroni di essa gli Conti di Nassau, detti poi Prencipe d'Orange; e quante volte in che maniera, ed in che tempo l'hanno persa, e recuperata, e come ultimamente s'è resa all'Eccellentissimo Sig. Marchese Spinola, con l'inventario delle monitioni, e stromenti militari trovati in essa nella sudetta resa (Milan: Malatesta, 1625), USTC 4005875.

Copia d'vna lettera scritta dal campo sotto Breda adi 5. giugno 1625. Quale racconta la resa di quella piazza, con le capitulationi stabilite trà l'eccellentiss. Sign. Marchese Spinola Generalissimo delli esserciti intrati per S.M. in Alemagna, e Governatore Generale nelli Stati di Fiandra. Et altri felici successi occorsi innanzi à questa resa (Milan: Malatesta, 1625), USTC 4004822.

Copia d'vna lettera scritta dal campo sotto Bredá. Adì 5. di Giugno 1625 (Rome: Grignani, 1625), USTC 4004796.

Copia duna lettera scritta dal campo sotto Breda adi 5. giugno 1625 (Piacenza: Ardizzoni, 1625), USTC 4007806.

Copia d'vna lettera scritta dal campo sotto Breda a 5. di giugno 1625 (Naples: Roncagliolo, 1625), USTC 4002675.

Copia d'vna lettera scritta dal campo sotto Breda. Alli 5. di Giugno 1625. Quale racconta la resa di quellq piazza, con le capitulationi stabilite trà l'eccellentiss. Sign. Marchese Spinola Generalissimo delli esserciti intrati per S.M. in Alemagna, e Governatore Generale nelli Stati di Fiandra. Et altri felici successi occorsi innanzi la detta resa (Bologna: Tebaldini and Barbieri, 1625), in Biblioteca Comunale dell'Archiginnasio, Shelfmark Fondo Spec Zambeccari 3. 285.

Dichiaratione delle allegrezze fatte nel solenne apparato fato nella chiesa di Santo Eustorgio di Milano per ringraziare Iddio nell'occasione della resa di Breda (Milan: Colonna, 1625), USTC 4007652.

Descors intorna a la resa de Brada in despresij di Navarin Nostran. Dà in lus da Battista da Miran ([Adrianopoli]: s.n., 1625), in BNB Shefmark RARI MELZI 027/07.

Milano, Andrea da, *Ragionamento fatto in lode di Bredà di Porta Noua, doue si contengono tutti i Bredà feste, giuochi, e fuochi fatti nella città di Milano per l'allegrezza della presa di detto Bredà* (Milan: Malatesta, 1625), USTC 4002785.

Ragguaglio della resa di Breda. Con le capitolazioni stabilite tra l'eccellentissimo signor marchese Spinola et altri felici successi (Milan: Malatesta, 1625), USTC 4043110.

Relacion de lo sucesso del armada, y exercito que fue a socorro del Brasil, desde que entro en la Bahia de Todos-Santos, hasta que entro en la ciudad del Salvador, que posseian los rebeldes de Olanda, sacada de una carta que don Fadrique de Toledo escrivio a su magestad (Naples: Roncagliolo, 1625), USTC 5042991.

Relatione certa, e vera della felice vittoria ch'hanno reportato nell'Indie Orientali gli portughesi contro una grand'armata de olandesi, e persiani, e tutti gli prosperi successu seguiti in essa questo anno 1624 (Milan: Malatesta, 1625), USTC 4007650.

Relatione della solenne entrata in Breda della Serenis. Infante D. Isabella Clara Eugenia arciduchessa d'Austria. Adi 12. Giugno 1625 (Milan: Malatesta, 1625), USTC 4005876.

Relatione della solenne entrata in Breda della Serenis. Infante D. Isabella Clara Eugenia arciduchessa d'Austria. Adi 12. Giugno 1625 (Rome: Grignani, 1625), USTC 4004797.

Valor eroico d'ottocento fanti spagnuoli contro diecimila fanti sbarcati dall'armata Inglese, nel porto di Cadiz, & altri prosperosi successi di Fiandra, & Alemagna per la Fede, e Rè Cattolico (Milan: Malatesta, 1625), USTC 4004823.

1626   Bergh, Giovanni, *Vera relatione del maraviglioso successo della perdita dell'armata Olandese appresso Donchirchen* (Milan: Malatesta, 1626), in BNM, Shelfmark: MISC 1157 (014).

Copia d'una lettera scritta dal campo cattolico a Issem adi 4 ottobre 1626. A. s.e. il sig. marchese Spinola dal Conte Henrico de Bergh generale dell'artiglieria di Fiandra. Qual l'avvisa d'una rotta datta alla cavalleria ollandese (Milan: Malatesta, 1626), USTC 4004762.

La vera relatione della battaglia, che hebbe Nugno Alvarew Boteglio, generale dell'armata Portoghesa d'Altobordo, nelli mari dell'India. Con l'armate d'Olanda, & Inghilterra nell Stretto d'Ormus (Rome: Grignani, 1626), in BAV, Stamp. Cappon.v.684 (int.14).

1629   Vaivod, Donato, *Assedio et sito della cittá di Boldvc in Brabantia, assediata da Hollandesi, dal primo di Maggio 1629 sotto la condotta di Federico Henrico Pr. d'Orangia* (s.l.: s.n., 1629), News print in RCT, RCIN 722043.

1632   *Parte presa nel gran consiglio de Malines per sua Maesta Cattolica li 5 Luglio 1632. Intorno la Fellonica retirata del Co Henrico di Bergh dal servitio della medesima Cattolica Maestà. Tradotta dal francese in italiano* (Milan: Malatesta, 1632), in BCB, Shelfmark B.S. XVII D 347.

1635   *Auuisi certissimi della rotta di molte troppe francesi seguita nella Lorena, Fiandra, Lucemburg, & altri luoghi. Tradotti in italiano da fidelissimo originale. Con aggiunta delle cose più vicine* (Milan: Ghisolfi, 1635), USTC 4012085.

Auuisi certissimi della rotta di molte troppe francesi seguita nella Lorena, Fiandra, Lucemburg, & altri luoghi. Tradotti in italiano da fidelissimo originale. Con aggiunta delle cose più vicine (Naples: Longo, 1635), USTC 4009367.

Auuisi di diuerse parti mandati alla Francia da vn suo affettionato, tradotti di francese in italiano (Naples: Longo, 1635), USTC 4008471.

Bianchi, Giovanni Paolo, *Vera Descrittione del famoso Forte di Schench, importato alli 28. Luglio 1635. Sotto gli Auspicij della Real Altezza del Sig. Cardinal Infante* (Milan: Gariboldi, 1635), News print, 359 × 392 mm, in RCT, RCIN 722090.

Breve relatione della vittoria ottenuta dall' armi di S.M. sotto il commando del Sig. Prencipe d'Oranges, & Signori marescialli di Sciattiglion & Bressè. Sopra l'armata del Serenissimo Caridanl Infante a Tirlemont in Fiandra (s.l.: s.n., s.d.), in ASF, MdP 4878.

Discritione [sic] *del sito è positura della gran fortezza di Schinhen e del modo con la quale la Guarnigione de Gheler commandata dal Luogotenente Colonello Anholt del Regimento del Conte di Embden ne fece la sopresa la notte de 27 di Luglio 1635* (Milan: Ghisolfi, 1635), News print, 195 × 307 mm, in RCT, RCIN 722089.

Distinta e vera relatione di quanto è successo al Serenissimo Cardinal Infante di Spagna et alle sue armi nella fiandra doppo la sopresa di treveri sino à Novembre 1635 (Milan: Malatesta, 1635), USTC 4010427.

Relatione delli successi di fiandra dal di che l'eserciti di Francia & Olanda vniti entrorono nelli stati obedienti di sua maesta cattolica sin alli dodeci di lugio, e della vittoria, ch'hebbe in questo giorno sua real altezza il signor infante cardinale contro gli eserciti inmici dedicata all'illustriss signor Don Fabritio Lanario & Aragona (Naples: Longo, 1635), USTC 4009368.

Relacion de diversos avisos del estado de las cosas de Lombardia, de Alemania, y otras partes, hasta los 24 de otubre 1635 (Naples: Longo 1635), USTC 5035096.

Prima relatione del seguito in Fiandra doppo ch'entrarono nelli Stati obedienti di Sua Maestà Cattolica li due esserciti di Francia & Olanda l'anno 1635 (Milan: Malatesta, 1635), in BCB, Shelfmark B.S. XVII D 346 and 354.

Seconda relatione del seguito in Fiandra et in altre diverse parti di Germania nel presente anno 1635 (Milan: Malatesta, 1635), in BCB, Shelfmark B.S. XVII D 349 and 355.

Seconda relatione del seguito in Fiandra et in diverse parti di Germania nel presente anno 1635 dedicata all'illustriss signor don Fabritio Lanario & Aragona (Naples: Longo, 1635), USTC 4008481.

1636 *Ferdinando Per gratia di Dio Infante di Spagna, Luogotenente Governatore, & Capitan General de Paesi Bassi, & di Borgogna &c.* (Milan: Ghisolfi, 1636), BCB, Shelfmark B.S. XVII D 352.

Copia di lettera scritta da Brusselle. Con il Manifesto publicato nell'entrata dell'armi cattoliche nella Fracia et la presa della Ciapella (Milan: Ghisolfi, 1636), BCB, Shelfmark B.S. XVII D 353.

1637 *Relatione della resa di Ruremonda con raguaglio de felici progressi segviti sotto Breda. Et d'altri parti della Fiandra, & Germania* (Milan: Malatesta, 1637), in BNB.

    Prosperi successi dell'arme Austriache in varie parti (Milan: Malatesta, [1637]), in BNB.

1638 Franchi, Lamberto (trans.), *I felici progressi dell'armi del Re Christianissimo nelle provincie di Spagna, Fiandra, Borgogna, & Alsatia, occorsi nelli mesi di Giugno, Luglio, & Agosto del 1638: descritti in lingua Francese, e tradotti nell'Italiana da L. Franchi* (Casale Monferatto: s.n. 1638), USTC 4046167.

    Relatione del gran rotta data dall'armi spagnuole all'olandesi, sotto il forte di Calò vicino Anuersa, con la ricuperatione del medesimo forte, acquisto de vascelli, e di quanto haueuano i medisimi olandesi portato in capo, seguita a 21. Di Giugno 1638 (Naples: Longo, 1638), USTC 4008488.

    Relatione del gran rotta data dall'armi spagnuole all'olandesi, sotto il forte di Calò vicino Anuersa, con la ricuperatione del medesimo forte, acquisto de vascelli, e di quanto haueuano i medisimi olandesi portato in capo, seguita a 21. Di Giugno 1638. e delle fattioni fatte da S.A. il principe Tommaso di Sauoia, e dal Conte Piccolomini contra l'arme francesi in soccorso di Sant'Omer, con hauergli fatto leuar l'assedio da quella piazza (Naples: Longo, 1638), USTC 4010711.

    Gabriel del Corral, *Relaciones de las victorias que las armas de su magestad catolica han tenido, desde de mayo asta junio deste ano de 1638 en Flandes, en alemania, en Milan y otras partes* (Naples: Molo a instancia de Giovanni Orlando, 1638), USTC 4046197 and 5032809.

    Ragguaglio della liberazione di S. Omer (Florence: Pignoni, 1638), USTC 404619.

1639 *Lettera scritta a S.M. Cesarea dal Marescial di Campo Sig. conte Picolomini sopra la vittoria da lui ottenuta contro l'essercito Francese sotto Thionville. Li sette giugno MDCXXXIX* (Genoa: Farroni, 1639), USTC 4012088.

    Relatione della grandissinma vittoria, che hà ottenuta S.M. Cattolica nel paese di Lucemburg (Naples: Mollo, 1639), USTC 4047071.

    Relatione somaria della battaglia di Tionuille trà l'armata imperiale commandata dall'eccellenza del sig. conte Picolomini d'Aragona (Milan: Malatesta, 1639), USTC 4012089.

1641 *Nuoua, e piu distinta relatione della vittoria ottenuta dall'armi delle M.ta Ces.a e Catt.ca comandate dal generale Lamboy vnite con quelle delli prencipi della Lega della pace, contro l'essercito del maresciale di Sciattiglione vicino a Sedan, li 6 luglio 1641* (Milan: Malatesta, 1641), USTC 4017672.

1642 *Breve relazione della segnalata vittoria ch'ha ottenuto l'esecito cattolico di Fiandra commandato dall' eccellentiss. Francesco del Melo* (Florence: Massi e Landi, 1642), USTC 4017673.

1644 *Relatione della conquista fatta per il duca d'Orleans della città e castello di Gravelinghe in Fiandra, con li articoli della capitualtione* (Florence: Stamperia alla Condotta, 1644), USTC 4048042.

1647 *Breve relatione dell'assedio & presa della città d'Armentieres nel contado di Fiandra*
fatta dal serenissimo Arciduca Leopoldo (Milan: Malatesta, 1647), USTC 4019712.

1648 *Relatione di quanto è successo nella ratification e publication della Pace tra Sua*
Maesta Cattolica e gli stati d'olanda, fattasi nella città di Munster in Vestfalia sotto
li 15. 16. e 17. Di Maggio 1648 (Naples: Cavalli, 1648), USTC 4019537.

Relatione di quanto è successo nella ratification e publication della Pace tra Sua
Maesta Cattolica e gli stati d'olanda, fattasi nella città di Munster in Vestfalia sotto
li 15. 16. e 17. Di Maggio 1648 (Rome: Grignani, 1648), USTC 4048542.

Relazione del combattimento seguito in Fiandra sotto Lens alli 20. Agosto 1648.
Trà l'Esercito del Re Cristianissimo comandato dal Principe di Condè, E l'altro del
Re Cattolico comandato dall'Arciduca Leopoldo (Florence: Stamperia S.A.S., 1648),
in BL, Shelfmark General Reference Collection 1323.

Capitoli della pace d'Olanda col potentissimo monarca Filippo IV. Tradotti
dallo spagnolo in italiano. Dedicati all'Altezza Serenissima del signor D. Giovanni
d'Austria (Naples: Orlando, 1648), USTC 4019538.

Seconda, e compita relatione della segnalata vittoria ottenuta dalle armi fran-
cesi in Fiandra, sotto il comando del prencipe di Conde, con disfatta della spag-
nuola comandata dall'arciduca Leopoldo (Piombino: s.n., 1648), USTC 4020043.

Pace di Olanda (Florence: Stamperia di S.A.S., 1648), USTC 4048592.

3   Printed Histories on the Revolt in the Low Countries

Abbondanti, Antonio, *Breviario delle guerre dei Paesi Bassi* (Cologne: Binghio, 1641),
USTC 2178521.

Adriani, Giovanni Battista, *Istoria de' suoi tempi di Giovambatista Adriani gentilhuomo*
fiorentino. Divisa in libri ventidue di nuovo mandata in luce. Con li sommarii, e, tavola
delle cose piu notabili (Florence: i Giunti, 1583), USTC 807801.

Adriani, Giovanni Battista, *Istoria de' suoi tempi di Giovambatista Adriani gentilhuomo*
fiorentino. Divisa in libri ventidue. Di nuovo mandata in luce. Con li sommarii, e, tavola
delle cose piu notabili, che in esse istorie si contengono (Venice: i Giunti, 1587), USTC
807802.

Bentivoglio, Guido, *Della guerra di Fiandra* (Cologne [Rome?]: s.n., 1632), USTC
4044867, 2172672.

Bentivoglio, Guido, *Della guerra di Fiandra. Con l'aggiunta del nono e decimo libro*
(Cologne [Rome?]: s.n., 1633), USTC 2113322.

Bentivoglio, Guido, *Della Guerra di Fiandra. Seconda parte* (Cologne: s.n., 1636), USTC
2522659.

Bentivoglio, Guido, *Della Guerra di Fiandra. Terza parte* (Cologne: s.n., 1639), USTC
2036098.

Bentivoglio, Guido, *Della guerra di Fiandra*, (Cologne: s.n., 1633–1639), USTC 2522659.

Bentivoglio, Guido, *Della guerra di Fiandra* (Leiden: Elzevier, 1635–1640), USTC 2514084, 1024205, 1011879.

Bentivoglio, Guido, *Della guerra di Fiandra* (Venice: Baba, 1637–1640), USTC 4012526.

Bentivoglio, Guido, *Della guerra di Fiandra* (Venice: Giunta and Baba, 1645), USTC 4018089.

Bentivoglio, Guido, Varen, Basilio (trans.), *Guerra de Flandes* (Madrid: Martinez, 1643), USTC 5011216.

Bentivoglio, Guido, *Histoire de la guerre de Flandre* (Paris: Sommaville, 1634), USTC 6028106.

Bentivoglio, Guido, *Opere del cardinal Bentivoglio, cioè le Relazioni di Fiandra e di Francia, l'Historia della guerra di Fiandra e le lettere scritte nel tempo delle sue nuntiature* (Paris: Redelichuysen, 1645), USTC 6036756.

Bentivoglio, Guido, *Opere del cardinal Bentivoglio, cioè le Relazioni di Fiandra e di Francia, l'Historia della guerra di Fiandra e le lettere scritte nel tempo delle sue nuntiature* (Paris: Jost, 1648), USTC 6006096, 6006058.

Bentivoglio, Guido, *Opere del cardinal Bentivoglio, cioè le Relazioni di Fiandra e di Francia, l'Historia della guerra di Fiandra e le lettere scritte nel tempo delle sue nuntiature* (Paris: Jost, 1650), USTC 6008730.

Bentivoglio, Guido, *Relationi fatte dall'ill.mo, e reu.mo sig.or cardinal Bentiuoglio in tempo delle sue nuntiature di Fiandra, e di Francia. Date in luce da Erycio Puteano* (Antwerp: Meerbeeck, 1629), USTC 1001516.

Bentivoglio, Guido, *Relationi del cardinal Bentivoglio* (Genoa: s.n., 1630), USTC 4012469.

Bentivoglio, Guido, *Relationi del cardinal Bentivoglio* (Paris: Sciappellain, 1631), USTC 6032223.

Bentivoglio, Guido, *Relationi del cardinale Bentiuoglio* (Venice: Ginammi, 1633), USTC 4012401.

Bentivoglio, Guido, *Relaciones del cardenal Bentivollo, publicadas por Enrico Puteano y traduzidas por Francisco de Mendoca y Cespede de Italiano en lengua castellana* (Naples: s.n., 1631), USTC 4008951.

Bentivoglio, Guido, *Les relations du cardinal Bentivoglio traduites, et dediees a monsigneur De Noyers* (Paris: Rouillard, 1642), USTC 6039563.

Bentivoglio, Guido, *Verhael-boecken van den Caerdinael Bentivoglio vertaelt door Roeland de Carpentier* (Rotterdam: Naeranus, 1648), USTC 1029096.

Bentivoglio, Guido, *Historicall relations of the United Provinces of Flandres*, (London: Moseley, 1652).

Bentivoglio, Guido, *The History of the Warss of Flanders, written in Italian by that learned and famous Cardinal Bentivoglio, englished by the Right Honourable Henry Earl of Monmouth, the whole Work illustrated, with a Map of the seventeen Provinces and above twenty Figures of the chief Personages mentioned in the History* (London: Moseley, 1654).

Bisaccioni, Maiolino, *Commentario delle guerre successe in Alemagna. Dal tempo, che il rè Gustauo Adolfo di Suetia, si leuò da Norimberga; doue s'intende la sua morte, e quello che è seguito doppo, fino alla dieta di Hailbrun, fatta di marzo 1633* (Venice: Baba, 1633), USTC 4012244.

Bisaccioni, Maiolino, *Del commentario parte seconda, che contiene le guerre successe in Alemagna, dalla dieta di Hailbruna, fatta di marzo 1633. fino all'assedio di Costanza; et altri fatti più notabili della Francia, Spagna, Fiandra, Italia, & altri luoghi* (Venice: Baba, 1636), USTC 4009319.

Bizzari, Pietro, *Historia della guerra fatta in Ungheria dall'invittissimo imperatore de christiani, contra quello de turchi: con la narratione di tutte quelle cose che sono avvenute in Europa dall'anno 1564, infino all'anno 1568* (Lyon: Rouillé, 1568), USTC 116065.

Campana, Cesare, *Assedio e racquisto d'Anversa, fatto dal serenissimo Alessandro Farnese prencipe di Parma, &c. Luogotenente, governatore, e capitan generale ne' Paesi Bassi, del Catholico, e potentissimo Filippo secondo re di Spagna. Historia di Cesare Campana, divisa in due libri. Con una breve narratione delle cose avvenute in Fiandra, dall'anno 1566 fin al 1584, che cominciò detto assedio; e con l'arbore de' conti di Fiandra* (Vicenza: Ciotti, 1595), USTC 818152.

Campana, Cesare, *Delle historie del mondo. Volume secondo che contiene libri sedici: nei quali diffusamente si narrano le cose avvenute dall' anno 1580 fino al 1596, con un Discorso intorno allo scrivere Historie* (Venice: Angelieri e Compagni, 1597), USTC 818157.

Campana, Cesare, *Della Guerra di Fiandra, Fatta per difesa di Religione dalla Maestà di Don Filippo Secondo Re di Spagna, e Filippo terzo di tal nome* (Vicenza: Greco, 1602), USTC 4034222.

Campana, Cesare, *Imprese nella Fiandra del serenissimo Alessandro Farnese Historia di Cesare Campana. Aggiontovi gl'arbori de' conti di Fiandra* (Cremona: Pellizari, 1595), USTC 818154.

Campana, Cesare, *Imprese nella Fiandra del serenissimo Alessandro Farnese Historia di Cesare Campana. Aggiontovi gl'arbori de' conti di Fiandra* (Cremona: Zanni, 1595), USTC 818153.

Conestaggio, Gerolamo, *Delle guerre della Germania inferiore, divisa in dieci libri* (Venice: Pinelli, 1614), USTC 4026677.

Conestaggio, Gerolamo, *Historia delle guerre della Germania inferiore, divisa in dieci libri* (s.l., s.n., 1634) [Leiden: Elzevier, 1634], USTC 1011778 and 2035333.

Gallucci, Angelo, *De Bello Belgico ab anno Christi 1593 ad inducias annorum 12 an 1609 pactas* (Rome: Corbelleti, 1671).

Gallucci, Angelo, Cellesi, Jacopo (trans.), *Historia della Guerra di Fiandra. Parte Prima* (Rome: Lazari, 1673).

Gallucci, Angelo, Cellesi, Jacopo (trans.), *Historia della Guerra di Fiandra. Parte Seconda* (Rome: Lazari, 1673).

Giustiniani, Pompeo, *Delle guerre di Fiandra libri VI di Pompeo Givstiniano del consiglio di guerra di s. m. c. e suo maestro di campo d'infanteria italiana. Posti in luce da Gioseppe Gamvrini gentil'huomo aretino con le figure delle cose piu notabili* (Antwerp: Trognesius, 1609), USTC 1003522.

Giustiniani, Pompeo, *Delle guerre di Fiandra libri VI* (Venice: Giunta e Ciotti, 1610), USTC 4026708.

Giustiniani, Pompeo, *Delle guerre di Fiandra libri VI* (Venice: Giunta e Ciotti, 1612), USTC 4028432.

Giustiniani, Pompeo, *Delle guerre di Fiandra libri VI* (Milan: Bidelli, 1615), USTC 4022169.

Giustiniani, Pompeo, *Bellvm Belgicvm siue Belgicarvm rervm, e commentariis Pompei Ivstiniani peditatvs italici tribvni, et a consiliis bellicis regis catholici. Libri sex. Supplemento auctoris aucti. Edente Iosepho Gamvrino* (Cologne: Kinckij, 1611), USTC 2120047, 2041789, 2107014, 2081051.

Lanario, Francesco, *Le guerre di Fiandra brevemente narrate* (Antwerp: Verdussen, 1615), USTC 1003607.

Lanario, Francesco, *Le guerre di Fiandra dal principio de' primi motivi in quelle parti, sino al presente breve, e diligentemente narrate da don Francesco Lanario* (Venezia: Baglioni, 1616), USTC 4021781.

Lanario, Francesco, *Le guerre di Fiandra brevemente narrate* (Milan: Bidelli, 1616), USTC 4022150.

Lanario, Francesco, *Le guerre di Fiandra brevemente narrate. Con l'agiunta de i successi dell'illustriss. et eccell. Sig. D. Pietro Girone duca d'Ossuna vicerè, e capitan generale in questo regno* (Naples: Rocagliolo, 1617), USTC 4025948.

Lanario, Francesco, *Las guerras de Flandes, desde el año de mil y quinientos y cincuenta y nueve hasta el seiscientos y neuve* (Madrid: Sánchez, 1623), USTC 5008178.

Manolesso, Emilio Maria, *Historia nova nella quale si contengono tutti i successi della guerra Turchesca, la congiura del duca de Norfolch, contra la Regina d'Inhilterra, la guerra di Fiandra, Flisinga, Zelanda & Holanda, l'uccisione d'Ugonotti, le morti de Prencipe, l'elettioni de novi, e finalmente tutto quello che nel mondo è occorso da l'anno MDLXX fin all' hora presente* (Padua: Pasquati, 1572), USTC 840139.

Mathieu, Pierre, Mártir Rizo, Juan Pablo (trans.), *Historia de las guerras de Flandes, contra la de Geronimo de Franqui Conestaggio* (Valencia: Mey, 1627), USTC 5005867.

Nicoletti, Gabriele, *Supplimento delle guerre di Fiandra dopo la Tregua, con l'origine dell'incendio dell'armi nella christianità et il maraviglioso assedio di Bredà coll'acquisto fatto dal Marchese Spinola scritto e lineato da Gabriele Nicoletti di Terni* (Terni: Arnazzini, 1650), USCT 4020789.

Pieri, Francesco, *Diario del seguito in Fiandra dalli xxi luglio mdcxxlv sino alli 25 d'agosto del 25 con l'assedio, e resa di Bredà col seguito del campo cattolio e dell'olandese, dal capitano Pier Francesco Pieri Fiorentino veduto, scritto e dedicato all'altezza serinissima di Toscana* (Bologna: Mascheroni, 1626), USTC 4006135.

Pieri, Francesco, *Nove gverre di Fiandra dalli XXI. Lvglio M.DC.XXIV. sino alli 25. d'Agosto del 1625. con l'assedio, e resa di Bredà, col seguìto del campo cattolico, e dell'olandese, dal capitano Pier Francesco Pieri fiorentino* (Milan: Besozzo, 1626), USTC 4002937.

Pieri, Francesco, *Nove gverre di Fiandra dalli XXI. Lvglio M.DC.XXIV. sino alli 25. d'Agosto del 1625. con l'assedio, e resa di Bredà, col seguìto del campo cattolico, e dell'olandese, dal capitano Pier Francesco Pieri fiorentino* (Venice: Ciotti, 1626), USTC 4007181.

Strada, Famiano, *De bello belgico decas prima ab excessu Caroli V. imp. Usque ad initia praefecturae Alexandri Farnesii Parmae, ac Placentiae Ducis III* (Rome: Corbelletti, 1632), USTC 4011524.

Strada, Famiano, *De Bello Belgico decas prima* (Antwerp: Cnobbaert, 1635), USTC 1003187.

Strada, Famiano, *De Bello Belgico decas prima* (Antwerp: Cnobbaert, 1636), USTC 1004327.

Strada, Famiano, *De Bello Belgico decas prima* (Rome: Scheus, 1637), USTC 4012466.

Strada, Famiano, *De Bello Belgico decas prima* (Rome: Scheus, 1640), USTC 4017806.

Strada, Famiano, *De Bello Belgico decas prima* (Antwerp: widow of Cnobbaert, 1640), USTC 1004417.

Strada, Famiano, *De bello belgico decas prima* (Leiden: Marcus, 1643), USTC 1011804.

Strada, Famiano, *De bello belgico decas prima* (Bologna: Zenero, 1646), USTC 4020827.

Strada, Famiano, *De Bello Belgico decas prima* (Amsterdam: Janssonius, 1648), USTC 1035890.

Strada, Famiano, *De Bello Belgico decas prima* (Rome [Amsterdam]: Scheus, [Blaeu] 1648), USTC 1028752, 1028753.

Strada, Famiano, *De Bello Belgico decas prima* (Antwerp: widow Cnobbaert, 1648), USTC 1035891.

Strada, Famiano, *De Bello Belgico decas prima* (Antwerp: widow Cnobbaert, 1649), USTC 103188.

Strada, Famiano, *De bello belgico decas secunda ab initio praefecturae Alexandri Farnesii Parmae Placentiaeque ducis III anno 1578 usque ad annum 1590* (Rome: Corbelletti, 1647), USTC 4033994.

Strada, Famiano, *De Bello Belgico decas secunda* (Antwerp: widow Cnobbaert, 1648), USTC 1003189, 1003190, 1000249.

Strada, Famiano, *De Bello Belgico decas secunda* (Rome [Amsterdam]: Corbelletti [Janssonius], 1648), USTC 1014159.

Strada, Famiano, *De Bello Belgico decas secunda* (Rome [Amsterdam]: Corbelletti [Blaeu], 1648), USTC 1028751.

Strada, Famiano, *De Bello Belgico decas secunda* (Amsterdam: Van Metelen, 1648), USTC 1035890.

Strada, Famiano, *De Bello Belgico decas secunda* (Paris: Duval, 1648), USTC 6035771.

Strada, Famiano, *De Bello Belgico decas secunda* (Rome: Diversin and Masotti, 1650), USTC 4037059.

Strada, Famiano, Papini, Carlo (trans.), *Della Guerra di Fiandra deca prima* (Rome: Scheuss, 1638), USTC 4011323.

Strada, Famiano, Segnere, Paolo (trans.), *Della Guerra di Fiandra deca seconda* (Rome: Corbelletti Heirs, 1648), USTC 4020566.

Strada, Famiano, Du Ryer, Pierre (trans.), *Histoire de la guerre de Flandre* (Paris: De Sommaville and Courbe, 1644), USTC 6041322.

Strada, Famiano, Du Ryer, Pierre (trans.), *Histoire de la guerre de Flandre* (Leiden: Elzevier, 1645), USTC 1034451.

Strada, Famiano, *Histoire de la guerre de Flandre* (Paris: Courbé, 1649), USTC 6007749.

Strada, Famiano, *Histoire de la guerre des Pays Bas. Seconde decade* (Tournay: widow of Quinqué, 1651).

Strada, Famiano, Van Aelst, Willem (trans.), *De thien eerste boecken der Nederlantsche oorloghe* (Antwerp: widow of Cnobbaert, 1645), USTC 1002333.

Strada, Famiano, Van Aelst, Willem (trans.), *De thien eerste boecken der Nederlantsche oorloghe* (Antwerp: widow of Cnobbaert, 1646), USTC 1001599.

Strada, Famiano, Van Aelst, Willem (trans.), *De thien eerste boecken der Nederlandsche oorloge* (Amsterdam: van Ravesteyn, 1646), USTC 1013813.

Strada, Famiano, Nees, Hubertus (trans.), *Nederlantsche oorloge* (Roermond: Du Pree, 1647), USTC 1035893.

Strada, Famiano, *Het tweede deel der Nederlandsche oorlogen* (Amsterdam: van Ravesteyn, 1649), USTC 1029357.

Strada, Famiano, Van Aelst, Willem (trans.), *De thien eerste boecken der Nederlandtsche oorloge en het tweede deel der Nederlandtsche oorlogen* (Dordrecht: Savry, 1655).

Strada, Famiano, *Het tweede deel der Nederlandsche oorlogen in Latijn beschreven in thien boecken* (Antwerp: Cnobbaert, 1662), STCV 3136024.

Strada, Famiano, Stapylton, Rob (trans.), *De bello Belgico The history of the Low-Countrey warres, written in Latine by Famianus Strada englished by sr. Rob. Stapylton* (London: Moseley, 1650), USTC 3062712.

Strada, Famiano, Lancaster, Thomas (trans.), *The Siege of Antwerp: Written in Latin by Famianus Strada, Englished by Tho Lancaster* (London, Moseley, 1656).

Strada, Famiano, Novar, Melchior de (trans.), *Primera decada de las guerras de Flandes* (Cologne, s.n., 1681), VD17 23:32350E.

Strada, Famiano, Novar, Melchior de (trans.), *Segunda década de las guerras de Flandes* (Cologne, s.n., 1681), VD17 23:323532V.

Ulloa, Alfonso, *Commentari del sig. Alfonso Ulloa, della guerra, che il sig. don Fernando Avarez di Toledo duca d'Alua et capitano generale del serenissimo re catolico ha fatto contra Giglielmo di Nansau principe di Oranges, et contra il conte Lodovico suo fratello, et altri ribelli di sua maesta catolica, in Fiandra. L'anno 1568 et della morte del principe di Condè, con le sue cose piu notabili successe nella Francia questo anno 1569* (Turin: Crieger, 1569), USTC 861581.

Ulloa, Alfonso, *Commentari del sig. Alfonso Ulloa, della guerra, che il sig. don Fernando Avarez di Toledo duca d'Alua et capitano generale del serenissimo re catolico ha fatto contra Giglielmo di Nansau principe di Oranges, et contra il conte Lodovico suo fratello, et altri ribelli di sua maesta catolica, in Fiandra. L'anno 1568 et della morte del principe di Condè, con le sue cose piu notabili successe nella Francia questo anno 1569* (Turin: Crieger, 1569), USTC 861581.

Ulloa, Alfonso, *Commentari del sig. Alfonso Ulloa, della guerra, che il sig. don Fernando Avarez di Toledo duca d'Alua, ha fatto contra Guglielmo di Nansau principe di Oranges nelli Paesi Bassi l'anno MDLXVIII. Insieme con le cose occorse tra la reina d'Inghilterra, l'ambasciatore catolico appresso quella maestà, & il sopradetto duca d'intorno all'arresto fatto di alcune navi Et quel che piu avvenne sino alla morte del principe di Condè in Francia questo anno MDLXIX* (Venice: Zaltieri, 1570), USTC 861583.

Ulloa, Alfonso, *Le historie di Europa del sig. Alfonso Ulloa, nuovamente mandate in luce. Nelle quali principalmente si contiene la guerra ultimamente fatta in Ungheria tra Massimiliano imperatore de' christiani, & sultan Solimano re de' turchi* (Venice: Zaltieri, 1570), USTC 861583.

Ulloa, Alfonso, *Comentarios (primero, segundo, tercero) de la guerra, que el illustriss, principe don Hernando Alvarez, duque de Alva, ha hecho contra Guillermo de Nasau, principe de Oranges, y otros rebeldes* (Venice: de Farris, 1569), USTC 340645.

Ulloa, Alfonso, *Guerre des Pais Bas entre le duc d'Albe et le prince d'Orange* (s.l.: s.n. 1569), USTC 14102.

Ulloa, Alfonso, *Gründliche beschreibung inn zwen thail verfast. Des Niderlaendischen kriegs so Herr don Fernando Alvares von Toledo, Hertzog von Alba kriegs obrister des durchleuchtigsten Catholischen Künigs Philippi gefuert hat wider Wilhalmen von Nassaw, Printzen von Oranien und Graven Ludwigen seinen bruder im Niderland des 1568. Jars* (Dillingen: Mayer, 1570), USTC 660875.

Ulloa, Alfonso, *Commentaire premier contenant le voyage du duc d'Albe en Flandres* (Paris: Dallier, 1570), USTC 10003.

Ulloa, Alfonso, *Commentaire premier contenant le voyage du duc d'Albe en Flandres* (Antwerp: Marcelin, 1570), USTC 16271.

Ulloa, Alfonso, *Le commentaire touchant les troubles advenuz en Flandres* (Brussels: s.n., 1570), USTC 94599.

4   Other Printed Primary Sources

Articles du traicté de trefve faict et conclu en la ville et cité d'Anvers, le neufiesme d'avril 1609 (The Hague: van Wouw, 1609), USTC 1032151.

Auuiso alla maestà del Re d'un buono e fedele Francesce circa le turbulenze d'Italia (Turin: Pizzamiglio, 1628), USTC 4005893.

Benedetti, Pietro, *Il Magico Legato tragicomedia pastorale di Pietro Benedetti Genovese dedicata all. ill. et ecc. Sig. Ambrosio Spinola Marchese di Venaffro, cavaliero dell' ordine del Toson d'oro, mastro di campo general, e governator de gl'esserciti per S.M. ne Paesi Bassi* (Antwerp: Keerberghen, 1607), USTC 1037642.

Benedetti, Pietro, *Il Magico Legato tragicomedia pastorale* (Venice: Alberti, 1607), USTC 4034604.

Bentivoglio, Guido, *Memorie del cardinal Bentivoglio, con le quali descriue la sua vita, e non solo le cose a lvi successe nel corso di essa, ma insieme le più notabili ancora occorse nella città di Roma, in Italia, & altrove. Divisi in due libri* (Venice: Heir of Giunta and Baba, 1648), USTC 4020325.

Bentivoglio, Guido, *Raccolta di lettere scritte dal Cardinale Bentivoglio in tempo delle sue nuntiature di Fiandra e di Francia* (Cologne: s.n., 1631), USTC 2522134.

Bergh, Giovanni (trans.), *Verissima relatione nella quale si narra la gran rotta che l'essercito di sua maesta cesarea ha dato nuouamente a quello del marchese di Baden ouero Durlach nel Palatinato doppo vna battaglia sanguinosa. Tradotta dalla lingua Alemanna da Giouanni Bergh* (Milan: Malatesta, 1622), USTC 4002889.

Bergh, Giovanni, *Relatione verissima della presa fatta per forza d'Assalti dal sig. Conte di Tilli tenente generale del serenissimo duca Massimiliano di Baviera, capo della lega cattolica, e commissario Cesareo, della città di Heidelbergh, metropoli del Palatinato, doppo l'assedio di tre settimane, seguita alli 16. di settembre M DCXXII publicata da Giovanni Bergh* (Rome: Fei, 1622), USTC 4042331.

Boccalini, Traiano, *Ragguagli di Parnaso. Centuria Seconda* (Venice: Farri, 1613), USTC 4029076.

Boccalini, Traiano, *Cetra d'Italia. Sopplimento de' ragguagli di Parnaso* (s.l.: s.n., 1614), USTC 4026743.

Bocchi, Francesco, *Discorso di Francesco Bocchi fiorentino a chi de' maggiori guerrieri, che insino à questo tempo sono stati, si dee la maggioranza attribuire* (Florence: Marescotti, 1573), USTC 815009.

Botero, Giovanni, *Relationi Universali di Giovanni Botero Benese. Parte tre* (Brescia: Compagnia Bresciana, 1599), USTC 816588.

Brancaccio, Lelio, *I carichi militari de Fra Lelio Brancaccio* (Antwerp: Trognesius, 1610), USTC 1003548.

Collectio in unum corpus. Omnium librorum Hebraeorum Graecorum Latinorum necnon germanice italice (Frankfurt: Bassai, 1592), USTC 623058.

Coloma, Carlos, *Las guerras de los Estados Baxos, desde el año de MDLXXXVIII hasta el de MDXCIX* (Cambrai: De la Rivière, 1622), USTC 1119766.

Coloma, Carlos, *Las guerras de los Estados Baxos, desde el año de MDLXXXVIII hasta el de MDXCIX* (Barcelona: Thomas, 1627), USTC 5005502.

Cornejo, Pedro, *Origen de la civil disension de Flandes con lo a la buelta de esta hoja en dos partes contenido, recopilado por el maestro Pedro Cornejo* (Turin: Belvicqua, 1579), USTC 824097.

Cornejo, Pedro, *Origen de la civil disension de Flandes con lo a la buelta de esta hoja en dos partes contenido, recopilado por el maestro Pedro Cornejo* (Turin: Belvicqua, 1580), USTC 344172.

Cornejo, Pedro, *Della historia di Fiandra libri X. Nella quale si vede l'origine delle civili dissensioni, & guerre universali dal principio fin a questi tempi; con la descrittione di tutto quel paese, in quante provincie sia diviso, la qualità de' Fiamenghi, i Stati generali, & come pervenisse nella casa d'Austria* (Brescia: Marchetti, 1582), USTC 824099.

Cort verhael van den Aenslach, ende veroveren der stadt Liere (Antwerp: Ballo, 1595), USTC 415575.

Costa, Giovanni, *Ragionamento di Giovanni Costa, gentil'huomo genovese, sopra la triegua de' Paesi bassi, conchiusa in Anuersa l'anno 1609* (Genoa: Pavoni, 1610), USTC 4026637.

Da Fano, Bartholomeo Dionigi, *Giardino di tutte l'historie piu notabili del mondo, nel quale si contiene, quanto è successo dalla venuta di S. Pietro a Roma, e dal principio del suo papato, per tutte le parti del mondo, fino all' anno MDCVI dalla nostra salute, cavato da tutti i più celebri e famosi Historici, che di tempo in tempo l'hanno descritte, & da veri e fedeli avisi de i nostri tempi* (Venice: Varisco, 1606), USTC 4033536.

Discours ende warachtich verhael van het inne nemen van de stadt van Liere door den vyant op den XIIII dach van Octob, int jaer MDXCV ende hoe de selve wederom is in genomen ghewesst op den zelven dach (Brussels: Velpius, 1595), USTC 402347.

Discours du succes des affaires passez en Phrise. Depuis le septiesme de juillet, jusques au quinziesme dudict moys, que fut le jour de la routte & defaicte de ceux de la Religion pretendue reformee (Antwerp: s.n., 1568), USTC 11365.

Discours sommier des justes causes et raisons qui ont contrainct les estats generaulx des Païs Bas de pourveoir à leur deffence (Antwerp: Silvius, 1577), USTC 4079.

Discours touchant la prise admirable de la grande et puissante ville d'Amiens (Arras: de La Rivière, 1597), USTC 13462.

Doglioni, Gio Nicolo, *Compendio historico universale di tutte le cose notabili già successe nel Mondo, dal principio della sua creazione, fino all' anno di Christo 1594* (Venice: Zenaro, 1594), USTC 827032.

Editto che predicatori non trattino nelle loro prediche, de reporti, & avvisi (Rome: Blado, 1590), USTC 821034.

Editto che predicatori non trattino nelle loro prediche, de reporti, & avvisi (Rome: Blado, 1590), USTC 870002.

Editto del re di Francia, sopra la pacificazione de tumulti del suo regno (Milan: Tini, 1576), USTC 830779.

Exemplaire des lettres patentes par lesquelles sa majesté donne grace absolue et pardon general, tant à estats, pays, villes et communautés, que tous particuliers (Lyon: Rigaud, 1574), USTC 6801.

Gascoigne, George, *The Spoile of Antwerp Faithfully Reported, by a True Englishman, Who Was Present. Nouem. 1576. Seene and allowed* (London: Jones, 1576), USTC 508187.

Giustificatione delle attioni di Spagna & manifestazione delle violenze di Francia (s.l.: s.n., s.d.) in BNB, Shelfmark XG.05 0032/22.

Giner, Miguel, *El sitio y toma de Anvers, dirigido al ilustrissimo y excel. Senor Rainuccio Farnese, Principe de Parma y Plasenzia* (Zaragoza: s.n., 1586), USTC 348807.

Giner, Miguel, *El sitio y toma de Anvers* (Milan: Da Ponte, 1587), USTC 345626.

Giner, Miguel, *El sitio y toma de Anveres por el serenissimo Alexandro Farnese, duque de Parma y Plasencia* (Antwerp: Plantin, 1588), USTC 440548.

Guarnello, Alessandro, *Canzone nella felicissima vittoria christiana contra infedeli al Sereniss. D. Gio D'Austria del Cavalier Guarnello* (Venice: Guerra, 1572), USTC 835033.

Guarnello, Alessandro, *Canzoni et sonetti al serenissimo principe di Parma et Piacenza del Cavalier Guarnello* (Rome: Heredi Blado, 1585), USTC 835035.

Guicciardini, Lodovico, *Descrittione de tutti i paesi bassi; altrimenti detti Germania Inferiore* (Antwerp: Silvius, 1567), USTC 405351.

Guicciardini, Lodovico, *Description des touts les pays-bas autrement appellez la Germanie Inferieure ou Basse Allemagne* (Amsterdam: Claesz, 1609), USTC 1033146.

Grillo, Angelo, *Delle lettere* (Venice: Ciotti, 1604), USTC 4036040.

Hugo, Herman, *Obsidio Bredana armis Philippi IIII* (Antwerp: Moretus, 1626), USTC 1007564.

Hugo, Herman, *Obsidio Bredana armis Philippi IIII* (Milan: Bidelli, 1627), USTC 4005552.

Ivsti Lipsii sent-brief, in welcke hy antwoorde gheeft aen een seker groot heer, op de vraghe, welck van dryen den coning van Hispaengien best gheraden ware, oorloghe oft peys, oft liever bestant met den Fransman, Engelsche ende Hollander (Dusseldorf: Horst, 1608), USTC 1033024, 1033026.

Insinuatione di un compendioso discorso delle giuste ragioni, che hà la casa di Nevers, unita hoggi con quella di Mantova, sopra li ducati di Brabant, Lothier, Limburgh et signoria di Anvers, ne' Paesi Bassi della Fiandra, dalla corona di Spagna occupati (Paris: s.n., 1628), USTC 6020580.

Istoria, o brevissima relatione della distruttione dell'Indie occidentali / di monsig. reverendiss. don Bartolomeo dalle Case, o Casaus; conforme al suo vero originale spagnuolo stampato in Siviglia, con la traduttione in italiano di Francesco Bersabita (Venice: Ginammi, 1626), USTC 4006104.

La seconda parte del Tesoro politico, nella quale si contengono trattati, discorsi, relationi, ragguagli, instruttioni di molta importanze per li maneggi, interessi, pretensioni, dipendenze e disegni de' Prencipi (Vicenza: Greco, 1602), USTC 4034267.

La terza parte del tesoro politico. Nella quale si contengono Relationi, Instruttioni, Trattati, et Discorsi non meno dotti et curiosi, che utili per conseguire la perfetta cognitione della Ragione di Stato. Non prima dati in luce (s.l.: Turnoni, 1605), USTC 6801413.

Lettere intercepte du Prince d'Orange au Duc d'Alençon avec quelques advertissemens sur icelle pour ouvrir le yeulx aux bons subiects (Mons: Velpius, 1580), USTC 13212.

Macini, Giacomo, *Descrizzione dell'arco trionfale fatto in Genova nel passaggio della maestà della Regina Catolica, del serenissimo Alberto arciduca d'Austria* (Genoa: Pavoni, 1599), USTC 839952.

Manifesto delle giustificate attioni della Corona di Spagna, e delle violenze della Corona di Francia. Tradotto dalla lingua castigliana nell'italiano (Naples: Longo, 1636), USTC 4011105.

Melzo, Lodovico, *Regole Militare del Cavalier Melzo sopra il governo e servitio della cavalleria* (Antwerp: Trognesius, 1611), USTC 1003563.

Oratione funebre dell'aggravato academico Delio in morte dell'illusstrissimo, & Eccellentissimo Sig. Gio Battista del Monte (Padova: Crivellari, 1615), USTC 4028536.

Ordine del Re christianissimo al suo residente in Bruselles di chieder in suo nome la liberatione dell'arcivescovo di Trevari, con ciò che è seguito dappoi, tradotto dal Francese (s.l.: s.n., s.d.), ASF, MdP 4878.

Ordonnance et edict provisional sur la pacification des troubles de la ville d'Anvers (Antwerpen: Silvius, 1567), USTC 13178.

Orsi, Aurelio, *De bello Belgico Ad Alexandrum Farnesium serenissimum Parmæ, & Placentiæ principem* (Perugia: Bresciano, 1586), USTC 845503.

Patrizi, Francesco, *Della historia diece dialoghi di m. Francesco Patritio ne' quali si ragiona di tutte le cose appartenenti all'historia, et allo scriverla, et all'osservarla* (Venice: Arrivabene, 1560), USTC 847039.

Patrizi, Francesco, *Paralleli militari, ne'quali si fa paragone delle milizie antiche* (Rome: Zannetti, 1594), USTC 847058.

Persico, Panfilo, *Del Segretario del sig. Panfilo Persico libri quattro, ne'quali si tratta dell'arte, e facolta del segreatrio, della istituione, e vita di lui nelle republiche e nelle corti* (Venice: Zenaro, 1643), USTC 4017857.

Placcaet ende ordonnantie daer by allen toevoer van leeftochten ende coopmanschappen naer de steden vanden vyandt wordt verboden, ende correspondentie te houden (Antwerp: Plantin, 1584), USTC 411712.

Recit de la descente des Hollandois a Calloo et de la victoire que Dieu a donnée sur eux aux armes du Roy Catholique, au mois de Iuin de l'année M.DC.XXXVIII (Brussels: Velpius, 1638) in ASF, MdP 4878.

Relatione della gran vittoria ottenuta dal generale conte di Tilli, con l'essercito della Lega cattolica, contro il re di Danimarca, e la sua armata nella giornata, e battaglia generale seguita tra di loro appresso il villaggio, e castello di Luter, nel paese di Brunsuich, a 27. d'agosto 1626 (Rome: Grignani, 1626), USTC 4004721.

Relatione della vittoria havuta dalli cattolici contro li Protestanti d'Alemagna & Svedesi sotto la città di Norlinghen (Milan: Malatesta, 1634), USTC 4012081.

Relacion nueva y muy verdadera de los sucessos del archiduque cardenal Alberto de austria en los estados de Flandes en este Anno de 1596 (Seville: Cabrera, 1596), USTC 338860.

Risposta per la riputazione spagnuola al finto conseglio di stato sopra la fuga de' Spagnuoli da Verrua (s.l.: s.n., [1625]), USTC 4000722.

Sansovino, Francesco, *Cronologia del mondo di M. Francesco Sansovino divisa in tre libri. Nel primo de quali s'abbraccia tutto quello ch'è avvenuto cosi in tempo di pace come di guerra fino all'anno presente* (Venice: Sansovino, 1580), USTC 854821.

Sanvitale, Fortuniano, *Anversa Conquistata* (Parma: Viotto, 1609), USTC 4030232.

Petit, Jean (trans.), *Sommaire recueil des raisons plus importantes qui doivent mouvoir Messieurs des Etats des Provinces unies du Païs Bas, de ne quitter point les Indes. Traduit de flamant en françois* (La Rochelle: Haultin, 1608), USTC 6026038.

Stopenro, Adriano, *Avertimenti sopra l'istoria delle guerre della Germania inferiore di Geronimo Conestaggio fatti da Adriano Stopenro ad instanza del Sig. Marchese N. Prencipe del sacro Imperio Tradotti dal Francese in Italiano per T.P.* (s.l.: s.n., 1619), USTC 4041510.

Tasso, Faustino, *Le historie de' successi de' nostri tempi, del R.P. Faustino Tasso vinitiano de' minori osseruanti, diuise in tredici libri. Nelle quali si contengono tumulti, ribellioni, seditioni, tradimenti, solleuationi, guerre de' popoli, prese di città, espugnationi di fortezze, diete di stati, saccheggiamenti di luoghi, incendij, tregue, accordi, rompimenti di pace, vccisioni di gente, morte de' principi, & altre cose occorse fra catolici, & heretici, dal fine dell'anno MDLXVI fino al principio dell'anno MDLXXX* (Venice: Guerra, 1583), USTC 858273.

Thesoro politico cioè relationi instruttioni trattati, discorsi varii d'amb.ri pertinenti alla cognitione, et intelligenza delli stati, interessi, et dipendenze de più gran Principi del Mondo. Nuovamente impresso a benefficio di chi si diletta intendere, et pertinentemente discorrere li negotii di stato (Cologne [Paris]: Coloresco, 1589), USTC 806507.

Tre discorsi appartenenti alla grandezza delle città. L'uno di m. Lodovico Guicciardini. L'altro di m. Claudio Tolomei. Il terzo di m. Giovanni Botero. Raccolti da m. Giovanni Martinelli (Rome: Martinelli, 1588), USTC 835453.

Verdugo, Francesco, *Li Commentari di Francesco Veduro delle cose successe in Frisia. Nel tempo, che egli fù governatore, & capitan generale, in quella provincia. Non mai prima messi in luce con la vita del medesimo Vedrugo dedicati da Girolamo Fracchetta all'illustriss. & Eccellentiss. Sig. Don Giovan Alfonso Pimentelo d'Herrera, Conte di Benvento, vicerè & capitan generale del regno di Napoli* (Naples: Stigliola, 1605), USTC 4036021.

Véritable récit des choses passees ès Pays-Bas depuis la venue du Siegneur Don Jehan d'Austriche Lieutenant, Gouverneur et Capitaine general pour le Roy en iceulx, avec solution des Objects contenus au Discours non veritables, mis en Lumière par les

Etats desdicts pays, touchant la rupture par eulx faicte de la Dernière Pacification (Luxemburg: Marchand, 1577), USTC 4085.

Von Isselt, Michael, *Mercurius gallobelgicus. Sive, rerum in Gallia et belgio potissimum: Hispania quoque, Italia, Anglia Germania, Polonia, vicinisque locis gestarum, nuncius* (Cologne: Von Kempen, 1592), USTC 675718.

Vray Discours et relation de la Bataille, donnée le xvij. de Iuing 1580. entre Hardenberge & Gransberge, païs d'Ouerysle, à trois heures apres midy, par les gens de guerre de sa Maiesté, conduicts par Marten Schenck de Nydeggen, au secours de Groningen. Et le Conte d'Hohenloe Chief des gens de la nouuelle vnion d'Vtrecht (Cologne [Leuven] : s.n. [Massius], 1580) USTC 13203.

5   Catalogues and Edited Sources

Albèri, E. (ed.), *Relazioni degli ambasciatori veneti al senato* (15 vols., Florence: Grazzini, 1839–1863).

Aristodemo, D. (ed.), *Descrittione di tutti i Paesi Bassi. Edizione critica*, (Amsterdam: unpublished dissertation, 1994).

Aristodemo, D. (ed.), *Descrittione di tutti i Paesi Bassi, vol II. Edizione critica e indici* (Rome: Edizioni di Storia e letteratura, 2020).

Battistini, M. (ed.), *Lettere di Giovan Battista Guicciardini a Cosimo e Francesco de Medici scritte dal Belgio dal 1559 al 1577* (Brussels/Rome: Academia Belgica, 1949).

Bioni, A., Bussi, R., Giovannini C. (eds.), *Cronaca di Modena, anni 1588–1602* (Modena: Franco Cosimo Panini, 1993).

Bitossi, C. (ed.), *Andrea Spinola. Scritti Scelti* (Genoa: Sagep, 1981).

Blok, P-J. (ed.), *Relazioni Veneziane. Venetiaansche Berichten over de Verenigde Nederlanden* (The Hague: Martinus Nijhoff, 1909).

Brom, G. (ed.), *Archivalia in Italië belangrijk voor de geschiedenis van Nederland* (3 vols., The Hague: Stockum, 1908–1914).

Brom, G., Hensen, A.H.L. (eds.), *Romeinsche Bronnen voor den Kerkelijk-Staatkundigen Toestand der Nederlanden in de 16de Eeuw* (The Hague: Nijhoff, 1922).

Brown, R., Cavendish Bentinck, G. (eds.), *Calendar of State Papers Relating to English Affairs in the Archives of Venice, Vol 7, 1558–1580* (London: Her Majesty's Stationery Office, 1890), pp. 575–579; available via *British History Online*.

Capron, L. (ed.), *Correspondance complete et autres écrits de Guy Patin* (Paris: Bibliothèque interuniversitatire de santé, 2018), available via <https://www.biusante.parisdescartes.fr/patin/>.

De Meester, B. (ed.), *Lettres de Philippe et de Jean-Jacques Chifflet sur les affaires des Pays-Bas* (Brussels: Palais des Academies, 1943).

De Meester, B. (ed.), *Correspondance du nonce Giovanni Francesco Guidi di Bagno (1621–1627)* (Brussels: Belgisch Historisch Instituut te Rome, 1938).

Cantagalli, R. (ed.), *Diario di Firenze e di altre parte della cristinità (1574–1579)* (Florence: Istituto Nazionale del Rinascimento, 1970).

Cauchie, A. (ed.), 'Episodes de l'histoire de la ville d'Anvers durant le second semestre de l'année 1566. Correspondance de Daniel di Bomalès avec François di Marchi', *Analectes pour servir à l'histoire ecclésiastique de la Belgique* 7 (1892), pp. 20–60.

Cauchie, A. (ed.), *Recueil des instructions générales aux nonces de Flandre (1596–1635)* (Brussel: Kiessling, 1904).

Cauchie, A., Van der Essen, L. (eds.), *Inventaire des archives Farnésiennes de Naples* (Brussels: Libraries Kiessling et Company, 1911).

Contini, A., Volpini, P. (eds.), *Istruzioni agli ambasciatori e inviati Medicei in Spagna e nell' "Italia Spagnola" (1536–1648) Tomo I: 1536–1586* (Rome: Beni Culturali, 2007).

Continisio, C. (ed.), *La Ragion di Stato* (Rome: Donzelli, 1997).

Colleción de documentos inéditos para la historia de Espana, tomo XXXI (Madrid: Academia de la Historia, 1857).

Firpo, L. (eds.), *Discorsi ai principi d'Italia ed altri scritti filo-ispanici* (Turin: Chiantore, 1945).

Gachard, M. (ed.), *Actes des États Généraux de 1600* (Brussels: Deltombe, 1849).

Génard, P. (ed.), 'La Furie Espagnole. Documents pour servir à l'histoire du sac d'Anvers en 1576', *Annales de Académie Royale d'Archéologie de Belgique* 32 (1876) pp. 5–728.

Giordano, S. (ed.), *Le istruzioni generali di Paolo V ai diplomatici pontifici 1605–1621* (Tübingen: Max Niemeyer, 2003).

Griffante, C. (ed.), *Le edizioni veneziane del seicento. Censimento* (Milan: Ed. Bibliografica, 2003–2006), 2 vols.

Japikse, N., *Resolutiën der Staten Generaal. Eerste deel 1576–1577* (Den Haag: Nijhoff, 1915).

Knuttel, W.P.C. (ed.), *Catalogus van de pamfletten-verzameling berustende in de Koninklijke Bibliotheek 9 vols.* (The Hague: Landsdrukkerij, 1889–1920). (also available via *TEMPO – Early Modern Pamphlets Online*).

Koller, A. (ed.), *Nuntiaturen des Giovanni Delfino und des Bartolomeo Portia (1577–1578)* (Tübingen: De Gruyter, 2003).

Mastellone, S., Haitsma Mulier, E.O.G. (eds.), *Relatione Delle Provincie Unite. Facsimile dell'edizione "Elzeviriana" Brusselles 1632* (Florence: Centro Editoriale Toscano, 1983).

Magdaleno, R., *Papeles de Estado de Venecia* (Valladolid: Martin, 1976).

Piot, C., Poullet, E. (ed.), *Correspondance du Cardinal de Granvelle, 1565–1586* (12 vols., Brussels: Hayez, 1877–1896).

Ronchini, A. (ed.), *Cento lettere del capitano F. Marchi Bolognese* (Parma: F. Carmignani, 1864).

Rooses, M., Ruelens, C. (eds.), *Correspondance de Rubens et documents épistolaires concernant sa vie et ses œuvres, publiés, traduits, annotés. Tome troisième du 27 jullet au 22 octobre 1626* (6 vols., Antwerp: Maes, 1900).

Skinner, Q., Price, R. (eds.), *The Prince* (Cambridge: Cambridge University Press, 1988).

Salsano, F. (ed.), *Anversa Liberata, tre canti inediti. De' Capelli di Sta Maria Maddalena, due odi inediti* (Bologna: Commissione per i testi di lingua, 1956).

Van der Essen, L. (ed.), 'Correspondance de Cosimo Masi, secrétaire d'Alexandre Farnèse, concernant le gouvernement de Mansfeld, de Fuentes et de l'Archiduc Ernest aux Pays-Bas, 1593–1594', *Bulletin de l'Institut historique belge de Rome*, 27 (1952), pp. 357–390.

Van der Essen, L., Louant, A. (eds.), *Correspondance d'Ottavio Mirto Frangipani (1596–1606)* (3 vols., Brussels: Belgisch Historisch Instituut te Rome, 1924–1942).

Van Meerbeeck, L. (ed.), *Correspondance des nonces Gesualdo, Morra, Sanseverino, avec la Secrétaire d'Etat pontificale (1615–1621)* (Brussels: Belgisch Historisch Instituut te Rome, 1937).

6   Secondary Literature

Akkerman, N., 'The Postmistress, the Diplomat, and a Black Chamber? Alexandrine of Taxis, Sir Balthazar Gerbier and the Power of Postal Control', in Adams, R., Cox, R. (eds.), *Diplomacy and Early Modern Culture* (Basingstoke: Palgrave, 2011), pp. 172–188.

Alfani, Guido, *Calamities and the Economy in Renaissance Italy. The Grand Tour of the Horsemen of the Apocalypse* (Basingstoke: Palgrave Macmillan, 2013).

Allen, Paul C., *Philip III and the Pax Hispanica, 1598–1621. The Failure of a Grand Strategy* (London, New Haven: Yale University Press, 2000).

Álvarez Garcia, Francisco Javier, *La Quietud de Italia ante la crisis del Monferrato (1612–1618) Gestión política y rétorica del conflicto* (Unpublished PhD thesis, Universidad Complutense de Madrid, 2019).

Álvarez-Ossorio Alvariño, A., 'La sombre del gobernador y cuello de la República: el Gran Canciller del Estado de Milán', in Mazzocchi, G. (ed.), *El corazón de la Monarquía. La Lombardia in età spagnola* (Como: Ibis, 2010), pp. 15–41.

Amadei, Giuseppe, 'I giornali manoscritti che erano letti dai Gonzaga', *Civiltà mantovana: rivista bimestrale*, 18 (1968), pp. 367–378.

Ancel, René, 'Étude critique sur quelques recueils d'avvisi. Contribution à l'histoire du journalisme en Italie', *Ecole Française de Rome. Mélanges d'Archéologie et d'Histoire*, 28 (1908), pp. 115–139.

Andretta, S., 'Scrivere di altri paesi: il Portogallo e le Fiandre nell'Opera di Girolamo Conestagio de' Franchi', in Firpo, M. (ed.), *"Nunc Alia tempora, alii mores" Storici e storia in età postridentina: atti del convengo internazionale* (Florence: Olschki, 2005), pp. 479–489.

Andriessen, Jozef, *De Jezuïeten en het Samenhorigheidsbesef der Nederlanden 1585–1648* (Antwerp: De Nederlandsche boekhandel, 1957).

Angiolini, Francesco, 'L'Italia nell'età di Filippo ii. Osservazioni preliminari', *Rivista Storica Italiana*, 92 (1980), pp. 432–469.

Ansaldi, Vittorio, 'Giovanni Botero coi principi sabaudi in Spagna', *Bollettino storico-bibliografico Subalpino*, 25 (1933), pp. 322–328.

Arblaster, P., 'Antwerp and Brussels and Inter-European Spaces in News Exchange', in Dooley, B. (ed.), *The Dissemination of News and the Emergence of Contemporaneity in Early Modern Europe* (Burlington: Ashgate, 2010), pp. 193–206.

Arblaster, Paul, *From Ghent to Aix. How They Brought the News in the Habsburg Netherlands, 1550–1700* (Leiden: Brill, 2014).

Arblaster, P., 'Our Valiant Dunkirk Romans': Glorifying the Habsburg War at Sea, 1622–1629', in Raymond, J., Moxham, N. (eds.), *News Networks in Early Modern Europe* (Leiden: Brill, 2016), pp. 583–596.

Arblaster et al., 'The Lexicons of early modern News', in Raymond, J., Moxham, N. (eds.), *News Networks in Early Modern Europe* (Leiden: Brill, 2016), pp. 64–101.

Arrendondo, Maria Soledad, *Literatura y propaganda en tiempo de Quevedo: guerras y plumas contra Francia, Cataluña y Portugal* (Madrid/Frankfurt am Main: Iberoamericana/Vervuert, 2011).

Arfaioli, Mario, 'Alla destra del duca: La figura di Chiappino Vitelli nel contesto degli Affreschi Vasariani del Salone dei Cinquecento', *Mitteilungen des Kunsthistorischen Institutes in Florenz*, 51 (2007), pp. 271–278.

Arfaioli, Mario, 'Bastion of Empire: The Italian *terzo vecchio* of the Army of Flanders (1597–1682)', *Journal of Military History*, 85 (2021), pp. 27–50.

Aristodemo, D., 'Giovan Battista Guicciardini', in *DBI*, 61 (2004).

Arnade, Peter, *Iconoclasts and Civic Patriots: The Political Culture of the Dutch Revolt* (New York: Ithaca, 2008).

Arndt, Johannes, *Das Heilige Römische Reich und die Niederlande 1566 bis 1648. Politisch-konfessionelle Verflechtung und Publizistik im Achtzigjährigen Krieg* (Keulen/Weimar/Wenen: Böhlau Verlag, 1998).

Astarita, T. (ed.), *A Companion to Early Modern Naples* (Leiden: Brill, 2013).

Assonitis, A., Van Veen, H.Th. (eds.), *A Companion to Cosimo I de' Medici* (Leiden: Brill, 2021).

Baars, Rosanne, *Rumours of Revolt: Civil War and the Emergence of a Transnational News Culture in France and the Netherlands, 1561–1598* (Leiden: Brill, 2021).

Baldacchini, L., 'Gottardo da Ponte', in *DBI*, 32 (1986).

Baldini, E. (ed.), *Botero e la "Ragion Di Stato": Atti del convegno in memoria di Luigi Firpo (Torino 8–10 Marzo 1990)* (Florence: Olschki, 1992).

Baldini, E., 'Girolamo Frachetta informatore politico al servizio della Spagna', in Continisio, C., Mozzarelli, C. (eds.), *Repubblica e virtù: Pensiero politico e monarchia Cattolica fra XVI e XVII secolo* (Rome: Bulzoni, 1995), pp. 465–482.

Balsamo, Jean, 'Les Origines Parisiennes du *Tesoro politico* (1589)', *Bibliothèque d'Humanisme et Renaissance*, 57 (1995), pp. 7–21.

Barbarics-Hermanik, Z., 'The Coexistence of Manuscript and Print: Handwritten Newsletters in the Second Century of Print, 1540–1640', in Kemp, G., Walsby, M. (eds.), *The Book Triumphant. Print in Transition in the Sixteenth and Seventeenth Centuries* (Leiden: Brill, 2011), pp. 347–368.

Barbarics-Hermanik, Z., 'Handwritten Newsletters as Interregional Information Sources in Central and Southeastern Europe', in Dooley, B. (ed.), *The Dissemination of News and the Emergence of Contemporaneity in Early Modern Europe* (Burlington: Ashgate, 2010), pp. 155–178.

Barbarics-Hermanik, Z. and Pieper, R., 'Handwritten newsletters as means of communication in early modern Europe', in Bethencourt, F., Egmond, F. (eds.), *Cultural Exchange in Early Modern Europe: Correspondence and Cultural Exchange in Europe, 1400–1700, Volume 3* (Cambridge: Cambridge University Press, 2007), pp. 53–79.

Barberi, F., 'Antonio Blado', in *DBI*, 10 (1968).

Bareggi, Claudio di Filippo, *Il mestiere di scrivere: lavoro intelletuale e mercato librari a Venezia nel Cinquecento* (Rome: Bulzoni, 1988).

Barcia, F., 'La Spagna negli scrittori politici italiani del xvi e xvii secolo', in Continisio, C., Mozzarelli, C. (eds.), *Repubblica e virtù. Pensiero politico e monarchia Cattolica* (Rome: Bulzoni, 1995), pp. 179–206.

Barilli, Arnaldo, 'Nuovi documenti su Alessandro Farnese', *Archivio storico per le province parmensi*, 15 (1938), pp. 73–92.

Barker, S., '"Newes Lately Come": European News Books in English Translation', in Barker, S., Hosington, B.M. (eds.), *Renaissance Cultural Crossroads: Translation, Print and Culture in Britain, 1473–1640* (Leiden: Brill, 2013), pp. 227–244.

Barker, S., 'Secret and Uncertain': A History of *Avvisi* at the Court of the Medici Grand Dukes', in Raymond, J., Moxham, N. (eds.), *News Networks in Early Modern Europe* (Leiden: Brill, 2016), pp. 716–738.

Bauer, Oswald, *Zeitungen vor der Zeitung. Die Fuggerzeitungen (1568–1605) und das Frühmoderne Nachrichtensystem* (Berlin: Akademie Verlag, 2011).

Bauer, O., 'Reichspolitik in den Fuggerzeitungen (1568–1605) – Der Kölner Krieg (1583–1589) als Medienereignis mit Reichspolitischer Relevanz', in Burkhardt, J. (ed.), *Die Fugger und das Reich – Ein neue Forschungsperspektive zum 500jährigen Jubiläum* (Augsburg: Wissner-Verlag, 2008), pp. 269–288.

Behringer, Wolfgang, *Im Zeichen des Merkur: Reichspost und Kommunikationsrevolution in der Frühen Neuzeit* (Göttingen: Vandenhoeck & Ruprecht, 2003).

Behringer, Wolfgang, 'Communications Revolutions. A Historiographical Concept', *German History*, 24 (2006), pp. 333–374.

Bellingradt, Daniel and Rospocher, Massimo, 'A History of Early Modern Communication', *Annali dell'Istituto storico italo-germanico in Trento/Jahrbuch des italienisch-deutschen historischen Instituts in Trient*, 45 (2019), pp. 7–22.

Bellingradt, D., 'The Dynamic of Communication and Media Recycling in Early Modern Europe: Popular Prints as Echoes and Feedback Loops', in Rospocher, M., Salman, J., Salmi, H. (eds.), *Crossing Borders, Crossing Cultures. Popular Print in Europe (1450–1900)* (Oldenbourg: De Gruyter, 2019), pp. 9–32.

Bellettini, Pierangelo, 'Le più antiche gazette a stampa di Milano (1640) e di Bologna (1642)', *La Bibliofilía*, 100 (1998), pp. 465–494.

Bellettini, P., 'Pietro Vecchi e il suo progetto di lettura pubblica, con ascolto a pagamento, delle notizie periodiche di attualità (Bologna 1596)', in Bellettini, P. (ed.), *Una città in piazza: comunicazione e vita quotidiana a Bologna tra Cinque e Seicento: Biblioteca dell'Archiginnasio, sala dello Stabat Mater, 24 Maggio–31 Agosto 2000* (Bologna: Compositori, 2000), pp. 68–76.

Belvederi, Raffaele, *Guido Bentivoglio e la politica europea del suo tempo* (Padua: Liviana editrice, 1962).

Belvederi, R. (ed.), *Rapporti Genova-Mediterraneo-Atlantico nell'età moderna* (Genoa: University of Genoa, 1985).

Belvederi, R., 'Il "Ragionamento di Giovanni Costa, Gentil'Huomo Genovese ..."', in Belvederi, R. (ed.), *Genova, la Liguria e l'Oltremare tra Medioevo ed età moderna: studi e ricerche d'archivio* (Genoa: Bozzi, 1981), pp. 175–360.

Benedict, Philip, *Graphic History: The Wars, Massacres and Troubles of Tortorel and Perrissin* (Geneva: Droz, 2007).

Bennassar, Bartolomé, *Don Juan de Austria. Un héroe para un imperio* (Madrid: Temas de Hoy, 2004).

Benzoni, G., 'Cesare Campana', in *DBI*, 17 (1974).

Berns, J.J., 'Parteylichkeit and the periodical press', in Murphy, K., Traninger, A. (eds.), *The Emergence of Impartiality* (Leiden: Brill, 2014), pp. 87–140.

Bertini, Giuseppe, *Ottavio Gonzaga di Guastalla. La carriera di un cadetto al servizio della monarchia spagnola (1543–1583)* (Guastalla: Biblioteca Maldotti, 2007).

Bertini, G., 'Cosimo Masi', *DBI*, 71 (2008).

Bertini, G. (ed.), *Militari Italiani dell'esercito di Alessandro Farnese* (Guastalla: Mattioli, 2013).

Bertini, Giuseppe, 'La nazione italiana nell'esercito di Alessandro Farnese nei Paesi Bassi: Nuove prostettive', *Philostrato*, 1 (2018), pp. 258–295.

Bertoli, Gustavo, 'Autori ed editori a Firenze nella seconda metà del sedicesimo secolo: il 'caso' Marescotti', *Annali di storia di Firenze*, 2 (2007), pp. 77–93.

Bethencourt, F. and Egmond, F. (eds.), *Cultural Exchange in Early Modern Europe: Correspondence and cultural exchange in Europe, 1400–1700, Volume 3* (Cambridge: Cambridge University Press, 2007).

Bicci, Antonella, 'Italiani ad Amsterdam nel Seicento', *Rivista Storica Italiana*, 102 (1990), pp. 899–934.

Biferali, F., 'Gabrio Serbelloni', *DBI*, 92 (2018).

Bireley, Robert, *The Counter-Reformation Prince: Anti-Machiavellianism or Catholic Statecraft in Early Modern Europe* (Chapel Hill, London: University of North Carolina Press, 1990).

Bireley, Robert, *The Jesuits and the Thirty Years War. Kings, Courts, and Confessors* (Cambridge: Cambridge University Press, 2003).

Bitossi, C., 'Le vicissitudini di una simbiosi: Genova e la Spagna nell'età di Filippo II', in Di Stefano, G., Fasano Guarini, E., Martinengo, A. (eds.), *Italia non spagnola e monarchia spagnola tra '500 e '600. Politica, cultura e letteratura* (Florence: Olschki, 2009), pp. 83–108.

Blanc, J., 'Hugo Grotius, Historiographe des Bataves au XVIIe siècle', in Grell, C. (ed.), *Les Historiographes en Europe de la fin du Moyen Âge à la Révolution* (Paris: Presses de l'université Paris-Sorbonne, 2006), pp. 297–311.

Blum, Anna, *La Diplomatie de la France en Italie du nord au temps de Richelieu et de Mazarin* (Paris: Garnier, 2014).

Bloemendaal, J., Van Dixhoorn, A. and Strietman, E. (eds.), *Literary Cultures and Public Opinion in the Low Countries, 1450–1650* (Leiden: Brill, 2011).

Boutcher, Warren, 'Collecting Manuscripts and Printed Books in the Late Renaissance and Naudé and the Last Duke of Urbino', *Italian Studies*, 66 (2011), pp. 206–220.

Boutier, J., Landi, S., Rouchon, O. (eds.) *La politique par correspondance. Les usages politiques de la lettre en Italie (XIV–XVIIIe siècle)* (Rennes: Presses Universitaires de Rennes, 2009).

Boute, B., 'Que ceulx de Flandres se disoijent tant catholicques, et ce neantmoings les hereticques mesmes ne scauroijent faire pir. The Multiplicity of Catholicism and Roman Attitudes in the Correspondence of the Nunciature of Flanders under Paul V (1605–1621)', in Koller, A. (ed.), *Die Aussenbeziehungen der römischen Kurie unter Paul V. Borghese (1605–1621)* (Tübingen: Max Niemeyer Verlag, 2008), pp. 457–492.

Boute, B., Cools, H., Visceglia, M.A. (eds.), *Fiandre e Italia tra monarchia universale e stati territoriali: cultura politica e dinamiche sociali. Dimensioni e problemi della ricerca storica 2* (Rome: Carroci, 2009).

Bouwsma, William, *Waning of the Renaissance 1550–1640* (New Haven: Yale University Press, 2000).

Borreguero Beltrán, C., 'Philip Of Spain: The Spider's Web of News and Information', in Dooley, B. (ed.), *The Dissemination of News and the Emergence of Contemporaneity in Early Modern Europe* (Burlington: Ashgate, 2010), pp. 23–50.

Buono, A. and Petta, M., 'Il racconto della battaglia. La Guerra e le notizie a stampa nella Milano degli Austrias (secoli XVI–XVII), in Buono, A., Civale G. (eds.), *Battaglie. L'evento, l'individuo, la memoria* (Palermo: Associazione Mediterranea, 2014), pp. 187–248.

Bulgarelli, Tullio, 'Bernardino Beccari da Sacile antesignano dei giornalisti italiani', *Accademie e Biblioteche d'Italia*, 34 (1966), pp. 123–126.

Bulgarelli, Tullio, *Gli avvisi a stampa in Roma nel Cinquecento* (Rome: Istituto Nazionale di Studi Romani, 1967).

Bulgarelli, Sandro and Bulgarelli, Tullio, *Il giornalismo a Roma nel Seicento* (Rome: Bulzoni, 1988).

Burke, Peter, 'A Survey of Popularity of Ancient Historians, 1450–1700', *History and Theory*, 5 (1966), pp. 135–152.

Burke, P., 'Rome as Center of Information and Communication for the Catholic World, 1550–1650', in Jones, P., Worchester, T. (eds.), *From Rome to eternity: Catholicism and the arts in Italy, ca. 1550–1650* (Leiden: Brill, 2002), pp. 253–269.

Burke, P., 'Early Modern Venice as a Center of Information and Communication', in Martin, J. (ed.), *Venice Reconsidered: The History and Civilization of an Italian City-State, 1297–1797* (Baltimore: Johns Hopkins University Press, 2000) pp. 389–419.

Busolini, D., 'Pompeo Giustiniani', in *DBI*, 57 (2001).

Braun, Guido, *Imagines Imperii: Die Wahrnehmung des Reiches und der Deutschen durch die römische Kurie im Reformationjahrhundert (1523–1585)* (Münster: Aschendorf Verlag, 2014).

Brege, Brian, *Tuscany in the Age of Empire* (Harvard University Press, 2021).

Brood, P., Kubben, R. (eds.), *The Act of Abjuration: Inspired or Inspirational* (Nijmegen: Wolf Legal Publishers, 2011).

Brown, Peter M., *Leonardo Salviati: A Critical Biography* (Oxford: Oxford University Press, 1974).

Bruni, F., Pettegree, A. (eds.), *Lost Books: Reconstructing the Print World of Pre-Industrial Europe* (Leiden: Brill, 2016).

Brunelli, G., 'L'eco di un paradigma: Gli *avvertimenti politici* di Vicenzo Vitelli a Giacomo Boncompagni', in Ossola, C., Verga, M., Visceglia, M.A. (eds.), *Religione cultura e politica nell' Europa dell' età moderna. Studi offerti a Mario Rosa dagli amici* (Florence: Olschki, 2003), pp. 251–261.

Brunelli, G., 'Canali di informazione politica degli Orsini di Bracciano fra Cinque e Seicento', in Fasano Guarini, E., Rosa, M. (eds.), *L'informazione politica in Italia (secoli XVI–XVIII)* (Pisa: Scuola Superiore Normale, 2001), pp. 281–301.

Brunelli, Giampiero, *Soldati del papa. Politica militare e nobiltà nello Stato della Chiesa (1560–1644)* (Rome: Carocci, 2003).

Bryce, Judith, *Cosimo Bartoli (1503–1572): The Career of a Florentine Polymath* (Geneva: Droz, 1983).

Casas Nadal, Montserrat, 'Sobre la difusión de l'unione del Regno di Portogallo alla corona di Castiglia' de Conestaggio (1585)', *EPOS*, 23 (2007), pp. 197–220.

Cantagalli, R. and de Blasi, N., 'Cosimo Bartoli', in *DBI*, 6 (1964).

Callard, Caroline, *Le prince et la république: histoire, pouvoir et société dans la Florence des Médicis au XVIIᵉ siècle* (Paris: Presses de l'Université Paris-Sorbonne, 2007).

Caputo, Vincenzo, *La 'bella maniera di scrivere vita': biografie di uomini d'arme e di stato nel secondo cinquecento* (Naples: Edizioni Scientifiche Italiane, 2009).

Capra, C., Sella, D. (eds.), *Il Ducato di Milano dal 1535 al 1796* (Turin: UTET, 1984).

Caracciolo, C.H., 'L'informazione a Bologna tra cinque e seicento: il caso degli avvisi a stampa', in Bellettini, P. (ed.), *Una Città in piazza: comunicazione e vita quotidiana a Bologna tra Cinque e Seicento: Biblioteca dell'Archiginnasio, Sala dello Stabat Mater, 24 Maggio–31 Agosto 2000* (Bologna: Compositori, 2000), pp. 77–88.

Carnelos, Laura, 'Cecità. La percezione di una (dis)abilità nella prima età moderna', in Carraro, S. (ed.), *Alter-habilitas. Perception of disability among people* (Verona: Alteritas, 2018), pp. 235–256.

Castronovo, V., 'I primi sviluppi della stampa periodica fra Cinque e Seicento', in Castronovo, V., Ricuperati, G., Capra, C. (eds.), *La stampa Italiana dal Cinquecento all'Ottocento* (Rome: Laterza, 1980), pp. 3–65.

Casetti Brach, C. and Carmela di Cesare, M., 'Lodovico Grignani', in *DBI*, 50 (2003).

Cavanna Ciappina, M., 'Gerolamo de Franchi Conestagio', in *DBI*, 27 (1982).

Clarke, P., 'The Villani Chronicles', in Dale, S., Williams Lewin, A., Osheim, D.J. (eds.), *Chronicling History: Chroniclers and Historians in Medieval and Renaissance Italy* (Pennsylvania: Pennsylvania State University Press, 2007), pp. 113–143.

Clerici, Alberto, 'Ragion di Stato e politica internazionale. Guido Bentivoglio e altri interpreti italiani della Tregua dei Dodici Anni (1609)', *Dimensione e problem della ricerca storica*, 2 (2009), pp. 188–223.

Cloulas, Ivan, 'La diplomatie pontificale médiatrice entre la France et l'Espagne: La mission de l'archevêque de Nazareth auprès de François d'Anjou (1578)', *Mélanges de la Casa de Velázquez*, 5 (1969), pp. 451–459.

Cioni, A., 'Benacci', *DBI*, 8 (1966).

Christ, Georg, 'A Newsletter in 1419? Antonio Morosini's Chronicle in the Light of Commercial Correspondence between Venice and Alexandria', *Mediterranean Historical Review*, 20 (2005), pp. 35–66.

Coldagelli, U., 'Giacomo Buoncompagni', in *DBI*, 11(1969).

Cochrane, Eric, *Historians and Historiography in Renaissance Italy* (Chicago: Chicago University Press, 1985).

Cochrane, Eric, 'The Transition from Renaissance to Baroque historiography: the case of Italian Historiography', *History and Theory*, 19 (1980), pp. 21–38.

Contini, A., 'L'informazione politica sugli stati italiani non spagnoli nelle relazioni veneziane a metà cinquecento (1558–1566)' in Fasano Guarini, E., Rosa, M. (eds.),

L'informazione politica in Italia (*secoli XVI–XVIII*) (Pisa: Scuola Superiore Normale, 2001), pp. 1–57.

Contini, A., 'Aspects of Medicean Diplomacy in the Sixteenth Century', in Frigo, D. (ed.), *Politics and Diplomacy in Early Modern Italy. The Structure of Diplomatic Practice, 1450–1800* (Cambridge: Cambridge University Press, 2000), pp. 49–94.

Contini, A., 'Dinastia, Patriziato e politica estera: ambasciatore e segretari medicei nel cinquecento', in Frigo, D. (ed.), *Ambasciatori e nunzi: figure della diplomazia in età moderna* (Rome: Bulzoni, 1999), pp. 57–131.

Cools, H., Keblusek, M., Noldus, B. (eds.), *Your Humble Servant: Agents in Early Modern Europe* (Hilversum: Verloren, 2006).

Cools, H., 'Some Italian voices on Dutch liberties', in Brood, P., Kubben, R. (eds.), *The Act of Abjuration. Inspired and Inspirational* (Nijmegen: Wolf Legal publishers, 2011), pp. 1–13.

Costantini, Claudio, *La Repubblica di Genova* (Turin: UTET, 1986).

Crinò, Anna, 'Avvisi di Londra di Petruccio Ubaldini, fiorentino, relativi agli anni 1579–1594, con notizie sulla guerra di Fiandra', *Archivio Storico Italiano*, 127 (1969), pp. 461–581.

Cruz, L., 'The Epic Story of the Little Republic that could: The Role of Patriotic Myths in the Dutch Golden Age', in Cruz, L., Frijhoff, W. (eds.), *Myth in History, History in Myth* (Leiden: Brill, 2009), pp. 159–173.

Cust, Richard, 'News and Politics in Early Seventeenth-Century England', *Past & Present*, 112 (1986), pp. 60–90.

Dall'Acqua, M. (ed.), *Pomponio Torelli tra assolutismo e controriforma. Mostra documentaria e bibliografica* (Parma: Baroni e Villani, 1976).

D'Alessio, Silvana, *Contagi. La rivolta napoletana del 1647–48: linguaggio e potere politico* (Florence: Centro Editoriale Toscana, 2003).

D'Amico, Stefano, *Spanish Milan. A City within the Empire 1535–1706* (New York: Palgrave, 2012).

Danet, Alexandra, 'El Rómulo del Fabricio Lanario de Aragón (Naples, 1635): notes sur une traduction espagnole méconnue du Romulo de Virgilio Malvezzi', *Studi secenteschi*, 50 (2009), pp. 63–87.

Dandelet, Thomas, *Spanish Rome 1500–1700* (New Haven, London: Yale University Press, 2001).

Dandelet, T., Marino, J. (eds.), *Spain in Italy: Politics, Society, and Religion 1500–1700* (Leiden: Brill, 2007).

Dauser, Regina, *Informationskultur und Beziehungswissen. Das Korrespondenznetz Hans Fuggers* (*1531–1598*) (Tübingen: Max Niemeyer, 2008).

Dauverd, Céline, *Imperial ambition in the Early Modern Mediterranean: Genoese merchants and the Spanish Crown* (Cambridge: Cambridge University Press, 2015).

Darnton, Robert, 'An Early Information Society: News and Media in Eighteenth-Century Paris', *American Historical Review*, 105 (2000), pp. 1–35.

Daybell, James, *The Material Letter: Manuscript Letters and the Culture and Practices of Letter-Writing in Early Modern England, 1580–1635* (Basingstoke: Palgrave, 2012).

Davies, S., Fletcher, P. (eds.), *News in Early Modern Europe: Currents and Connections* (Leiden: Brill, 2014).

De Brézé, N., 'L'histoire des Bataves et des Romains dans la peinture des Pays-Bas aux XVII et XVIIᵉ siècles', in Soen, V., Junot, Y. (eds.), *Les identités aux pluriel. Jeux et enjeux des appartenances autour des anciens Pays-Bas* (Villeneuve d'Asq: Revue du Nord, Hors Serie, 2014), pp. 95–112.

Debruyne, Nicolas, 'Een Gentse Staatsgreep. De Gevangenneming van de Hertog van Aarschot en andere edelen te Gent op 28 oktober 1577', *Handelingen der Maatschappij voor Geschiedenis en Oudheidkunde te Gent*, 64 (2010), pp. 167–212.

Denarosi, Lucia, *L'accademia degli Innominati di Parma: teorie letterarie e progetti di scrittura (1574–1608)* (Florence: Società Editrice Fiorentina, 2003).

De Groof, B., 'Alexander Farnese and the origins of modern Belgium', in De Groof, B., Galdieri, E. (eds.), *La dimensione europea dei Farnese* (Turnhout: Brepols, 1993), pp. 195–219.

De Groof, B., 'A noble courtier and a gentleman warrior. Some aspects of the creation of the Spinola image', in Fenoulhet, J., Gilbert, L. (eds.), *Presenting the Past: History, Art, Language, Literature* (London: Centre Low Countries Studies, 1996), pp. 39–52.

De Jonge, Johannes C., *Nederland en Venetië* (The Hague: Van Cleef, 1852).

De Keyser, Joey, *Vreemde Ogen. Een kijk op de Zuidelijke Nederlanden (1400–1600)* (Antwerp: Meulenhof/Manteua, 2010).

De Landtsheer, J., 'Justus Lipsius' *De militia romana*. Polybius revived, or How an ancient historian was turned into a manual of early modern warfare', in Enenkel, K., De Jong, J.L., De Landtsheer, J. (eds.), *Recreating Ancient History: Episodes from the Greek and Roman Past in the Arts and Literature of the Early Modern Period* (Leiden: Brill, 2001), pp. 101–122.

De Meester, Bernard, *Le Saint-Siège et les Troubles des Pays-Bas 1566–1579* (Leuven: Bibliothèque de Louvain, 1934).

De Ridder, B. and Soen, V., 'The Act of Cession, the 1598 and 1600 States General in Brussels and the Peace Negotiations during the Dutch Revolt', in Lesaffer, R. (ed.), *The Twelve Years Truce (1609). Peace, Truce, War and Law in the Low Countries at the Turn of the 17th Century* (Leiden/Boston: Brill/Nijhoff, 2014) pp. 48–68.

Derks, S., 'Le ricompense della guerra: giustificazione e rappresentazione di Alessandro Farnese nel *Liber relationum* di Paolo Rinaldi', in Bertini, G. (ed.), *Militari Italiani dell' esercito di Alessandro Farnese nelle Fiandre* (Fidenza: Mattioli 1885, 2013), pp. 211–219.

Descendere, Romain, *L'état du monde. Giovanni Botero entre raison d'état et geopolitique* (Geneva: Droz, 2006).

Descimon, Robert and Ruiz Ibáñez, José Javier, *Les Ligueurs de l'exil: Le refuge catholique français après 1594* (Seyssel: Editions Champ Vallon, 2005).

De Vivo, Filippo, 'Paolo Sarpi and the Uses of Information in Seventeenth-Century Venice', *Media History*, 11 (2005), pp. 37–51.

De Vivo, Filippo, *Information & Communication in Venice. Rethinking Early Modern Politics* (Oxford: Oxford University Press, 2007).

De Vivo, Filippo, 'Pharmacies as centres of communication in early modern Venice', *Renaissance Studies*, 21 (2007), pp. 505–521.

De Vivo, Filippo, 'Coeur de l'Etat, lieu de tension. Le tournant archivistique vu de Venise (xvᵉ–xviiᵉ siècle)', *Annales. Histoire, Sciences Sociales*, 68 (2013), pp. 699–728.

De Vivo, Filippo, 'Microhistories of Long-Distance information: Space, Movement and Agency in the Early Modern News', *Past & Present*, 242 Supplement 14 (2019), pp. 179–214.

Dierickx, Michel, 'Les "Carte Farnesiane" de Naples par rapport à l'histoire des anciens Pays-Bas, après l'incendie du 30 septembre 1943', *Bulletin de la Commission Royal d'Histoire/Handelingen van de Koninklijke Commissie voor Geschiedenis*, 112 (1947), pp. 111–126.

Dooley, B., Baron, S.A. (eds.), *The Politics of Information in Early Modern Europe* (London: Routledge, 2001).

Dooley, B. (ed.), *The Dissemination of News and the Emergence of Contemporaneity in Early Modern Europe* (Burlington: Ashgate, 2010).

Dooley, Brendan, *The Social History of Skepticism. Experience and Doubt in Early Modern Culture* (Baltimore, London: John Hopkins University Press, 1999).

Dooley, B., 'Sources and methods in information history. The case of Medici Florence, the Armada and the Siege of Ostende', in Koopmans, J. (ed.), *News and Politics in Early Modern Europe (1600–1800)* (Leuven: Peeters, 2005), pp. 29–45.

Doria, G., 'Conoscenza del Mercato e sistema informativo: il know-how dei mercanti-finanzieri genovesi nei secoli xvi e xvii', in De Maddelena, A., Kellenbenz, H. (eds.), *La Repubblica internazionale del denaro tra xv e xvii secolo* (Bologna: Il Mulino, 1986), pp. 57–115.

Dover, P.M., 'Philip ii, Information Overload, and the Early Modern Moment', in Andrade, T., Reger, W. (eds.), *The Limits of Empire: European Imperial Formation in Early Modern Europe. Essays in Honor of Geoffrey Parker* (Burlington: Ashgate, 2012), pp. 99–120.

Dover, Paul M., *The Information Revolution in Early Modern Europe* (Cambridge: Cambridge University Press, 2021).

Duerloo, Luc, *Dynasty and Piety. Archduke Albert (1598–1621) and Habsburg Political Culture in an Age of Religious Wars* (Farnham: Ashgate, 2012).

Duquenne, Frédéric, *L'Entreprise du duc d'Anjou aux Pays-Bas de 1580 à 1584. Les responsabilités d'un échec à partager* (Villeneuve d'Ascq: Septentrion, 1998).

Dumont, George Henri, *Marguerite de Parme bâtarde de Charles Quint (1522–1586). Biographie* (Brussels: Le Cri, 1999).

Dunthorne, H., 'Resisting Monarchy: The Netherlands as Britain's School of Revolution in the Late Sixteenth and Seventeenth Centuries', in Oresko, R., Gibbs, G.C., Scott, H.M. (eds.), *Royal and Republican Sovereignty in Early Modern Europe: Essays in Memory of Ragnhild Hatton* (Cambridge: Cambridge University Press, 1997), pp. 125–148.

Dunthorne, Hugh, *Britain and the Dutch Revolt 1560–1700* (Cambridge: Cambridge University Press, 2013).

Dursteler, Eric R., 'Speaking in Tongues: Language and Communication in the Early Modern Mediterranean', *Past & Present*, 217 (2012), pp. 47–77.

Droste, Heiko, *The Business of News* (Leiden: Brill, 2021).

Elliott, John H., *Spain and Its World 1500–1700: Selected Essays* (New Haven, London: Yale University Press, 1989).

Elliott, John H., 'A Europe of Composite Monarchies', *Past & Present*, 137 (1992), pp. 48–71.

Engels, Marie-Christine, *Merchants, Interlopers, Seamen and Corsairs. The Flemish community in Livorno and Genoa (1615–1635)* (Hilversum: Verloren, 1997).

Ernst, Germana, *Tommaso Campanella: The Book and the Body of Nature* (Dordrecht/New York: Springer, 2010).

Evenden, Elizabeth and Freeman, Thomas S., *Religion and the Book in Early Modern England: The Making of John Foxe's 'Book of Martyrs'* (Cambridge: Cambridge University Press, 2011).

Espejo, Carmen, 'The Prince of Transylvania: Spanish News of the War against the Turks, 1595–1600', in Raymond, J., Moxham, N. (eds.), *News Networks in Early Modern Europe* (Leiden: Brill, 2016), pp. 512–541.

Ettinghausen, Henry, *How the Press Began. The Pre-Periodical Printed News in Early Modern Europe* (Coruña: Janus, 2015).

Ettinghausen, Henry, 'Los avvisi a stampa: las relaciones de sucesos italianas, en relación con las españolas', in Andres, G. (ed.), *Proto-giornalismo e letterature: avvisi a stampa, relaciones de sucesos* (Rome: FrancoAngeli, 2013), pp. 13–24.

Ettinghausen, Henry, 'The Golden Age of Single Event Printed Newsletter: *Relaciones de sucesos*, 1601–1650', Wilkinson, A.S., Ulla Lorenzo, A. (eds.), *A Maturing Market: The Iberian Book World in the first half of the Seventeenth Century* (Leiden: Brill, 2017), pp. 241–258.

Eysinga, Willem J.M., *De wording van het Twaalfjarig Bestand van 9 april 1609* (Amsterdam: Noord-Hollandsche Uitgevers Maatschappij, 1959).

Externbrink, Sven, *Le Coeur du monde. Frankreich und die norditalienischen Staaten (Mantua, Parma, Savoyen) im Zeitalter Richelieus 1624–1635* (Munster: Lit Verlag, 1997).

Externbrink, S., 'The Thirty Years' War in Italy 1628–1659', in Asbach, O., Schröder, P. (eds.), *Ashgate Research Companion to the Thirty Years' War* (Farnham: Ashgate, 2014), pp. 177–190.

Fagel, R., 'The Duke of Alba and the Low Countries 1520–1573', in Ebben, M., Lacy-Bruijn, M., van Hövell, R. (eds.), *Alba: General and Servant to the Crown* (Maastricht: Karwansaray, 2013), pp. 257–285.

Fagel, R., Francés Álvarez, L., Santiago Belmonte, B. (eds.), *Early modern war narratives and the Revolt in the Low Countries* (Manchester: Manchester University Press, 2020).

Fagel, R., Santiago Belmonte, B., Francés Álvarez, L., 'Eer en Schuld. Heiligerlee en Jemmingen in Spaanse ogen', in S. van der Hoek (ed.), *Heiligerlee. Strijd in een landschap van glorie en nederlaag* (Gorredijk, Uitgeverij Noordboek, 2021) pp. 79–89.

Fagel, Raymond, *Protagonists of War. Spanish Army Commanders and the Revolt in the Low Countries* (Leuven: Leuven University Press, 2021).

Fagel, Raymond, and Pollmann, Judith, *1572. Burgeroorlog in de Nederlanden* (Amsterdam: Promotheus, 2022).

Fantoni, M., 'Il "Perfetto Capitano": storia e mitografia', in Fantoni, M. (ed.), *Il "Perfetto Capitano": immagini e realtà (secoli XV–XVII): atti dei Seminari* (Rome: Bulzoni, 2001), pp. 15–67.

Fasano Guarini, E. (ed.), *L'Informazione politica in Italia (secoli XVI–XVIII): Atti del seminario organizzato presso la scuola normale superiore Pisa, 23 e 24 Giugno 1997* (Pisa: Scuola Normale Superiore, 2001).

Fasano Guarini, E., 'Italia non spagnola e Spagna nel tempo di Filippo II', in Lotti, L. and Villari, R. (eds.), *Filippo II e il Mediterraneo* (Rome: Laterza, 2003), pp. 5–23.

Fasano Guarini, E., 'Committenza del principe e storiografia pubblica: Benedetto Varchi e Giovan Battista Adriani', in Fasano Guarini, E., Angiolini, F. (eds.), *La pratica della Storia in Toscana. Continuità e mutamenti tra la fine del '400 e la fine del '700* (Milan: FrancoAngeli 2009), pp. 79–100.

Fasano Guarini, Elena, *Repubbliche e Principi. Istituzioni e pratiche di potere nella Toscana Granducale del '500–'600* (Bologna: Il Mulino, 2010).

Fernandez Collado, Angel, *Gregorio XIII y Felipe II en la nunciatura de Felipe Sega (1577–1581). Aspectos político, jurisdiccional y de reforma* (Toledo: Estudios teologicas de San Idlefonse, 1990).

Findlen, P., and Sutherland, S. (eds.), *The Renaissance of Letters. Knowlegde and Community in Italy, 1300–1650* (London: Routledge, 2020).

Firpo, L., 'Tommaso Campanella', in *DBI*, 17 (1974).

Firpo, Luigi, 'In Margine al processo di Giordano Bruno. Francesco Maria Vialardi', *Rivista Storica Italiana*, 68 (1956), pp. 325–364.

Firpo, Massimo, *Pietro Bizzarri. Esule italiano del Cinquecento* (Turin: G. Giappichelli, 1971).

Firpo, Massimo, *Il sacco di Roma del 1527 tra profezia, propaganda politica e riforma religiosa* (Cagliari: Ceuc editrice, 1990).

Formica, Marina, *Lo Specchio Turco. Immagini dell'altro e riflessi del sé nella cultura italiana d'èta moderna* (Rome: Donzelli, 2012).

Fontana, A., 'Les Provinces Unies dans les Relations des Ambassadeurs Vénitiens au XVIIᵉ siècle', in Blanco-Morel, M., Piéjus, M-F. (eds.), *Les Flandres et la culture Espagnole et Italienne aux XVIᵉ et XVIIᵉ siècles* (Lille: Travaux et Recherches, 1998), pp. 139–150.

Fournel, J-L., 'Du bon usage historique de l'hérésie. La Révolte des Flandres dans la pensée politique de Campanella', in Blanco-Morel, M., Piéjus, M-F. (eds.), *Les Flandres et la culture Espagnole et Italienne aux XVIᵉ et XVIIᵉ siècles* (Lille: Travaux et Recherches, 1998), pp. 121–138.

Frajese, V., 'Campanella e la monarchia di Spagna', in Lotti, L. and Villari, R. (eds.), *Filippo II e il Mediterraneo* (Rome: Laterza, 2003), pp. 357–386.

Frigo, D., 'Pubblicistica e storiografia nella sultura veneta del primo seicento', in Fasano Guarini, E. (ed.), *L'informazione politica in Italia (secoli XVI–XVIII): Atti del seminario organizzato presso la Scuola Normale Superiore Pisa, 23 e 24 Giugno 1997* (Pisa: Scuola Normale Superiore, 2001), pp. 83–136.

Frigo, D., '"Small States" and Diplomacy: Mantua and Modena', in Frigo, D. (ed.), *Politics and Diplomacy in Early Modern Italy. The Structure of Diplomatic Practice, 1450–1800* (Cambridge: Cambridge University Press, 2000), pp. 147–175.

Frigo, D. (eds.), *Politics and Diplomacy in Early Modern Italy. The Structure of Diplomatic Practice, 1450–1800* (Cambridge: Cambridge University Press, 2000).

Frigo, D., 'Il ducato Mantovano e la corte di Filippo II', in Martinez Millán, J. (eds.), *Felipe II (1527–1598). Europa y la Monarquía Católica* (Madrid: Parteluz, 1998), pp. 283–305.

Galasso, G., 'L'Italia una e diversa nel sistema degli Stati Europei (1450–1750)', in Galasso, G. (ed.), *Storia d'Italia vol XIX: L'Italia moderna e l'unità nazionale* (Turin: Einaudi, 1998) pp. 1–492.

García García, Bernardo, *La Pax Hispánica: Política Exterior del Duque de Lerma* (Leuven: Leuven University Press, 1996).

García de la Fuente, V., 'Relaciones de Sucesos en forma de carta: estructura, temática y lenguaje', in Ettinghausen, H. (ed.), *Las Relaciones de sucesos en España (1500–1750)* (Alcalá de Henares: Universidad de Alcalá, 1996), pp. 175–184.

Gachard, Louis-Prosper, 'Les archives Farnéssienes, à Naples', *Compte Rendu des séances de la commission royale d'histoire*, 11 (1870), pp. 301–311.

Grafton, Anthony, *What was History? The Art of History in Early Modern Europe* (Cambridge: Cambridge University Press, 2007).

Giachery, A., 'Pinelli', *DBI*, 83 (2015).

Giannini, M., 'Giuliano Gosellini', *DBI*, 58 (2002).

Giansante, M., 'Cappello Annibale', *DBI*, 18 (1975).

Gilbert, F., 'Italy', in Ranum, O. (ed.), *National consciousness, history and political culture in Early Modern Europe* (Baltimore/London: John Hopkins University Press, 1975), pp. 21–42.

Geurts, Pieter A.M., *De Nederlandse opstand in pamfletten 1566–1584* (Nijmegen: Centrale drukkerij, 1956).

Geyl, Pieter, *Christofforo Suriano, resident van de Serenissime Republiek van Venetië in Den Haag, 1616–1623* (The Hague: Martinus Nijhoff, 1913).

Goldthwaite, Richard A., *Private Wealth in Renaissance Florence, A Study of Four Families* (Princeton: Princeton University Press, 1968).

Goldthwaite, Richard A., *The Economy of Renaissance Florence* (Baltimore: John Hopkins University Press, 2009).

Goris, Jan-Albert, *Etude sur les colonies merchandes méridionales à Anvers de 1488 à 1567* (Leuven: Librairie Universitaire, 1925).

Gouwens, Kenneth, *Remembering the Renaissance: Humanist narratives of the Sack of Rome*, (Leiden: Brill, 1998).

Grendler, Paul, 'Francesco Sansovino and Italian Popular History 1560–1600', *Studies in the Renaissance*, 16 (1969), pp. 139–180.

Groenveld, Simon, *Unie- Bestand- Vrede. Drie fundamentele wetten van de Republiek der Verenigde Nederlanden* (Hilversum: Verloren, 2009).

Groenveld, Simon, *Het Twaalfjarig Bestand 1609–1621. De Jongelingsjaren van de Republiek der Verenigde Nederlanden* (The Hague: Haags Historisch Museum, 2009).

Grootveld, Emma and Lamal, Nina, 'Impious heretics or simple Birds? Alexander Farnese and Dutch rebels in Post-Tassian Italian poems', *Quaderni d'Italianistica*, 35 (2014), pp. 63–97.

Grootveld, Emma and Lamal, Nina, 'Cultural translation and glocal dynamics between Italy and the Low Countries during the sixteenth and seventeenth century', *Incontri. Rivista europea di studi italiani*, 30 (2015), pp. 3–12.

Haitsma Mulier, E.O.G., 'Willem van Oranje in de historiografie van de zeventiende eeuw', in Haitsma Mulier, E.O.G., Janssen, A.E.M. (eds.), *Willem van Oranje in de Historie 1584–1984: Vier Eeuwen Beeldvorming en Geschiedschrijving* (Utrecht: Hes, 1984), pp. 32–46.

Haitsma Mulier, E.O.G., 'Genova e l'Olanda nel Seicento: contatti mercantili e ispirazione politica', in Belvederi, R. (ed.), *Atti del Congresso internazionale di studi Rapporti Genova-Mediterraneo-Atlantico nell'età moderna* (Genoa: Istituto di scienze storiche, 1983) pp. 431–444.

Haitsma Mulier, Eco O.G., *The Myth of Venice and Dutch Republican Thought in the Seventeenth Century* (Assen: Van Gorcum, 1980).

Haitsma Mulier, Eco O.G., 'De Bataafse mythe opnieuw bekeken', *Bijdragen en Mededelingen betrefferende de Geschiedenis der Nederlanden*, 111 (1996), pp. 344–367.

Hanlon, Gregory, *The Twilight of a Military Tradition : Italian Aristocrats and European Conflicts, 1560–1800* (London: UCL, 1998).

Hanlon, Gregory, *The Hero of Italy: Odoardo Farnese, Duke of Parma, His soldiers, His Subjects during the Thirty Years' War* (Oxford: Oxford University Press, 2014).

Hanlon, Gregory, *Italy 1636: Cemetries of Armies* (Oxford: Oxford University Press, 2016).

Harline, Craig, *Pamphlets, Printing and Political Culture in the Early Dutch Republic* (Dordrecht: Martinus Nijhoff, 1987).

Hayez, J., 'Avviso, informazione, novella, nuova: La notion de l'information dans les correspondances marchandes toscanes vers 1400', in Boudreau, C., Fianu, K., Gauvard, C. (eds.), *Information et société en Occident à la fin du Moyen Age. Actes du colloque international tenu à l'université du Québec à Montréal et à l'université d'Ottawa (9–11 Mai 2002)* (Paris: Publication de la Sorbonne, 2004), pp. 113–133.

Helmers, Helmer J., 'Public Diplomacy in Early Modern Europe: Towards a New History of News', *Media History*, 22 (2016), pp. 401–420.

Herrero Sánchez, Manuel, 'The Business Relations, Identities and Political Resources of Italia Merchants in the early-modern Spanish monarchy: some introductory remarks', *European Review of History*, 23 (2016), pp. 1–12.

Hill, Alexandra, *Lost Books and Printing in London 1557–1640: An Analysis of the Stationer's Company* (Leiden: Brill, 2018).

Holenstein, H., Maissen, T. and Prak, M. (eds.), *The Republican Alternative. The Netherlands and Switzerland Compared* (Amsterdam: Amsterdam University Press, 2008).

Holt, Mack, *The Duke of Anjou and the Politique Struggle during the Wars of Religion* (Cambridge: Cambridge University Press, 1986).

Hook, Judith, *The Sack of Rome* (London: Palgrave Macmillan, 1972).

Hunt, John M., 'The Conclave from the "Outside In": Rumor, Speculation, and Disorder in Rome during Early Modern Papal Elections', *Journal of Early Modern History*, 16 (2012), pp. 355–382.

Hyde, J.K., 'Diplomatic correspondence and reporting', in Waley, D. (ed.), *Literacy and Its Uses: studies on late Medieval Italy* (Manchester: Manchester University Press, 1993).

Infelise, Mario, *Prima dei giornali: alle origini della pubblica informazione, secoli XVI e XVII* (Rome, Bari: Laterza, 2002).

Infelise, M., 'From Merchants' Letters to Handwritten Political Avvisi: Notes on the Origins of Public Information', in Bethencourt, F., Egmond, F. (eds.), *Correspondence and Cultural Exchange in Europe 1400–1700* (Cambridge: Cambridge University Press, 2007), pp. 33–52.

Infelise, M., 'News Networks between Italy and Europe', in Dooley, B. (ed.), *The Dissemination of News and the Emergence of Contemporaneity in Early Modern Europe* (Farnham: Ashgate, 2010), pp. 51–68.

Iordanou, Ioanna, *Venice's Secret Service. Organizing Intelligence in the Renaissance* (Oxford: Oxford University Press, 2019).

Israel, Jonathan, *The Dutch Republic. Its Rise, Greatness, and Fall 1477–1806* (Oxford: Oxford University Press, 1998).

Israel, Jonathan, *Dutch Primacy in World Trade 1585–1640* (Oxford: Oxford University Press, 2002).

Jacqmain, Monique, 'Een minder bekende "vlaamse" G.: G.B., de korrespondent van de Medici's', *Ons erfdeel*, 18 (1975), pp. 321–396.

Janssen, A.E.M., 'Prins van Oranje in het oordeel van tijdgenoten', in Haitsma Mulier, E.O.G., Janssen, A.E.M. (eds.), *Willem van Oranje in de Historie 1584–1984: Vier Eeuwen Beeldvorming en Geschiedschrijving* (Utrecht: Hes, 1984), pp. 9–31.

Janssen, Geert H., 'The Counter-Reformation of the Refugee: Exile and the Shaping of Catholic militancy in the Dutch Revolt', *The Journal of Ecclesiastical History*, 63 (2012), pp. 671–692.

Janssens, Gustaaf, 'De ordonnantie betreffende de pacificatie van de beroerten te Antwerpen (24 mei 1567): breekpunt voor de politiek van Filips II ten overstaan van de Nederlanden', *Handelingen van de Koninklijke Commissie voor de Uitgave der Oude Wetten en Verordeningen*, 50 (2009), pp. 105–132.

Janssens, Gustaaf, *Brabant in het verweer. Loyale oppositie tegen Spanje's bewind in de Nederlanden van Alva tot Farnese, 1567–1578* (Kortrijk: Heule, 1989).

Janssens, G., 'Cardinal Granvelle and the Revolt in the Netherlands. The evolution of this thought on a desirable political approach to the problem 1567–1578', in De Jonge, K., Janssens, G. (eds.), *Les Granvelle et les anciens Pays-Bas* (Leuven: Universitaire Pers, 2000), pp. 135–156.

Jensen, Freyja Cox, 'The Popularity of Ancient Historians 1450–1600', *The Historical Journal*, 61 (2018), pp. 561–595.

Kagan, Richard L., *Clio and the Crown. The Politics of History in Medieval and Early Modern Spain* (Baltimore: The John Hopkins University Press, 2009).

Kamen, Henry, *The Duke of Alba* (New Haven/London: Yale University Press, 2004).

Kattenberg, Lisa, *The Power of Necessity. Reason of State in the Spanish Monarchy ca. 1590–1650* (Unpublished PhD, University of Amsterdam, 2018).

Keblusek, M. and Noldus, B. (eds.), *Double Agents: Cultural and Political Brokerage in Early Modern Europe* (Leiden: Brill, 2011).

Keblusek, M., 'Double Agents in Early Modern Europe', in Keblusek, M., Noldus, B. (eds.), *Double Agents: Cultural and Political Brokerage in Early Modern Europe* (Leiden: Brill, 2011), pp. 1–9.

Keller, Katrin and Molino, Paola, *Die Fuggerzeitungen im Kontext. Zeitungssammlungen im Alten Reich und in Italien* (Vienna: Böhlau, 2015).

Kessel, Pieter Jan, *Van Fiandra naar Olanda. Veranderende visie in het vroegmoderne Italië op de Nederlandse identiteit* (Amsterdam: Noord Hollandse Uitgeverij, 1993).

Keenan, Charles R., 'English News in Papal Rome: Cross-Confessional Information Exchange in Reformation Europe', *Journal of Early Modern History*, 23 (2019), pp. 350–366.

Kirk, Thomas A., *Genoa and the Sea. Policy and Power in an Early Modern Maritime Republic, 1559–1684* (Baltimore: John Hopkins University Press, 2005).

Kittler, Juraj, 'Caught between business, war and politics: late medieval roots of the early modern European news networks', *Mediterranean Historical Review*, 33 (2018), pp. 199–222.

Koenigsberger, Helmut, *Monarchies, States Generals and Parliaments. The Netherlands in the Fifteenth and Sixteenth Centuries* (Cambridge: Cambridge University press, 2001).

Kohler, A., Piergentili, P.P., Venditti, G. (eds.), *I Codici Minucciani dell'Istituto Storico Germanico. Inventario* (Rome: Online Publication of the German Historical Institute, 2009).

Kohler, A., 'Minucci' in *DBI*, 74 (2010).

Koller, A. (ed.), *Kurie und Politik, Stand und Perspektiven der Nunziaturberichtsforschung* (Tübingen: Max Niemeyer Verlag, 1998).

Koopmans, J. (ed.), *News and Politics in Early Modern Europe (1600–1800)* (Leuven: Peeters, 2005).

Kuijpers, E. and Pollmann, J., 'Why remember terror? Memories of violence in the Dutch Revolt', in Ohlmeyer, J., Siochrú, M.Ó (eds.), *Ireland 1641: Contexts and Reactions* (Manchester: Manchester University Press 2013), pp. 176–196.

Klinkert, Christi M., *Nassau in het nieuws: nieuwsprenten van Maurits van Nassaus militaire ondernamingen uit periode 1590–1600* (Zupthen: Walburg, 2005).

Lamal, Nina, *'Beter een oprechten crijgh dan een geveynsden peys' Pamfletten en publieke opinie in de aanloop naar het Twaalfjarig Bestand (1607–1609)* (Unpublished MA thesis, KU Leuven, 2010).

Lamal, Nina, 'De belichaming van christelijke liefde. Gevoelens en lichamelijkheid in zestiende-eeuwse franciscaanse martelaarsverhalen', in *Tijdschrift voor geschiedenis*, 126 (2013), pp. 505–508.

Lamal, N. and Cools, H., 'An Italian Voice on the Dutch Revolt: The Work of Francesco Lanario in a European perspective', in Van Bruaene, A-L., Kavaler, M. (eds.), *Urban Perspectives on sixteenth-century Netherlandish Art & Culture* (Brepols: Turnhout, 2018), pp. 375–388.

Lamal, N., '"Translated and Often Printed in Most Languages of Europe": Movement and Translation of Italian Histories on the Dutch Revolt across Europe', in McLean,

M., Barker, S.K. (eds.), *International Exchange in the Early Modern Book World* (Leiden: Brill, 2016), pp. 124–146.

Lamal, N., 'The circulation and collections of Italian books in the Low Countries at the beginning of the seventeenth century', in Adam, R., Lastraioli, C. (eds.), *Itinéraires du livre italien à la Renaissance Suisse romande, anciens Pays-Bas et Liège* (Paris: Garnier, 2019), pp. 103–126.

Lamal, N., 'Promoting the Catholic cause on the Italian Peninsula: Printed Avvisi on the Dutch Revolt and the French Wars of Religion, 1562–1600', in Raymond, J., Moxham, N. (eds.), *News Networks in Early Modern Europe* (Leiden: Brill, 2016), pp. 675–694.

Lamal, N., Cumby, J., Helmers, H.J. (eds.), *Print and Power in Early Modern Europe* (Leiden: Brill, 2021).

Lamal, Nina, 'Communicating conflict: early modern soldiers as information-gatherers', *Journal of Medieval and Early Modern Studies*, 50 (2020), pp. 13–31.

Lamal, N. and Arblaster, P., 'Spinola's fame in the news press', in Mostaccio, S., García García, B.J., Lo Basso, L. (eds.), *Ambrogio Spinola between Genoa, Flanders and Spain* (Leuven: Leuven University Press, 2022), pp. 213–250.

Lamberini, D., 'Francesco de Marchi', in *DBI*, 38 (1990).

Landi, Sandro, *Il governo delle opinioni: censura e formazione del consenso nella Toscana del Settecento* (Bologna: il Mulino, 2000).

Langereis, Sandra, *Geschiedenis als ambacht. Oudheidkunde in de Gouden Eeuw: Arnoldus Buchelius en Petrus Scriverius* (Hilversum: Verloren, 2001).

Laspéras, Jean-Michel, 'La biblioteca de Cristóbal de Salazar, humanista y bibliófilo ejemplar', *Criticón*, 22 (1983), pp. 5–132.

Lavenia, Vincenzo *Il catechismo dei soldati. Guerra e cura d'anime in età moderna* (Bologna: edb, 2014).

Lazzarini, Isabella, *Communication & Conflict. Italian Diplomacy in the Early Renaissance, 1350–1520* (Oxford: Oxford University Press, 2015).

Leuschner, Eckhard, 'Francesco Villamena's "apotheosis of Alessandro Farnese" and Engraved Reproductions of Contemporary Sculpture around 1600', *Simiolus: Netherlands Quarterly for the History of Art*, 27 (1999), pp. 144–167.

Leuschner, Eckhard, *Antonio Tempesta. Ein Bahnbrecher des römischen Barock und seine europäische Wirkung* (Petersberg: Michael Imhof, 2005).

Levin, Michael, *Agents of Empire. Spanish Ambassadors in Sixteenth Century Italy* (Ithaca, London: Cornell University Press, 2005).

Levin, M., 'Italy and the Limits of the Spanish Empire', in Reger, W., Andrade, T., *The Limits of Empire: European Imperial Formations in Early Modern World History. Essays in Honor of Geoffrey Parker* (Farnham: Ashgate, 2012), pp. 121–136.

Lievens, Anne Marie, *Il caso Ulloa: uno spagnolo "irregolare" nella editoria veneziana del Cinquecento* (Rome: Pellicani, 2002).

Lievens, A.M., 'Ulloa', in *DBI*, 97 (2020).

Lombardi, Giovanni, *Tra le pagine di San Biagio. L'economia della stampa a Napoli in età moderna* (Naples: Edizioni, Scientifiche Italiane, 2000).

Louthan, Howard, *The Quest for Compromise. Peacemakers in Counter-Reformation Vienna* (Cambridge: Cambridge University Press, 1997).

Love, Harold, *Scribal publication in Seventeenth-Century England* (Oxford: Clarendon Press, 1993).

Lowe, Kate, 'Africa in the News in Renaissance Italy: News Extracts from Portugal About Western Africa Circulating in Northern and Central Italy in the 1480s and 1490s', *IS*, 65 (2010), pp. 310–328.

Luzzati Laganà, F., 'Giovanni Calandrini', *DBI*, 16 (1973).

Maclean, Ian, 'Ciotti and Plantin: Italy, Antwerp and the Frankfurt Book Fair', *La Bibliofilía*, 115 (2013), pp. 135–146.

Maira Niri, Maria, *La tipografia a Genova e in Liguria nel XVII secolo* (Florence: Olschki, 1998).

Maffi, D., 'Cacciatori di gloria: la presenza degli italiani nell'esercito di Fiandra (1621–1700)', in Bianchi, P., Maffi, D., Stumpo, E. (eds.), *Italiani al servizio straniero in età moderna* (Milan: Angeli, 2008), pp. 73–103.

Marnef, G., 'Een Gente Proost in Keulen: Buccho Aytta en zijn rol in de Opstand, 1579–1581', in Jans, A. (ed.), *Liber amicorum Dr J. Scheerder. Tijdingen uit Leuven over de Spaanse Nederlanden, de Leuvense universiteit en Historiografie* (Leuven: Vereniging Historici Lovanienses, 1987), pp.75–86.

Marino Parenti, *Dizionario di luoghi di stampa falsi, inventati o supposti* (Florence: Sassoni, 1951).

Marrara, D., 'I rapporti giuridici fra la Toscana e l'impero (1530–1576)', in Garfagnini, G.C. (ed.), *Firenze e la Toscana dei Medici nell' Europa del 500. Strumenti e veicoli della cultura relazioni politiche ed economiche* (Florence: Olschki, 1981), pp. 217–222.

Martin, Collin and Parker, Geoffrey, *The Spanish Armada: Revised Edition* (Manchester: Mandolin, 1999).

Martin, J.J., 'The Venetian territorial State: Constructing Boundaries in the Shadow of Spain', in Dandelet, T.J., Marino, J.A. (eds.), *Spain in Italy: Politics, Society, and Religion 1500–1700* (Leiden: Brill, 2007), pp. 226–248.

Martin Lynn, A., 'Fabio Mirto Frangipani and Papal Policy in France. The case of an independent minded nuncio', *Archivum Historiae Pontificae* XVII (1979), pp. 197–240.

Martinez Millán, J. (ed.), *La monarquía de Felipe III: los reinos* (Madrid: Fundación Mapfre, 2008).

Mastellone, Salvo, 'Holland as a political model in Italy', *Bijdragen en Mededelingen betrefferende de Geschiedenis der Nederlanden*, 98 (1983), pp. 568–582.

Mastellone, Salvo, 'I Republicani del Seicento ed il Modello Politico Olandese', *Il Pensiero Politico*, 18 (1985), pp. 145–163.

Mavilla, Francesca, 'Committenti e collezionisti tra l'Italia e le Fiandre, il ruolo di Paolo e Chiappino Vitelli nel contesto artistico e culturale del Cinquecento' (unpublished doctoral dissertation, Università degli Studi di Perugia, 2016).

Mavilla, Francesca, '"Sua signoria è qua in molta buona riputatione con ciascuno": Chiappino Vitelli e i fratelli Guicciardini', *Horti Hesperidum*, 8 (2018), pp. 321–348.

McCusker, John J. and Gravesteijn, Cora, *The Beginnings of Commercial and Financial Journalism* (Amsterdam: Centraal Boekhuis, 1991).

McDonald, Mark, *The Print collection of Cassiano dal Pozzo. 2: Architecture, Topography and Military Maps* (London: Royal Collection Trust, 2019).

Mears, Natalie, 'Love-making and Diplomacy: Elizabeth I and the Anjou Marriage Negotiations, c. 1578 1582', *History*, 86 (2001), pp. 442–466.

Meerbergen, J. and Vermaseren, B.A., 'De martelaren Van Roermond in 1572', in Smeets, M.J.K., Van Rijswijck, A., Vermaseren, B.A. (eds.), *Historische Opstellen over Roermond en Omgeving* (Roermond: Bisschoppelijk College, 1951), pp. 257–287.

Meserve, Margaret, 'News from Negroponte: Politics, Popular Opinion, and Information Exchange in the First Decade of the Italian Press', *Renaissance Quarterly*, 59 (2006) pp. 440–480.

Merola, A., 'Guido Bentivoglio', in *DBI*, 8 (1966).

Merlin, P.P., 'Spagna e Savoia nella politica italiana ed europea da Cateau-Cambresis a Vervins (1559–1598)', in Martinez Millán, J. (ed.), *Felipe II (1527–1598). Europa y la Monarquía Católica* (Madrid: Parteluz, 1998), pp. 513–530.

Miccoli, G., 'Giovanni Battista Adriani' in *DBI*, 1 (1960).

Molino, Paola, 'Connected News. German Zeitungen and Italian avvisi in the Fugger collection (1568–1604)', *Media History*, 22 (2016), pp. 267–295.

Montone, Tina, *Pietro Benedetti (ca. 1579–ca. 1630) een Italiaan in het Antwerpse literaire leven van de vroege zeventiende eeuw* (unpublished PhD dissertation, KU Leuven, 2004).

Mout, N., 'Justus Lipsius between war and peace', in Pollmann, J., Spicer, A. (eds.), *Public Opinion and Changing Identities in the Early Modern Netherlands: Essays in Honour of Alastair Duke* (Leiden: Brill, 2007), pp. 141–162.

Moore, R.I., 'Heresy as disease', in Lourdeaux, W., Verhelst, D. (eds.), *The Concept of Heresy in the Middle Ages* (Leuven: Peeters, 1976), pp. 1–12.

Motta, Uberto, *Antonio Querenghi (1546–1633): un letterato Padovano nella Roma del tardo Rinascimento* (Milan: Vita e Pensiero, 1997).

Moretti, Silvia, 'La trattatistica italiana e la guerra: il conflitto tra la Spagna e le Fiandre', *Annali dell'Istituto storico italo-germanico in Trento/ Jahrbuch des ialienisch-deutschen historischen Instituts in Trient*, 20 (1994), pp. 129–164.

Muir, Edward, *Civic Ritual in Renaissance Venice* (New Jersey: Princeton University Press, 1986).

Mulryne, J.R., Watanabe- O'Kelly, H., Shewring, M. (eds.), *Europa Triumphans. Court and Civic Festival in Early Modern Europe* (Aldershot: Ashgate, 2004).

Musi, A. (ed.), *Alle origini di una nazione. Antispagnolismo e identità italiana* (Milan: Guerini, 2003).

Musi, Aurelio, *L'impero dei viceré* (Bologna: Il Mulino, 2013).

Neumann, Florian, *Geschichtsschreibung als Kunst: Famiano Strada S.I. (1572–1649) und Die Ars Historica in Italien* (Berlin: Walter de Gruyter, 2013).

Nevola, Fabrizio, *Street Life in Renaissance Italy* (New Haven/London: Yale University Press, 2020).

Nori, Gabriele, 'Una biografie parallela di Alessandro Farnese: Pomponio Torelli e Cesare Campana', *Aurea Parma*, 62 (1978), pp. 33–41.

Nuovo, Angela, 'Manuscript Writings on Politics and Current Affairs in the Collection of Gian Vincenzo Pinelli (1535–1601)', *Italian Studies*, 66 (2011), pp. 193–205.

Nuovo, Angela, *The Book Trade in the Italian Renaissance* (Leiden: Brill, 2013).

Nuovo, Angela, and Christian Coppens, *I Giolito e la stampa: nell'Italia del XVI secolo* (Geneva: Droz, 2005).

Nuti, G., 'Giovanni Costa', in *DBI*, 30 (1984).

'Oral Culture in Early Modern Italy: Performance, Language, Religion' in *The Italianist* 34 (2014).

Ognibene, Giovanni, 'Le relazioni della casa d'Este coll'estero, comunicazione fatta in Roma al congresso internazionale di Scienze Storiche nel 5 Aprile 1903', *Atti e memorie della R. Deputazione di Storia Patria per le Provincie Modenesi*, 8 (1904), pp. 223–319.

Olof de Törne, Per, *Don Juan d'Autriche et les projets de conquête de l'Angleterre: Étude historique sur dix années du seizième siècle (1568–1578)* (Helsinki: Acta Academia Aboentis, 1915–1928).

Oresko, R., 'The House of Savoy in search for a Royal crown in the seventeenth century', in Oresko, R., Gibbs, G.C., Scott, H.M. (eds.), *Royal and Republican Sovereignty in Early Modern Europe: Essays in Memory of Ragnhild Hatton* (Cambridge: Cambridge University Press, 1997), pp. 272–350.

Oresko, R. and Parrott, D., 'The House of Savoy and the Thirty Years War', in Schilling, H., Busmann, K. (eds.), *1648, War and Peace in Europe: Politics, Religion, Law and Society* (Münster: Veranstaltungsgesellschaft 350 Jahre Westfälischer Friede, 1998), pp. 141–160.

Osborne, Toby, 'The Surrogate War between the Savoys and the Medici: Sovereignty and Precedence in Early Modern Italy', *The International History Review*, 29 (2007), pp. 1–21.

Pacini, A., '"Pignatte di vetro". Being a republic in Philip II's empire', in Dandelet, T.J., Marino, J.A. (eds.), *Spain in Italy: Politics, Society, and Religion 1500–1700* (Leiden: Brill, 2007), pp. 197–225.

Parker, Geoffrey, 'Spain, her Enemies and the Revolt of the Netherlands', *Past & Present*, 99 (1970), pp. 72–95.

Parker, Geoffrey, *The Army of Flanders and the Spanish Road 1567–1659* (Cambridge: Cambridge University Press, 1972).

Parker, Geoffrey, *The Dutch Revolt* (Hamondsworth: Penguin, 1979).

Parker, Geoffrey, *Spain and the Netherlands 1559–1659. Ten Studies* (London: Collins, 1979).

Parker, Geoffrey, *The Grand Strategy of Philip II* (New Haven/London: Yale University Press, 1998).

Parrott, D., 'The Role of Fortifications in Early Modern Europe; the Farnese and the security of the duchies of Parma and Piacenza', in Mozzarelli, C. (ed.), *I Farnese. Corte, guerra e nobiltà in antico regime* (Rome: Bulzoni, 1997), pp. 243–311.

Parrott, David, 'The Mantuan succession crisis 1627–1631: A Sovereignty Dispute in Early Modern Europe', *The English Historical Review*, 112 (1997), pp. 20–65.

Parrott, D., 'Italian soldiers in French service 1500–1700. The Collapse of a Military tradition', in Bianchi, P., Maffi, D., Stumpo, E. (eds.), *Italiani al servizio straniero in età moderna* (Milan: Angeli, 2008), pp. 15–39.

Parrott, David, *The Business of War: Military Enterprise and Military Revolution in Early Modern Europe* (Cambridge: Cambridge University Press, 2012).

Patrick Robinson, Adam, *The Career of Cardinal Morone* (Burlington: Ashgate, 2002).

Peacey, J., '"My Friend the Gazetier": Diplomacy and News in Seventeenth-Century Europe', in Raymond, J., Moxham, N. (eds.), *News Networks in Early Modern Europe* (Leiden: Brill, 2016), pp. 420–442.

Pelizzari, P., 'Echi letterari della prima guerra del Monferrato: la prosa di Alessandro Tassoni', in Merlin, P., Ieva, F. (eds.), *Monferrato 1613. La viglia di una crisi europea* (Rome: Viella, 2016), pp. 179–196.

Petitjean, Johann, 'Mots et pratiques de l'information. Ce que aviser veut dire (XVI–XVIIᵉ Siècles)', *Mélanges de l'école française de Rome, Italie- Méditerranée*, 122 (2010), pp. 107–121.

Petitjean, Johann, *L'intelligence des choses. Une histoire de l'information entre Italie et Mediterranee (XVIᵉ–XVIIᵉ Siècle)* (Rome: Ecole Française de Rome, 2013).

Pattenden, M., 'Rome as a 'Spanish Avignon'? The Spanish Faction and the Monarchy of Philip II', in Baker-Bates, P., Pattenden, M. (eds.), *Spanish Presence in Sixteenth-Century Italy: Images of Iberia* (Farnham: Ashgate, 2015), pp. 65–78.

Peter Grell, Ole, *Brethren in Christ: A Calvinist Network in Reformation Europe* (Cambridge: Cambridge University Press, 2011).

Petta, M., 'Wars News in Early Modern Milan: the birth and shaping of printed news pamphlets', in Raymond, J., Moxham, N. (eds.), *News Networks in Early Modern Europe* (Leiden: Brill, 2016), pp. 287–290.

Petta, Massimo, *In Milano, per li Malatesti, stampatori regij e camerali. Una impresa editoriale al servizio delle istituzioni nella Milano spagnola: le botteghe dei primi Malatesta (1594–1664)* (Unpublished PhD thesis, Università degli studi di Milano, 2010).

Petta, M., 'Networks of Printers and the Dissemination of News: the case of Milan in the sixteenth and seventeenth Centuries', in Kirwan, R., Mullins, S. (eds.), *Specialist Markets in the Early Modern Book World* (Leiden: Brill, 2015), pp. 64–84.

Pettegree, Andrew, *The Invention of News: How the World Came to know about itself* (London: Yale University Press, 2014).

Pettegree, Andrew, *Reformation and the Culture of Persuasion* (Cambridge: Cambridge University Press, 2005).

Pettegree, Andrew (ed.), *Broadsheets: Single-sheet Publishing in the First Age of Print* (Leiden: Brill, 2017).

Pezzolo, L., 'The Venetian economy', in Dursteler, E. (ed.), *A Companion to Venice* (Leiden: Brill, 2013), pp. 255–288.

Pieper, Renate, *Die Vermittlung einer Neuen Welt: Amerika im Nachrichtennetz des Habsburgischen Imperiums 1493–1598* (Mainz: Philipp von Zabern, 2000).

Pignatti, F., 'Aurelio Orsi', in *DBI*, 79 (2013).

Piscini, A., 'Domenichi, Lodovico', in *DBI*, 40 (1991).

Poelhekke, Jan J., 'Het thema "Nederlanden" bij Trajano Boccalini', *Tijdschrift voor Geschiedenis*, 62 (1949), pp. 262–272.

Pollak, Martha, *Cities at War in Early Modern Europe* (Cambridge: Cambridge University Press, 2010).

Pollmann, Judith, 'Internationalisering en de Nederlandse Opstand', *Bijdragen en Mededelingen betreffende de Geschiedenis der Nederlanden*, 124 (2009), pp. 515–535.

Pollmann, Judith, 'Hogenberg's Ghost: New books on the Eighty Years' War', in *Early Modern Low Countries*, 4 (2020), pp. 124–138.

Pollmann, J. and Stensland, M., 'Alba's reputation in the Early Modern Low Countries', in Ebben, M., Lacy-Bruijn, M., Van Hövell, R. (eds.), *Alba: General and Servant to the Crown* (Rotterdam: Karwan Aray publisher, 2013), pp. 308–325.

Pommier Vincelli, F., 'Il concetto di reputazione e i giudizi sulla monarchia spagnola', in Lotti, L., Villari, R. (eds.), *Filippo II e il Mediterraneo* (Rome: Laterza, 2003), pp. 289–324.

Preto, P., 'Venezia, la Spagna, i Turchi', in di Stefano, G., Fasano Guarini, E., Martinengo, A. (eds.), *Italia non Spagnola e Monarchia Spagnola tra '500 e '600* (Florence: Olschki, 2009), pp. 113–121.

Orlandelli, G.F., 'Antonio Abbondanti' in *DBI*, 1 (1960).

Randall, David, *Credibility in Elizabethan and Early Stuart Military News* (London: Pickering & Chatto, 2008).

Randall, David, 'Epistolary Rhetoric, the Newspaper and the Public Sphere', *Past & Present*, 128 (2008), pp. 3–32.

Raugei, Anna Maria, *Gian Vincenzo Pinelli e la sua biblioteca* (Geneva: Droz, 2018).

Raymond, Joad, *The Invention of the Newspaper: English Newsbook 1641–1649* (Oxford: Clarendon Press, 2005).

Raymond, J. (ed.), *News Networks in Seventeenth Century Britain and Europe* (London: Routledge, 2006).

Raymond, Joad, 'Newspapers: a National or an International phenomenon', *Media History*, 11 (2012), pp. 1–9.

Raymond, J., Salman, J., Harms, R. (eds.), *Not Dead Things. The Dissemination of Popular print in England and Wales, Italy and the Low Countries, 1500–1820* (Leiden: Brill, 2014).

Raymond, J., 'Exporting impartiality', in Murphy, K., Traninger, A. (eds.), *The Emergence of Impartiality* (Leiden: Brill, 2014), pp. 141–168.

Raymond, J., Moxham, N. (eds.), *News Networks in Early Modern Europe* (Leiden: Brill, 2016).

Raviola, Blythe Alice, 'Sabaudian Propaganda and the Wars of Succession of Mantua and Monferrato, 1613–1631', in Stacey, S.A. (ed.), *Political, Religious and Social Conflict in the States of Savoy, 1400–1700* (Bern: Lang, 2014), pp. 53–76.

Reijner, Cees, 'Een Italiaanse verdediger van de Opstand? De internationale controverse rond het werk van Gerolamo Conestaggio', *Tijdschrift voor Geschiedenis*, 2 (2013), pp. 173–187.

Reijner, Cees, 'Gesprekken in Genua over het Twaalfjarig Bestand', *De Zeventiende Eeuw*, 30 (2014), pp. 76–96.

Reijner, Cees, 'Het eerste Italiaanse geschiedwerk over de Opstand: Francesco Bocchi's kroniek van een oorlog of biografie van een Italiaanse oorlogsheld?', *Belgisch tijdschrift voor filologie en geschiedenis*, 95 (2017), pp. 297–320.

Reijner, Cees, *Italiaanse geschiedschrijvers over de Nederlandse Opstand, 1585–1650. Een transnationale geschiedenis* (Unpublished PhD, University Leiden, 2020).

Retortillo Atienza, Asunción, *Ambrosio Spínola, de Génova a Ostende (1569–1604)* (Madrid: Ministerio de Defensa, 2017).

Ricci, Vittorio, *La Monarchia Cattolica nel governo degli Stati Italiani. Il ruolo dei fratelli Luis de Requesens e Juan de Zúñiga, cavalieri di Santiago* (Cassino: Francesco Ciolfi Editore, 2011).

Richardson, Brian, *Manuscript Culture in Renaissance Italy* (Cambridge: Cambridge University Press, 2009).

Richardson, Brian, 'A scribal publisher of political information: Francesco Marcaldi', *Italian Studies*, 64 (2009), pp. 296–313.

Rittersma, Rengenier, *Egmont da Capo: Eine mythogenetische studie* (Münster: Waxmann, 2009).

Rittersma, Rengenier, 'Le orrecchie sì piene di Fiandra. Famiano Strada (1572–1649) und Guido Bentivoglio (1577–1644) und ihr Interesse am niederländischen Aufstand', *Quellen und Forschungen aus italienischen Archiven und Bibliotheken*, 89 (2009), pp. 263–283.

Rizzo, M., 'Milano e le forze del principe. Agenti, relazioni e risorse per la difesa dell'impero di Filippo II', in Martinez Millán, J. (ed.), *Felipe II (1527–1598). Europa y la Monarquía Católica* (Madrid: Parteluz, 1998), pp. 743–759.

Roberts, Sean, *Printing a Mediterranean World: Florence, Constantinople and Geography* (Harvard: Harvard University Press, 2013).

Rodríguez Pérez, Yolanda, *De Tachtigjarige Oorlog in Spaanse ogen* (Nijmegen: Vantilt, 2003).

Rodríguez Pérez, Yolanda, *The Dutch Revolt through Spanish eyes: self and other in historical and literary texts in Golden Age Spain (c. 1548–1673)* (Bern: Peter Lang, 2008).

Rodríguez Pérez, Yolanda, 'The Pelican and its ungrateful Children: The Construction and Evolution of Dutch rebelliousness in Golden Age Spain', *Journal of Early Modern History*, 11 (2007), pp. 286–302.

Rodríguez-Salgado, M.J., 'Capo dei Capi: the Duke of Alba in Italy', in Ebben, M., Lacy-Bruijn, M., Van Hövell, R. (eds.), *Alba: General and Servant to the Crown* (Rotterdam: Karwansaray Publishers, 2013), pp. 227–255.

Rodríguez-Salgado, M.J., 'Do not reveal that I wrote this': diplomatic correspondence, news and narratives in the early years of the civil war in the Low Countries', in Fagel, R.P., Francés Álvarez, L., Santiago Belmonte, B. (eds.), *Early modern war narratives and the Revolt in the Low Countries* (Manchester: Manchester University Press, 2020), pp. 24–27.

Rodriguez Villa, Antonio, *Ambrosio Spínola, primer marqués de los Balbases* (Madrid: Fortanet, 1905).

Roello, M., 'Gio Nicolo Doglioni', in *DBI*, 40 (1990).

Rosa, M., 'The World's Theatre: The Court of Rome and Politics in the first half of the seventeenth century', in Visceglia, M.A., Signorotto, G. (eds.), *Court and Politics in Papal Rome, 1492–1700* (Cambridge: Cambridge University Press, 2002), pp. 78–98.

Rosenthal, D., 'The Tailor's Song: Notes from the Savonarolan Underground in Grand-Ducal Florence', in Howard, P.F., Hewlett, C. (eds.), *Studies on Florence and the Italian Renaissance in Honour of F.W. Kent* (Turnhout: Brepols, 2016), pp. 359–372.

Rospocher, M. (ed.), *Beyond the Public Sphere. Opinions, Publics and Spaces in Early Modern Europe* (Bologna: il Mulino, 2012).

Rozzo, Ugo, *La Strage Ignorata. I fogli volanti a stampa nell' Italia dei secoli XV e XVI* (Udine: Forum, 2008).

Sabbadini, R., 'L'uso della memoria. I Farnese e le immagini di Alessandro, duca e capitano', in Fantoni, M. (ed.), *Il perfetto capitano: immagini e realtà, secoli 15–17* (Rome: Bulzoni, 2001), pp. 155–182.

Salsano, Fernando, 'Fortuniano Sanvitale', *Studi Secenteschi*, 5 (1964), pp. 69–72.

Salzberg, Rosa, 'In the mouth of charlatans. Street performers and the dissemination of pamphlets in Renaissance Italy', *Renaissance Studies*, 24 (2010), pp. 638–654.

Salzberg, Rosa, *Ephemeral city. Cheap print and urban culture in Renaissance Venice* (Manchester: Manchester University Press, 2014).

Salzberg, Rosa, and Rospocher, Massimo, 'Street Singers in Italian Renaissance Urban Culture and Communication', *Cultural and Social History*, 9 (2012), pp. 9–26.

Sanchez, J.H., 'Naples and Florence in Charles V's Italy: Family, Court and Government in the Toledo-Medici Alliance', in Dandelet, T., Marino, J. (eds.), *Spain in Italy: Politics, Society, and Religion 1500–1700* (Leiden: Brill, 2007), pp. 135–180.

Sánchez García, Encarnació, *Imprenta y cultura en la Nápoles virreinal: los signos de la presencia Española* (Florence: Alinea, 2007).

Sardella, Pierre, *Nouvelles et spéculations à Venise au début du XVIᵉ siècle* (Paris: Colin, 1949).

Sautter, Karl, 'Auffindung einer grossen Anzahl verschlossener Briefe aus dem Jahre 1585', *Archiv für Post und Telegraphie*, 4 (1909), pp. 97–115.

Sbordone, S., 'Editori e tipografi a Napoli nel 600', *Quaderni dell'Accademia Pontaniana*, 12 (1990), pp. 5–93.

Schellekens, Christophe, *Merchants and their hometown: Florentines in Antwerp and the Duchy of Florence* (ca 1500–1585), (Unpublished PhD thesis, European University Institute, 2018).

Schneider, Gary, *The Culture of Epistolarity: Vernacular Letters and Letter Writing in Early Modern England, 1500–1700* (Newark: University of Delaware Press, 2005).

Schobesberger, N., Arblaster, P., Belo, A., Espejo C., Infelise, M., Moxham, N., Raymond, J., 'European Postal Networks', in Raymond, J., Moxham, N. (eds.), *News Networks in Early Modern Europe* (Leiden: Brill, 2016), pp. 19–63.

Schöffer, I., 'The Batavian myth during the Sixteenth and Seventeenth Centuries', in Bromley, S. (ed.), *Britain and the Netherlands* (The Hague: Martinus Nijhoff, 1975), pp. 78–101.

Scott Baker, N., 'The Emperor and the Duke: Cosimo I, Charles V; and the Negotiation of Sovereignty', in Assonitis, A., Van Veen, H. Th. (eds.), *A Companion to Cosimo I de' Medici* (Leiden: Brill, 2021), pp. 115–159.

Signorotto, G., 'Urbino nell' età di Filippo II', in Martinez Millán, J. (ed.), *Felipe II (1527–1598). Europa y la Monarquía Católica* (Madrid: Parteluz 1998), pp. 833–879.

Simoni, Anna E.C., *The Ostend Story. Early Tales of the great siege and the mediating role of Henrick van Haestens* ('t Goy-Houten: Hes & De Graaf, 2003).

Simonin, Michel, *Vivre de sa plume au XVIᵉ siècle ou la carrière de François de Belleforest* (Genève: Droz, 1992).

Soen, Violet, 'Philip II's Quest. The Appointment of Governors-General during the Dutch Revolt (1559–1598)', *Bijdragen en Mededelingen betreffende de Geschiedenis der Nederlanden*, 126 (2011), pp. 3–29.

Soen, Violet, "'C'estoit comme songe et mocquerie de parler de pardon". Obstructie bij een Pacificatiemaatregel (1566–1567)', *Bijdragen en Mededelingen betreffende de Geschiedenis der Nederlanden*, 119 (2004), pp. 309–328.

Soen, Violet, *Vredehandel. Adellijke en Habsburgse verzoeningspogingen tijdens de Nederlandse Opstand* (Amsterdam: Amsterdam University Press, 2012).

Soll, Jacob, *Publishing the Prince. History, Reading, and the Birth of Political Criticism* (Ann Arbor: University of Michigan Press, 2008).

Sowerby, T., 'Elizabethan Diplomatic Networks and the Spread of News', in Raymond, J., Moxham, N. (eds.), *News Networks in Early Modern Europe* (Leiden: Brill, 2016), pp. 305–327.

Spagnoletti, Angelantonio, *Le dinastie italiane nella prima età moderna* (Bologna: Il Mulino, 2003).

Spagnoletti, Angelantonio, 'La tregua di Anversa e la pace di Asti. Ovvero come la Spagna persa la propria reputazione', *Dimensioni e problemi della ricerca storica*, 2 (2009), pp. 163–185.

Spagnoletti, Angelantonio, 'Le dinastie italiane e la guerra delle Fiandre', *Storia e società*, 125 (2009), pp. 423–443.

Spagnoletti, A., 'Paz y quietud' in Italia negli anni di Filippo II', in di Stefano, G., Fasano, Guarini, E., Martinengo, A. (eds.), *Italia non spagnola e monarchia spagnola tra '500 e '600. Politica, cultura e letterature* (Florence: Olschki, 2009), pp. 29–41.

Spina, R., 'Rossi', *DBI*, 88 (2017).

Spini, G., 'Historiography: The Art of History in the Italian Counter Reformation', in Cochrane, E. (eds.), *The Late Italian Renaissance* (London: Macmillan, 1970), pp. 92–133.

Spini, Giorgio, *Architettura e Politica da Cosimo I a Ferdinando I* (Florence: Olschki, 1976).

Spini, G., 'Il Principato dei Medici e il sistema degli Stati europei del Cinquecento', in Garfagnini, G.C. (ed.), *Firenze e la Toscana dei Medici nell' Europa del' 500. Strumenti e veicoli della cultura relazioni politiche ed economiche* (Florence: Olschki, 1983), pp. 155–216.

Stabel, P., 'Italian Merchants and the Fairs in the Low Countries (12th–16th centuries)', in P. Lanario (ed.), *La Pratica dello scambio. Sisteme di fiere, mercanti e città in Europa (1400–1700)* (Venice: Marsilio, 2003), pp. 131–160.

Stallybrass, P., "'Little jobs": broadsides and the printing revolution', in Alcorn Baron, S., Lindquist, E.N., Shevlin, E.F. (eds.), *Agent of Change: Print Culture Studies after Elizabeth L. Eisenstein* (Amherst: MA, 2007), pp. 315–341.

Stensland, Monica, *Habsburg Communication in the Dutch Revolt* (Amsterdam: Amsterdam University Press, 2011).

Stensland, Monica, 'Not as bad as all that: The strategies and effectiveness of Loyalist propaganda in the early years of Alexander Farnese's governorship', *Dutch Crossing*, 31 (2007), pp. 91–112.

Stevens, Kevin M. and Gehl, Paul F., 'Cheap print: a look inside the Lucini/Sirtori stationery shop at Milan (1597–1613)', *La Bibliofilía*, 112 (2010), pp. 281–327.

Subacchi, P., 'Italians in Antwerp in the second half of the sixteenth century', in Soly, H., Thijs, A.K.L. (eds.), *Minderheden in Westeuropese steden (16de–20ste eeuw). Minorities in Western European Cities (sixteenth-twentieth century)* (Rome: Belgisch Historisch Instituut te Rome, 1995), pp. 73–90.

Swart, Koenraad, 'The Black Legend during the Eighty Years War', in Broomley, J.S., Kossmann, E.H. (eds.), *Britain and the Netherlands. Volume V. Some political mythologies* (The Hague: Nijhof, 1975), pp. 36–75.

Testa, Simone, *Scipione di Castro e il suo trattato politico. Testo critico e traduzione inglese inedita del seicento* (Rome: Vecchiarelli, 2012).

Testa, Simone, 'Did Giovanni Maria Manelli publish the Thesoro Politico (1589)?', *Renaissance Studies*, 19 (2005), pp. 380–393.

Testa, Simone, 'Per una interpretazione del Thesoro Politico (1589)', *Nuova Rivista Storica*, 85 (2001), pp. 347–362.

Testa, Simone, 'Death of a political informer. Camillo Volta, Roman agent of Louis de Gonzague Duc de Nevers', *Lives and Letters*, 2:1 (2010).

Tilmans, Karen, *Aurelius en de Divisiekroniek van 1517. Historiografie en Humanisme in Holland in de tijd van Erasmus* (Hilversum: Verloren, 1988).

Thøfner, Margaret, *A Common Art, Urban ceremonial in Antwerp and Brussels during the Dutch Revolt* (Zwolle: Waanders, 1997).

Thomas, W. (ed.), *De Val van het Nieuwe Troje. Het beleg van Oostende (1601–1604)* (Leuven: Davidfonds, 2004).

Thomas, W., 'Andromeda Unbound, the Reign of Albert and Isabella in the Southern Netherlands, 1598–1621', in Duerloo, L., Thomas, W. (eds.), *Albrecht en Isabella 1598–1621: essays* (Turnhout: Brepols, 1998), pp. 1–13.

Toffetti, M., 'Tini', in *DBI*, 95 (2019).

Vaccaro, L., 'Francesco Maria Vialardi', in *DBI*, 99 (2020).

Vanderhaeghen, Ferdinand, 'Fam. Strada De bello Belgico decas prima et decas secunda: description des diverses éditions de cet ouvrage', in *Extrait des livraisons de la Bibliotheca Belgica ou Bibliographie générale des Pays-Bas* (Ghent: Vyt, 1881).

Van Bruaene, Anne-Laure, '50 jaar Tachtig Jaar Oorlog in de BMGN', *Bijdragen en Mededelingen betreffende de Geschiedenis der Nederlanden*, 136 (2021), pp. 124–134.

Van Deursen, A.Th., 'Tussen eenheid en zelfstandigheid. De toepassing van de unie als fundamentele wet', in Van Deursen, A.Th. (ed.), *De hartslag van het leven, studies over de Republiek der Verenigde Nederlanden* (Amsterdam: Bert Bakker, 1996), pp. 307–321.

Van den Heuvel, Charles, *'Papiere bolwercken'. De introductie van de Italiaanse stede- en vestingbouw in de Nederlanden (1540–1609) en het gebruik van tekeningen* (Alphen aan de Rijn: Canaletto, 1991).

Van der Essen, Léon, *Les Italiens en Flandre au XVI et au XVII siècle* (Brussels: La Lecture au Foyer, 1926).

Van der Essen, Léon, *Alexander Farnèse, prince de parme, gouverneur général des Pays-Bas (1545–1592)* (5 vols., Brussels: Librairie nationale d'art et d'histoire, 1933–1937).

Van der Lem, Anton and Turkoglu, Bahar, 'L'anti-apolgie de 1581 de Pedro Cornjeo', *LIAS*, 31 (2004), pp. 185–237.

Van der Steen, Jasper, *Memory Wars in the Low Countries, 1566–1700* (Leiden: Brill, 2015).

Van den Broek, Jan, *Voor God en mijn koning. Het verslag van colonel Francisco Verdugo over zijn Jaren als legerleider en gouverneur namens Filips II in Stad en Lande van Groningen, Drenthe, Friesland, Overijssel en Lingen (1581–1595)* (Assen: Van Gorcum, 2009).

Van Gelder, M., 'In liefde en werk met de Lage Landen verbonden: de Genuese koopman en literator Girolamo Conestaggio (ca. 1530–1614/1615)', in Van Gelder, M., Meijers, E. (eds.), *Internationale handelsnetwerken en culturele contacten in de vroegmoderne Nederlanden*, (Maastricht: Shaker, 2009), pp. 43–53.

Van Gelder, Maartje, *Trading Places: The Netherlandish Mercants in Early Modern Venice* (Leiden: Brill, 2009).

Van Gelder, Maartje, 'Supplying the *Serenissima*. The role of Flemish merchants in the Venetian grain trade during the first phase of the *Straatvaart*', *International Journal of Maritime History*, 16 (2004), pp. 39–60.

Van Gelderen, Martin, *The Political Thought of the Dutch Revolt 1555–1590* (Cambridge: Cambridge University Press, 2002).

Van Gelderen, M., 'Aristotelians, Monarchomachs and Republicans: Sovereignty and respublica mista in Dutch and German Political Thought, 1580–1650', in Van Gelderen, M., Skinner, Q. (eds.), *Republicanism and Constitutionalism in Early Modern Europe* (Cambridge: Cambridge University Press, 2002), pp. 195–218.

Van Houtte, Hubert, 'Un journal manuscrit intéressant (1557–1648): les Avvisi du fonds Urbinat et d'autres fonds de la Bibliothèque Vaticane', *Bulletin de la Commission Royal d'Histoire/Handelingen van de Koninklijke Commissie voor Geschiedenis*, 89 (1925), pp. 359–440.

Van Ittersum, Martine, *Profit and Principle: Hugo Grotius, Natural Rights Theories and the Rise of the Dutch Power in the East Indies (1595–1615)* (Leiden: Brill, 2006).

Van Stipriaan, René, *De zwijger. Het leven van Willem van Oranje* (Amsterdam/Antwerpen: Querido, 2021).

Van Tielhof, Milja, *The 'Mother of All Trades': The Baltic Grain Trade in Amsterdam from the Late Sixteenth to the Early Nineteenth Century* (Leiden: Brill, 2002).

Van Zuilen, V., 'Les Placards de Philippe II en Flandres et Brabants', in Ertlé, B., Gosman, M. (eds.), *Les écrits courts à vocation polémique* (Frankfurt am Main: Peter Lang, 2006), pp. 113–129.

Vermaseren, Bernard, *De Katholieke Nederlandsche geschiedschrijving in de XVIe en XVIIe eeuw over den Opstand* (Maastricht: Van Aelst, 1941).

Verrier, Fréderique, *Les Armes de Minerve. L'Humanisme militaire dans l'Italie du XVIe siècle* (Paris: Presses de l'université de Paris-Sorbonne, 1997).

Vialardi di Sandigliano, Tomaso, 'Un cortigiano e letterato piemontese del cinquecento: Francesco Maria Vialardi', *Studi Piemontesi*, 34 (2005), pp. 299–312.

Viroli, Maurizio, *From Politics to Reason of State: the Acquisition and Transformation of the Language of Politics 1250–1600* (Cambridge: Cambridge University Press, 1992).

Visceglia, Maria Antonietta, 'The International Policy of the Papacy: Critical Approaches to the Concepts of Universalism and *Italianità,* Peace and War', in Visceglia, M.A. (ed.), *Papato e politica internazionale nella prima età moderna* (Rome: Viella, 2013), pp. 17–62.

Voges, Ramon, *Das Auge der Geschichte: Der Aufstand der Niederlande und die Französischen Religionskriege im Spiegel der Bildberichte Franz Hogenbergs (ca. 1560–1610)* (Leiden/Boston: Brill, 2019).

Volpini, Paola, *Los Medici y España: príncipes, embajadores y agentes en la Edad Moderna* (Madrid: silex, 2017).

Vosters, S.A., *Het beleg van Breda in het wereldnieuws* (Delft: Eburon, 1987).

Vosters, S.A., *Het beleg en de overgave van Breda in geschiedenis, literatuur en kunst* (Breda: Gemeentelijke archiefdienst, 1993).

Wauters, Frédéric, *L'audience de Don Juan D'Autriche: essai sur le séjour dans les Flandres (1576–1578)* (Brussels: Le Cri éditions, 2000).

Weis, Monique, *Les Pays-Bas Espagnols et les états du Saint-Empire (1559–1579): priorités et enjeux de la diplomatie en temps de troubles* (Brussels: Universitè de Bruxelles, 2003).

Weststeijn, Arthur, 'Antonio Pérez y la formación de la política española respecto a la rebelión de los Países Bajos, 1576–1578', *Historia y Política*, 19 (2008), pp. 231–254.

Wilkinson, Alexander S., 'Bum Fodder & Kindling: Cheap Print in Renaissance Spain', *Bulletin of Spanish Studies*, 90 (2013), pp. 871–893.

Witcombe, Christopher, *Copyright in the Renaissance: Prints and the Privilegio in Sixteenth Century Venice and Rome* (Leiden: Brill, 2004).

Witcombe, Christopher L.C.E., *Print Publishing in Sixteenth-Century Rome. Growth and Expansion, Rivalry and Murder* (Turnhout: Brepols, 2009).

Wrigth, Antony D., 'Why the Venetian Interdict?', *English Historical Review*, 89 (1974), pp. 534–550.

Zago, R., 'Emiliano Manolesso', in *DBI*, 69 (2007).

Zapperi, R., 'Scipio di Castro', in *DBI*, 22 (1979).

Zapperi, Roberto, *Don Scipio di Castro. Storia di un impostore* (Rome: Carucci Beniamino, 1977).

Zapperi, Roberto, 'Annibale Carracci e Odoardo Farnese', *Bollettino d'arte*, 84 (1999), pp. 87–102.

Zatti, Sergio, *The Quest for Epic: From Ariosto to Tasso* (Toronto: Toronto University Press, 2006).

Zucchi, E., 'Contesting the Spanish Myth. Republican Shaping of Ambrogio Spinola's image in Genoese literature', in in Mostaccio, S., García García, B.J., Lo Basso, L. (eds.), *Ambrogio Spinola between Genoa, Flanders and Spain* (Leuven: Leuven University Press, 2022), pp. 251–270.

Zwierlein, Cornel, *Discorso und Lex Dei. Die Entstehung neuer Denkrahmen im 16. Jahrhundert un die Wahrnehmung der französischen Religionskriege in Italien und Deutschland* (Göttingen: Vandenhoeck & Ruprecht, 2006).

Zwierlein, Cornel, 'Fuggerzeitungen als Ergebnis von italienisch-deutschem Kulturtransfer 1552–1570', *Quellen und Forschungen aus italienischen Archiven und Bibliotheken*, 90 (2010), pp. 1–56.

Websites

EURONEWS project: <https://www.euronewsproject.org>.

Digital exhibition on the siege of Ostend: <http://omeka.euronewsproject.org/omeka/neatline/fullscreen/the-exciting-news-of-ostende>.

Fuggerzeitungen: https://fuggerzeitungen.univie.ac.at/.

1572 Geboorte van Nederland: <https://geboortevannederland.nl/> and <https://geboortevannederland.nl/gebeurtenissen-1572/>.

Index